BATTLE OF BRITAIN

BATTLE OF BRITAIN

PATRICK BISHOP

ISIS
LARGE PRINT
Oxford

First published in Great Britain 2009
by
Quercus Publishing Plc

Published in Large Print 2010 by ISIS Publishing Ltd.,
7 Centremead, Osney Mead, Oxford OX2 0ES
by arrangement with
Quercus Publishing Plc

British Library Cataloguing in Publication Data
Bishop, Patrick (Patrick Joseph).
    Battle of Britain.
    1. Britain, Battle of, Great Britain, 1940.
    2. Britain, Battle of, Great Britain, 1940 - -
    Chronology.
    3. Large type books.
    I. Title
    940.5'4211–dc22

        ISBN 978–0–7531–8778–4 (hb)
        ISBN 978–0–7531–8779–1 (pb)

    Printed and bound in Great Britain by
    T. J. International Ltd., Padstow, Cornwall

Contents

INTRODUCTION

A Life and Death Struggle

history or myth?

The Battle of Britain was unique. Nothing like it had happened before. Nothing like it was to happen again. For the first time in history a great military encounter was fought in the air.

Appropriately for the Age of the Common Man it took place, spectacularly, in the full sight of ordinary people, above fields and villages, streets and cities. The visibility of the combat helped to give the battle its pre-eminent place in the British folk memory of the Second World War, becoming a towering legend of skill, determination and sacrifice that seems to become more fascinating with the passing of time.

Since the end of the Second World War, the episode has been under constant reappraisal, however. The processes of historical revisionism have sought to shrink the legend to less epic proportions. But the point of a legend is that it has outgrown mere facts. No amount of

1

academic reappraisal is likely to change the larger, more resonant, sense of the battle as a David-and-Goliath contest, in which virtue triumphed over the forces of evil.

In researching the history of the battle, one is struck by how remarkably sound some of the myth's underpinnings actually are. Many of the scenes popularly associated with the event are, indeed, true, and the heroes of the tale closely match their propaganda images. Pilots really were, by and large, young, modest and surprisingly carefree, and would conclude a hard day's flying and fighting by climbing into jalopies and heading to the nearest pub.

The country was gripped by the feeling that, to use Churchill's phrase, "a great climacteric" had been reached. However much historians might subsequently have questioned the seriousness of Hitler's invasion plans, a sense of impending onslaught felt frighteningly real to the people of Britain in the middle of 1940. Though later assessments might seek to downgrade the contribution the victory made to Germany's eventual defeat, that was not how it was seen at the time. In a BBC broadcast in September 1942, George Orwell described it as one of the greatest events in history. "It is becoming clear," he said, "that the Battle of Britain ranks in importance with Trafalgar, Salamis, the defeat of the Spanish Armada and other battles of the past in which the invading forces of a seemingly invincible monarch or dictator have been beaten back and which have formed a turning point in history."

This judgement may have been rather premature; but it has turned out to be essentially true. The Battle of Britain did not make eventual victory certain, but it made it possible. It provided the answers to some crucial questions, and those answers were to shape the future direction of the war.

The first question was a basic one: would Britain fight? It is difficult now to imagine how dark the future seemed from Britain's perspective at the end of June 1940. The British Army was licking its wounds, having been beaten back across the Channel from Dunkirk. France had fallen with unimagined suddenness, its army and air force collapsing in a matter of a few weeks from the shock of a collision with an enemy that was bold, skilful and superbly equipped. Britain really did stand alone. It had friends, but no real allies. The United States was supportive, but remained prudent and watchful. It sensibly stood and awaited the evidence of Britain's fighting resolve before making any firm commitment.

The decision to stand and fight was by no means as inevitable as it has come to appear. Hitler seems to have genuinely hoped he could avoid a direct assault on Britain, and he believed that ultimately the country's rulers would see where their interests lay. It was for that reason that plans for invasion — codenamed *Seelöwe* (Sea Lion) — were drawn up only tardily. Even as late as 19 July, when the initial skirmishing in what has come to be seen as the battle period proper was well advanced, Hitler issued another appeal to British "reason and common sense".

A positive response would not have spared Britain from essential servitude. Hitler had reasonable grounds for thinking, though, that his overture might be favourably received. Churchill had come to power only in May, and his appointment was not regarded with universal approval. To many, such as those for whom the memory of his responsibility regarding the inglorious Dardanelles campaign of the First World War was still fresh, he was a romantic and an adventurer who would make a disastrous war leader. He was flanked by ministers whose instincts were for a negotiated peace.

It was piquant, then, that it was the man most associated with compromise with Nazi Germany, Foreign Secretary Lord Halifax, who was instructed to tell Hitler that his "Appeal to Reason" had been rejected. The public quickly caught the mood of defiance. The isolation brought about by the French defeat in June even brought a sense of relief. "Thank God we are on our own and not saddled with a craven ally" was the reaction of Peter Brothers, a No. 32 Squadron pilot at Biggin Hill, when he heard the news. It was a feeling shared by his monarch, George VI. But it was not until the Luftwaffe had been swept from Britain's daytime skies that Churchill's approach won general approval.

The second question was: having chosen to fight, could the British actually win? Did they have enough men and aircraft to do so? If they did, were they of the right sort? What about the assertion, made repeatedly in the interwar years by those who ought to know, that "the bomber would always get through"?

The mythologizing that started within a few days of battle being joined has created a distorted picture of Britain's preparedness for the fight. The impression has been created of a grossly unequal struggle, in which the eventual victory of the RAF was little short of a miracle. It is easy to see how this distortion came about. The image of a handful of tiny fighter planes diving into a rolling phalanx of bombers is an indelible one. It also happened, on many occasions, to be accurate. But the notion of "the Few" pitted against "the Many" does not faithfully portray the strategic truth. In reality, the odds were more finely balanced. The Luftwaffe might have had more aircraft than the RAF — perhaps twice as many — at the outset. But the RAF had enough of the right type needed to mount a serious defence. The outcome would depend, to a large extent, on the quality of the fighter planes, the availability and skill of men to fly them and the ability of commanders to avoid major blunders. The RAF had the Spitfire — which was at least as good as its German counterpart, the Messerschmitt Me109 — and the Hurricane, which was sturdy and fast enough to hold its own. In the battle of attrition that followed, thanks to organizational foresight, the supply of aircraft and pilots managed to keep pace with losses.

The defenders had two other great assets as they faced up to the German attack. They had the wonderful advantage of radar, which allowed those controlling the fighting to get early warning of the German raids as they formed up in the skies of northern France, and to make their dispositions to tackle them. In addition, the pilots were operating from their own soil, which brought obvious logistical benefits as well as the psychological boost of fighting in sight of the people and places they were chancing their lives to protect.

The fact that Britain's air defences were strong enough to meet the German challenge owed as much to judgement as to luck. As one recent historian of the battle has demonstrated convincingly, in some respects the national stereotypes were reversed: in this story it was often the British who were the professionals and the Germans the romantic amateurs.[1] However, in keeping with another durable cliché about Britain there was a certain amount of muddle during the preparations for war, which add a touch of suspense to the proceedings. In the interwar years conventional thinking at the top of the air force had been firmly against the idea of large fleets of fighter aircraft. The bomber was the weapon that would win the war by landing a "knockout blow" on the enemy. To deter the Germans from striking first, the energy of the air marshals was poured into matching the Germans heavy plane for heavy plane. It was an obscure politician, Sir Thomas Inskip, who had the vision to realize that it was a waste of effort. His providential intervention made it possible for the Battle of Britain to be fought. Inskip was made minister for coordination of defence in 1936. In December 1937, this unregarded lawyer came to the wise judgement that "the role of our Air Force is not an early knockout blow . . . but to prevent the Germans from knocking us out."

His conclusion was opposed fiercely by service experts, who claimed that this was a recipe for losing the next war. But Inskip stuck to his guns. He argued that this approach was not only better but cheaper. Fighters cost much less to produce than bombers. He succeeded in persuading the Cabinet, and for the time being the emphasis was on churning out fighters and the men to fly them.

It was the RAF's great good fortune that two superb fighter designs were already in existence — Sydney Camm's Hurricane and R. J. Mitchell's Spitfire. Britain's fortunes were further strengthened by the presence at the head of Fighter Command of Hugh Dowding. He was an awkward man, distant and unconvivial; but he possessed a strong understanding of how fighters should be used to the maximum effect, as well as the strength of character to force his views through, even over the objections of colleagues and politicians.

Dowding resisted Churchill's demand for Fighter Command to be thrown into the hopeless fight to save France and insisted that it be held back to build up its strength for the real battle ahead. While the opposing forces may not have been so unbalanced as the myth suggests, elements of Fighter Command were to be stretched to snapping point several times during the course of the Battle of Britain. Dowding and his lieutenants were operating on tight margins. They had to make constant, vital calculations as to how best to use their slender resources. One in particular — Keith Park — proved superbly matched to the task, barely putting a foot wrong while commanding 11 Group, which bore the brunt of the fighting. The defenders were helped by serious German miscalculations, such as the decision in September to switch the weight of the attack away from the infrastructure of Fighter Command and onto British cities.

The prevailing orthodoxy now is that, so long as it kept its head and its nerve, the RAF was on course to win the Battle of Britain. But no matter how logical that result might seem in hindsight, there was no feeling of certain victory at the time. In the summer of 1940 any confrontation with Germany appeared likely to end in defeat and Europe's fate seemed sealed. The land and air armies of France, so impressive-looking on paper, had been swept aside in no time. Who was to say that the RAF would not go the same way?

The first significance of the Battle of Britain was that it proved that the Germans could be resisted. In the first year of war, Hitler had enjoyed a run of swift, relatively easy successes. This was his first setback. The Battle of Britain did not destroy the Luftwaffe, which was to carry on bombing British cities by night until the spring of 1941, undeterred by the RAF. But it prevented the Luftwaffe from achieving the aim ordered by Hitler — the destruction of the British air force as a precondition for launching an invasion. When the Luftwaffe failed to achieve that goal, there was no chance that the conditions for an invasion could be established and Operation Sea Lion was postponed — indefinitely, as it turned out.

The outcome of what was essentially a small battle was to have great psychological implications, which were, in turn, to have even greater strategic consequences. The victory persuaded the British of the virtue of defiance. It encouraged the belief that Hitler could not only be resisted, but also beaten. No-one imagined that Britain could do that on its own. It needed the United States, and here the Battle of Britain played a crucial role. The RAF's success in driving back the Luftwaffe created the circumstances in which America could be steered towards the path of intervention, invasion and victory. This element of the battle was never far from Churchill's mind. The propaganda was managed with one eye trained on transatlantic public opinion. The British authorities gave US newspaper correspondents and newsreel teams preferential treatment over their home-grown colleagues. The approach was effective. An American *March of Time* newsreel released in October 1940 carried a commentary declaring: "Today as the world watches the Battle of Britain it sees England still mistress of the seas and, in over a year of solid war, the Royal Air Force still unconquered not only over Britain but in the Near East and Far East."

The message sent to an undecided America, and received loud and clear, was that Britain was a reliable ally who was engaged in an open-ended fight. The fact of its survival would give America a launching pad into Europe, should it choose to join the struggle against

9

Nazism. Had the battle been lost, and had Operation Sea Lion succeeded in spite of the Royal Navy, this option would no longer have been open and all Europe would indeed have sunk into the "new Dark Age" predicted by Churchill.

Seen in purely military terms, the achievement of the pilots of Fighter Command was limited. It was to avoid defeat rather than to achieve a crushing victory. But it is, ultimately, in ideological terms that the Battle of Britain should be judged. The skill and fortitude of the almost 3,000 men who flew in it ensured Britain's survival as a beacon of freedom and decency to inspire and rally the rest of the world. Seen in that light, the battle was a triumph, not just for Britain but for humanity.

CHAPTER ONE

Origins

The British people had lived with the knowledge of what war from the air might mean for a quarter of a century before the 1940 Blitz. Zeppelin airships commenced their attacks in January 1915, and on the night of 31 May one of them dropped a ton of explosives on East London, killing seven people. By the end of the First World War, the British civilian death toll had risen to 670. The psychological effect was greater, though, than the numbers suggest. Aerial bombardment emphasized the fact that henceforth civilians could expect to find themselves in the front line, liable to random death from an enemy that had broadened its military repertoire to include the terrorizing of the enemy population. The prospect both repelled and fascinated — people travelled miles to examine the debris. The appearance of hostile aircraft in hitherto inviolate skies underlined another disturbing truth. Britain could no longer rely on its naval supremacy to ensure its national security.

The transformation of aeroplanes from objects of delight that opened up the skies to instruments of destruction was depressingly swift. When the First

World War began, powered flight was only ten years old. To begin with, the embryonic air forces of Britain and Germany used their planes for reconnaissance, and to direct artillery fire. As the early biplanes acquired machine-guns and developed into fighting machines, the era of aerial duelling began as each side tried to drive the other from the skies over the trenches. The contest produced the great fighter aces, whose exploits provided a romantic contrast to the grim bloodletting on the ground.

ALBERT BALL

The culture of fighter "aces" was born during the First World War in the skies over the trenches of Flanders. Many Battle of Britain pilots were brought up on the exploits of such famous air warriors as Albert Ball (1896–1917) and Edward "Mick" Mannock (1887–1918), whose spirit would permeate the culture of Fighter Command. These characters had been adventurous, dashing and independent-minded to the point of eccentricity, and their feats seemed to belong to the era of knightly combat rather than to the ghastly industrial warfare being waged in the trenches below them.

Albert Ball was brought up in a middle-class home in Nottingham. His father had started his life as a plumber but rose to be mayor of the city. Albert initially joined the infantry, but while waiting to be sent to France took private flying lessons, which propelled him into the Royal Flying Corps. He was posted to France as a lieutenant in the RFC at the time of the Somme offensive. A solitary figure, he had no interest in the camaraderie of the mess or the attractions of local women, preferring to spend hours playing the violin or chatting with his aeroplane's riggers and fixers, making endless adjustments to improve its efficiency. He would go up alone, and he soon adopted an effective, but highly dangerous, tactic of flying directly at packs of enemy aircraft, getting as near as he could before firing off his Lewis gun at close range. "He had but one idea," said a fellow pilot, Roderic Hill, "that was to kill as many Huns as possible."[1] But in a letter home he described his wish to "leave all this beastly killing for a time".

His courage and aggression quickly made him a hero to the younger pilots, although, as one commented, "One felt that it could only be a matter of time before he 'bought it', as he was shot about so often." By the end of 1916 he was the most famous pilot in the RFC and was taken off operations. He was invited to breakfast by the prime minister and showered with attention and honours, but, finding life away from the front difficult, he was soon agitating to return to action. Ball's aircraft crashed during combat in May 1917, killing him. He was awarded, posthumously, the Victoria Cross.

The advent of aeroplanes used as "strategic" bombers came relatively late in the war, but on 25 May 1917 German Gotha G.IV bombers based in Ghent crossed the English Channel and attacked Folkestone, killing 71 people. More devastatingly, on 13 June 1917, a bombing run on London and Southeast England killed 158 people, including a number of children in a school in Poplar, East London.

The "slaughter of the innocents" as the newspapers called it, and the indiscriminate nature of the attacks, intensified popular outrage against the Germans. It persuaded King George V to drop his Germanic "Saxe-Coburg" family name in favour of the homely and patriotic "Windsor". Strategic thinking and planning intensified to reflect the reality that aerial warfare would play a central role in future conflicts. Under Jan Smuts, the South African prime minister and British Cabinet member, a government committee in 1917 made proposals for invigorating air defences and for establishing better offensive capabilities. The results were profound. By January 1918, Britain had acquired a separate Air Ministry. On 1 April 1918, the Royal Air Force was born out of the army's Royal Flying Corps and the Royal Naval Air Service. It was the first independent air arm in the world.

The new chief of the air staff, Sir Hugh Trenchard (1873–1956), insisted that the RAF have its own independent training schools, and a cadet college opened at Cranwell in Lincolnshire in 1920 to provide a core of permanent officers. Selection criteria were stringent, and most recruits were from the public schools. To provide a stream of skilled mechanics, riggers and fitters to maintain the aircraft, Trenchard established a training school at Halton in Buckinghamshire. Here, boys would serve a three-year apprenticeship before joining the ranks, and the best three apprentices from each year were offered places at Cranwell. In late 1921 it was announced that outstanding candidates from the ranks would also be offered the chance to learn to fly, serving for five years as sergeant pilots before returning to their trades. The highly technical nature of the service ensured a narrowing of the gap between officers and skilled "other ranks".

It was not long before the RAF's existence was threatened. In the years following the war Trenchard had to fight for its life, as the force was cut from 188 squadrons to 33 and its assets were eyed up greedily by the army and the navy, who had never fully accepted the need for an independent air service. Trenchard, supported by Winston Churchill who at the time was secretary of state for war and air, argued that an independent RAF could become "a force that will profoundly alter the strategy of the future". Indeed, in the 1920s and 1930s a growing group of military strategists looked to air power as the means of avoiding static trench warfare, and to aerial bombing as the means of delivering decisive victory. Influential figures included the Italian Giulio Douhet, whose 1921 book *Il dominio dell'aria* (*The Command of the Air*) advocated strategic bombing as the best means to undermine an enemy, and the British military thinker

Sir Basil Liddell Hart. Trenchard, too, was a leading voice in the pro-bomber chorus.

Underlying the theory of aerial bombing was a sense that there was no effective defence against bombers, either from the ground or from fighter aircraft. It seemed unlikely that a home-based fighter could make a successful interception of an incoming bomber force. If the attackers flew at 10,000 feet and at 200 miles per hour, they would be over London long before a defending fighter could climb to reach them. In Trenchard's eyes, the answer to the problem was the creation of a deterrent bomber force that could match the enemy blow for blow. In order for the deterrence factor to work, the fear of retributive annihilation had to be so great as to dissuade aggressors. In such a view, the advent of the bomber seemed to have made the traditional battlefield more or less irrelevant: future wars would be won, or lost, by the extent to which a civilian population could be demoralized and a national infrastructure could be bombed into ruins.

Projections of what bombing could wreak tended to be stark. A 1924 defence committee report chaired by Sir John Anderson predicted 28,000 deaths in one month of bombing. A later medical report warned of the likelihood of "three to four million cases of acute panic, hysteria and other neurotic conditions during the first six months of air attack." It was believed that armed forces would be needed to keep order at home. The philosopher (and pacifist) Bertrand Russell predicted in 1936 that London under bombing would become "one vast raving bedlam, the hospitals will be stormed, traffic will cease, the homeless will shriek for peace, the city will be a pandemonium". The commonly held view was that the city would be powerless to resist these attacks which were likely to come without warning.

The gloom was encapsulated by Conservative Party leader Stanley Baldwin, who, during a debate in the House of Commons on 10 November 1932, bluntly stated that "it is well for the man in the street to realise that there is no power on earth that can protect him from being bombed. Whatever people may tell him, the bomber will always get through . . ." Reminding *MPs* that "aerial warfare is still in its infancy, and its potentialities are incalculable and inconceivable", he echoed the view that "the only defence is in offence, which means that you have to kill more women and children more quickly than the enemy if you want to save yourselves."[2] The Japanese bombing of Shanghai in 1932, and — five years later — the destruction of the Basque town of Guernica by German aircraft serving General Franco's Nationalist cause, during the Spanish Civil War, seemed to bear out theories of the bomber's irresistible force.

Such fears did not necessarily work to bolster the RAF's resources. A widespread pacificist mood, and an understandable reluctance to consider the appalling prospect of another war so soon after the last one, created a reluctance to take action. The RAF's annual budget remained under £20 million until 1935.

It took events in international politics and technology to change things. In August 1934, Adolf Hitler —

already Germany's chancellor — consolidated the Nazi grip on the country by appropriating the presidency on the death of the old war hero Hindenberg. The potential menace of a resurgent, re-armed, expansionist Germany soon became clear. On 20 April 1935, the full might of the new German Luftwaffe ("air force") was revealed at a huge air parade held in Berlin to mark Hitler's birthday. British observers were startled at the show of strength. The realization grew that "Britain was an island no more".

A rearmament scheme, known as Expansion Plan A, had been launched in 1934 in response to German events, and it now took on a greater urgency. Forty-five new air stations were ordered in 1935, and plans were laid to increase the number of home-based squadrons to one hundred-and-twenty-three. In 1937, for the first time, more money was spent on the Royal Air Force than on the British Army. RAF personnel increased fivefold between 1934 and the beginning of the Second World War, by which time the service had a strength of 118,000, with 45,000 reserves. The number of Auxiliary squadrons increased from eight to twenty, and another reserve force was established, the Royal Air Force Volunteer Reserve (RAFVR).

The Auxiliary Air Force (AAF) had been set up in 1924, with its first four squadrons formed the following year — No. 600 (City of London), No. 601 (County of London), No. 602 (City of Glasgow) and No. 603 (City of Edinburgh). Applicants were required to have learned to fly, which was expensive, and so the first Auxiliary squadrons were socially rather exclusive, in spite of Hugh Trenchard's wish that the ranks be open to all. Legend had it that 601, which became known as the "Millionaire's Squadron", was founded at White's, grandest of the London clubs, by the son of the Duke of Westminster. The scheme was enlarged as part of the 1934 expansion, and the Auxiliary pilots switched to fighter planes. By the time of the Battle of Britain, there were 21 Auxiliary squadrons, making up a quarter of Britain's fighter strength. (The high number of casualties in the early period of the battle meant that they would gradually lose their tight social cohesion.)

In marked contrast, the Royal Air Force Volunteer Reserve, launched in 1936, was a more egalitarian and democratic organization. This inspired creation gave adventurous, "air-minded" young men — many of them doing dull jobs in offices and factories — the chance to learn to fly in their spare time, at no cost. Men aged between 18 and 25 joined as "airmen under training", and they received commissions only on merit. The aim of the RAFVR was to train 800 airmen a year. Volunteers received £25 per year in pay and had to attend an annual 15-day flying course. By spring 1939, there were 2,500 RAFVR pilots in training, with 310 of them flying fighters when war broke out. They would play an essential role in the Battle of Britain, as pilots from the regular RAF fell from the skies in the first months of the fighting.

Before the Expansion Plan of 1934, all regular pilots and crew had been trained by the RAF; but as the numbers increased it became necessary to farm out the basic aviation training to civilian flying schools, 13 of which were operational by 1936. New pilots trained in two-seater planes — Avro Tutors or de Havilland Tiger Moths — and during a course lasting between eight and twelve weeks pupils were taken through twenty-two different stages, from the first "air experience" through to aerobatics, flying blind and recovering from a spin. Those without a natural feel for flying were "washed out". Those who were successful proceeded to the RAF Depot at Uxbridge, where for two weeks they drilled, trained and learned the customs of the air force. This phase was followed by a six-week stint at an operational training unit (OTU), where the pilots would, in theory, fly the aircraft they would fight in and practise formation flying and combat tactics.

In 1936, the RAF was restructured into four Commands: Fighter, Bomber, Coastal and Training. Sir Hugh Dowding (1882–1970), then the head of research and development on the Air Council, was put in charge of Fighter Command, which would include responsibility for anti-aircraft assets such as guns and searchlights. At the same time, the strategic focus was shifting. Those strategists and officials who had argued that it *was* possible to mount a plausible and effective defence against aerial bombers were gathering strength. They were aided by two important developments.

First, the prototypes of faster, monoplane fighters — the Hawker Hurricane (designed by Sydney Camm) and the Supermarine Spitfire (designed by Reginald Mitchell) — suggested that perhaps, after all, the bomber would *not* always get through. If these aircraft could climb sufficiently quickly, they could then

20

intercept what (it was anticipated) would be ranks of unprotected bombers. Second, a group of innovators had hit upon a crucial breakthrough in gaining advance warning of approaching aircraft long before human observers could see with their own eyes: "radio detection and ranging", which was to become famous by its acronym: radar.

Pioneering work on radar had been carried out by German, French, Soviet and American scientists. But it was British experimentation that produced the breakthrough. At the end of 1934, the director of scientific research at the Air Ministry, W. E. Wimperis, suggested that a committee be set up to explore any ideas, however unlikely, that might contribute to air defence. The Aeronautical Research Committee, under the leadership of Henry Tizard, first met in January 1935. Wimperis had already approached Robert Watson-Watt (1892–1973), a radio expert, and asked him about rumours concerning a German "death ray", an electromagnetic weapon that, it was suggested, could shut down the engine of a hostile plane in mid-air. A descendant of James Watt, the 18th-century inventor and pioneer of the steam engine, Watson-Watt had worked for the Meteorological Office, experimenting with equipment that could detect at long range the radio signals given off by thunderstorms. In late 1934 he was superintendent of the radio department at the National Physical Laboratory at Teddington, West London.

Watson-Watt brushed aside the idea of a "death ray": it would not be possible to generate a powerful enough signal to interfere with an engine and, anyway, the aircraft would have to be located first. But he did come up with another idea, which, though less dramatic, turned out to be of supreme importance. His work with weather detection had shown him that radio waves were bounced back to earth not only by certain atmospheric conditions but also by the metal fuselages of aircraft overhead. On 12 February 1935, he and his assistant Arnold Wilkins produced a draft report entitled *The Detection and Location of Aircraft by Radio Methods*. Tizard's committee was impressed. So too was Dowding, who was then still heading research and development at the Air Ministry.

Less than two weeks later Watson-Watt and Wilkins demonstrated a basic system to a member of Tizard's committee, A. P. Rowe. A Handley Page Heyford bomber was flown along the centre line of the 50-metre radio beam transmitted by the BBC's station at Daventry. In a field near Upper Stowe, Northamptonshire, receiving equipment had been set up linked to a cathode-ray oscilloscope to display the beam's signal. As the bomber passed within eight miles of the transmitter, the beam was measurably displaced.

Tizard's committee backed further development, establishing an experimental unit under Watson-Watt at Orford Ness on the Suffolk coast. Before the end of 1935, the range of the equipment had been expanded to 50 miles, and plans had been drawn up to create a chain of 20 coastal "Chain Home" radar stations covering the approaches from Germany, and to make the new technology a cornerstone of air defence. When Dowding took over Fighter Command in 1936, he thus brought with him both an understanding of radar and strong support for Watson-Watt's work.

Top-secret research continued on the project, which was known, partly in the interests of vagueness, as "Radio Direction Finding" or RDF. At Bawdsey Manor, near Orford Ness, an experimental station was opened in September 1936, with two more following the next year, at Dover and Canewdon, Essex. By now, the accuracy of the equipment had improved, and the range increased to 100 miles.

By February 1940, the 20 original Chain Home (CH) stations had been constructed, as well as a further 12 covering the west and the north of England. Each consisted of a number of 350-ft transmitter aerial masts, 250-ft receiver aerial masts, a transmitter and a receiver block, and an office where the radar displays were situated. These Chain Home "High" stations, however, could not detect incoming aircraft at low altitude, and to fill this gap a second system of "low-looking" Chain Home Low stations — and mobile units — was established from November 1939. These operated on a lower frequency and had a shorter range, but together with the Chain Home High stations they gave the RAF an excellent chance of detecting attacks in time to react effectively.

Radar's development and deployment had been supported by many, from King George down, and certainly Dowding's enthusiasm was enormously beneficial. But the greatest share of the credit belongs to Watson-Watt, who now turned from the technical side of radar to building up a usable network of machines and the people to run them, as well as a layered organization that efficiently passed information along the chain of command. His contributions to the war effort earned him a knighthood in 1942. A decade later he was awarded £50,000 by the British government for his work.

In September 1938, Prime Minister Neville Chamberlain made his last attempt to buy peace in Europe by feeding Hitler another slice of territory. Earlier in the year Germany had annexed Austria. Now Hitler was demanding Czechoslovakia's German-speaking Sudetenland region. At a summit at Munich, Britain and France acceded. Publicly, Chamberlain was lauded for preserving the peace, appearing on the balcony of Buckingham Palace to rapturous crowds below. Privately, even he now thought Hitler was unhinged and untrustworthy, and British military preparations intensified further.

A few months later, in December 1938, the long debate about whether the RAF should invest in fighters for defence, or bombers for offence, was settled in favour — for the time being at least — of the fighters. This crucial change was led not by the colourful figures and substantial egos in the debate, but by a lawyer-cum-politician, Sir Thomas Inskip, who had been appointed the minister in charge of defence coordination in 1936. Rejecting the "early knockout blow" argument of the pro-bomber lobby, he sided with Dowding in deciding that the RAF's principal role had to be "to prevent the Germans from knocking us out". His argument was strengthened by the fact that fighters were a lot cheaper to produce than bombers. Now, the proportion of fighter to bomber squadrons started to near parity.

When, in March 1939, German and Hungarian troops occupied the rest of the Czech lands, Chamberlain's "peace in our time" sentiments of Autumn 1938 were exposed as delusions. Poland was next on the Nazi menu. Both Britain and France had guaranteed its security. War now seemed inevitable. The pilots of Fighter Command prepared for the daunting duty of defending Britain's skies.

It was still assumed that their task would be to bring the maximum amount of firepower to bear on heavily armoured enemy fleets of invading bombers. The premise was that the bombers would be unescorted. For one thing, the German airfields were judged as being too far from British shores to allow the Luftwaffe to send fighter escorts. This reinforced a tactical presumption that fighter-to-fighter combat was a thing of the past — that the dogfights reminiscent of the First World War were obsolete in the new bomber age. Accordingly, fighter pilots were trained to carry out set-piece attack patterns from varying directions. The basic formation for carrying out the attacks was the "vic" — three fighters flying in a close horizontal arrow-head relation, with a leader and two wingmen.

★ ★ ★

As was often the case in war, the RAF peacetime theoretical orthodoxies were soon bent out of shape by the realities of battle. But the Luftwaffe too found that their anticipated methods of waging war required significant modification.

The German air force that so astonished British observers in 1935 had been born in secret. Forbidden by the 1919 Treaty of Versailles to support a military air force, Germany had instead channelled energy, technical expertise and substantial state subsidy into the development of civil aviation. Hugo Junkers (1859–1935), the pioneer of metal aircraft, Claude Dornier (1884–1969), Ernst Heinkel (1888–1958) and Willy Messerschmitt (1898–1978) — who all gave their names to Luftwaffe combat aircraft — started out designing and manufacturing civilian, or "sporting", aircraft in the 1920s. A state carrier, Deutsche Lufthansa, was created in 1926 under the chairmanship of Erhard Milch, who had commanded a fighter *Geschwader* (wing) in the First World War. Within two years, it was Europe's most efficient airline, and by 1930 it was bigger than the British and French civil airlines combined. At the same time, years before the advent of the Nazi regime, "air-mindedness" was encouraged, with state-sponsored gliding and flying clubs attracting tens of thousands of members. At a time when elsewhere flying was the preserve of the rich, in Germany it was a new and exciting sport for all.

As early as 1923, a top-secret memorandum laid out plans for an independent military air force. Lufthansa openly and quite legally trained many hundreds of pilots, who in time would form a core for the Luftwaffe. It also deliberately developed designs for commercial aircraft that could be easily convertible into bombers, such as the Junkers 52. More secret were agreements with the Russian authorities, who, from the end of 1923, allowed the setting-up of a secluded base 200 miles southeast of Moscow. There, far from the eyes of western Europe, many of the future Luftwaffe's senior personnel underwent thorough military training. By the time the Luftwaffe was unveiled to the world in 1935, it had behind it the strongest aircraft industry in Europe. Generous subsidies and loans to Dornier, Heinkel and Junkers allowed a massive expansion of aircraft production, by more than 800 per cent in the two years after 1933.

Hermann Goering, the senior Nazi and First World War flying ace, was the Luftwaffe's commander; reporting to him was Erhard Milch (1892–1972) who, as state secretary of the new *Reichsluftfahrtministerium* (Reich Aviation Ministry), exercised close control of a force that already numbered 20,000 men and nearly 2,000 aircraft. Milch calculated that he needed ten years to build a Luftwaffe ready to fight a major war. Goering cemented his position by appointing First World War colleagues to senior positions. Meanwhile, Milch drove forward a vigorous expansion plan, which, by late 1935, was delivering 300 new aircraft a month.

All Lufthansa pilots now became Luftwaffe reservists, and training programmes for combat pilots were also massively expanded through the 1930s. At the outbreak of the Second World War, Luftwaffe training units were producing pilots of a very high standard at the rate of 15,000 a year. Pilots had 250 hours' flying time behind them before being transferred to an operational flying school to receive specialist training in fighter, bombing or dive-bombing skills.

Many interwar German strategists endorsed the prevailing notions of the primacy of the bomber. The first chief of the air staff of the new Luftwaffe, Walther Wever, supported by Milch, ordered the development of heavy four-engined bombers that would be able to deliver a significant bomb load from Germany as far away as Scotland or the Urals. But in June 1936 Wever was killed in an air crash, and Goering, jealous of Milch's influence, sidelined Milch in favour of a First World War fighter ace crony, Ernst Udet. Udet had been a superb pilot but was inadequate to the tasks of aircraft procurement and production. Under his influence, supported by Goering and by Wever's successor as chief of the air staff, ex-army officer Albert Kesselring (1885–1960), the Luftwaffe abandoned the heavy-bomber project in favour of shaping a force for infantry support, with lighter, faster bombers able to dive on ground targets.

The outbreak of the Spanish Civil War in July 1936 gave Goering a chance to measure the capabilities of his new force. Before the end of the year, the Condor Legion had come into being, made up of Luftwaffe "volunteers" under the command first of General Hugo Sperrle (1885–1953), and then of General Wolfram von Richthofen, cousin of the famous First World War ace Baron von Richthofen. The war provided a test bed for the Luftwaffe's latest models and combat experience for its pilots. It was also the first time that a coordinated air and ground war had been fought, and the results were devastating. Von Richthofen returned to Berlin to press the case for continuing to develop air policy in the direction of ground support.

Thus, the Luftwaffe that confronted Fighter Command in the summer of 1940 had been designed to support the army rather than to fight a strategic battle on its own. Those tactics, though, delivered demonstrable success in the first months of war.

CHAPTER TWO

Watching, Waiting . . . and Withdrawing

The events of the ten months leading up to the Battle of Britain left the country in the most perilous position of her modern history. On 3 September 1939, two days after Hitler invaded Poland, France and Britain reluctantly declared war in support of their ally, honouring their agreement of 1 April that year. By then, Poland was already reeling. Her army had been spread thinly over the long frontiers with Germany, Czechoslovakia and East Prussia (the latter divided from the rest of Germany by the "Polish Corridor" established after the First World War). Much of her air force was destroyed on the ground in the first few days of the war by a Luftwaffe that was ready, well trained, and combat-tested in the Spanish Civil War — and which outnumbered the Poles by at least four to one. It was a grossly unequal contest. German combat aircraft were five years more advanced in design and performance. German air superiority was immediate, and it was used to crushing effect as supply lines were ruptured, troops bombed and machine-gunned, and cities threatened with annihilation from above.

The Polish pilots proved skilful, despite their poor machines, destroying nearly 300 German aircraft during the course of the fighting. But by 17 September the Polish capital, Warsaw, was surrounded, as Red Army troops invaded Poland from the east to swallow the rest of the country (under secret terms of the Nazi-Soviet Pact agreed in August). By 6 October the battle for Poland was over. But for many Polish soldiers and airmen it was only the beginning of their war. Some 100,000 managed to escape through Romania, and they would go on to fight hard for the Allies, including during the Battle of Britain. Within a year Wladyslaw Gnys, who had been the first Polish fighter pilot of the war to shoot down a German aircraft, would be flying Hurricane fighters out of Northolt in Middlesex.

The rape of Poland produced no answering intervention from the French and British allies. They were in no position to do anything, and, apart from sporadic skirmishing, nothing very much happened in the way of hostilities. In Britain, the period from September 1939 to May 1940 became known as the "Phoney War". In Germany it was called the *Sitzkrieg*, the "sitting war".

Britain busied herself instead with preparing her defences. After the Munich Summit crisis in September 1938, the Air Raid Precaution (ARP) budget had been tripled. By the end of the year, 90 per cent of Londoners had been issued with gas masks and over a million feet of trenches had been dug, zigzagging across parks and commons. Plans for more substantial public shelters lagged behind, partly because of a fear of a direct hit killing a large concentration of people. It was thought preferable that people should build their own protection in the shape of "Anderson" shelters, named after Lord Privy Seal (and soon Home Secretary) Sir John Anderson (1882–1958), who held responsibility for ARP measures.

The Anderson shelter was cheap and easy to construct, made out of six curved sections of corrugated steel bolted together at the top and sunk into the ground over a shallow square-shaped hole about four feet deep and ten feet wide, lined with five other metal sheets. It was suggested that at least 18 inches of soil be loaded on top, which, it was hoped, would save the shelter's occupants from anything other than a direct hit. The great flaw — apart from the need for a garden to place it in — was the lack of drainage, and many shelters quickly filled up with dirty water. The discomfort was compounded by the sacking, soaked in water, which was supposed to be hung over the entrance as a defence against the possibility of poison gas. Despite these deficiencies, by September 1939 nearly 1.5 million Anderson shelters had been distributed free to families with incomes of less than £250 per year. The more comfortably off were expected to pay for their own.

With the outbreak of war, people practised putting out fires and crawling through smoke-filled rooms, underwent first-aid training, and were told what to do if caught outside in a raid: lie face down, with hands over the ears, mouths half open and teeth parted. Works of art were removed from the National Gallery and the Tate Gallery to caves in Wales. Irreplaceable volumes and documents from the Public Records Office were shipped out of London or stored deep underground. London Zoo took the precaution of destroying its snakes in case they escaped during an air raid.

At the same time, the transformation of London, and Britain's other main cities, gathered pace. Famous Oxford Street stores boarded up their windows and converted their basements into air-raid shelters for their customers. Landmarks such as the Albert Memorial in Kensington were boxed up to minimize bomb damage. Sandbags, filled from pits dug in Hampstead Heath, appeared everywhere, stacked against windows and doors as blast-proofing. They soon turned mouldy. Windows were webbed with tape to prevent injuries from flying glass. Heavy dark curtains hung from every window, to keep the light in and make the blackout complete.

The blackout proved one of the most unpopular of the new restrictions. London became as "dark as a pocket", and it was frightening to be out at night. It was easy to get lost or hit by cars, which travelled with hoods over their headlamps. The dishonest thrived in the darkness, and petty crime soared. The local ARP wardens were ruthless in enforcing the blackout regulations, with a shout of "Put that light out!" Estimates of what could be seen from an aircraft at altitude were ludicrously inaccurate. A German-Swiss resident of Kensington was even accused of trying to provide guidance for the enemy by puffing too hard on his cigar.

The start of war also witnessed the evacuation of millions from the towns and built-up areas, particularly London. Evacuation lists for threatened cities had been drawn up before September 1939, and those on them included children, the handicapped, the ill and the blind. But registration was neither complete nor obligatory, and parents could decide for themselves whether or not their children should be sent away. Three days before the war started, the government began moving 39,000 people from towns in Southeast England considered to be in the bombers' likely path. In London, about half the population of children departed. Around 1.5 million people travelled on the government scheme, with a further 2 million making their own arrangements. For the rich, this meant moving to hotels in the north or the countryside. Ten thousand children from well-to-do families were sent abroad in the first year of the war, mainly to Canada or the United States. It did not necessarily make them safer: in September 1939, the liner *City of Benares* was torpedoed on the way to Canada, and only 13 of the 90 children on board survived.

Most evacuated children in Britain were taken in by rural families, with varying degrees of enthusiasm. Some children from London's East End found it difficult adjusting to their new surroundings. Used to a diet of bread, margarine, fish, chips and sweets, they viewed the fruit and vegetables now on offer with suspicion. Some of their middle-class hosts, cushioned from the reality of urban poverty, were appalled by their new charges. One Women's Institute reported that "the children were filthy, and in this district we have never seen so many verminous children lacking any knowledge of clean and hygienic habits . . . it appeared they were unbathed for months".[1]

As autumn 1939 turned to winter, and the expected waves of German bombers failed to materialize, many people drifted back to their homes, as shelters filled with water and the miles of trenches dug in public parks crumbled and collapsed. The absence of an immediate threat made the rules and restrictions under which people had to live — rules on movement, meetings, free expression and especially the blackout — all the more irksome.

The early days of war were characterized, too, by false alarms and accidents. The most dramatic incident involved two friendly aircraft being shot up by their own side. On 6 September, a searchlight battery in the Blackwater estuary in Essex reported a hostile aircraft crossing the coast. Hurricanes from No. 56 Squadron were ordered up from North Weald to intercept. As they climbed on the hunt for the intruder, they were picked up by a radar station in Essex, which mistook them for a large enemy formation. Further fighters were scrambled, which, in turn, confused the radar picture even more. Among them were 12 Spitfires from No. 74 Squadron at Hornchurch, Essex. A three-man section led by Adolph "Sailor" Malan took off first, followed by another section led by Flying Officer

"Paddy" Byrne. Behind Byrne was John Freeborn, who remembered "looking down and seeing we had cut a line through the haze where we had taken off . . . Malan was well in front . . . We saw these aircraft and Malan gave the order: 'Number One attack — go!' "[2] Malan's section went in, then Byrne's. Byrne and Freeborn opened fire and saw two aircraft go down. Freeborn remembers feeling "exhilarated". But when he landed, he learned the truth: the aircraft they had shot down — the first ever to fall to a Spitfire's guns — had been Hurricanes. One pilot was dead, another missing.

Byrne and Freeborn were put under arrest, and a general court martial was held on 7 October. According to Freeborn, Malan denied ever giving the order. Nevertheless, both men were acquitted. The so-called "Battle of Barking Creek" was hushed up, but harsh lessons were learned about the vital importance of positive identification of aircraft. (By coincidence, on the same day that the tragedy occurred, film director Alexander Korda was at the Hornchurch airfield filming an RAF propaganda picture, *The Lion Has Wings*.)

Despite the deceptive calm of the Phoney War, everyone understood that the respite was only temporary. In anticipation of a German attack westwards, the RAF set up bases in France at the very outset of the war. The deployment had two elements. The Advanced Air Striking Force, consisting of eight squadrons of Battle and Blenheim bombers and two squadrons (Nos 1 and 73) of Hurricane fighters, was to reinforce the French army along the frontier with Germany. The Air Component, with fighter-bombers and another two squadrons of Hurricanes (Nos 85 and 87), was to support the army's British Expeditionary Force (BEF), which started arriving in France as early as 10 September 1939. Britain's regular army of about five divisions, reinforced with Territorial Army units, was tiny compared with the French conscript army of eighty-eight divisions.

On the Franco-German border the fixed defences of the Maginot and Siegfried lines faced each other. The BEF, along with the First French Army, was positioned along the unprotected border between France and the neutral Low Countries, ready to move forward to the River Dyle (Dijle) in central Belgium should the Germans repeat their 1914 Schlieffen Plan and attack through Belgium.

The small RAF contingent, reinforced in the north by two squadrons (Nos 607 and 615), equipped with Gladiator biplanes, flew reconnaissance missions and patrols when the poor weather allowed and worked hard to improve the soggy French airfields, most of which were primitive and uncomfortable. The pilots had arrived in France full of excitement, only to find they had little to do. Bombing of Germany was forbidden for fear of reprisals. There were few enemy intruders. Those that appeared were often high-level reconnaissance planes, long gone by the time the Allied aircraft could climb high enough to meet them.

Nevertheless, on 30 September 1939, Flying Officer Peter "Boy" Mould from No. 1 Squadron scored the first British success of the war, shooting down a Dornier Do17 reconnaissance plane that had appeared over his airfield. Attacking from behind, he seems to have taken the Germans by surprise "as no evasive tactics were employed and no fire was encountered". Raked from top to toe with bullets, the Dornier caught fire and crashed after a vertical dive. The squadron later found the wreckage, with the only discernible remains of the crew being five disembodied hands. Mould got very drunk that night, telling a friend: "I'm bloody sorry I went and looked at the wreck. What gets me down is the thought that I did it."[3]

On the morning of 16 October 1939, the first serious aerial raid on Britain's navy occurred, when 12 Junkers Ju88s attacked shipping at the Royal Navy base at Rosyth. A fault with the local radar station meant that the arrival of the bombers came as a surprise, and they were able to damage a destroyer, killing sixteen. Spitfires arrived only as the Junkers were leaving, chasing them out to sea and downing two.

The winter of 1939–40 was a bitter one. Snow and thick cloud prevented flying for weeks on end. Pilots became bored and frustrated. But in March 1940, the weather improved, there was more patrolling and a greater number of encounters between the Luftwaffe and RAF. On 2 March, the first Messerschmitt Me109 fighter (also known as the Bf109) was shot down; at the end of the month, the first Messerschmitt Me110 twin-engine fighter-bomber was downed near Metz.

These encounters were analysed closely for what they could reveal about the shape of things to come, and the shot-down aircraft were salvaged and studied.

Such aerial skirmishing as there was in France in the months prior to the Battle of Britain taught the British a number of useful lessons as well as familiarizing them with the ways of their opponents. The RAF began to copy Luftwaffe practices, painting the underside of its fighters duck-egg blue to make them less visible against the sky, and fitting steel plates behind the pilot's seat to increase protection. The Hurricane's propeller was altered to improve climbing speed. Tactics were adjusted too, including the adoption of a "tail-end-Charlie", a single fighter weaving around behind the formation to guard against surprise attack from the rear.

The squadrons based in Britain were learning too. The German air force and army had been ordered to preserve their strength for the battles ahead, and Luftwaffe pilots on the Franco-German border were forbidden to seek combat, so that activities were limited to reconnaissance, mine-laying in northern waters and some sporadic raiding of British naval bases. These operations meant that British-based squadrons, although hardly busy compared with the times to follow, probably had more to do than did their colleagues in France. Most of the German attacks that did take place were performed by high-level bombers — harassing attacks, designed to stretch British nerves. They provoked constant alarms, but offered little chance of a "kill" for the British fighters.

British pilots came to dislike the frequent patrols carried out to protect shipping around the coast, which were monotonous, tiring and nerve-wracking, with worries of mechanical failure, ditching and death never far away. There was little at that stage, though, to fear from the Luftwaffe. As in France, the lack of action was frustrating. The pilots in the outlying stations, where there were no towns to distract them, grew bored. In the satellite stations the harsh winter was made worse by the spartan conditions.

In spring 1940, the military hibernation was drawing to an end. Germany was stirring again. Before launching his main attack in the west, Hitler wished to secure Germany's northern flank by occupying neutral Denmark and Norway. Control of the latter would also safeguard Germany's vital supplies of iron ore from Sweden via the northern Norwegian port of Narvik, as well as providing bases for an aerial attack on Britain from the east. The strategic importance of Norway was understood in London and, as the German High Command was well aware, Britain was simultaneously preparing a force to seize the port and looking at basing fighter and bomber aircraft in Norway.

The German invasion, ostensibly designed to protect Denmark and Norway from Anglo-French aggression, was launched shortly after 5a.m. in the morning of 9 April 1940, with a simultaneous advance of land forces in Denmark and seaborne landings on the Danish islands and in Norwegian ports. Denmark fell in a day, as did key cities and airfields in Norway, the latter secured by history's first ever paratroop attacks. The valiant shore batteries on the Oslo fjord, equipped with Krupp guns installed in 1893, succeeded in sinking the German heavy cruiser *Blücher*, thereby giving the Norwegian government and royal family a chance to flee the country. But control of the air gave the invaders a vital advantage.

As the Germans crushed resistance in the south of Norway, British infantrymen landed on the west coast near Trondheim and at Narvik to the north. Later in the month they were reinforced by French and then Polish troops. But the poorly equipped Allied effort lacked both clear objectives and a unified command.

The RAF's contribution was touched with the same chaotic, amateur feel that characterized the whole campaign. The first squadron dispatched to Norway — No. 263 — was made up of Gloster Gladiators, biplanes that belonged to a bygone generation of fighter aircraft. Carried to within 50 miles of the Norwegian coast by the carrier HMS *Glorious*, the squadron landed on a makeshift airfield on the frozen ice of the *Lesjaskogsvatnet* (Lake Lesjaskog) on 24 April. In theory, the Gladiators were adapted to winter conditions, but vital supplies to keep the engines de-iced failed to turn up and the airfield lacked radar or adequate anti-aircraft guns. During the first night the wheels of many of the machines froze to the ice, leaving the squadron sitting ducks when an attack of Heinkel He111 bombers came in at just before eight in the morning. Eight of the Gladiators were destroyed, and those that managed to take off found themselves heavily

41

outnumbered. By the end of the day, eleven had been lost and two had been destroyed and were beyond repair. Two days later there were no aircraft left.

In May, No. 263 Squadron returned to Norway as Allied troops, driven out from the south, fought the Germans at Narvik. This time, they were accompanied by No. 43 Squadron of Hurricanes, which struggled to find a usable base. For a time they operated from "a strip by a fjord", remembered Flight Sergeant Richard Earp. "The troops had been working very hard out there and they'd covered the place with coconut matting and wire netting." There was no running water and only cramped tents to sleep in. "All I had was a groundsheet and two blankets," said Earp. "You couldn't sleep. It was daylight all the time." Above all, he remembered that it "was terribly bloody cold".[4]

The emerging débâcle in Norway fed dissatisfaction in the House of Commons, and in the country at large, with Neville Chamberlain's government. It seemed incompetent and irresolute, quite unfit to lead the country at the time of its greatest peril. On 30 April the well-connected Conservative MP Henry "Chips" Channon wrote in his diary that there was a "cabal against poor Neville. 'They' are saying . . . that Winston should be Prime Minister as he has more vigour and the country behind him." During a long career Churchill had made many enemies in the country and in the House. But before the war he had established himself as the leading advocate of rearmament and Hitler's fiercest enemy. Now that his predictions had come true, he was being viewed with a new respect.

The political intrigues and manoeuvrings reached a climax on 7 May, as the House of Commons met to debate the failures of the Norway campaign. Chamberlain had lost the confidence of the House. The announcement of the result of a vote of censure brought shouts of "Out! Out! Out!" from the Opposition benches. Chamberlain tried and failed to form a cross-party national government under his premiership. On 10 May, he resigned his office, and the task fell to Churchill, the fervent pre-war opponent of appeasement who had been summoned from the backbenches in September 1939 to become First Lord of the Admiralty.

Churchill immediately brought senior Opposition figures into a new Cabinet, and appointed his friend Lord Beaverbrook as head of a new ministry for aircraft production. Churchill felt touched by the hand of history. "At last I had the authority to give directions over the whole scene," he later wrote. "I felt as if I were walking with destiny, and that all my past life had been but a preparation for this hour and for this trial."[5] There was to be no honeymoon period for the new prime minister. Churchill's first crisis came the very same day, as the Germans launched *Blitzkrieg* in the west.

The opening blow came at first light, when more than 300 German bombers attacked 22 airfields in the Netherlands, Belgium and northeastern France. The assailants regarded control of the air as essential for swift victory. In men and tanks the two sides were evenly matched, but the Germans had almost twice as many aircraft than all their opponents combined, amounting to some 4,000 planes, of which over 1,000 were Messerschmitt Me109s. The German air force was divided into two *Luftflotten* ("air fleets"): *Luftflotte 2*, in the north under Generaloberst Albert Kesselring, and *Luftflotte 3*, on the central front under Generaloberst Hugo Sperrle. Both reported to Generalfeldmarschall (Field Marshal) — and soon to be Reichsmarschall — Goering.

The Belgian and Dutch air forces were soon destroyed. German reconnaissance planes roved ahead of the advancing forces, spotting targets and triggering devastating dive-bombing attacks. These raids were followed by airborne assaults on key bridges, airfields and fortresses. Meanwhile, tanks and motorized infantry units crossed the borders, swept aside resistance and raced to meet up with their advance units.

Positioned to support the British Expeditionary Force, No. 87 Hurricane Squadron had been put on alert the night before and told to expect *Blitzkrieg* the next morning. "There was nothing unusual in that . . . people had become a little sceptical," reported the squadron's diary. But "we were awakened at dawn by a tremendous anti-aircraft barrage, the drone of many aero engines and a deep thudding sound we had never previously heard, BOMBS!" Most of the RAF contingent escaped being hit on the ground and was immediately in action. No. 1 Squadron took off at 5a.m. and was active for almost the entire day, shooting down several Dorniers. As soon as the attack had started, four more

Hurricane squadrons — Nos 3, 79, 501 and 504 — were rushed to France. Most were in action almost immediately, and their first day turned out to be their best. Much of the German bomber force had arrived without fighter escort. It was easy to find targets, as there were simply so many German aircraft in the skies. The RAF fighters flew 208 sorties and shot down at least 33 bombers, losing in the process only 7 Hurricanes, with 8 damaged and not a single pilot killed.

But each day thereafter was worse than the day before. Bombers now came escorted by swarms of Messerschmitts. Hurricane pilots were flying up to five sorties a day, taking off from under-equipped airfields that were the target of regular attacks from dive-bombers. Perpetual exhaustion sapped the strength of the airmen, as the German aircraft roamed deeper and deeper into France. "Our nerves were getting somewhat frayed," wrote Paul Richey of No. 1 Squadron. "We were jumpy and morose. Few of the boys smiled now — we were no longer the merry band of days gone by." Richey had already baled out once, and the experience had shaken him greatly: "I had a hell of a headache and was jumpy and snappy. Often I dared not speak for fear of bursting into tears."[6] But on the ground, the situation was soon even worse.

To the surprise of the Allies, the main German armoured thrust crashed through the supposedly "untankable" Ardennes forest in southwestern Belgium (and bypassed the Maginot Line), aiming to establish a bridgehead across the Meuse, the most formidable river barrier protecting France. Here again, air superiority was decisive, with the key French fortress of Sedan, just to the east of the Meuse, pounded by "airborne artillery": waves of dive-bombers that delivered the firepower of conventional big guns, but with much greater flexibility. Once successfully over the river, the German armoured columns headed northwest, hurrying towards the sea in order to split the Allied forces and pin the BEF and First French Army against the Channel.

The BEF had advanced, as planned, to the River Dijle in central Belgium. The British now threw their Blenheim and near obsolete Fairey Battle bombers against the advancing German columns, but with disastrous results. On 14 May, the Netherlands capitulated, her government and royal family having already evacuated to England.

For the French leadership, the fall of Sedan had a huge psychological as well as strategic impact. What remained of the Allies' bomber force was now sent *en masse* against the Meuse bridge-head, but the only result was appalling losses from flak and German fighters. On 15 May, French Prime Minister Paul Reynaud telephoned Churchill and told him, in English, "We have been defeated." Nonetheless, he pleaded for further fighter squadrons to be sent from England.

Air Chief Marshal Dowding was already dismayed at how his precious Fighter Command assets were being sacrificed in actions that did little to change a hopeless situation. He insisted that the bleeding stop. He was allowed into the War Cabinet meeting of 15 May to make his case. If the same rate of attrition continued for the next ten days, he argued, there would not be a single Hurricane left in France or Britain. "If the Home Defence Force is drained away in desperate attempts to remedy the situation in France," he wrote in an official letter that night to the under-secretary of state for air, "defeat in France will involve the final, complete and irremediable defeat of this country."

Churchill, however, was still set on giving "the last chance to the French army to rally its bravery and strength". The next day, 16 May, he flew to Paris in an effort to reinforce the morale of the French leadership. All he found, though, was disillusion and despair. "Utter dejection was written on every face," Churchill later wrote. "Where is the strategic reserve?" he asked the French commander-in-chief, General Gamelin. "Gamelin turned to me," wrote Churchill, "and with a shake of the head and a shrug, said '*Aucune*' [there is none]. There was another long pause. Outside in the garden of the Quai d'Orsay clouds of smoke arose from large bonfires, and I saw from the window venerable officials pushing wheelbarrows of archives on to them. Already, therefore, the evacuation of Paris was being prepared."[7]

In spite of the evidence of his eyes, and in the face of Dowding's dire warning, Churchill authorized the deployment of four further Hurricane squadrons after his return to London. They were to fly each day from England, because there were now not enough airfields and facilities left in French hands to support them.

Nevertheless, by 17 May Churchill had succumbed to reality. He ordered a contingency plan for the complete withdrawal of the BEF and RAF from France. Churchill's assistant private secretary, John ("Jock") Colville, noted in his diary: "Winston is depressed. He says the French are crumbling up as completely as did the Poles . . . There is a risk that the BEF may be cut off if the French do not rally in time."

The BEF began retreating and the airmen fell back with them, hopping from one vulnerable airfield to another. The withdrawal was painful. Nos 1 and 73 Squadrons lost 19 aircraft and 12 pilots in 7 days. In the three days from 16 May, Fighter Command lost sixty-two precious Hurricanes. The pilots of 32 Squadron were now flying in daily from Biggin Hill, Kent, an exhausting schedule that meant being woken up at 2.30a.m. and sometimes not getting back until as late as 10.30p.m. Across the English Channel they found chaos and despair. Peter Brothers remembered that "We'd go to a French airfield, refuel and try to get some instructions but everything was chaotic and so we'd just go off and do a patrol around to see what we could find . . . it was pretty ghastly and the French, I'm afraid, were totally demoralized by this time."[8] There was no effective control from the ground and few men were left to refuel and rearm the aircraft. Nor was there any effective early-warning system to get the Hurricanes airborne in time to intercept a raid. Above all, the British pilots were massively outnumbered in the air.

For the troops below, the situation was also desperate. Refugees clogged the roads, and overhead the terrifying Junkers Ju87 "Stuka" dive-bombers attacked seemingly at will. It was now clear that the French Ninth Army, originally positioned opposite the southern thrust from the Ardennes, had suffered a serious defeat. As the German Panzers raced for the Channel, they encountered virtually no resistance, covering on some days up to 40 miles. On 20 May, Amiens fell, cutting the Allied armies in two. The same day Gamelin was sacked, and his replacement, General Weygand, immediately ordered a French counter-attack on the German armoured column. The British also counter-attacked near Arras, but the delay to the German advance was only brief.

The airmen were not immune to the ravages or exhaustion, physical and emotional, of the rapidly deteriorating situation. On 21 May, Sergeant Eric Bann, of No. 238 Squadron, wrote to his parents in Macclesfield:

Have been having a real rough time, lost nearly all my clothes and have been sleeping in any old place, plus getting into some real hot places. We have bagged about forty German planes in the last four days but their numbers are terrific. Have been going in for about six of us to forty or fifty of theirs, the air was thick. I think we lost the Flight Commander yesterday, what a nice chap, they said he was engaged by about ten fighters and went down fighting madly. Our Squadron had been flying every day and we are very tired . . .

Believe me to see the German dive-bombers in their
hundred cutting at our poor troops makes you only
too glad to help — it's terrible.

On 22 May, the Germans reached the outskirts of
Boulogne and Calais, cutting off the BEF's supply
route, and the army was put on half rations. There was
no option now but to retreat to the coast. As the scale
of the disaster filtered down the ranks, there was
disbelief and anger. To the British High Command, the
army seemed doomed. Alan Brooke, commanding II
Corps, wrote on 23 May that "Nothing but a miracle
can save the BEF now."

From 24 May, British troops poured into Dunkirk
(Dunkerque), on the coast east of Calais. The town and
docks were already under attack from the air. The oil
depot was soon on fire, gushing thick smoke that lay in
a fat, black pall over the town and the shoreline. By 26
May, the port was wrecked beyond use. There was no
salvation there, and the men were ordered onto the
beaches. Hermann Goering was confident that his
Luftwaffe could prevent the escape of the trapped men.
"I hope the Tommies are good swimmers," he declared
delightedly on 26 May.

Lance-Bombardier Peter Lambert, a 22-year-old
volunteer who had swapped life as an insurance clerk
for the Territorial Army in April 1939, recollected the
bewildering chaos in an unpublished memoir:

The very thought of the British army being in retreat to
the extent that we had to abandon everything was

unbelievable. Despite all the meandering around northern France one felt that, sooner or later, things would stabilize and we could get into action.

Then came that night when we were told by our sergeant that the British Army was to retreat to the coast around Dunkirk where we were to be taken off by the Royal Navy. Not one of the gun positions we had so diligently surveyed during the Phoney War was used. Instead we had trundled these large things around the northern French countryside, preparing for action only once, but not firing a single shot. We were told to leave our vehicles having made them as useless as possible. The guns were too damaged and dumped in the La Bassée canal and we were to make our way on foot to Dunkirk.

So began our trek to the coast. We moved at night to avoid the bombing, accompanied everywhere by the barking of dogs whose owners had fled, leaving them to fend for themselves. Everyone was afraid of becoming detached from their comrades and lost. We had no sense of order. Morale was low. We could hardly be described as a military unit and on several occasions I remember hearing tanks all around us not knowing whether whey were friend or foe.

Hermann Goering

Born in 1893 in Bavaria, Hermann Wilhelm Göring (usually Anglicized as "Goering") served in the German infantry during the First World War, before transferring to the air force. He was an outstanding pilot, with a reported 22 kills and numerous decorations, including the "Blue Max" award for valour. In July 1918 he took over as commander of the "Flying Circus" unit made famous by the "Red Baron" Manfred von Richthofen.

Disgusted with the postwar settlement, he joined the Nazi Party in 1922 and for a time was in charge of its paramilitary *Sturmabteihung* (SA, "Storm Troop"). He played a part in the failed Munich Putsch of November 1923, when he was wounded in the groin and forced to flee to Austria. During painful treatment for his injury, he was given morphia, starting an addiction that he would battle for several years. He returned to Germany in 1927,

where his distinguished war record and charm made him an effective promoter of the party among the wary upper classes. He was elected as a deputy to Germany's parliament, the *Reichstag*, in the following year, becoming its president in 1932.

With Hitler's assumption of power in 1933, Goering was in the first Cabinet and in charge of the powerful Prussian police force, which he soon turned into a political weapon for the Nazis. During the 1930s he played key roles in the Nazification of the country, in the suppression of internal opposition, and in international and economic affairs. He was also given the post of special commissioner for aviation, then, shortly afterwards, minister for air, and he oversaw the secret expansion of the Luftwaffe. When the new air force became public in 1935, Goering was appointed its commander. In 1938, he became the first *Generalfeldmarschall* (field marshal) of the Luftwaffe, the promotion making him the highest ranking officer in Germany. Hitler named him his successor as leader of Germany and on 19 July 1940 made him the country's only *Reichsmarschall*.

Goering was an immensely powerful figure in the Third Reich, but he was also avaricious, vain, corrupt and decadent. Many years after the war, Me109 pilot Hans-Ekkehard Bob remembered meeting Goering on being presented with the Knight's Cross: "He showed up wearing a raw silk shirt with puffed sleeves, a silk cravat with a great big emerald on the throat, light grey riding breeches and red boots. Even by today's standards, it was a pretty daring get-up."[9] Goering liked to be called "The Iron Man", but at around 20 stone he was seriously overweight.

Goering's military reputation began to decline after the Luftwaffe failed to stop the Allied evacuation at Dunkirk. It fell further when the air force could not make good his boast to smash the RAF in weeks, nor prevent Berlin from being bombed. His ignorant, impetuous approach added greatly to the Luftwaffe's difficulties during the Battle of Britain.

"At the beginning we had great respect for him," said one Luftwaffe pilot, Gerhard Schöpfel. "But later our feelings changed. He began to complain that we were not doing enough, but we needed far more machines and manpower to achieve what he wanted."[10] The failure to supply the German Sixth Army at Stalingrad was the final blow to the reputation of Goering and his Luftwaffe. In April 1945, he sent a message to Hitler in his Berlin bunker offering to take over the leadership of the Reich, an action which Hitler regarded as high treason: Goering was placed under arrest, before his surrender to US forces in early May 1945.

Goering was convicted at the Nuremberg trials of war crimes and crimes against humanity, and sentenced to death. Poison was smuggled into his cell and he took his own life the night before his scheduled execution by hanging. The following morning his dead body was displayed by the gallows for the inspection of official witnesses.

Goering never accepted that the Battle of Britain had been a defeat for the Luftwaffe. He told one interrogator that he regarded the result as a draw.

On the night of 26 May, a hastily organized evacuation plan — Operation Dynamo — was launched. Over the previous few days every available ship had been gathered to form a rescue armada, comprising nearly 850 vessels, from destroyers, to transports, down to ferries and pleasure boats. The great evacuation started that evening. It was a slow and laborious business ferrying the men in dinghies from the beaches to the waiting boats, but on this occasion luck was siding with the British.

The next morning, 27 May, was grey and overcast, and the smoke in the air gave a measure of protection from the Luftwaffe. Then, when a breakwater in the harbour was adapted as a jetty, and piers were improvised on sunken lorries, the rate of evacuation improved dramatically. Some 47,000 were taken off on 29 May, and 68,000 on 31 May.

The overall speed of the evacuation took the Germans by surprise. It was only with improving weather on 1 June, by which time about three-quarters of the BEF had escaped, that an all-out German air assault was ordered against the beaches and town of Dunkirk. The German armour also returned to the attack, but the delay had given the Allies a chance to throw a makeshift defensive perimeter around the pocket.

While Stuka dive-bombers attacked the beaches, the port and any shipping present, Me109 fighters circled high above. The soldiers below would later bitterly complain that the "Brylcreem Boys" of the RAF had left them to their fate, but in fact Fighter Command threw itself fully into the task of trying to shield the evacuation. Dowding at last deployed his precious Spitfires, and many squadrons based around London were ordered into the fight, some seeing action for the first time. Fighter Command flew 2,739 sorties over the heads of the BEF, but much of this activity was hidden from the beaches by smoke or took place inland and out of sight, as fighters tried to get to the attacking bombers before they could discharge their loads. Many pilots were in the air for two, three or even four hours a day.

Sometimes the clouds cleared sufficiently to allow the full awfulness of the scene below to reveal itself. Brian Kingcome, a pilot with No. 92 Squadron, vividly remembered the contrasts of order and chaos:

> The beaches were a shambles, littered with the smoking wreckage of engines and equipment, destroyed either by enemy fire or else by our own troops to stop them falling into German hands. The sands erupted into huge geysers from exploding bombs and shells, while a backdrop to the scene of the carnage and destruction was provided by the palls of oily black smoke rising from the burning harbour and houses of Dunkirk and hanging high in the still air. And yet there the orderly lines of our troops stood, chaos and Armageddon at their backs, patiently waiting their turn to wade into the sea towards the boats, or holding their weapons above their heads as their turn finally came and they waded in up to their waists.[11]

One combat novice, Tim Vigors, a pilot officer with 222 Squadron based at Duxford, vividly remembered the sheer terror of his induction into the art of war over Dunkirk:

I walked over to my aircraft to make sure everything was in order. My mouth was dry and for the first time I understood the meaning of the expression "taste of fear". I suddenly realized that the moment had arrived . . . within an hour I would be battling for my life, being shot at with real bullets by a man whose one desire in life was to kill me. Up until now it had all somehow been a game, like a Biggles book where the heroes always survived the battles and it was generally only the baddies who got the chop. I was dead scared and knew I had somehow to control this fear and not show it to my fellow pilots.

Near Dunkirk, his flight — led by Douglas Bader — climbed to attack some Me109s. In the dogfight that followed Vigors found himself being chased by a Messerschmitt, which fired white tracer past his port wingtip. In that moment his first reaction was "extreme fear which temporarily froze my ability to think. This was quickly replaced by an overwhelming desire for self-preservation." He escaped unharmed and later managed to get some shots into another Me109. As he returned home after one-and-a-half exhausting hours, he examined his feelings. His biggest concern was "how deadly scared I'd been when I first saw those enemy bullets streaming past my wingtip. I had never known any fear like that before in my life . . . I just fervently hoped I could keep it under control." Vigors succeeded and went on to shoot down five German aircraft and gather a further four probable kills.[12]

The general rule was, though, that "green" pilots suffered against their more experienced enemies. The Intelligence Officer for 609 Spitfire Squadron later wrote: "It was a bit like sending a football eleven, whose members had never played together before, against a crack team that had never tasted defeat." Of the eighteen 609 pilots who fought over Dunkirk, five were killed and one was seriously injured.

The RAF was heavily outnumbered, partly because its fighters could not carry enough fuel to last over Dunkirk for more than half an hour, much less if in high-throttle combat. At first, small groups were sent out on rotation, but they found themselves so outnumbered as to be ineffective. Thereafter, the fighters were deployed in "wings" of several squadrons combined, which inevitably left gaps in the air cover. But the evacuation continued below.

The British government was keen to keep news of the BEF's retreat and evacuation from the people at home. On 28 May, the Director of Military Intelligence called together the press at a London hotel. They should act, he told them, as "shock absorbers" after the stunning defeat. That same day, Belgium's King Leopold surrendered his country — in the face of Franco-British opposition and that of his own Cabinet — thus giving German forces easier passage to the coast. In spite of the tens of thousands of British troops now being carried on trains away from the south coast of England, the press and radio declined to report the evacuation until 30 May. Then, at 6p.m., the BBC announced that: "All day men of the undefeated British

Expeditionary Force have been coming home . . . it is clear that if they have not come back in triumph they have come back in glory . . . they are anxious only to be back again soon — as they put it — 'to have another crack at Jerry'."

The manipulation worked. The troops returned, shattered after a nightmare of confused retreat in darkness, hunger, thirst and sleeplessness, to an enthusiastic welcome. "We expected to slink back, a defeated army," remembered Peter Lambert, one of the last of those evacuated on 31 May. "Instead there were cups of tea, food, waving flags. There were cheers, even."

The handling of the Dunkirk evacuation for public consumption was a masterpiece of news management. The BEF had been smashed, leaving behind in France over 30,000 men and pretty much all its equipment; but the whole episode set a new tone of defiance. The press duly followed the government's line, reporting that the evacuation had been "terrible, but glorious". The BEF, wrote the *Daily Mail*, had survived despite the "treachery" of the Belgian surrender. "Bloody Marvellous" was the *Mirror's* headline. The small, civilian sea vessels became a shining symbol of resourcefulness and resolve. J.B. Priestley, the novelist whose morale-lifting broadcasts were widely trusted, rhapsodized on the BBC about how "the little holiday steamers made an excursion to Hell and came back glorious". The implication was clear: this was a war of civilians as well as soldiers. Crucially, the new mood carried across the Atlantic. "As long as the English tongue survives, the word Dunkirk will be spoken with reverence," declared the *New York Times* on 1 June.

The resilience of public morale buoyed Churchill's argument that salvation lay in fighting on. He constantly stressed to his colleagues the necessity of persuading the United States that Britain was a solid ally, which could be relied on to continue the struggle. At a meeting at the end of May he had gathered together his junior ministers and declared: "If this long island story of ours is to end at last, let it end only when each one of us lies choking in his blood upon the ground." The rhetoric had its effect and he won their complete support amidst tears and backslapping.

Envigorated by their backing, Churchill headed for the House of Commons a few days later, on 4 June, having just that morning received the final, miraculous figures for the Dunkirk evacuation: 338,000 Allied soldiers rescued. He also heard encouraging reports from Fighter Command about aircraft production and received news that the US Congress was to debate giving more extensive help for Britain. The speech that he then delivered to Parliament was a classic and immortal oration, delivered by one of the great artists of the English language. He started by emphasizing how the evacuation from Dunkirk had far exceeded planners' estimates. The architects of Operation Dynamo had hardly dared hope to rescue more than 30,000 troops. The real figure had exceeded that number tenfold. Thus, the "root and core and brain" of the army had been saved, Churchill said, "on which and around which . . . great British armies" could be built. Britain had survived and Britain would fight on. For Berlin the words were a message of defiance, for Washington a plea for help:

> Even though large tracts of Europe and many old and
> famous states have fallen or may fall into the grip of
> the Gestapo and all the odious apparatus of Nazi rule,
> we shall not flag or fail. We shall go on to the end.
> We shall fight in France, we shall fight on the seas and
> oceans, we shall fight with growing confidence and
> growing strength in the air, we shall defend our island,
> whatever the cost may be. We shall fight on the
> beaches, we shall fight on the landing grounds, we
> shall fight in the fields and in the streets, we shall
> fight in the hills, we shall never surrender, and even if,
> which I do not for a moment believe, this island or a
> large part of it were subjugated and starving, then our
> Empire beyond the seas, armed and guarded by the
> British Fleet, would carry on the struggle, until, in
> God's good time, the New World, with all its power
> and might, steps forth to the rescue and liberation of
> the Old.

It is now forgotten that much of the speech was devoted to the achievements of the Royal Navy in bringing about the "miracle of deliverance" at Dunkirk and highlighting its future role in defending the British Isles from invasion. Remembered rather better are the relatively short passages devoted to the RAF. The air force needed the balm of praise. Churchill was careful to laud its role in the rescue, countering the charges that it had failed to offer adequate protection from the Luftwaffe. At the same time he put the RAF and Fighter Command at the centre of the next phase of the crisis, laying the foundations of the myth before the Battle of Britain had properly begun. "There has never been, I suppose in all the world, in all the history of war, such an opportunity for youth," Churchill declared. The fighter pilots of the RAF, the prime minister went on, were like the Knights of the Round Table, but "holding in their hands these instruments of colossal and shattering power". Such paladins, he said, "could outlive the menace of tyranny, if necessary for years, if necessary alone".

As he spoke, Fighter Command was licking its wounds and scarcely in any condition to rise to the challenge. During the Dunkirk campaign it had lost 60 fighter pilots killed, 15 injured, and 2 more were missing, presumed dead. Those lost to Fighter Command included three squadron commanders killed and one taken prisoner, as well as about twelve section leaders. The last RAF squadrons based in France withdrew on 18 June, taking with them only 66 of the 452 fighters sent out to the Continent. The rest had been shot down, abandoned or in many cases destroyed to deny them to the Germans.

Furthermore, while the public and politicians gave thanks for the relative deliverance that was Dunkirk, the RAF was still embroiled in the much less "glorious" withdrawal from Norway, Nos 263 and 43 Squadrons had been fighting hard during May, in bad weather, and were heavily outnumbered covering the evacuation of the Allied troops. By 7 June, No. 263 Squadron had flown 389 sorties over 12 days, been in combat 69 times and claimed 26 successes. Over the same time, 43 Squadron had taken part in 26 fights and claimed 11 kills. On 7 June, the remaining eight Gladiators flew out to the waiting HMS *Glorious*. Orders were given for the Hurricanes to be destroyed to prevent them falling into the enemy's hands. But, after a protest, their pilots were allowed to attempt to land their planes on the *Glorious*, in spite of the lack of "arrester hooks" — the restraints to catch planes as they touched down — and the fact that none of the pilots had performed a deck landing before.

In the event, all of the remaining ten Hurricanes landed safely: an amazing feat. Yet it was to no avail. Because of a lack of fuel, the *Glorious* was forced to steer a direct line home. It was therefore unable to avoid the attentions of the German battlecruisers *Scharnhorst* and *Gneisenau*, patrolling off the coast. The *Scharnhorst* opened fire at long range, hitting the carrier and setting it on fire. Within an hour it had sunk, together with 1,471 officers and men of the Royal Navy and 41 RAF personnel, including all but two of the pilots. It was the final tragedy in a disastrous campaign.

On 22 June, a new French government, headed by the First World War veteran Marshal Philippe Pétain, formalized its surrender and signed the German terms of armistice. Britain was now alone, with a hostile and powerful enemy surveying it from Cap Gris Nez, within sight of the White Cliffs of Dover. On 30 June and 1 July the undefended Channel Islands were occupied, and German soldiers stood on British soil. German fighter bases were quickly established in the occupied area. From Europe came rumours of a huge fleet of invasion barges being prepared and paratroopers mustered.

The reaction in Britain to its isolation was, in hindsight, extraordinary. The exit of France from the war was regarded by some as a relief, clearing the ground and simplifying matters. A newspaper headline after the French armistice terms were agreed on 18 June read: "French sign peace treaty: we're in the finals." The Labour Party leader, Clement Attlee, and his deputy, Arthur Greenwood, reassured Churchill that the working classes supported his defiant stand. Certainly it was the end of the feeling of detachment that had characterized the Phoney War. It was now a war of national survival.

The process by which disaster encouraged a mood of national defiance was eagerly fostered by officialdom. The transformation was caricatured by Evelyn Waugh in his 1942 novel, *Put Out More Flags*:

Finally when it was plain, even to Sir Joseph [Mainwaring], that in the space of a few days England had lost both the entire stores and equipment of her regular army and her only ally; that the enemy were less than twenty-five miles from her shores; that there were only a few battalions of fully armed, fully trained troops in the country; that she was committed to a war in the Mediterranean with a numerically superior enemy; that her cities lay open to air attack from fields closer to home than the extremities of her own islands; that her sea-routes were threatened from a dozen new bases, Sir Joseph said: "Seen in the proper perspective I regard this as a great and tangible success . . . The war has entered into a new and glorious phase."

George Orwell characterized things rather differently in 1941: "After eight months of vaguely wondering what the war was about, the people suddenly knew what they had to do . . . it was like the awakening of a giant."

CHAPTER
THREE

Squaring Up

Following the fall of France, the Luftwaffe moved with great speed to redeploy for an attack on Britain. In Poland, Norway and France, the German air force had demonstrated its ability to push forward quickly, a key component of the success of *Blitzkrieg*. Soon, Luftwaffe bases were established in a huge arc on the Continent, threatening Britain from Norway in the north, through Denmark, Holland, Belgium and France as far west as the Atlantic coast of Brittany.

Its forces were organized into three *Luftflotten* (air fleets). Hugo Sperrle's *Luftflotte 3*, with its headquarters in Paris, was based in northwestern France, with Kesselring's *Luftflotte 2*, commanded from Brussels, operating from northeastern France and the Low Countries. A further *Luftflotte*, No. 5, was deployed to Denmark and Norway to threaten Britain's eastern coast all the way north to Scapa Flow in the Orkneys.

The *Luftflotten* were divided into a number of *Fliegerkorps* (air corps), usually two or three, which in turn contained *Geschwader* (wings) of fighters, bombers, dive-bombers and so on. Bombers were organized in "battle wings" (*Kampfgeschwader*, or

KG), while dedicated fighter wings were *Jagdgeschwader* (JG), literally "hunter groups". The twin-engine Me110 heavy-fighters fought in "destroyer wings" (*Zerstörergeschwader*, or ZG), and the Ju87 dive-bombers were organized in *Sturzkampfgeschwader* (or stG). It was the German words for dive-bomber — *Sturzkampflugzeug* and *Sturzkampfbomber* — that fostered the name "Stuka" for the Ju87, the aircraft so closely identified with the tactics of *Blitzkrieg*.

The Luftwaffe possessed other types of *Geschwader* too, the most significant (for the Battle of Britain) being the mixed-aircraft "teaching wings" (*Lehrgeschwader*, or LG), so called because they were staffed largely by former instructors.

Each *Geschwader* contained, at full strength, some 90–120 aircraft, usually divided into 3 *Gruppen* (groups). The equivalent of the British squadron was the *Staffel* (echelon) numbering about 10–12 aircraft. Each *Gruppe* contained three or four *Staffeln*.

The Luftwaffe units were now poised to put all they had learned at the service of an assault on Britain. Until relatively recently, Goering's pilots had forgotten the lessons of aerial combat learned in the First World War — as had the RAF — and during their involvement in the Spanish Civil War they had flown in very close wingtip-to-wingtip formation. But the German fighter pilots soon realized the vulnerability of such tactics and adopted the formation, still in use today, of the two-aircraft *Rotte* (pair) and the four-aircraft *Schwarm* (swarm). As Me109 pilot Hans-Ekkehard Bob explained:

The Messerschmitt Me 109s used the *Schwarm* four aircraft formation. Two aircraft [a *Rotte*] would fly together at the same altitude with a distance of 50 metres between them. Another two aircraft were flying alongside, further away, again with a distance of 50 metres between them, so that we were flying in a broad row about 200 metres long. Each of the pilots was able to monitor to the rear and to the front and so see what was where. The wingman protected his leader from attack, or was in a position to fasten onto the tail of an enemy diving on the forward aircraft, while the leader navigated and was ready, in turn, to protect his wingman. Flying in this fashion meant that a Messerschmitt *Staffel* of 12 fighters stretched about a mile and a half across the sky, with each *Schwarm* at varying heights.[1]

The Luftwaffe had proved itself a decisive force in the war so far, and German confidence was high. In France and the Low Countries, it had shot down or destroyed on the ground more than 3,000 enemy aircraft. Luftwaffe losses from the earlier campaigns were quickly made good. As early as mid-June, the new airfields in the conquered northern European countries began launching exploratory raids on Britain on their own initiative. There were even training missions flown over British soil. The first large-scale raid came in on the night of 18 June, when 100 bombers attacked scattered and diverse targets between Yorkshire and Kent. Now, the full strength of the force was gathered for the battle ahead.

★ ★ ★

With their opponents arrayed against them across the Channel and the North Sea, Fighter Command's task was clear yet daunting: to prove that the bomber would *not*, as the pre-war theory claimed, always get through. Its role was made more difficult by the fact that the anticipated fleets of bombers would be protected by nimble fighter aircraft, well within range of Britain now that they occupied the airbases of the vanquished nations.

For the purposes of organization, the British Isles was divided into geographical areas, each defended by a Fighter Command group, and controlled from Dowding's headquarters at Bentley Priory, Stanmore, on the outskirts of Northwest London. At the beginning of 1940 there were three groups: No. 11 (southern England and London), No. 12 (central England and Wales), and No. 13 (northern England and Scotland). A fourth group, No. 10, for the defence of the southwest, became operational in July 1940, so that 11 Group's remit became just the southeast. Each group was subdivided into local sectors, with a sector station controlling satellite airfields.

The basic unit of Fighter Command was the squadron. At full strength, this consisted of about 20 pilots and 12–14 fighter aircraft. Within a squadron there were two "flights", each with two "sections" of three aircraft each.

For the defenders, the earliest possible warning of an attack was vital. That initial detection depended first on radar, and then for greater detail on human observation by the Observer Corps, whose origins went back to the First World War. In 1914–18, the reporting of enemy aircraft overhead had switched from the police to the army, then back to the police. A network of telephone communications had been established linking police stations with operations rooms. At the end of the war, the system had been dismantled, but a pilot scheme with volunteer observers was launched in the 1920s. By 1925, the Observer Corps had been formed with over 100 observation posts in Southeast England, manned by uniformed civilian volunteers. The Air Ministry took over the Observer Corps from the Home Office in 1929, and it now became linked to local sector airfields. By mid-1940, there were some 30,000 Observers, of whom about 4,000 were women, keeping watch at more than 1,000 posts.

Once radar picked up incoming aircraft over the sea, the Fighter Command group HQ would alert the local Observer Corps group HQ, which would in turn notify the relevant posts. Radar could not tell the types or number of aircraft coming over, nor their precise height. This information, vital for a successful interception, had to come from the Observer Corps. When enemy aircraft were over land, radar lost them altogether and only the Observer Corps could track them.

A Fighter Command group controlled about 30–40 Observer posts. At group HQ were 12 plotters seated around a map, each receiving and noting information from two or three posts. From here, the plots were passed up the chain of command as well as direct to the nearest sector station.

Observation posts were sited anywhere that provided a good field of vision: rooftops, clifftops or simply high ground. Many were in basic sandbagged enclosures, open to the elements and vulnerable to enemy attack, although a number of standard-design positions were constructed of brick or concrete, usually two-storey with an open observation platform above a small lower-level room where the crew rested. Each post usually had a crew of two or three, all highly trained in aircraft recognition. Their equipment, though, was rudimentary — binoculars, earphones and a chest-mounted telephone, and a simple sextant device to calculate the height of an incoming raid. Nevertheless, their contribution to the Battle of Britain fully affirmed their motto — "Forewarned is forearmed" — and earned them the "Royal" prefix in 1941.

At Fighter Command headquarters, Dowding organized a system that, after much practice, reduced the time from detection to getting the intercepting fighters airborne to just six minutes. Radar and Observer Corps reports — with the estimated type, strength, height and position of aircraft — were telephoned through to the Filter Room at Bentley Priory, which would ascertain whether the planes were friendly or hostile and attempt to deal with inevitable inconsistencies in the reports. The processed information was then passed to the operations (Ops) room next door, where the raid was plotted on a large map table, providing a striking visual representation of the

71

situation. At the same time, the information was passed to the relevant groups and sectors, which had their own operations rooms and GSMs (general situation maps).

These maps were constantly updated by plotters wearing headphones, through which they received filtered information about sightings by radar, by members of the Observer Corps and by pilots themselves. Using what looked like long-handled croupiers' rakes, the plotters pushed arrows across the map, each marked with an "F" for friendly, "H" for hostile, or "X" for unknown and colour-coded to show the time of the report. Group and sector "ops" rooms would usually include among their personnel liaison officers from the Observer Corps and Royal Artillery. Both would relay information to their larger organizations, and the latter would attempt — sometimes unsuccessfully — to warn his anti-aircraft batteries when friendly aircraft were flying above them.

Bentley Priory was the brain of the Fighter Command system, while the radar and Observer stations were the eyes and ears, and the group and sector stations the arms and hands. Minute-by-minute tactical control was decentralized, while Bentley Priory took on the vital role of processing, analysing and then communicating incoming information. An American military attaché, Raymond Lee, visiting the Priory in August 1940 found in two great subterranean chambers one of "the most intricate and modern organizations in the world", which was "almost silent — only a soft murmur of voices as messages come and go over headsets, and only a little movement as operators move counters and markers from point to point and others tend electric bulletins and switchboards . . . I had no idea the British could evolve and operate so intricate, so scientific and rapid an organization."[2]

Once a raid was confirmed, the controller of the Fighter Command sector or sectors affected would scramble his fighters and guide them to meet the attackers. The perfect interception was from above, when the enemy fighter escort was low on fuel (or, even better, already heading home), and before the bombers hit their target. Too early and the RAF aircraft might already be short of fuel, or back on the ground, by the time the raid came in. Too late and they would fail to disrupt the attack and expose themselves to being shot down by the escorts.

Once the aircraft were in place, control passed to the pilots, as Squadron Leader Peter Devitt, the sector controller at RAF Tangmere, explained:

The controller controlled the aircraft once they got off the ground. I might be told by Group to get them up to a height of 18,000 feet over a certain place and to wait for further instructions. We used to get the further instructions and then we would tell the pilots where to go, what to expect and the number of German aircraft coming through. We were controlling them to get into the right position to attack the enemy. When I heard "Tally Ho!" from the pilots, I was finished with them and ready for anybody else going up.[3]

Controllers also had to consider the limits of pilots and machines. Time was needed for men to recuperate and aircraft to be patched up. To manage this, commanders maintained their precious squadrons at various states of availability. "Released" meant that, usually, they were free to leave the station for short periods. "Available" required them to be ready to take off at 10, 15, 30 or 60 minutes' notice. "Readiness" demanded that they should be able to run to their aircraft to take off within five minutes. "'Standby' meant that you were sitting in the cockpit with your helmet on, your hood slid back, listening on the radio for start-up," said Flying Officer John Young of 249 Squadron. From this state, the fighter should have been able to be airborne within two minutes. On the wall of the sector and group operations rooms were slates with each squadron's ordered status marked, usually with coloured bulbs, as well as the number of aircraft each had operational.

Pilots became familiar with the mixture of boredom, anticipation and fear that these states of availability induced. "Readiness meant that you were sitting in the dispersal hut, togged up in your 'Mae West' life vest, your aeroplane all ready for instant departure," explained John Young.[4] "The most stressful thing in the Battle of Britain was sitting at readiness waiting for the scramble telephone bell to ring," said Sergeant Cyril "Bam" Bamberger of 610 and 41 Squadrons. "I couldn't relax. You tried to read a book or you tried to play draughts or you pretended to doze. The phone would ring and immediately you jumped up but it was probably to say that the NAAFI van was coming with tea. Then you flopped back and tried to relax again."[5]

Vital to the preparedeness of Fighter Command's aircraft were the speed and skills of the mechanics. Each fighter had a dedicated team of armourer, fitter and rigger. There were also specialist technicians for the radio, the instruments and the electrics. Fred Roberts was an armourer for No. 19 Squadron Spitfires at Fowlmere. He explained how two-man teams would work on each wing to reload the machine-guns after combat:

> First we'd drop the empty tanks out, and while I was pushing the full tanks back up in and pulling the belt through, my assistant would be running the cleaning rod down the barrel. This had to be done before the plane was re-armed, otherwise the first round in the belt would already be in the breech. So you had to push the cleaning rod down, clean it out quick, a bit of oily four-by-two, and as soon as the assistant pushed that through, we pulled the belt through and let the breech rod go forward. Once we'd done that with each of the four guns on each side, the plane was fully loaded.[6]

The whole process took the men about three and a half minutes.

The rigger had responsibility for wheels, tyres, airframe and the hood. Often he could be identified by his ever-present polish and cloth — pilots insisted that the glass be totally free of specks, which might be mistaken for German aircraft. The fitter looked after the engine. Leading Aircraftman Joe Roddis, a fitter with No. 234 Squadron, described his role:

When the aircraft returned, I'd refuel the engine and put oil in it. If there was a snag and it was within my capability to fix it, I would, and then I'd run it up to see that I'd resolved the problem. I would always do an "afterflight". That meant giving the engine a real good going-over. You might look at it and think that nothing's happened but a bullet could have gone through the cowling or the propeller. It would take about half an hour and they'd bring us back on readiness when all the other trades had finished their jobs.[7]

"Of course the pilot, he became part of the team of armourer, rigger and fitter," said Fred Roberts:

We three and the pilot were a team of four. The radio operator, the electrician and the instrument mechanic, they probably had three or four aircraft to look after, so they weren't part of our team. But we three were always together and usually when we had a scramble, you were there, the fitter was in the cockpit starting the engine up, the armourer was there, sometimes he would be on the starter trolley pressing the accumulator to start the engine. The airframe wallah, he was there with us ready to pull the chocks away. As soon as the engine was warmed up, the pilot came, he got into the cockpit, the rigger was on one side, the fitter was the other side, I'd be there strapping him into his harness. When that was done, the other two would come back to the tail with me and all three of us lay across the tail, to hold it down while the pilot revved. As soon as he had revved the engine up, then the rigger, the fitter and the armourer went to each wing tip to guide him out onto the airfield. We worked as a team and we became close to the pilot like that".[8]

Some pilots were friendly with their groundcrew, taking care to learn their first names and nicknames. Peter Brothers, while his squadron was "commuting" to France, made a habit of bringing his crew a crate of beer at the end of the day and spending some time discussing the day's action. "We wouldn't have got off the ground but for them," he said. "They were all super. And of course, their aircraft had to be the best in the squadron, naturally."[9] Other pilots were "a bit stand-offish". Most of them, particularly at the start of the war, said Joe Roddis, "were university graduates, clever lads from well-to-do families, and they'd not been brought up to mix with mechanics". Fred Roberts said that, on the whole, the crew looked up to the pilots, "and we looked up more to the NCO pilots because they understood us better, they had been through the ranks with us". Generally, there was a feeling of mutual respect and admiration between pilot and crew, but there remained a social divide. "I would never ever call an officer by his first name," said Roddis. "But we got on with them because they realized our worth as much as we realized theirs . . . We didn't go out drinking with them. It was pilots and groundcrews and that's the way we liked it."

Fred Roberts and Joe Roddis describe a highly masculine world of men and machines, and at the hard edge of combat the participants were always men. But women made up a large proportion of the personnel operating the communications infrastructure of Fighter Command. The vital role played by the Women's Auxiliary Air Force (WAAF) ensured them a leading place in the mythology of the Battle of Britain. Their qualities were encapsulated in images showing them in slate blue tunics, hair shiny and curled just below the neck, bosom thrust forward, looking skywards with firm determination.

The WAAF succeeded the Women's Royal Air Force (WRAF), formed at the same time as the RAF on 1 April 1918. Its personnel acted in a wide variety of jobs, from sailmakers and "dopers" of planes to engine fitters and electricians. At its height, the WRAF contained over 24,000 members, but it was disbanded after the First World War. The Munich crisis of September 1938 hastened the formation of a new organization, of the Auxiliary Territorial Service (ATS), designed to engage women in service work. In June 1939, two specialist offshoots emerged: the WAAF and the Women's Royal Naval Service (WRNS). During the course of the war, the ATS, WAAF and WRNS would recruit more than 600,000 women into the services.

The WAAF's first commander was Katherine Trefusis-Forbes. She was described by one WAAF as being "neat as a new pin, and given to roaring to work on her motorbike".[10] Long after the war, in 1966, she would marry Watson-Watt, the man behind British radar.

There was no shortage of candidates for the WAAF. The glamour of the air and the "fighter boys" meant that over half of women volunteers marked the WAAF as their first choice. It offered a chance for adventure and a stake in the struggle against a hated enemy. The WAAF also presented a challenge to social norms. Many boyfriends, husbands or fathers were unenthusiastic at the thought of their womenfolk mixing relatively freely with men at their bases. Women in uniform had acquired a "fast" reputation during the previous war, however unfairly. "You used to see women in uniform, and it all seemed rather glamorous," said WAAF NCO Vera King. "But my father was very service-oriented and his memory for the women's services from the First World War was that they had bad reputations. His theme was, if you go into the services, no decent man will want to marry you."[11] Hazel Williams remembers leaving home to report for duty with the WAAF: "I shall always remember my mother, tears streaming down her face, at the door. Then she called me back and said 'Don't sit on strange lavatory seats,' and pointing to my bosom, 'Don't let any man touch you there!'"[12]

Those women taken on were supposed to be between 17½ and 43 years old, but there were few checks on age. Some as young as 15 were recruited, but the majority were 18 or 19 years old. Most early volunteers were educated and well-to-do. "At the start, there were a whole lot of titled people in the WAAFs. It was the upper strata of society," said WAAF Marian Orley. "But a lot of them couldn't take it. Out of 60 of us, about 30 didn't come back after a week's leave at Christmas. I had to parcel up their effects and send them back."

The more privileged volunteers arrived at a very different world to that they had known at home. Accommodation was basic and cramped, with three to a billet, and discipline was strict. On their first night, many women wept into their straw pillows. "Hair had to be kept off the collar," said Marian Orley. "No jewellery was allowed except a wedding ring. And no-one plastered their faces with make up."[13] Male NCOs treated their female charges with condescension. "They thought we were in it for the fun," said one WAAF.

"We all grew up very quickly in those days. We had to," said WAAF Kay France. "When I became a sergeant I discovered I had to be both disciplinarian, the spoil-sport sergeant, and mother, comforting girls whose boyfriends had been shot down or whose parents were killed in bombing raids."

Initially there were limited roles for the new recruits. They worked as equipment assistants, mess and kitchen workers, cooks, drivers and clerks. But it was soon realized that women were not only as proficient as men in almost all of the support roles, but in some cases better, particularly as radar operators and plotters, where precision and thoroughness were vital. Those operating the top-secret radar equipment were known as "Clerks, Special Duties". They had to have above-average educational achievement and were sworn to secrecy about their true role.

Many succeeded in alleviating some of the hardships, smuggling in non-regulation shoes and underwear as well as feather mattresses to cushion the uncomfortable straw ones they were issued with. During quiet periods, they wrote letters, knitted, sewed and embroidered. WAAF Hazel Gregory spent much of her time making underwear: "It was the fashionable thing to do at the time — we were all hand-stitching glamorous undies. Most of the men were very intrigued."[14]

The WAAF's role may have seemed like a step towards equality, but to many the attitude of the authorities still seemed belittling and unfair. After a raid on Kenley airfield in Surrey, the pilots were released to enjoy themselves. The WAAFs on the airfield, however, were sent to bed "in case of any nervous reaction". Women were given inferior rations and were paid only two-thirds of what their male counterparts made for doing the same job. "I began to get a bee in my bonnet about equal pay," said Marian Orley. "The NCO in charge of the watch was a woman sergeant — she was paid less than an ordinary airman on the switchboard. That got under my skin a little."[15]

By mid-1940, WAAFs were performing virtually every role in Fighter Command, save combat flying. But some did fly in other capacities: 30 of them worked for the Air Transport Auxiliary, piloting Spitfires and Hurricanes from factories or repair yards to the squadron airfields. Others bercame switchboard operators, parachute packers, plotters, RDF operators or barrage-balloon operators.

A number of WAAFS worked with codes and ciphers, analysed reconnaissance photographs, and performed intelligence operations. Some became important members of the new "Y Service", established to pick up enemy radio traffic. In the first three months of the war, the only messages picked up were in Morse code using the W/T (wireless telegraphy) method; encrypted messages were sent to the Government Code and Cypher School established at Bletchley Park in Buckinghamshire. But soon ham radio operators reported picking up voice messages in a foreign language on the 40-megacycle band using R/T (radio telephony). By March 1940, with the aid of some American Hallicrafters 510 units set up at Hawkinge aerodrome, RAF Intelligence was able to pick up the transmissions. The RAF mounted a rapid recruiting drive within the WAAF to find women with an expert knowledge of idiomatic and regional German. By the beginning of the Battle of Britain, half a dozen had been identified and were installed as intelligence operators at a new base at Fairlight in East Sussex. There they eavesdropped on conversations among the German aircrews that often revealed the numbers of aircraft in their formations and their destinations. Soon, more branches of the "Y Service" were set up around the country.

As the Battle of Britain became more intense, WAAF plotters would work four-hour watches — four hours on and two hours off. One night in three there was a watch of eight hours during the day, giving the women a full night in bed. "Everybody worked very hard," said plotter Edith Kup. "Everybody wanted to do their best. I mean, we didn't think about it, we just did it."

Proximity between aircrew and WAAFs inevitably led to romances, so that working in the operations rooms meant that women could sometimes hear from the "R/T" what was happening to their boyfriends in the skies above. One WAAF was working in the Debden Sector operations room when she heard that "Blue Four" was heading into the sea, his aircraft on fire. Without having to wait for confirmation, she knew that the man she was about to marry was dead.[16]

When the Luftwaffe onslaught started hitting airfields and sector stations in summer 1940, the women of the WAAF found themselves in the frontline. During the war, 191 WAAFs were killed and 420 wounded. But for most of them, danger increased the pride they took in their work and their contribution to the war effort. The press and public, too, took the WAAFs to their hearts.

While Fighter Command braced itself, Churchill was also anxious to create an atmosphere of alertness and action among the population as a whole. Small civilian vessels, fishing boats and other craft were diverted to watch Britain's long coastline for an invasion fleet. Armaments factories churned out weapons and the training centres churned out troops. Almost half a million men were put in uniform between May and the end of July 1940.

As part of the effort, by mid-June a further 400,000 were enrolled in the Local Defence Volunteer force — better known by the name given to it by Churchill in July 1940: the Home Guard. Now everyone could feel part of the war effort. The secretary of state for war, Anthony Eden, launched the organization in a radio broadcast on 14 May. He appealed to those between the ages of 17 and 65 to come forward to create an auxiliary force to counter any invasion, be it from the sea or the air. Within a day, a quarter of a million men had volunteered, and by the end of the month 400,000 were listed, about three times the expected number.

Among them, and in spite of the supposed age ceiling, were some as old as 84 who had fought in Sudan for Queen Victoria. About a third were First World War veterans. To be back in uniform stirred many memories: "I think none of us will forget our first LDV route march," wrote one veteran. "On it a quarter of a century slipped away in a flash. There came memories of the Menin Road . . . of the smell of cordite and the scream of shrapnel, of the mud and stench and misery of Flanders, of hopes and fears in battles long ago."

Some organizations formed their own units. Both Houses of Parliament had battalions, as did the BBC, the court at Buckingham Palace, London taxi drivers and dustmen, and the printers and typesetters of Fleet Street. To the dismay of the pro-Hitler US ambassador, Joseph P. Kennedy, an American battalion was formed of expatriates living in London. In Sussex a group was assembled complete with horses, and soon a 50-strong unit known as the Lewes Cossacks was patrolling the South Downs.

All volunteers were unpaid, provided their own food, and had to commit to ten hours' service a week. Uniforms and weapons were in very short supply. Pressed into service were rifles dating from the Indian Mutiny, pikes from theatre props rooms, golf clubs, hockey sticks and missiles made from potatoes studded with razor blades. Armbands were issued, and slowly the army released its unwanted uniforms to the LDV — the very large and very small sizes.

Sceptics, of whom there were plenty, said that LDV stood for "Look, Duck and Vanish" or "Last Desperate Venture". "We were prepared to lean out of a bedroom window, light a piece of rag in the neck of a bottle and throw it at a tank," said Stanley Brand of the Middlesbrough Home Guard. "How long would we have survived?" But Brand acknowledged that the force was not entirely useless and had useful morale benefits: "My unit would have achieved something but nothing permanent," he said. "We couldn't ever have defeated the Germans — only delayed them. The Home Guard was really a civilian morale builder. It made us feel we could do something useful."[17]

In truth, the large numbers were misleading, and the Home Guard, made up of those men too old or too young for regular service, was of minimal military value, while regular troops in key positions facing the likely landing sites in Kent and Sussex were barely equipped and only partly trained.

The landscape of England became transformed during these months, and feverish activity to combat an enemy landing was visible everywhere by mid-July 1940. Liquid fuel pipes were installed in the sea off likely landing beaches, with the purpose of setting the waves ablaze if necessary. The most vulnerable stretches of the coastline were strung with barbed wire and sown with mines.

The main defence line, however, was inland, stretching from Somerset to Essex to protect London and the heart of England — the "GHQ Line". It was designed to be a continuous anti-tank obstacle, using natural features such as rivers and canals and, in between, huge anti-tank ditches and other obstructions. It was originally about 400 miles (640km) long, before being extended northwards via Newcastle to Edinburgh.

In front of the GHQ Line in the south were other "stop-lines" based as much as possible on natural features. Concrete bollards — "dragon's teeth" — were sown along roads and railway lines to impede the German armour. Ugly brick-and-concrete pill-boxes and strong-points were set up all over the countryside. By the end of July 1940, there were some 8,000 of them, with a further 17,000 planned or under construction — so many that supplies of both concrete and timber were dwindling fast.

Should the main British force have to retreat to the GHQ Line, the plan was for secret auxiliary units hiding out in well-stocked bases in caves and woods to strike the enemy behind their lines. "We would have booby-trapped German stores and vehicles," said Percy

Clark, attached to one such unit in Kent. "We'd have tried to do something about any bridges that weren't blown up. We'd have stretched wires across the road to catch necks. We were trained to be silent killers."[18] "They told us our expected lifetime after the invasion would be seven days," said George Pellet, another recruit to the underground organization. "They reckoned that after seven days either Jerry would be back out of it or we'd all be finished."[19]

General Sir Edmund Ironside was appointed commander of Britain's defences on 27 May, but things were to change when, on 20 July, General Sir Alan Brooke took over. He considered the existing defences too static, and British leaders from Churchill down were concerned about their soldiers becoming "Maginot-minded", infected with the defensive mindset that, it was believed, had led to the defeat of France. So the huge number of men now in uniform were deliberately kept busy with marches and exercises as well as helping with the construction of defences. Weapons and ammunition remained in very short supply, though.

To Bombardier Douglas Goddard, it was "really rather comical. We had rifles with five rounds of ammunition, we had one 1914 Lewis gun and we had three London taxis. We patrolled the coast between Camber Sands and Dymchurch — where the invasion was due to land — in taxis."[20] Captain Kenneth Johnstone of the 11th Battalion, Durham Light Infantry, remembered "one officer being put on a charge by the brigadier because he didn't have a revolver, until it was explained to the brigadier that it wasn't his turn to wear the revolver, because we only had one between six of us".[21]

Preparing for "the enemy without" obsessed politicians and planners. But the potential enemy within was not forgotten. When the fighting in western Europe erupted in May, acts of popular outrage replaced what had been a relatively tolerant atmosphere thus far in Britain. On 12 May "enemy aliens" began to be rounded up and placed in internment camps or sent abroad.

Some of them had been in Britain for years. Since 1933 there had been a steady exodus from Germany to Britain of those who feared for their lives and security under the Nazis because of their politics or their Jewish blood. They were subsequently joined by refugees from Austria, and then Czechoslovakia. They had been met with sympathy on the whole, though the mounting alarm engendered by Hitler's voracious pre-war demands had given rise to some scare stories in the press. One such appeared in the London *Evening Standard* in February 1939, under the headline "Hitler's Gestapo employing Jews for spying in England".

At the start of the war there were about 80,000 Germans and Austrians in Britain. As citizens of an enemy power, they were automatically suspect as potential spies, saboteurs or Nazi supporters. All those over the age of 16 had been summoned to tribunals to be assessed, where they were divided into three categories. Group A comprised high-risk Nazi sympathizers, of whom there were nearly 600, and they were immediately interned. Group B was made up of 6,500 "doubtful cases", who were subject to restrictions on their movements and kept under supervision. Group C, by far the largest at 55,000, was designated "no security risk" and left alone. The great majority of them were Jewish.

After Hitler launched *Blitzkrieg* in the west, "enemy aliens", the majority refugees from fascism, were rounded up and imprisoned. The net was widened to include the 19,000 Italians resident in Britain, many of whom had lived there for decades. When Italy entered the war on 10 June 1940, Italian cafés and restaurants in Glasgow, Manchester and London's Soho district were attacked and wrecked. One long-assimilated restaurateur in London felt compelled to put up a notice in his window stating that all four of his sons were in the British Army.

Spartan camps were set up on racecourses and half-finished housing estates. Most of the internees were sent to the Isle of Man, while another 7,000 were deported, mainly to Canada and Australia, though not all of those ever made it into exile. The liner *Arandora Star*, which left for Canada on 1 July 1940, was torpedoed with the loss of 714 lives. The dead included the Italian ex-head chefs of the Savoy and the Ritz, as well as prominent German and Austrian anti-Nazi politicians and labour leaders.

In all, the British authorities interned 30,000 people, most of them fervent anti-Nazis. They included a high proportion of engineers, physicists, chemists and university professors, who had a potential contribution to make to the war effort. Opposition to the policy began to be voiced almost immediately in Parliament, and the first releases from the internment camps would take place in August 1940, as the Battle of Britain was reaching fever pitch. By the summer of 1942, only 5,000 internees were left.

British subjects, too, were interned — 1,769 in total, of whom nearly half had been members of the British Union of Fascists. Its leader, Sir Oswald Mosley, and his wife were among them, held in Brixton prison, London.

Allied to the suspicions about enemy aliens and home-bred Nazi supporters was the fear of invasion from the air — launched by German paratroopers (*Fallschirmjäger*) followed by gliders or transport aircraft, and aided by fifth columnists among the British public. The successes of the German parachutists earlier in the year had made a strong impression on British civilians. The *Fallschirmjäger* had struck first in Denmark, where they captured Aalborg airport at the start of the German invasion, and dropped into Norway. On 10 May, they scored their most dramatic victory, when a force of 78 men seized the supposedly impregnable Belgian fort of Eben-Emael, between Liège and Maastricht. The *Illustrated London News* that month carried a "wonderful double page spread" showing the parachutists' methods.

It was widely anticipated that paratroopers would be used in an invasion of Britain, and they were not expected to confine themselves to conventional military activities or appearance. On 21 May, the Dutch foreign minister alleged, quite inaccurately, that German paratroopers had descended on his country disguised as nurses, tramcar conductors, nuns and monks. The military correspondent of the *Chichester and Southern Post* warned his readers on 28 June to be on the lookout for parachutists, "mostly young men of the desperado type" whose task was to "organize local fifth column members and arm them . . . [and] create panic and confusion and spread false news among the civil population".

Such advice made people panicky. A commercial traveller who failed to stop his car in time at a checkpoint near Wrexham, manned by Local Defence Volunteers, was shot dead. Enemy aliens were moved away from coastal areas, and innocents were arrested on suspicion of being spies, often after tip-offs from neighbours.

What, with hindsight, looks like paranoia was by no means confined to the ignorant or overly nervous. Neither General Ironside nor Admiral Ramsay, the architect of Operation Dynamo at Dunkirk, were immune to concerns about fifth columnist activity. On 30 May, Ironside wrote in his diary: "Important telegraph poles marked, suspicious men moving at night all over the country."[22]

Many Fighter Command pilots shared this fear. During the Battle of Britain, Sergeant Geoffrey Goodman of No. 85 Squadron found on one sortie that only his port guns were firing. On returning to his base he discovered, according to a squadron report, that matchsticks had been forced into the airlines of his guns — clear evidence, it seemed, of sabotage "by some German sympathiser at the depot", according to Squadron Leader Peter Townsend. Stories of RAF parachutes being sabotaged by Irish Republican Army (IRA) sympathizers also did the rounds.

In order to make life difficult for the *Fallschirmjäger* once they had landed, road signs were uprooted and postal districts were blanked out on the nameplates on London streets. On 13 June, orders were given that church bells should only be rung to signal a parachute attack, and in mid-June a leaflet was distributed with instructions about what to do "If the Invader Comes". The population was told to disregard rumours, to take orders only from a British officer — having first established that he was "really British" and not "pretending to be so" — and to immobilize transport, cars and bicycles. The basic order was to "stay put" to avoid clogging the roads, as had happened in France, Belgium and the Netherlands.

As early as 12 May, Churchill's scientific adviser Professor Frederick Lindemann was recommending that holes be dug in all flat areas more than 400 yards (365 metres) long that were within 5 (later extended to 10) miles of any vulnerable and strategically important site. This was to defend against airborne landings. Fields, even those under crops, were planted with sharp obstructions — wooden stakes or old farm machinery — to prevent German gliders landing on them. These measures would prove equally hazardous to stricken friendly aeroplanes when they attempted to crash-land.

The Home Guard patrolled the streets and lanes or manned roadblocks, at first with just their improvised weapons. Their primary role was to be the first on the scene of any German invasion from the air. Such was their vigilance that it led to problems for Fighter Command, with RAF pilots descending on parachutes being shot at by over-eager guards. By 5 September 1940, the Air Ministry was forced to issue a notice reminding the public that not all parachutists were enemies.

The cumulative fear of invasion that gripped the country did help to maintain energy and unity, essential in a "people's war" when the civilians were now at the centre of events. The "great invasion scare", Churchill told his assistant private secretary, "Jock" Colville, "is serving a very useful purpose . . . it is keeping every man and woman tuned to a high pitch of readiness".[23] In many cases there was a real expectation of German occupation. People kept packed suitcases sitting in their halls for the seemingly inevitable flight. The writer Virginia Woolf and her husband Leonard, the publisher Victor Gollancz and many others prepared the means for suicide. Even 19-year-olds were to be found writing their wills. Mollie Panter-Downes, writing for the *New Yorker* (24 May 1940), reported that: "The Channel had now shrunk in men's minds to the size of the Thames."

Nevertheless, as Hitler appreciated, the invasion of Britain was an enormously difficult task. The most obvious obstacle facing the Germans was the Royal Navy, still majestically intact. Colville had used a vivid metaphor when describing the relative strengths of Germany and Britain. One was the elephant, a mighty terrestial beast. The other was the whale, king of the seas. Neither was able to bring its strength to bear on the other. That only left the third element in which modern wars were fought — the air. As Hitler considered how to tame the British, one thing seemed clear. In order for victory over Britain to be achieved, through invasion, blockade or demoralization, there was an essential precondition. Germany must have mastery of the skies.

Churchill's rhetorical response to the challenge, given to the House of Commons before being broadcast to the nation on 18 June, was a masterpiece:

What General Weygand called the Battle of France is over. I expect that the Battle of Britain is about to begin. Upon this battle depends the survival of Christian civilization . . . the whole fury and might of the enemy must very soon be turned on us. Hitler knows that he will have to break us in this Island or lose the War. If we can stand up to him, all Europe may be free and the life of the world may move forward into broad sunlit uplands. But if we fail, then the whole world, including the United States, including all that we have known and cared for, will sink into the abyss of a new Dark Age made more sinister, and perhaps more protracted, by the lights of perverted science. Let us therefore brace ourselves to our duties, and so bear ourselves that, if the British Empire and its

Commonwealth last for a thousand years, men will still say, "This was their finest hour."

The scene was set for the greatest air battle in history.

CHAPTER
FOUR

Beginning the Duel

1 July to 16 July 1940

As first light smudged the horizon on 10 July, the sky over the English Channel was cloaked in dense cloud. All along the clifftops, perched on sandbagged platforms, men and women of the Observer Corps peered into the swirling rain, searching for German aircraft. The likelihood was that, whatever the weather, sooner or later the Luftwaffe would appear. Events were settling into a routine. The previous ten days had seen more than a dozen raids, each of fifty or more aircraft. But history would judge this day to be special. It was the hour, historians would later decide, when the Battle of Britain proper began.

Above the heads of the Observer Corps, the fingers of Britain's radar stations probed the clouds, looking for enemy intruders. They were not long in finding one. It was the Chain Home radar station at West Beckham on the Norfolk coast that picked up the first ominous blip on one of its small cathode-tube screens. The mechanisms of Britain's air defences clicked into action. At 7.30a.m., No. 66 Squadron based at

Coltishall, Norfolk, received an order to "scramble" and three of its Spitfires climbed into the wet skies. Led by Pilot Officer Charles Cooke, the section climbed fast through the rain and cloud, and then at about 10,000 feet broke through into brilliant sunshine. Cooke was given a vector bearing that led him to where the enemy aircraft was last spotted. At 8.15a.m. the intruder came into view. It was a lone Dornier Do17 twin-engine bomber, probably on a reconnaissance mission to report back on the weather over the coast.

One by one, the Spitfires peeled off to attack. As they swooped down, the pilot of the Dornier threw his aircraft around the sky in a desperate effort to avoid the stream of incoming fire and to give his gunners a chance to shoot back. One bullet from the bomber's 7.9mm MG machine-guns hit Cooke's windscreen, flooding the cockpit with icy air. The Spitfires continued to harass the bomber until one fighter, attacking from underneath, raked the Dornier at close range with its eight Browning machine-guns. Smoke billowed from the bomber. It went into a banking turn, gliding steadily down until it struck the grey seas off Great Yarmouth and swiftly sank. None of the four-man crew survived, and the Spitfire section returned home to celebrate their success.

The German aeroplane had been one of several searching Britain's coastal waters for signs of convoys. That morning there were eight convoys at sea, slowly butting through the choppy waters, protected by naval escorts and the occasional fighter patrol. The largest of the convoys, codenamed Bread, had set sail on the early

97

morning tide from the Thames Estuary. At about 10a.m. it rounded the North Foreland where it was spotted by another Do17 reconnaissance aircraft, this one guarded by about 30 Messerschmitt Me109 single-engine fighters. As the Germans radioed back the position of a tempting target, six Spitfires, alerted by radar, were racing to the scene from Manston airfield in Kent, the nearest Fighter Command station.

At just before 11a.m., battle was joined. The Spitfires of No. 74 Squadron headed straight for the Dornier. The escorting Luftwaffe fighters were waiting, however, and turned fast behind them, opening fire and damaging two of the attackers. The British pilots held their course, concentrating on the Dornier, scoring hits on the cockpit and setting it on fire. But soon the Me109s were on top of them and the battle turned into a series of wheeling dogfights that drifted over the genteel Kent seaside town of Margate. The Dornier managed to limp away back across the Channel carrying one dead crewman and several injured, before crash-landing near Boulogne. One of the Me109s was hit but not badly damaged, and the rest escaped unscathed. The two Spitfires damaged during the first moments of the attack both managed to return to Manston. Their aircraft were just repairable, the pilots shaken but unhurt.

Meanwhile, pressure was mounting elsewhere. At almost exactly the time that the Spitfires of 74 Squadron were clashing with the Dornier and its escorts, the order to scramble had been given at Biggin Hill. Radar plots and Observer Corps reports had shown a *Staffel* of Me109s — about a dozen aircraft — roaring over Dover, searching for targets of opportunity. Nine Spitfires of No. 610 Squadron took off and raced to intercept. Combat was brief and inconclusive; one Spitfire was shot down and the raiders escaped unharmed.

The convoys were not the Germans' only targets that morning. Seventy German bombers, flying in from the west and taking the radar stations by surprise, attacked Swansea, killing thirty people and damaging ships, railways, a power station and a munitions factory. The shift of direction delayed Fighter Command's response, and when No. 92 Squadron, based in Pembrey in South Wales, was ordered to scramble, the planes arrived to find the raiders had gone. The appearance of the bombers provoked Wing Commander Ira Jones, a veteran of the First World War Flying Corps, to fly to the defence of his native Wales. He was in charge of the training airfield at Stormy Down, and he seized a Hawker Henley "target tug" — a light bomber now used for towing targets in shooting practice — to take to the air and pursue a German Ju88 bomber. His sole weapon, however, was a Verey signal pistol, which failed to make any impression on the raider.

The main fighting of the day was focused on the Bread convoy. Although the Dornier reconnaissance aeroplane had been damaged, it had still been able to report the whereabouts of the ships. At 1.30p.m., radar picked up an ominously heavy enemy build-up over the Pas de Calais. Twenty minutes later the sky above the convoy was crowded with hostile aircraft — a swarm of

26 Do17s, operating as bombers rather than reconnaissance aircraft, shielded by nearly 40 Me110 fighter-bombers and some 24 Me109s. The convoy's aerial protection amounted to a mere six Hurricanes from No. 32 Squadron.

Mistaking the twin-engine Me110s for Do17s, the British pilots reported "sixty Dorniers" and called for help. Among the first to arrive were the Hurricanes of 111 Squadron, who brought with them their own unique approach to tackling the bombers. With the entire formation flying abreast in a shallow V-shaped "vic", the squadron headed at full speed head on into the German bomber pack. For those conducting the attack it was an extraordinarily risky tactic, but it delivered a devastating effect. "You could see the front of the aircraft crumple," said 111 Squadron pilot Ben Bowring. Pilots observed the panic-stricken bomber crews rearing up from their seats and stumbling backwards to try to avoid the blast of bullets. The aircraft were forced to break their tight self-defending formations and veer off course, missing their aim and making them easier prey for the British fighters.

As Flying Officer Brian Kingcome of No. 92 Squadron testified, "A head-on attack did far more to destroy the morale of the German bombers than anything else. It upset the poor old pilot so much that he turned tail. When he was sitting and couldn't see the attack and he was protected by a nice sheet of metal behind him and he could hear his gunners firing away, he was in a much more relaxed state of mind than when we were coming straight at him and he had nothing between himself and the guns."[1]

Inevitably with such a tactic, there were collisions. Flying Officer Tom Higgs, aged 23, was still firing when he clipped his target Dornier. With one wing missing, the Hurricane span seawards, closely followed by the wrecked German bomber. Higgs seems to have baled out, but the launch that rescued the Dornier pilot and another member of his crew could find no sign of Higgs, nor of the two other Germans. Higgs's body eventually washed up on the Dutch coast at Noordwijk more than a month later.

By now the order to "scramble" had gone out to five Fighter Command airfields. German bombers had not been seen in such numbers before. At Fighter Command HQ, at Bentley Priory, the realization was growing that the Luftwaffe effort had moved to a higher and more dangerous tempo.

Soon, a huge dogfight developed over the Bread convoy, with more than 100 aircraft looping and circling, climbing and diving. High above, the Spitfires concentrated on their counterparts, the Messerschmitt Me109s, driving them away from their charges, letting the slower and less nimble Hurricanes in to harry the bomber formations and the sluggish Me110s. It was a Spitfire, though, flown by Flying Officer John Mungo-Park, that scored the first hit on a Dornier. Mungo-Park, slim and dark-haired, who was later regarded by his comrades as encapsulating the humour, courage and modesty of the Battle of Britain pilots, described watching the bomber "turn lazily on its back and dive into the sea".

Now that every fighter pilot was on his own, coordination became impossible, with the radio jammed by excited voices. Flying Officer Henry Ferriss, a little short of his 23rd birthday but already an experienced fighter pilot, arrived at the scene in his Hurricane as the second wave of German bombers prepared their attack on the convoy. "It was a thrilling sight I must confess," he told a BBC radio interviewer later. "I looked down on the tiny ships below and saw two long lines of broken water where the first lot of bombs had fallen . . . Just ahead were fountains of water leaping skywards from bombs newly dropped. In a second or two the sea down below spouted up to the height of about fifty feet or more in two lines alongside the convoy." Ferris led his flight in an attack on the second wave of Dorniers. "We went screaming down and pumped lead into our targets. We shook them up quite a bit."

Although neither side had gained the upper hand in the fighter dogfight, the bombing formation was starting to break up. After further damaging a stricken Dornier from the first wave, Ferriss chased a Messerschmitt Me109 far out to sea. "He was going very fast, and I had to do 400 miles an hour to catch him up. Then, before I could fire, he flattened out to no more than fifty feet above the sea level, and went streaking for home." But Ferriss stayed on his tail and got in five short bursts, "all aimed very deliberately. Suddenly the Messerschmitt's port wing dropped down. The starboard wing went up, and then in a flash his nose went down and he was gone. He simply vanished into the sea." Just then Ferriss felt a sharp stinging sensation in his leg, and knew he had been hit. "There were some Messerschmitt 109s right on my tail ... I did a quick turn and made for home, but it wasn't quite so easy as that." Ferriss's port aileron had been damaged, and his engine was running rough. There followed a 20-mile pursuit back to the English coast, with Ferriss throwing his Hurricane to the right each time the Me109s caught up with him and opened fire. As the beaches came into view, the pursuers turned back, and Ferriss managed to land his damaged plane. Almost immediately he "got a fresh Hurricane, and rejoined my squadron before going on another patrol".[2] Ferriss, who had been a medical student before joining the RAF in 1937, would become one of the victims of No. 111 Squadron's aggressive, front-on tactics. He was killed on 16 August in a collision with a Dornier Do17.

One further Hurricane was hit that day, but also made it down safely. The Germans lost four aircraft, and several limped back with dead and dying on board. One hundred and fifty bombs had been dropped, but the attack had been successfully broken up. Only one ship in the convoy was struck.

Thus ended the first day of the Battle of Britain. It had been a good one for the RAF. The results seemed to endorse the soundness of the defensive preparations that had been made. Air Chief Marshal Dowding judged that "for this victory, we must thank the radar which placed us in readiness and allowed us to send our fighter squadrons out to meet them". Looking back to the start of the summer, he comforted himself with the thought that the RAF had learned lessons from its bruising encounters with the Luftwaffe during the German surge westwards, achieving a kind of "maturity".

Sir Hugh Dowding

Sir Hugh Caswell Tremenheere Dowding (1882–1970), air chief marshal in charge of RAF Fighter Command, was 58 years old in the summer of 1940, and a remote figure to the pilots who flew under him. His stiff manner, feathery moustache and pained demeanour made him appear a relict of the Edwardian era in which he had done his early soldiering as an artillery officer in imperial outposts. He seemed to suit his nickname, "Stuffy". But in other respects Dowding belonged firmly in the modern era.

He had taken up the dangerous and dashing occupation of flying early on, gaining his pilot's certificate in December 1913, and he served with distinction in the Royal Flying Corps during the First World War, partly on active service in France and partly in logistics and training roles. In the interwar years that followed, he stood out against the pro-bomber theories that prevailed in the RAF and understood better than any other senior officer the vital importance of a strong, well-equipped fighter force. In July 1936, he became head of the new Fighter Command, and the following year was promoted to air chief marshal.

Many found it difficult to warm to Dowding personally. But behind his awkward manner there beat a warm heart, and he cared deeply for his men. (His son, Derek, was one of them, a Battle of Britain fighter pilot.) He made this clear at the close of the Dunkirk crisis, in a letter of 2 June directed to "My Dear Fighter Boys" — the name by which the men who flew the Spitfires and Hurricanes were becoming known.

My Dear Fighter Boys

I don't send out many congratulatory letters and signals but I feel that I must take this occasion, when the intensive fighting in northern France is for the time being over, to tell you how proud I am of you and the way in which you have fought since the "Blitzkrieg" started.

I wish I could have spent my time visiting you and hearing your accounts of the fighting but I have occupied my self in working for you in other ways.

I want you to know that my thoughts are always with you and that it is you and your fighting spirit which will crack the morale of the German Air Force and preserve our Country through the trials which yet lie ahead.

Good luck to you.

His men felt their lives were in responsible hands. "Even junior people like myself had enormous

105

confidence in him," said Christopher Foxley-Norris, then a young pilot with No. 3 Squadron. "He was a father figure. You felt that as long as his hand was on the tiller, all was going to be well."[3]

The women who worked with him at Fighter Command's Bentley Priory HQ could sense the warmth behind the stiffness. "We all admired our Stuffy enormously," said Elizabeth Quayle, a WAAF plotter in the operations room. "We had great loyalty to him. I think you might call it affection. He built up a tremendous *esprit de corps* among us. He was very remote but if you met him he was always very considerate."[4]

During the Battle of Britain, Dowding was the right man in the right job. Once it was done, Churchill unsentimentally moved him on. He was considered dour, stubborn and defensive-minded by jealous colleagues. But it was these very qualities that saved Fighter Command from destruction. In 1943, Dowding accepted a barony. He died in 1970, and his ashes were placed in Westminster Abbey, in the RAF chapel.

---

10 July has been chosen as marking the start of the Battle of Britain proper because the scale of the attacks that day demonstrated that the raids of the preceding week were merely the overture to a symphony of violence that was to last the rest of the summer. The showdown had finally come.

The decision to launch a full-scale aerial assault was taken by the German Armed Forces Supreme Command (*Oberkommando der Wehrmacht*, or OKW) once it was confident that its assets were in place. From the start of July, the Luftwaffe probed the RAF's defences, looking for weak spots and aiming to wear down the defenders. A small raid could cause a disproportionate amount of wear and tear. On the night of 31 June/1 July, a force of only 20 bombers caused sirens to be sounded in 20 counties. The following day saw the first daylight raids, on Wick in Scotland and on Hull. Thereafter *Luftflotte* 5 commenced fairly regular operations over northeastern Britain from its base at Stavanger, Norway, bringing home the reality of the huge front the British had to defend. Britain now felt vulnerable in the west, too, where it was exposed to attacks from the airfields near Brest and Cherbourg. To counter the threat, the new RAF group, 10 Group, was formed in the West Country and South Wales, under Air Vice-Marshal Sir Quintin Brand, with sector stations at Filton, near Bristol, and later Middle Wallop, Hampshire.

On 2 July, a Luftwaffe operational order set two objectives: to close the Channel to British shipping and to clear the air of British fighters. This was in keeping with a Hitler directive issued in November 1939, which had envisaged the Luftwaffe "waging war against the English economy" once the Anglo-French armies had been disposed of. What happened next was largely dependent on how the British reacted to the assault on their economic existence. As will be seen, the approach taken by Hitler and his commanders to the problem of Britain was always clouded with vagueness.

The aircraft for the task of blockading the Channel from the air would be provided by two *Fliegerkorps* formations. The main bomber force would be augmented by two groups of Stuka dive-bombers and protected by two *Jagdgeschwader* (fighter wings), Nos 26 and 53. The battle was to be called the *Kanalkampf* (Channel Battle) and the *Kanalkampfführer* was to be Oberst (Colonel) Johannes Fink, a sombre, religious-minded 45-year-old, who had been one of the few men allowed to be trained as pilots each year under the draconian terms imposed on Germany at Versailles in 1919.

German operations began tentatively on 3 July. About 50 aeroplanes flew towards Britain, of which about a quarter were on reconnaissance missions, tasked with photographing airfields and ports in preparation for future attacks. The day was full of alarms as patrolling aircraft and civilians in the streets of southern England caught glimpses of the intruders. One event that day brought home an uncomfortable truth: henceforth, no-one under the skies in which battle would be fought could consider themselves entirely safe. In the village of Holmbury St Mary, near Dorking in Surrey, a policeman walking his beat caught sight of a low-flying bomber and alerted RAF Biggin Hill. Ten minutes later, two large bombs fell close by, on the market town of Guildford, killing 15 innocents.

Countering the Luftwaffe's probes that day cost a lot of effort. By evening, 28 fighter squadrons had flown more than 120 patrols, each involving three or six aircraft. The result of all this effort was only five German aircraft shot down. In the months ahead, controllers from the top down would have to make constant fine judgements as to how to combat an ever-present but fluctuating threat while trying to preserve aircraft and men.

Thursday 4 July saw a bolder approach from the Germans. At first light, about 30 Ju87 "Stukas" attacked the naval base at Portland, Dorset. A merchant tanker suffered a direct hit from a 500 kg bomb and was set on fire. Next, the Stukas sank the largest vessel in the naval base, the 5,500-ton HMS *Foyle Bank*. Further small ships were sunk or damaged, buildings battered and civilians killed. By the time fighters from 609 Squadron arrived from Middle Wallop, Hampshire, the Stukas were long gone.

At 2p.m. about 20 Dorniers, guarded by Messerschmitt Me109s, attacked a convoy of 9 ships as they passed through the Straits of Dover. High-flying German spotter planes had called in the attack when the convoy was without a fighter escort. The bombs struck several vessels, encouraging the Germans to linger over the area long enough for them to be caught by eight Hurricanes from No. 79 Squadron. But as the Hurricanes arrived, the escorting Me109 fighters dived to the rescue, shooting down a Hurricane over St Margaret's Bay, killing the pilot, and driving the rest of the squadron away.

★ ★ ★

The convoys transporting food, coal, raw materials and machinery were vital to the maintenance of Britain's very existence; but having to defend them around the country's coast was not a welcome prospect for Fighter Command. RAF planes frequently came under fire from overeager Royal Navy anti-aircraft gunners. In operations against shipping, the Germans had a crucial advantage. Before engaging offshore targets, attackers could form up out of range of radar and be over the vessels in ten minutes. It took British fighters at least 15 minutes to get sufficient altitude to make a successful attack possible. On several occasions during the first week of July, the intercepting British fighters arrived over a convoy only to find the bombers gone and the damage already done. Soon the Germans were timing Me109 fighter sweeps to coincide with the belated arrival of the British defenders, "bouncing" the Spitfires or Hurricanes — charging at them from out of the glare of the sun — as the British fighters dived on the bomber stragglers.

At this stage the RAF pilots' lack of combat experience was often revealed. Patrolling near Manston, Kent, on 4 July, a threeman section from 54 Squadron came across a formation of Messerschmitt Me110s crossing the coast near Dungeness. They were just about to attack "when they were jumped from above by a formation of escorting Me109s". According to 54 Squadron's Al Deere, "This was a classic example of 'beware the Hun in the sun'. The Spitfire pilots, to put it bluntly, were caught with their trousers down and two of our aircraft were shot down and a third damaged."[5] The pilots all escaped with their lives.

Even with the benefit of radar, it was proving difficult to locate incoming German aircraft. The defenders had to fall back on the unsatisfactory precaution of constant patrolling, hoping that some of their aircraft would be in the air at the right time and place to intercept a raid. On Sunday 7 July a large convoy was making its way eastwards through the English Channel when it was spotted by a Dornier Do17, one of a number scanning the coast. No. 145 Squadron happened to be patrolling over the Isle of Wight at the time. They managed to down the Do17, but then another appeared. It too was chased away and shot down, this time by No. 43 Squadron from Tangmere, Sussex, which had taken over patrol duties as the convoy headed eastwards. Next on station was 601 Squadron, which also destroyed a Do17.

By now, however, Kesselring had all the reconnaissance information he needed. The main attack on the convoy was ready. At 7.30p.m. British time, 45 Dorniers took off from their base at Arras. Fifty-five minutes later they were over the convoy, sinking one ship and damaging three others. Fighters from Kenley, near Croydon, and Hornchurch, in outer East London, were too late to stop the attack, but they arrived in time to be caught by a "free sweep" of Me109s timed to meet any Fighter Command response. As well as carrying out exhausting patrolling, the pilots of Fighter Command were having to rise to the challenges of "free

111

sweeps", whereby small groups of Messerschmitt Me109s would range over the south coast looking for British patrols or trying to tempt aircraft up into combats — in which the RAF tended to come off worse. On this occasion, the Messerschmitts caught No. 65 Squadron from above, and all three pilots of its Green Section were shot down and killed.

Albert Kesselring

Albert Kesselring (1885–1960) was a versatile commander and accomplished administrator, but he was arguably more effective in charge of ground troops than air forces. During the First World War, he served in the German artillery and in various staff positions. He remained in the army after the war, but in 1933 was transferred to the *Reichskommissariat für die Luftfahrt* (Aviation Commission), a cover organization for planning the then clandestine Luftwaffe. In April 1936 he was made Luftwaffe chief of staff and, as an ex-army man, was firmly on the side of those who wished to steer the new force towards concentrating on tactical ground support.

At the beginning of the Second World War, Kesselring held the rank of general and was in charge of *Luftflotte 1*, which, in support of Generalfeldmarschall von Bock's Army Group North, was instrumental in the rapid destruction of Polish forces. He had similar success in command of *Luftflotte 2* during the battle in the west, and in both campaigns he worked very closely with army commanders on the ground.

During the Battle of Britain, the newly promoted Generalfeldmarschall Kesselring's *Luftflotte 2* was based in eastern France and the Low Countries. Like Goering, Kesselring consistently underestimated the strength of Fighter Command. He was also a strong proponent of the terror bombing of London, a decision that, more than any other, eventually lost Germany the battle.

In late 1941, after the dazzling success of his air forces in the opening months of Operation Barbarossa against the Soviet Union, Kesselring was appointed commander-in-chief of all German forces in the Mediterranean and North African theatres. His conduct of the Italian campaign, where superior Allied forces were successfully sucked into a battle of attrition in terrain that greatly favoured the defenders, earned him a reputation as one of Hitler's most able commanders.

At the end of the war Kesselring was charged with responsibility for atrocities committed in northern Italy by the SS and regular Wehrmacht soldiers after the surrender of Italy. He was sentenced to death, but this was commuted to life imprisonment. Freed because of ill health in 1952, he died eight years later.

Fighter Command was also carrying out sweeps of its own, with reconnaissance patrols across the Channel to report back on activity in the Pas de Calais. Interception by hostile enemy fighters was almost inevitable, and pilots on constant lookout in the air found themselves struggling to provide sufficient information about military activity on the ground to make the missions worthwhile. Furthermore, their presence confused the vital radar picture over the Channel. Soon such operations were ended, although specially adapted Spitfires continued to fly on lone missions over northern Europe, photographing the preparations for the invasion of Britain.

With seven convoys at sea on 8 July, there was no respite for Fighter Command. Heavy cloud failed to prevent German planes from shadowing, from the early morning, one convoy sailing up the Bristol Channel and another heading from the Thames Estuary to the Straits of Dover. By midday, Kent's radar stations were showing a build-up over the Pas de Calais. This time an interception was made, with a section of 610 Squadron encountering a *Staffel* of unescorted Dorniers. The absence of German fighter protection did not mean that the bombers were easy targets. They were forced to scatter their bombs harmlessly, but then they moved into a defensive formation that maximized the crossfire from their guns, and enabled them to pump out an effective barrage. One of the British pilots was hit by several gunners at once and his aircraft burst into flames. Pilot Officer A. L. B. Raven baled out and was seen by one of his section swimming in the sea, but he drowned before he could be reached.

Nine Hurricanes from 79 Squadron were ordered off from Hawkinge, but they were bounced by a free chase of enemy fighters between Dover and the convoy. By the time the German planes were spotted, two Hurricanes were already spinning in flames towards the Channel. One pilot baled out and was rescued, but he died from his burns. The other died in his cockpit.

The day's events showed that even attacks on unescorted bombers were loaded with danger. On other occasions, fighters would be scrambled to intercept a bombing attack, only to discover that the intruders were in fact Me109 fighters. At this early stage, the heavily outnumbered British fighters were finding themselves capable of picking off stragglers or lone reconnaissance aircraft, and of breaking up bombing attacks — but little else. By the end of 10 July, with battle properly joined, Fighter Command's resources were already being stretched. It now seemed likely that there was little chance of any respite until the contest was settled.

In one respect, the RAF possessed a much-needed advantage. Its aircraft gained a significant power increase from using 100-octane fuel, while the Luftwaffe had to make do with 60- or 70-octane. Achieving an octane rating of 100 required a very complicated process and a large and expensive refinery plant. The necessary "alkylation" process had been pioneered by scientists at the Anglo-Iranian Oil

115

Company's (AIOC) laboratory at Sunbury-on-Thames, but it was the US Army Air Corps that first produced 100-octane aviation fuel. In 1937, engine-specialist Air Commodore Rod Banks urged the RAF to adopt engines able to use it, "even if the supply of such fuel were limited, because the use of high-duty equipment might prove decisive in the air in the early stages of a war".[6] So two British engines, one of them the Merlin, were tested and developed to run on 100-octane.

In June 1939, the first cargo of "BAM.100" (British Air Ministry 100) was shipped from the Lago (Esso) refinery on the island of Aruba, part of the Dutch West Indies. The valuable fuel was dyed a distinctive green and secretly stockpiled by the Air Ministry. In May 1940, the RAF began to use the special fuel in the Merlins of Hurricanes and Spitfires. At a stroke the maximum boost was doubled from 6 pounds (in metric pressure measurements, 1.36ata) to 12 pounds (1.82ata), resulting in an increase in maximum power from 1,130 horsepower to 1,310 horsepower. This made a major difference to the Hurricane and Spitfire, bringing the former broadly up to the level of the Me109E and delivering to the Spitfire a vital edge.

Thursday 11 July was overcast in the south, with thunder and bright intervals elsewhere. Early in the morning, radar reported a formation approaching a convoy off the Dorset coast. No. 501 Squadron, patrolling above the vessels, was vectored to intercept, but before it reached the ten or so Ju87 dive-bombers, the squadron was attacked by escorting Me109 fighters, with one Hurricane shot down. The pilot,

21-year-old Sergeant Frederick Dixon, baled out, only to drown before he could be rescued.

In the meantime, 609 Squadron had been scrambled to help. The unit was an Auxiliary squadron, drawn originally from the West Riding of Yorkshire, one of the 12 Auxiliary squadrons created in 1936 to boost the number of pilots available to the RAF. No. 609 Squadron had been blooded over Dunkirk, where it had lost six of its pilots, and with them much of its territorial identity. The vigorous leadership of a regular RAF officer, Squadron Leader H. S. "George" Darley, had restored shattered morale, and on 9 July the squadron had moved from Middle Wallop, Hampshire, to a satellite station at Warmwell, Dorset, nearer the coast. The primary role of the station was to help protect Portland naval base, which had been hit in the 4 July incident. By 11 July the airfield had only just become operational and conditions were spartan. It was described by one of its flight lieutenants, John Dundas, as "possessing the two chief characteristics of a forward station — action and discomfort".[7] There was no running water or sanitation, and the pilots were forced to sleep in the dispersal tent. It was very dry and the tent would become filled with dust and stones whenever an aircraft passed nearby.

Six 609 Spitfires from Warmwell arrived just as the Stukas were preparing to dive on the convoy. One section went for the bombers, while the other tried to hold off the escort. Although the convoy escaped serious damage, the encounter was otherwise a disaster for 609 Squadron. Facing odds of six-to-one, it failed to hit any of the German attackers but lost two Spitfires and with them two pilots. Flight Lieutenant "Pip" Barran was one of the squadron's founder members, a son of wealthy Yorkshire colliery owners and universally liked and respected. The other casualty was Pilot Officer Gordon Mitchell, another popular figure. The squadron was shaken and angry. David Crook, another 609 pilot officer, had been at school and university with Mitchell and felt his loss deeply. "I just could not get used to the idea that we would not see him again," he wrote later. "He was a delightful person, a very amusing and charming companion and one of the most generous people. He was also a brilliant athlete, a Cambridge hockey blue and Scots international. He played any game with natural grace and ease."

Others wondered whether the convoys they were laying down their lives to protect were actually necessary. "They could have stopped at Plymouth or somewhere and put all their stuff on a train. But they went on and on with these convoys," said the 609 pilot John Bisdee.[8] David Crook summed up the emotions of the shattered squadron after the action:

> It is difficult to describe my feelings during the next few days. We had just lost three pilots in thirty-six hours, all of them in fights in which we had been hopelessly out-numbered, and I felt that there was now nothing left to care about, because obviously from the law of probability, one could not expect to survive many more encounters of a similar nature.[9]

Through the morning of 11 July, all three German *Luftflotten* sent reconnaissance aircraft, eighty in number, over British coastal waters, from the tip of Cornwall to the north of Scotland. Several were intercepted and shot down, including one by Squadron Leader Douglas Bader. Bader had lost both his legs in a flying accident in the 1930s and been invalided out of the RAF. Once equipped with artificial legs, he resumed flying, overcoming strong official opposition. He had taken part in the actions over Dunkirk, shooting down a Messerschmitt Me109 on 1 June, and was subsequently given command of 242 Squadron, made up mainly of Canadian pilots, where he imposed forceful discipline. The Dornier Do17 he downed on 11 July was his first kill of the Battle of Britain.

Experience such as Bader possessed was undoubtedly a huge help in staying alive and scoring victories, but it was no guarantee of success. In February, the highly skilled Squadron Leader Peter Townsend of 85 Squadron had taken part in the downing of the first German bomber to be brought down on British soil since the First World War. But on 11 July, on a lone patrol near Harwich, he had a narrow escape from a watery end, colourfully recorded in his memoir *Duel of Eagles* (pp. 298-301). "I was at 8000 feet and still climbing in and out of grey soggy rain clouds. Below yawned a dark, blue-grey void and somewhere at its bottom the sea. Suddenly an aircraft appeared out of the cloud above, going the other way. A Dornier 17!" Townsend wheeled his Hurricane around, craning his head backwards, his eyes riveted on the German

119

bomber. But he felt "enormously visible", and could only dimly see the Dornier through his rain-lashed windscreen. He opened the hood and slanted his head out into the battering slipstream to get a better view. Then he was spotted. The rear gunner, Werner Borner, spotted the Hurricane and opened fire. Townsend pressed closer and then hit the fire button. Suddenly "pieces of metal and other fragments were flying everywhere", said Borner. Leutnant Berchein, on the starboard rear gun of the German plane, was hit in the head and slumped to the floor of the cabin. Moments later, Feldwebel (Sergeant) Lohrer collapsed on top of him, hit in the head and throat. The bomber was now awash with blood. But Borner continued firing as the Hurricane came so close that he could see the pilot.

"I was still firing when suddenly there was a bright orange explosion in the cockpit in front of me," recorded Townsend. "The engine was hit." As he glided down through the rain clouds, Townsend attempted to radio his position. There was no ship in sight. "Now only two things mattered, life and death." Townsend dived out head first and then pulled the rip cord. "Far below I could see my Hurricane diving vertically towards the sea to disappear in an eruption of spume and spray." He hit the water. "When the big splash came I hit the harness release knob and sank, it seemed fathoms deep, into green obscurity . . . when at last I broke the surface I saw a little ship lying less than a mile away." The ship, the trawler *Cap Finisterre*, lowered a boat that was soon alongside the downed pilot. One of the sailors was brandishing a boat hook.

"Blimey, if he ain't a fucking Hun!" he shouted. "I'm not," replied Townsend. "I'm a fucking Englishman!"

That day, the weather remained clearest in the west, and here the Germans struck again, with a force of two *Staffeln* of Ju87 Stukas, accompanied by about 40 Me110s, appearing over Portland at about 11am. It was fortunate timing for the attackers as almost all the fighters in the Middle Wallop sector were on the ground refuelling. So six Hurricanes of 601 Squadron were sent from Tangmere, more than 50 miles away. They nonetheless arrived in time to disperse the raid and to down two of the Me110s. The squadron was in action again at 5.15p.m., breaking up a smaller raid on the naval base at Portsmouth. Two Heinkel He111s were destroyed when they collided, and a third was badly damaged. One of the Hurricanes, however, was shot down by friendly fire from anti-aircraft guns on the Isle of Wight.

By now the Spitfires of No. 54 Squadron had been allocated a gruelling routine, which meant leaving at first light from RAF Rochford, Essex, to the forward base at Manston, Kent. Late in the day on 11 July, two sections of the squadron's Spitfires, led by flight lieutenants Al Deere and Johnny Allen, were sent to investigate activity five miles east of Deal. It was Deere's fourth sortie of the day. "We had just crossed the coast at a height of 1,500 feet when I spotted an aircraft flying at wave top height." It was a Heinkel He59 seaplane, with Red Cross markings. The Luftwaffe had lost six aircraft into the waters of the

Channel that day and was hoping to pick up survivors. Deere was wondering what to do when Allen's voice "burst though on the R/T [radio telephone]. 'Red Leader there are about a dozen 109s flying in loose formation, well behind and slightly above the seaplane.'" "Thanks, Johnny," Deere replied, "That makes the seaplane enemy as far as I am concerned."[10]

While Deere's attitude towards the Red Cross plane might smack of callousness, he had good reasons to be suspicious. The Germans had inaugurated a service during the early part of the war to rescue airmen downed over the sea, using Heinkel He59 and Dornier Do18 seaplanes, operating from bases in Norway, Denmark, Belgium and along the French coast. However, although these aircraft were painted white and adorned with numerous red crosses, they also often carried armaments and had been observed carrying out reconnaissance tasks.

While Allen's Yellow Section went for the seaplane, Deere led his own section against the escort, banking around to get behind them. But as the section levelled out behind the Me109s, it was spotted, and at once the enemy formation split in two, each breaking upwards in a steep turn, one half to the left, one to the right. Although outnumbered six-to-one, the Spitfires attacked, breaking formation, each pilot choosing his target. Deere managed to fasten onto the tail of one of the yellow-nosed Messerschmitts and opened fire. "There was an immediate response from my eight Brownings which, to the accompaniment of a slight bucketing from my aircraft, spat a stream of lethal lead targetwards," he wrote. But just as he saw his bullets strike home, he spotted Me109s on his tail. "I broke hard into the attack, pulling my Spitfire into a climbing, spiralling turn as I did so." The action was gratifyingly effective. "The Messerschmitts literally 'fell out of the sky' as they stalled in an attempt to follow me."[11]

Deere was aware that at least one of the squadron's Spitfires had gone down in flames — he heard Allen's number two "screaming for help over the R/T"; but Deere now fastened onto a new target, an Me109 turning to re-enter the fray. The German spotted him almost immediately "and rolled out of his turn towards me so that a head-on attack became inevitable. Using both hands on the control column to steady the aircraft . . . I peered through the reflector sight at the rapidly closing enemy aircraft. We opened fire together, and immediately a hail of lead thudded into my Spitfire. One moment the Messerschmitt was a clearly defined shape, its wingspan nicely enclosed within the circle of my reflector sight, and the next it was on top of me, a terrifying blur which blotted out the sky ahead. Then we hit."

Deere was catapulted forwards. He realized immediately that his Spitfire was terminally damaged. He was amazed to be still alive. The engine, now on fire, vibrated wildly, throwing the control column around the cockpit. Then it abruptly stopped. He could see that the propeller blades had been "bent almost double with the impact of the collision". "With smoke now pouring into the cockpit I reached blindly forward for the emergency hood release toggle and tugged at it violently." But there was no welcoming rush of cold air into the cockpit, and the normal release catch did not work either. Gathering his strength, struggling to stay calm, Deere steered his now powerless aircraft into a glide towards the coast. With eyes streaming from the smoke, he peered forward, searching for open space in which to crash-land. "Through a . . . cloud of flame and smoke the ground suddenly appeared ahead of me. The next moment a post flashed by my wingtip and then the aircraft struck the ground and ricocheted into the air again finally returning to earth with a jarring impact." The aircraft ploughed through a succession of wooden posts, driven into the open ground to deter German landings, before at last coming to a rest. "With my bare hands wielding the strength of desperation, I battered at the Perspex hood which entombed me. With a splintering crash it finally cracked open." Deere scrambled to a safe distance as his aircraft, enveloped by flames, started giving off a series of explosions. "My hands were cut and bleeding," he wrote, "my eyebrows singed; both knees were badly bruised; and blood trickled into my mouth from a slightly cut lip. But I was alive!"

Others had been less lucky. The squadron had two Spitfires shot down during the fight with the seaplane escort. Neither pilot escaped his burning cockpit.

Three days after the encounter, the British government issued a communiqué declaring, in effect, that German Red Cross seaplanes would be considered legitimate targets:

Enemy aircraft bearing civil markings and marked with the Red Cross have recently flown over British ships at sea and in the vicinity of the British coast, and they are being employed for purposes which His Majesty's Government cannot regard as being consistent with the privileges generally accorded to the Red Cross.

His Majesty's Government desire to accord to ambulance aircraft reasonable facilities for the transportation of the sick and wounded, in accordance with the Red Cross Convention, and aircraft engaged in the direct evacuation of the sick and wounded will be respected, provided that they comply with the relevant provisions of the Convention.

His Majesty's Government are unable, however, to grant immunity to such aircraft flying over areas in which operations are in progress on land or at sea, or approaching British or Allied territory, or territory in British occupation, or British or Allied ships. Ambulance aircraft which do not comply with the above requirements will do so at their own risk and peril.

Friday 12 July dawned grey and wet, but the pattern of attacks continued, with raids on convoys — this time concentrated off the east coast — together with small, scattered actions across the whole front. The heaviest fighting took place over a convoy codenamed Booty, as it steamed southwards off Harwich. A flight of six aircraft from No. 17 Squadron was patrolling overhead, and when the Germans arrived further fighters were scrambled from Nos 85, 242, 264 and 151 Squadrons.

The RAF lost two aircraft in the fighting, with both pilots — L. Jowitt and New Zealander J. H. L. Allen — killed. Five Luftwaffe bombers were put out of action, either shot down or crash-landing on return to their bases.

Deterioration in the weather kept further heavy German raids at bay, as it did the next day when fog hampered both air forces. But convoys were still shadowed by high-flying reconnaissance aircraft, and, as the sky cleared during Saturday 13 July, the Germans returned to the attack. Shortly before 3p.m., elements of the two squadrons now roughing it at the forward base at Warmwell, Dorset, were scrambled to intercept an incoming raid on a convoy off Lyme Regis. Three Spitfires from 609 Squadron and twelve Hurricanes of 238 Squadron took off and roared into a steep climb. No. 238 had been battered over France. It had been reinforced with a wave of new pilots, including Sergeant Eric Seabourne, who was setting off on his first combat. He had received little preparation for the test ahead. Before taking off he had only spent seven hours at the controls of a Hurricane.

The British fighters met the 50-strong attacking formation before either side reached the convoy. A flight of No. 238, led by the Australian Flight Lieutenant John Kennedy, swooped on some straggling Dorniers, while the flight containing Seabourne squared up to the accompanying Me110s, which now formed themselves into a defensive ring. This manoeuvre, much practised by Me110 pilots, was known in the Luftwaffe as a "death circle". Each aircraft followed the one in front, rotating over a fixed point, thereby giving the rear gunners the best chance of providing defensive fire-power, while each aircraft protected the tail of the one in front. This time, though, the attack by Seabourne's flight managed to break up the formation.

Moments later, one of the German planes swooped down just above Seabourne's cockpit. "It was pale blue underneath," he remembered, "with black crosses on the wings, so I thought, it's not one of ours, and pressed the gun button and gave it a good blast. As I did so another appeared and I did the same again. They clearly took objection to this because then large holes started appearing in my port mainframe and I could feel bullets hitting the armour plating behind my seat." Seabourne threw his Hurricane into a steep vertical dive. For a few seconds it did not seem that he could get out of it, as he tugged and heaved at the control column. Then, "very slowly I started winding the tail trim back, something we had been told never to do. But it worked and I came out in a beautiful, gentle curve and I was again flying straight and level."[12] When Seabourne got back to Middle Wallop, his engineer expressed his amazement that the wing hadn't been pulled off in the dive, as two armour-piercing bullets had lodged in the main spar. He would not be the last pilot to be thankful for the Hurricane's rugged construction, which allowed it to sustain far more damage than the Spitfire or Me109 and still stay in the air.

John Kennedy, who had shot down one of his target Dorniers over Chesil Beach, Dorset, and damaged another, must have sustained battle damage during the combat. Returning to the airfield, he crashed and was killed. Seabourne's reaction to the loss was less emotional than that expressed by David Crook over the loss of his friend Gordon Mitchell two days previously. It would be echoed many times in the months ahead, as the pilots learned to contain and suppress their responses to the violent deaths of comrades. "It was just hard luck. You were all right and he wasn't. There simply wasn't the time to grieve. You registered — Oh God, that's awful — but then you had to get on."[13]

The haemorrhaging of experienced and aggressive pilots like Kennedy would now come to pose a serious threat to the effectiveness of Fighter Command. The aircraft factories were pumping out planes. But men were harder to replace. In the first two weeks of July, thirty-one of Dowding's "fighter boys" had been killed. That was a significant figure given that there had been only 1,104 trained pilots available at the start of the month and the fighting had clearly hardly begun. Three new operational training units had been set up after the losses of May and June, where in theory the pilots would learn formation flying and tactics of combat. But from 10 July the overall training period was drastically truncated from six months to four weeks. Such was the pressure for new pilots that by the middle of the summer of 1940 many pilots were skipping the OTU stage altogether and posted to squadrons straight from flying school. There would be many novices like Eric Seabourne with only a handful of hours' experience in "Spits" or "Hurris" arriving fresh at squadrons throughout the rest of the battle. Some of them fired their new aircraft's guns for the first time when they were in actual combat.

On the afternoon of 13 July, the Luftwaffe's strength was again thrown against a Channel target. Just to the east of where 238 Squadron had fought off the morning attack, another convoy was risking the Dover Straits, within sight of German observation posts on the Pas de Calais coast. This time the attack was by a *Staffel* of Stuka dive-bombers, with at least three *Staffeln* of Me109s and Me110s circling high above. Eleven Hurricanes from No. 56 Squadron were on patrol between Calais and Dover, and they intercepted the raid at around 4p.m. While some made for the dive-bombers, blasting them at short range before the escort could intervene, others peeled off to attack the German fighters, climbing as fast as they could. By the time the latter made contact, "our three Hurricanes had managed to climb above the level of the twin-engine Me110s, but we were still below the single-seater Me109s," wrote 56 Squadron pilot Geoffrey Page. Then, led by Flight Lieutenant Edward "Jumbo" Gracie, the section swooped into the attack, forcing the Me110s into a defensive circle. "Being uncertain as to the best way to assail this orbiting group," wrote Page, "I decided to spray the area near two of the enemy before diving through the centre of the circle. The eight Browning machine-guns chattered away happily in the wings." Page ducked his head as the return fire came in, which he described as "orange glowing electric bulbs suspended in the air", before finding himself through the lethal zone. He climbed again and attacked from the other side, but to no visible effect except for a loosening of the formation. Then he found the Me109s on him.

"At that point the fight became a nightmare . . . for the next few minutes I registered nothing but flashing wings bearing iron crosses and streaks of tracer searing the sunlit sky." Then, as so often happened, suddenly the sky was clear, "as if the hand of God has wiped the slate clean". Moments later, Page spotted a lone Me109 circling towards him. He turned his aircraft and the two sped towards each other in a frontal attack. "Winking lights appeared on the leading edge of the enemy's wing." Page returned fire. "Both our aircraft roared by within inches of each other."[14] Then, again, the sky was empty. At the time Page did not think he had hit his target. The Me109, though, was fatally damaged, its engine perforated by Page's bullets. The pilot somehow nursed his machine back over the Channel to make a belly landing near Boulogne.

Page got back safely, but it had been a bad day for 56 Squadron. Sergeant James Cowsill, 20 years old, and Sergeant Joseph Whitfield, aged 21, were both shot down and killed by the Me109s.

Variable weather on Sunday 14 July protected most of the nine convoys braving the coastal waters. However, Fighter Command continued to mount an exhausting watch over the Channel, with 597 sorties flown on patrol or to intercept enemy reconnaissance flights or raids. The heaviest German attack was on a convoy between Eastbourne and Dover; it was led again by Stukas, protected by about thirty Me109s. Twelve Spitfires from No. 610 Squadron, together with seven Hurricanes from No. 151 and nine from No. 615, made the interception.

The action became one of the most famous in the Battle of Britain thanks to the presence on the ground of BBC reporter Charles Gardner, whose excited commentary caused an immediate controversy. He donned a tin helmet and strapped a mattress to the roof of his car to watch the action high above the white cliffs, near Dover:

> The Germans are dive-bombing a convoy out to sea; there are one, two, three, four, five, six, seven German dive-bombers, Junkers 87s. There's one going down on its target now — bomb! No, he missed the ships . . . Now the British fighters are coming up. Here they come. The Germans are coming in an absolute steep dive, and you can see their bombs actually leave the machines and come into the water. You can hear our guns going like anything now. I am looking round now. I can hear machine-gun fire, but I can't see our Spitfires. They must be somewhere there. Oh! Here's one coming down.
>
> There's one going down in flames. Somebody's hit a German and he's coming down with a long streak — coming down completely out of control — a long

streak of smoke — and now a man's baled out by
parachute.

The pilot's baled out by parachute. He's a Junkers
87, and he's going slap into the sea — and there he
goes. Smash! A terrific column of water and there was
a Junkers 87. Only one man got out by parachute, so
presumably there was only a crew of one in it. Now
then, ho, there's a terrific mix-up over the Channel!
It's impossible to tell which are our machines and
which are Germans . . . there are fighters right over our
heads . . . Oh boy! I've never seen anything as good
as this.[15]

The "Junkers" Gardner described going down was, in
fact, a Hurricane. The pilot who baled out was rescued
by the navy, but he died of his injuries the next day.
After the broadcast, which had contrasted sharply with
the style of the BBC's output thus far, there were
numerous complaints about it being undignified and
sensational, reducing the struggle to the level of a
sporting contest, and the experiment was not repeated.
But Gardner's broadcast also touched a chord. His
reactions were those of any of the hundreds of ordinary
citizens who were watching the same event from the
streets and fields below. By the end of the summer
many — perhaps most — of the inhabitants of southern
England would have witnessed an aerial battle.

Poor flying conditions on Monday 15 July turned out
to be the beginning of several days of reduced activity
due to the low cloud and heavy rain, which forced the

Luftwaffe to scale down its operations. But the bad weather brought no advantages to the defenders. Training of replacement pilots had to be curtailed. And the hazards of foul-weather flying wore down pilots who were still flying convoy patrols, and so caused numerous accidents. On this day there were more aircraft damaged through mishap than enemy attacks, which were limited to a light raid against an aircraft works at Yeovil in Somerset and half-hearted forays against convoys, driven off by the interceptions of Nos 56 and 151 Squadrons.

Tuesday 16 July saw a slight improvement in the weather late in the afternoon. At 5.05p.m., Flying Officer William Rhodes-Moorhouse, leading six Hurricanes of 601 Squadron from the fighter station at Tangmere, on the Sussex coast, shot down a Ju88 bomber near the Isle of Wight. Rhodes-Moorhouse's father (also called William) had been a First World War pilot who had died of his wounds in April 1915, after a bombing raid that won him the first Victoria Cross awarded for valour in the air. His son, Willie, had gained his pilot's licence when only 17 years old, while still at school at Eton.

Willie had flown Blenheim bombers at the start of the war, before No. 601 Squadron switched to Hurricanes, and took part in the Battle of France, where he had successfully downed a Heinkel and an Me109. He was not to survive the Battle of Britain; he was shot down and killed over Tunbridge Wells on 6 September.

By mid-July, it was becoming clearer that both sides were fighting a war of attrition. The question of how many aircraft your enemy had at his disposal was a vital one. Major Josef Schmid, chief of *Abteilung* (Department) V of the German intelligence service, had tried to answer it in a report entitled *A Comparative Appreciation of the Striking Power of the RAF and the Luftwaffe*, to be delivered to Hitler on 16 July. Schmid estimated that the RAF had 900 first-line fighters, of which 675 were fully operational. The figure was, if anything, an overestimation of the average fighter strength of the period. Schmid had come to the optimistic conclusion that "the Hurricane and Spitfire are both inferior to the Messerschmitt 109", although he conceded that the Spitfire could have the edge over the Me110 if the former were "well piloted". An intensification of the air war — "decisive daylight operations" — would be to the advantage of the Luftwaffe, he concluded, "so long as the large-scale operations are begun early enough to permit the exploitation of the relatively favourable meteorological conditions of July to early October". Major Schmid also estimated British aircraft production at 180–300 first-line fighters per month, and predicted that the figure would fall once the German blockade and air attacks took their toll. Here, he was badly mistaken: his estimate was too low.

The quantity of aircraft now emerging from British factories had significantly increased from what it had been a mere two months previously. Behind much of this increase in output was the newspaper magnate

Lord Beaverbrook, a crony of Winston Churchill, whom the prime minister had appointed on 11 May to the task of galvanizing the aero factories. The new minister for aircraft production was abrasive but very effective. Churchill's secretary, Colville, described Beaverbrook as "twenty-five per cent thug, fifteen per cent crook and the remainder a combination of genius and real goodness of heart". From the start of his appointment, he set about wresting control from the Air Ministry and injecting his energy and gusto into the fighter-aircraft factories. He recruited lieutenants from the commercial world, cut through red tape and defied labour regulations to keep factories busy. He caught the public's imagination in the struggle to produce more aircraft, famously appealing for donations of pots and pans and garden railings to be turned into fighters and enabling citizens to contribute to the purchase of their "own" Spitfire.

The results were impressive. May's production figure of 325 fighters was nearly double that of the previous two months. In June, the figure jumped again by a further 120 aircraft. At the end of June, Beaverbrook informed Churchill with justifiable pride that there were now 1,040 operational aircraft of all types available for service. "I would remind you," he continued, "that there were 45 aircraft ready for service when your Administration began." During July, just short of 500 fighters were produced — 200 more than Major Schmid estimated the British were capable of producing. Furthermore, technical improvements, such as the change from variable pitch propellors to more efficient constant speed ones, were carried out at an impressive pace.

Aircraft were not only being manufactured, but also patched up. By now the Civilian Repair Organization (CRO) was in full swing. Aircraft too badly damaged for the airfield workshops were collected by civilian mechanics, who in mid-July were returning 160 fighters a week to the squadrons. In Oxford, No. 1 Civilian Repair Unit was working a 14-hour day, 7 days a week, and pilots could fly there directly for repairs. Some aircraft returned two or three times. Even seemingly total wrecks could be salvaged for spare parts, including German aircraft.

By the beginning of August, the RAF would have more serviceable aircraft than it had possessed at the beginning of July. By contrast, German factories produced only 164 Me109s in June and 220 in July. If the Luftwaffe's initial clear superiority was to have a decisive effect, it would have to move quickly.

In truth, the Luftwaffe offensive had been launched in a spirit of reckless optimism. Goering had boasted at the start of the *Kanalkampf* that "my Luftwaffe is invincible". The next victory, he predicted, would not be slow in coming. "And so now we turn to England," he mused. "How long will this one last — two, three weeks?"[16] But by mid-July, the Luftwaffe had failed to achieve anything like the galloping success to which it had become accustomed. The start of the campaign had been cautious and the weather thus far had hampered its efforts. But it seemed obvious now that the goal of air superiority — the necessary prerequisite of the defeat of Britain, whether by capitulation or conquest — was still far away.

On 16 July, Hitler issued a directive which indicated that he no longer believed the subjugation of Britain was likely to be achieved by air battle and economic strangulation alone. In the preface to Directive No. 16 he ordered the preparation of an invasion plan to "eliminate the English motherland as a base from which war against Germany can be continued and, if this should become unavoidable, to occupy it to the full extent":

For this purpose I order the following:

1. The landing must take the form of a surprise crossing on a broad front, approximately from Ramsgate to the region west of the Isle of Wight, whereby elements of the Luftwaffe will play the role of artillery and elements of the *Kriegsmarine* [navy] the role of engineers. Whether it is appropriate to conduct partial operations in advance of the main one, such as the occupation of the Isle of Wight or the country of Cornwall, is to be studied from the point of view of each branch of the Wehrmacht, and the results reported to me. I reserve the right to decide.

    Preparations for the total operation must be completed by mid-August.

2. Included in these preparations is the bringing about of those preconditions which make a landing in England possible:

    a) The English air force must have been beaten

137

down to such an extent morally and in actual fact that it can no longer muster any power of attack worth mentioning against the German crossing.

b) Mine-free routes must have been created.

c) The Straits of Dover on both flanks, as well as the western entrance to the Channel approximately on a line Alderney-Portland, must have been blocked by a dense mine barrier.

d) The coastal foreland must be dominated and secured artillery-wise by a strong coastal artillery.

e) Tying down of English naval forces shortly before the crossing both on the North Sea and in the Mediterranean (by the Italians) is desirable, in the course of which every effort must now be made to reduce English naval forces stationed in the home country through air and torpedo attacks.[17]

The operation was to be codenamed *Seelöwe* — Operation Sea Lion.

CHAPTER
FIVE

Prodding and Probing

17 July to 31 July 1940

Operation Sea Lion looks now like something of an afterthought. Hitler's war preparations had taken little account of potential British intransigence. It was an inconvenient possibility that he appeared unwilling to think about. The swift and relatively painless seizure of France had induced a holiday mood. Hitler relaxed by heading off with a couple of old comrades to visit the battlefields where he had fought bravely a quarter of a century before. On 28 June, he made a sightseeing trip to Paris, a city that had haunted his architectural fantasies. He was photographed, the diabolical tourist, in front of the Eiffel Tower. In northern France preparations had been made to send up to 40 divisions home to Germany.

Hitler had all along hoped that Britain could be accommodated into his plans for continental Europe. This view was based partially on a logical appreciation of Britain's military position. The British Army had been smashed at Dunkirk, where its equipment lay rusting in the dunes. The air force and navy could still mount a daunting challenge to any attempted invasion. But they posed no substantial offensive threat to Germany, although the now almost nightly bombing raids by the RAF on Germany were certainly an embarrassment, even if they did little damage. Without France, and with the United States only a sympathetic onlooker, how long could Britain hold out?

It was a question also being asked by the US ambassador in London, Joseph P. Kennedy, whose warnings to Washington about Britain's hopeless situation ran counter to Churchill's efforts to rally the New World to the aid of the Old. Throughout the fighting in the spring of 1940, Churchill had kept Roosevelt vividly informed, writing to him on 15 May that: "The small countries are simply smashed up, one by one, like matchwood." In his speeches, the half-American Churchill frequently mentioned the United States, implying that it was a natural ally against Nazi barbarism. Churchill also played on a potential strategic threat to the United States should the Royal Navy fall into German hands. But the cause of inveigling America into the war was hampered by the personality and attitudes of Kennedy, whose Irish ancestry had nurtured in him a dislike of Britain and who also harboured an admiration for Hitler.

Churchill had asked Roosevelt for the loan of 50 obsolete US destroyers to help in home waters and on convoy patrols. But the president was wary. Although personally sympathetic to Churchill and Britain, he was reluctant to challenge the popular domestic isolationist feeling before the presidential election in November

1940. Opinion in the United States was deeply divided. The traditionally more Europhile East Coast was in favour of helping Britain, but there was significant opposition to the idea of getting dragged into another European war.

Roosevelt's caution disappointed Churchill. On 27 May, the British prime minister commented bitterly that "it would be very nice for him [Roosevelt] to pick up the bits of the British Empire if this country was overrun".[1] In Washington, worries were centred on the empire's credit-worthiness. Huge orders for US armaments were flowing in, with little solid capital to pay the bills. No-one wanted to lend money to a country about to fall. For Churchill, it became a prime aim of British diplomacy to convince the United States that Britain meant to fight on. The "miracle of Dunkirk" helped: it impressed many in the United States and led to a relaxing of laws concerning the supply of arms to nations at war. Soon, half a million used American rifles were on their way across the Atlantic.

Shortly afterwards, the British had another chance to demonstrate their resolve. Churchill had repeatedly urged the French to avoid letting their warships fall into enemy hands. But after the armistice with Germany in June 1940, trust had broken down. The French had freed 400 captive German pilots, in direct contravention of a promise made to Churchill. Now, confused and contradictory messages were coming back about the French fleet. On 3 July, those French ships that had slipped away to British ports were seized

141

by force, and at Mers-el-Kébir in Algeria a concentration of French vessels was attacked by a Royal Navy task force after failing to conform to an ultimatum. Within a very short time, much of the French fleet was destroyed and 1,297 of its officers and men died.

It was a ruthless move, and it demonstrated, as the US military attaché in London Raymond Lee commented, that "the British are not going to sit quietly and watch Hitler's plans mature".[2] Harry Hopkins, Roosevelt's secretary of state in 1940, later told Churchill that the action at Mers-el-Kébir, more than anything else, had convinced the president that Britain meant to fight on whatever the cost. But it was not until February 1941, after the US presidential election was safely won, that Roosevelt was able to send his envoy Averell Harriman to London to "recommend everything we can do, short of war, to keep the British Isles afloat".[3]

For now, though, British isolation remained complete, bolstering Hitler's instinctive feeling that Britain would have to see sense and come to terms. The *Führer* held a strategic aversion to the idea of invading. His attitude was tinged with a certain sentimentality based on notions of shared racial identity. Crushing Britain would mean the destruction of its empire, an outcome that would not benefit Germany. The real winners, he told his generals, would be Japan, the United States and even the Soviet Union.

There were good political reasons for thinking that an invasion would not be needed. The attitude of the

142

British government, prior to the arrival of Churchill, had suggested that a deal was not only possible, but likely.

Thus, no invasion plan for Britain had been drawn up when Hitler and his commanders prepared for the great European expansion. The inevitable defeat of Poland and France would leave Britain in a hopeless situation. In the unlikely event of her leaders choosing to hold out, a blockade was planned, using aircraft and U-boats, aimed at disrupting Britain's severe dependence on imported food and raw materials. This was the thinking that sustained the *Kanalkampf*.

The approach suited the German navy, the *Kriegsmarine*, and its commander *Grossadmiral* (Grand-Admiral) Erich Raeder. He was a complex figure. Raeder was 64, and he held strong opinions, which he was prepared to defend. He believed in a strategy that maximized the use of U-boats and small surface vessels to disrupt supply lines, rather than seeking a head-on confrontation with the Royal Navy. The British Home Fleet overmatched the German navy in northern waters. Raeder had little faith in the Luftwaffe's ability to win the mastery of the air over the Channel that he thought necessary to prevent his ships being smashed by the British navy.

Shortly after war began, Hitler had assured his *Grossadmiral* that he shared his view of the limitations of German sea power. His attitude had been reinforced by the loss of the "pocket battleship" *Graf Spee*, cornered by a British naval force off the coast of Uruguay, and the destruction of a number of valuable ships during the fighting for Norway. In naval matters, Hitler's customary boldness was reversed. "On land I am a hero," he told Raeder, "at sea I am a coward."[4]

Nonetheless, in November 1939 Raeder had felt it prudent to order that a study be made for an invasion across the Channel. The resulting report stressed the threat posed by the Royal Navy and the RAF, as well as the awkward tides, shallows and currents of the Channel. The army, too, carried out a study that envisaged airborne and infantry landings in East Anglia, with a diversionary action north of the Humber. The aim was to cut off London from the north. The plan was predicated on the other two services achieving daunting goals — the navy was to close the Straits of Dover to British ships from the south, and the Luftwaffe was to carry out the airborne landings as well as guarantee command of the air over the landing sites.

The Luftwaffe responded that the plan demanded "total air superiority" and "total surprise". It should only proceed, they said, as "the final act in an already victorious war". The navy, for its part, baulked at anything that looked like taking on the whole might of the Home Fleet and argued that the shipping required for transporting the 100,000 men that the army envisaged necessary would take at least a year to assemble. One thing that all three branches of the armed forces were able to agree on was that overwhelming local air superiority was a prerequisite of any landing attempt.

144

In the euphoric atmosphere that followed the victories in the west, German caution tended to fade. Without any prompting from Hitler, the army began preparing invasion plans. Only 21 miles (34 kilometres) of water separated the victorious Germans from the obstinate British. A landing began to appear not only desirable, but comfortably achievable. The army plan proposed landings between Margate in Kent and the Isle of Wight. Divisions were to form up in northern France, thirteen in total, split into two waves. The first was to be made up of 90,000 men, the second of a further 170,000 troops, together with heavy weapons, 34,000 vehicles, 57,000 horses and 26,000 bicycles. Raeder's subordinates, anxious not to exclude the navy from a stake in future glory, gave positive cooperation. Raeder himself, though, continued to raise objections.

On 13 July, the generals von Brauchitsch and Halder presented their proposals to the *Führer* at a meeting at his Alpine refuge at Berchtesgaden. As Egbert Kieser, the leading German historian of Sea Lion, recorded, to their great surprise and "completely at odds with his normal practice he [Hitler] asked no questions on specific operations, was not interested in details and recommended no improvements". The plan, Hitler declared, was practicable and preparations were to begin immediately.

Taking the decision did nothing to make the Luftwaffe's task easier. It was now faced with a number of objectives, each of which was daunting enough on its own. It had to continue its attacks on British shipping, wear down the RAF in the continuing battle of attrition and do what it could to reduce the Royal Navy's ability to menace a landing.

Reichsmarschall Goering could, though, report little progress on 17 July, the first day of operations following Hitler's invasion directive. The weather remained so bad that even many of the Luftwaffe's regular reconnaissance patrols were cancelled. Occasionally, though, the attackers could make clever use of the cloud. At around 2p.m., a patrol of 12 Spitfires of No. 64 Squadron was over Beachy Head when suddenly Flying Officer Donald Taylor was hit and went plunging downwards. He crash-landed near Hailsham in Sussex and was taken to Eastbourne Hospital. No-one in the squadron caught a glimpse of their attackers, who had vanished back into the cloud. The heaviest raid was in Scotland, coming from Stavanger, with half a dozen He111s bombing the Imperial Chemical Industries' factory at Ardeer, Ayrshire. One of the raiders was caught on its way back and shot down by three Spitfires of 603 Squadron.

The next day saw an increase in activity in spite of continuing poor weather. In northern France, more Luftwaffe units had finished their preparations and were becoming operational. It was dawning on the Germans that their raids were being "seen" by radar, and they started to take countermeasures. One method was to try to fool the watchers into reacting to spoof attacks. (The tactic was to be adopted by the British themselves in their bombing campaign against Germany.) Thursday 18 July saw the first "dummy raid". As a convoy passed through the Dover Straits shortly before nine in the morning, an enemy formation appeared on the radar moving towards it. No. 11 Group chief Sir Keith Park ordered up a dozen Spitfires from 610 Squadron at Biggin Hill, and they were duly vectored towards the raid. But it was a trap. Suddenly they were set on by a *Staffel* of Me109s, which shot down one of their number and then escaped unscathed into the low cloud. There were no bombers in attendance.

Sir Keith Park

A New Zealander by birth, Sir Keith Park (1892–1975) had been a distinguished aviator in the First World War, having transferred to the Royal Flying Corps after being wounded at Gallipoli in 1915 while serving with the New Zealand army. He was credited with downing 20 enemy aircraft and won an MC and Bar, DFC and Croix de Guerre for his exploits.

In spring 1940, promoted to air vice-marshal, he was given command of 11 Group. He was thus in charge of the most strategically sensitive area of Fighter Command's regional division, with responsibility for the section of the coastline most exposed to enemy attack as well as for the defence of London. In June 1940, he came in for severe criticism over the perceived failure of his pilots to do more to protect the British Expeditionary Force on the Dunkirk beaches. But Park maintained that his duty was to preserve what was a largely untried force for the great battle ahead, and that 11 Group had done all it could within that crucial constraint.

Park had direct and exhausting responsibility for the Battle of Britain in vital areas at crucial times. It was said that while Dowding controlled events from day to day, Park controlled them from hour to hour. He made a point of visiting his men, flying around the bases in his own Hurricane, taking a seat unannounced in the mess, listening rather than talking. Many pilots seem to have seen his long, lined face at some time during the summer of 1940.

Park's removal from command after the battle was a source of bitterness to him for the rest of his life. However, his contribution to the victory was appreciated fully by those who understood it. Lord Tedder, then chief of the RAF, wrote in 1947: "If any one man won the Battle of Britain he did. I do not believe it is realized how much that one man, with his leadership, his calm judgement and his skill, did to save not only this country, but the world."

In 2009 Park's importance was recognized when a temporary statue of him was unveiled on the fourth plinth in Trafalgar Square, prior to a permanent memorial to him being established in a Central London site.

This was just the sort of combat that Dowding and Park were desperate to avoid. They had urged the pilots repeatedly to concentrate on bombers and avoid the temptation to tangle with the raiding Me109s. The instruction was usually heeded and fighter sweeps by Me109s would often go unchallenged as they roared over southern England and the Channel.

In the afternoon the bombers were back, though, with several raids on convoys along the south coast, and the squadrons at Tangmere and Middle Wallop were in constant action. It was another hard day for 609 Squadron, which had a further two Spitfires shot down while taking on a formation of Ju88s. Both pilots survived. At one point in the afternoon, a large dogfight developed over Beachy Head, when 28 Messerschmitt Me109s were engaged by 16 Spitfires from Nos 152 and 610 Squadrons. One aircraft from the latter was shot down, but no enemy fighters were hit. It had been an ominous day. For the first time since the start of the battle on 10 July, the RAF lost more aircraft than the Germans.

With the increase in aircraft production, the loss of machines was less drastic than it would have been a month before. But if the trend continued, the potential impact on morale, civilian as well as military, would be considerable. The newspapers and the BBC were presenting the daily "scores", and it was important that the home side was seen to be on a winning streak. However, nerves were taut and the south of England was electrified by the prospect of imminent invasion.

On Friday 19 July the weather cleared, and Fighter Command was expecting trouble because there were nine British convoys at sea. Squadrons flew to forward airfields to cut the time it would take to get into action. At around 8a.m., four Dorniers appeared over Glasgow, arriving from the west to confuse the radar operators. They made a pinpoint attack on the Rolls Royce works, causing heavy damage and casualties, before escaping unscathed. In the south, interceptions were made on Stuka attacks on Dover and Portland, but the British pilots, having driven away the bombers, soon found themselves embroiled in dogfights with the Me109 escorts.

Among the units moved forward that morning was No. 141 Squadron. It had been formed only a month previously and was equipped with Boulton Paul Defiants. The Defiant was similar to the Hurricane, except that it had a large gun turret with four Browning machine-guns mounted to the rear of the cockpit and operated by a second crew-member. No. 141's sister squadron, No. 264, had enjoyed great success over Dunkirk, where its backward-firing guns had taken German attackers by surprise. However, 141 Squadron had flown only a few patrols and had yet to be tested in combat. Early in the afternoon, 12 Defiants of No. 141 were ordered to patrol at 5,000 feet over Folkestone, Kent. Three of the pilots experienced engine trouble, but the remaining nine, led by Squadron Leader William Richardson, and including New Zealand Pilot Officer John Gard'ner, took off from Hawkinge and headed south.

Northeast of Dover an armed trawler was under attack from Me110s, escorted by 20 Me109s of *Jagdgeschwader 51*, led by Hauptmann (Captain)

Hannes Trautloft. Having shepherded the Me110s back to France, Trautloft decided to return to the English coast on a free hunt. He soon spotted the Defiants far below flying in a tight formation, seemingly unaware of his presence. This time, the British planes were correctly identified for what they were. Checking that there were no Spitfires or Hurricanes about, Trautloft led his Me109s in a dive out of the sun. "I aimed at the right Defiant . . . my guns fired . . . pieces of the Defiant . . . broke off and came hurtling towards me . . . I saw a thin trail of smoke . . . then suddenly just a fiery ball."[5]

In this first attack, John Gard'ner's Defiant was also hit. "The first that I knew," he said, "was suddenly I had white tracer bullets going through the cockpit and then I had a flash of airplanes right and left under fire. I thought, I'm going to get out of this. I dived down. The prop was dead in front of me. I was lucky I didn't catch fire. There was a dreadful smell of cordite and bluey smoke in the cockpit." Meanwhile, the Me109s attacked again. Clearly, they had worked out the Defiant's debilitating weakness: an attack from the front and below met no resistance, as the Defiants had no forward-facing guns. In effect, as one pilot later complained, you had to fly past the enemy to fire at him. But as the Defiant was also slow — with a top speed of only 298mph — there was little chance of this happening when matched against Me109s. The Germans now attacked from head-on and below, and two more Defiants went down.

151

Meanwhile, Gard'ner wrestled with the controls of his stricken aircraft: "There was no engine and the rudder pedal was just loose under my foot. I don't know how I managed to keep it level. I saw this boat and I thought, I'm going to have to crash by that boat, but I was going so fast it was impossible. For some reason or other I stupidly undid my safety straps and I thought, I'm going to get into the water so I wanted to get out quickly, forgetting that I would hit at 100 m.p.h." Gard'ner hurriedly pulled the hook back on the hood. "At the moment of impact," he says, "I was thrown forward and hit my head. I blacked out and came to deep down in blackness. But the hood was open and I could get out. There was a big flap of skin that was hanging loose from my forehead and I had been hit on the back of the head as well."[6]

Up above, the five surviving Defiants swerved into cloud to try to escape the Me109s. One, flown by Flight Lieutenant Ian Donald, was hit and set on fire. Unlike any of the other men on the downed Defiants, the gunner, Pilot Officer Arthur Hamilton, did manage to bale out but drowned. The pilot was killed and the aircraft hit the ground in Elmsvale Road, Dover. The carnage would have almost certainly been worse, had it not been for the arrival of Hurricanes from 111 Squadron, sent to the rescue from Hawkinge.

The remaining Defiants limped back to their airfield. One of them crashed on landing; another was so badly damaged as to be irreparable. The squadron was effectively a write-off. In just a quarter of an hour, six machines had been destroyed and ten men killed. John

Gard'ner, quickly picked up by a coastguard launch, was the only survivor of any of the downed crews.

It was the worst part of another bad day for the RAF. Over 700 sorties were flown, but only 4 of the enemy had been shot down, and these had, for the most part, been stragglers or single aircraft on reconnaissance or mine-laying duties. For its part, Fighter Command lost a further five pilots killed, five wounded, and eleven fighter aircraft destroyed in combat. When dogfights had developed, the British had been all but overwhelmed.

Hugo Sperrle

Born in February 1885, the son of a brewer, Hugo Sperrle joined the German army in 1903 and, like Goering, had served in the Luftwaffe's forerunner, the *Flieger-truppen des deutschen Kaiserreiches* (Imperial German Flying Service), during the First World War. At the end of the war, like many disaffected soldiers, he joined the right-wing paramilitary *Freikorps*, before returning to the army. In 1925, he was taken onto the staff of General Hans von Seeckt, the defence minister and effective army chief of staff, and was involved in the secret planning for a future independent Luftwaffe. During the 1920s Sperrle was one of the airmen sent for secret military training at Lipetsk, near Moscow. By the time of the Spanish Civil War he was a *generalmajor* (major-general) and was given command of the Condor Legion operating in Spain, before handing over to his chief of staff, Wolfram Freiherr von Richthofen.

At the beginning of February 1939, Sperrle took over *Luftflotte 3*, with headquarters in Munich. The air fleet did not fight in Poland, but when unleashed in support of von Rundstedt's Army Group "A" during the *Blitzkrieg* in western Europe, his tactical forces — in particular the Ju87 "Stuka" dive-bombers — made a significant contribution to the rapid German victory. He received the rank of *Generalfeldmarschall* (field marshal) in July 1940. During the Battle of Britain, his air fleet was to be deployed in northwestern France.

With his thick neck, huge frame and habitual monocle, Sperrle struck Hitler as one of his "most brutal looking generals". In reality, he was a highly experienced and intelligent officer, noted for his "unusual vitality". Unlike Goering and Kesselring, Sperrle did not underestimate Fighter Command's strength — in fact, he even overestimated the resources left to Dowding by the end of August. He argued unsuccessfully that daylight attacks should continue against Fighter Command rather than switch to London.

After capture by the Allies, Sperrle was tried by a US military tribunal for war crimes, along with other senior German officers, in 1947–8, but he was acquitted. He died in 1953.

Later that day, Reichsmarschall Goering held a meeting with senior Luftwaffe commanders in which he told his lieutenants Sperrle and Kesselring that: "Fighting alone all these weeks on the Channel Front, *Jagdgeschwader 51* has already shot down 150 of the enemy's aircraft: quite enough to have weakened him seriously. Think now of all the bombers we can parade in the English sky. The few RAF fighters will not be able to cope."[7]

Such assessments sustained Hitler's hopes that a British capitulation would avert the need for an invasion. On the evening of 19 July, Hitler made a speech that came to be known as "The Last Appeal to Reason". It was an appeal for a settlement with the British Empire, but it made no mention of negotiations and was, in effect, a surrender demand. Hitler delivered it in front of the Nazi elite and *Reichstag* deputies crammed into the Kroll Opera House, Berlin, for a ceremony to mark the elevation of 11 generals to the rank of *Generalfeldmarschall* (field marshal) in recognition of their contribution to the victories in western Europe. Goering was awarded the yet more exalted title of *Reichsmarschall* (Marshal of the Reich). He had ordered a special uniform, light blue and encrusted with gold braid, for the occasion.

Hitler told his audience that "if this struggle continues, it can only end in the annihilation of one of us. Mr Churchill thinks it will be Germany. I know it will be Britain. I am not the vanquished, begging for mercy. I speak as a victor." He warned his opponent: "Mr Churchill ought perhaps, for once, to believe me

155

when I prophesy that a great empire will be destroyed — an empire which it was never my intention to destroy or even harm."

In the audience was the American correspondent William L. Shirer, who was reporting on events for CBS Radio. "Under one roof I have never seen so many gold-braided generals before," he observed in his diary. "Massed together, their chests heaving with crosses and other decorations, they filled a third of the first balcony." Hitler used his best oratorical techniques. His hands moved eloquently to emphasize his words; his body swayed in almost hypnotic fashion, and the crowd responded with cheers and outstretched saluting arms. But the German generals, politicians and diplomats fell silent as Hitler came to the core of his speech. "In this hour I feel it my duty before my own conscience to appeal once more to reason and common sense [to Great Britain]. I can see no reason why this war must go on." Shirer caught the reaction: "There was no applause, no cheering and no stamping of heavy boots. There was silence. And it was tense. For in their hearts, the Germans longed for peace now." Hitler waited a moment to allow tension to build up and then added with a subdued, almost sad voice: "I am grieved to think of the sacrifices which it will claim. I should like to avert them, also for my own people."[8]

The next day, Saturday 20 July, the aerial defence continued. All morning there were isolated enemy incursions, from Scotland to Dorset, but most action was centred again on the Channel, on a convoy codenamed Bosom.

In the Lyme Bay area, the patrolling duties fell to No. 238 Squadron, which lost a pilot and aircraft driving away a small number of Me109s. In mid-afternoon, 501 Squadron from Middle Wallop was scrambled to intercept an incoming force of Stukas escorted by Me109s. The enemy planes were encountered half way between Jersey and Portland Bill. The combat saw the first kill of the battle by Sergeant J. H. "Ginger" Lacey; he would go on to become one of the most successful RAF pilots of the Battle of Britain. He turned sharply on the inside of an Me109 that was heading for him and got three bursts off as he glued his Hurricane to the German's tail. "I can clearly remember watching him slanting down the sky at a hell of a steep angle," said Lacey. "A beautiful little blue and grey mottled aircraft with white and black crosses standing out startlingly clear, getting smaller and smaller; and thinking what a terribly small splash he made when he went straight into the Channel."

Lacey then tailed another fighter heading north, knowing that he would have to turn for home at some point, "and then I've got him". The turn, when it came, was sharp enough to nearly cause a collision with the Hurricane, but Lacey opened fire and "I suddenly saw the aeroplane almost stagger as I hit it. Its propeller started to slow down. We flashed past each other a few feet apart."[9] Another Hurricane would finish off the second Me109 moments later.

157

Other squadrons took over as the convoy moved eastwards, watched by the shadowing German aircraft. As an attack seemed inevitable, Air Vice-Marshal Park was determined that this time his fighters would not be overwhelmed, and he increased the strength of patrols to as many as 24 aircraft. Convoy Bosom was opposite Dover when, at around 6p.m., the attacking force came into sight — Stukas protected by some 50 Me109s and Me110s. But in flying towards the convoy, the Germans were facing the sun, and they were "bounced" by the Hurricanes of No. 32 Squadron, which flew straight through the Me109s and plunged onto the Stukas below, shooting down two and severely damaging four. Hurricanes of 615 Squadron and Spitfires of 610 Squadron then engaged the German fighters.

"Ginger" Lacey

Sergeant James Harry "Ginger" Lacey (1917–89) was an exceptionally talented pilot and a supremely accurate marksman, who shot down at least 15 aircraft in the Battle of Britain. An exact total can never be known, because the confusion endemic to aerial combat means that even now, after close examination of records and excavation of crash sites, the scores of leading aces will never be accurately known.

Called "Ginger" in reference to his hair colour, Lacey was born in Wetherby, Yorkshire, the son of a farmer. He attributed his later marksmanship to having shot rabbits when young.

The grammar-school-educated boy did not, however, take up the farming life, and was instead working as a trainee pharmacist when, in 1937, he applied to join the RAF Volunteer Reserve. He was called up at the outbreak of war, joined No. 501 Squadron and went with it to France on 10 May 1940. By the time the squadron withdrew on 19 June, Lacey had accounted for one Me109, an Me110 and two Heinkel He111s.

Lacey narrowly escaped death on numerous occasions during the Battle of Britain, and was shot down or forced to land because of combat damage no less than nine times. On 23 August, he was awarded the Distinguished Flying Medal (DFM), and the following month came his celebrated shooting down of a Heinkel He111 that had earlier bombed Buckingham Palace.

A commission came in 1941, and from 1943 he was in action against the Japanese in Burma. After 1945, he remained in RAF service until his 1967 retirement as a squadron leader — with the reputation as one of the most skilful and determined pilots of the battle.

The twin-engine Me110s retreated by forming a defensive orbiting circle, while the single-engine fighters clashed in a mass dogfight. The result was a clear victory for the pilots of Fighter Command. As well as the damage inflicted on the Stuka force, Fighter Command had shot down five Me109s while losing only two of its own fighters. After the previous few days, it was a very welcome boost.

The pilots were learning fast. The tempo of the fighting was beginning to turn even untried pilots into veterans within the space of a few days. They talked incessantly about their experiences, drawing from each other and sharing tips. There was no substitute for grim experience when it came to understanding how to survive — and, if you were lucky, to kill.

Pilots often said that they were fighting against machines rather than men. But it could still be a disturbingly intimate and vivid business, and the act of killing produced complex reactions. John Bisdee, of 609 Squadron, remembered the first time he hit an Me110: "It had a solitary tail gunner behind the pilot in the fuselage and he was shooting at me. I let off a burst and I saw him actually collapse. I lost quite a lot of sleep that night. To see a chap die in front of you was rather unnerving. In fact it was pretty ghastly."[10] But each man reacted differently. On 9 July, the same squadron's David Crook had shot down a Stuka, killing both crew-members. "I had often wondered what would be my feelings when killing somebody like this, and especially seeing them go down in flames," he wrote in his 1942 book *Spitfire Pilot*. "I was rather surprised to reflect afterwards that my only feeling had been one of considerable elation — and a sort of bewildered surprise because it had all been so easy . . . I also rang up home and told the family with considerable pride that I had at last been in action and managed to bag a Hun." He later described the episode as "the most

160

exciting and wildly exhilarating moment of my life". Other airmen felt a certain emotional confusion. Peter Townsend, who was commanding 85 Squadron, was initially elated by the "rapture of combat" when downing a Heinkel on 3 February 1940; but then he felt remorse when visiting the two surviving crew-members in hospital. He then returned to a champagne celebration in the mess. It was, he later wrote, "a horribly uncivilized way of behaving, really, when you have just killed someone. But an enemy bomber down was proof of our prowess, and that was legitimate cause for celebration."[11]

On the following day, 21 July, a patrol from 238 Squadron started by shooting down a Dornier that was shadowing a convoy. Two more aircraft joined the patrol, and between them they shot down an Me110, which was also engaged in watching the convoy as it headed westwards off the Dorset coast. When the flotilla was about ten miles south of the Needles, the chalky outcrops west of the Isle of Wight, it ran into an attacking force of a *Gruppe* of Dorniers together with about 50 Me109s and Me110s. Hurricanes from No. 43 Squadron made an interception, successfully breaking up the bomber formation and shooting down one of the escorts. Yet more Hurricanes arrived from 238 Squadron, just as the Me110s, which had formed their usual defensive circle, started dive-bombing the convoy — the first time this tactic had been seen. One of the Me110s was severely damaged by a 238 pilot before the attackers made for home.

Home for 238 Squadron was currently the uncomfortable Warmwell. In theory, forward bases such as this reduced the pilots' time to interception; but that also meant that the aircraft did not have time to climb as high as their operators would have liked. "One of the great advantages of Middle Wallop," said John Bisdee of 609 Squadron, "was that it was about sixty miles from Portland and those sort of places, which gave you enough time when you scrambled to climb up and attack from the top." Otherwise, you "had to climb up underneath the Germans". Eric Seabourne of 238 Squadron quickly learned that "When the ground controller said, 'Angels twelve', meaning at 12,000 feet, the squadron would go to 14,000. You always wanted maximum height. Once you'd got height you were in the driving seat."[12]

It was from Warmwell that Bisdee was scrambled in mid-July to protect the Portland naval base: "the first time I'd ever seen a really large German formation. The controller on the R/T said, 'One hundred-plus bandits' and then told us the direction. Moments later he said, 'Two hundred-plus bandits' and then finally he said, 'Very many bandits!' . . . I remember the incredible sight of this great swarm of rotating German aircraft, each following their own tail, going round and round emitting condensation trails." Indignation spurred Bisdee and his fellow pilots on. "The feeling I had, and a lot of us had, was, What are these buggers doing here? How dare they? It was really quite a shock to see this vast number of black crosses and swastikas in the sky over our country. Then we all plunged in."[13]

★ ★ ★

Hitler summoned his military commanders on Sunday 21 July to discuss the invasion of Britain. They examined the logistics of occupation in detail. Already, organizations that were considered particularly hostile to Germany had been identified. These included trade unions, the Freemasons, the universities — and even the Boy Scouts, described as "a disguised instrument of power for British cultural propaganda". A list of nearly 3,000 names for immediate arrest had been drawn up for use by the *Einsatzgruppen*, the Gestapo-led units formed to follow in the wake of the army to crush possible dissent. At Sunday's meeting, planning was carried out for detailed civil regulations and a currency conversion rate — at £1 Sterling to 9.6 Deutschmarks, designed to ensure that much of Britain's wealth flowed to Berlin, following the pattern imposed in France and other occupied lands. There was also a scheme to deport all males between the ages of 17 and 45.

But Hitler's enthusiasm for an amphibious attack was waning again. His attention was inclining towards the Soviet Union, and Operation Sea Lion was appearing a wasteful and risky diversion. "The invasion of Britain is an exceptionally dangerous undertaking," he told Grossadmiral Raeder. "Even if the way is short this is not just a river crossing, but the crossing of sea which is dominated by the enemy . . . Operational surprise cannot be expected; a defensively prepared and utterly determined enemy face us and dominate the sea area we must use . . . The prerequisites," he concluded, "are complete mastery of the air, the operational use of powerful artillery in the Straits of Dover and protection by minefields. The time of year is an important factor, too . . . if it is not certain that preparations can be completed by the beginning of September, other plans must be considered."[14]

With a lack of firm and enthusiastic leadership of the operation at the top, the various service chiefs argued among themselves. The German navy pleaded for more attacks on Britain's naval assets in the Channel, including the bombing and mining of the ports of Dover, Plymouth, Portland and Portsmouth. Other ports on the south coast were to be left undamaged for the use of the Wehrmacht invasion forces. The army said that it would not guarantee success unless the navy transported forty divisions; but the navy accepted responsibility for only ten. Generalfeldmarschall Halder, chief of the army general staff, considered this smaller number suicidal. Goering, with his habitual blind optimism, then declared that, given five days of good weather, he could so reduce the British defences that ten divisions would be more than enough. He then summoned Kesselring and Sperrle and ordered them to make plans for the successful conclusion of the *Kanalkampf*. There was, however, general agreement about one thing: the first priority was the destruction of Fighter Command.

On Monday 22 July it was clear to the Nazi leadership that the fighting would have to continue. That morning, Britain gave its defiant response to Hitler's speech of 19 July. On behalf of the British government, Lord Halifax, who had hitherto been an advocate of a negotiated peace, delivered the reply to Hitler's "Last Appeal to Reason", and his words were broadcast to the nation:

Many of you will have read two days ago the speech in which Herr Hitler summoned Great Britain to capitulate to his will. I will not waste your time by dealing with his distortion of almost every main event since the war began. He says he has no desire to destroy the British Empire. But there was in his speech no suggestion that peace must be based on justice, no word of recognition that the other nations of Europe had any right to self determination, the principle that he has so often invoked for Germans. His only appeal was to the base instincts of fear, and his only arguments were threats . . .

Hitler has now made it plain that he is preparing to direct the whole weight of German might against this country. That is why in every part of Britain there is only one spirit, a spirit of indomitable resolution. Nor has anyone any doubt that if Hitler were to succeed it would be the end, for many besides ourselves, of all those things which make life worth living. We realize that the struggle may cost us everything, but just because the things we are defending are worth any sacrifice, it is a noble privilege to be the defenders of things so precious . . .

We never wanted the war. Certainly no one here wants the war to go on for a day longer than is necessary. But we shall not stop fighting till freedom, for ourselves and others, is secure.

165

Up in the skies, there was little activity during the hours of daylight, with only sporadic reconnaissance and occasional ineffective attacks on shipping. But that night, from bases of all three *Luftflotten*, German aircraft flew over 100 mine-laying sorties. The mines sown were about 1100 pounds in weight, and the bombers usually carried two each. It was a difficult task technically, requiring accurate navigation and low-altitude, low-speed flying.

One of these sorties would provide the RAF with a considerable breakthrough. For the first time, a night raider was intercepted using airborne radar. The invention of radar had opened up the possibility that defending aircraft operating at night-time would be able to "see in the dark". But to make a night-time interception, the defending fighter plane had to be able to make visual contact with the raider, and this required it to be only some 325 yards (300 metres) away. The Chain Home High and Low radar were simply not accurate enough to be able to guide the fighter this close. This meant that the night-fighter had to have its own onboard radar system, which presented enormous difficulties. Radar in 1940 was based on low-frequency signals and needed large antennae, making it impractical for mounting on a ship or aircraft.

As early as 1936 it was realized that the Luftwaffe might turn to night-time bombing if a daylight campaign faltered. Watson-Watt had put another of the staff from the Radio Research Station, Edward Bowen, in charge of developing a radar that could be carried by a fighter. Bowen decided that an airborne radar should not exceed 200 pounds (90kg) in weight, and require no more than 500 watts of power. To reduce the drag of the antennae, the operating wavelength could not be much greater than one metre, difficult for the electronics of that time. Nevertheless, such a system, known as "AI" (Airborne Interception), was developed by 1940. In due course, it would prove instrumental in ending the Blitz in 1941. Bowen also fitted airborne radar to maritime patrol aircraft to reduce the threat from submarines.

On 22 July, the first victim of airborne radar was a Dornier, picked up by the Chain Home Low radar station at Poling, Kent. The position of the Dornier was tracked and passed to the operations room at Tangmere, where the Fighter Interception Unit, made up of Blenheims equipped with onboard radar, was based. The controller guided one of the Blenheims towards the inbound aircraft, and soon one of the first AI Mark III sets located the intruder south of Brighton. Then the observer, Pilot Officer Geoffrey Morris, glimpsed the Dornier crossing ahead and above and shouted to the pilot, Flying Officer Glynn Ashfield, to turn. He swung the aircraft around so that the bomber lay dead ahead, silhouetted by the moon. Ashfield fired a ten-second burst, which set the Dornier's fuel tanks on fire, and the German plane went flaming down into the sea.

Even with airborne radar, the problem of intercepting night raids was a formidable one, and the vast majority of sorties in darkness failed to find enemy

167

aircraft. On the same busy night of 22/23 July, however, "Ginger" Lacey had a piece of luck. "After being vectored all over the sky by the controller, I unexpectedly saw a Heinkel 111 caught in the searchlights some two miles ahead and slightly above, so I started to climb after it."[15] But then some of the searchlights switched to his Hurricane. The procedure to identify oneself as a friend was for a bomber to fire the Verey-light colours of the day, and for a fighter to flash the "letters of the day" on its downward light. This Lacey duly did, but then the Heinkel fired a red light followed by a green, which through luck or excellent intelligence was the correct signal of the day. Thereupon, all the searchlights switched to Lacey; ten seconds later the anti-aircraft guns opened up at him. Blinded by the lights, and in danger of being shot down, he lost the Heinkel.

The threat posed by barrage balloons to low-flying German aircraft was brought home to Hauptmann Hans-Joachim ("Hajo") Herrmann that night when, with three other Ju88 dive-bombers, he was attempting to lay mines in Plymouth Sound. He planned to descend to about 300 feet to drop his cargo along the harbour breakwater. As he lost height he saw the great outline of a balloon wallowing ahead, and his aircraft became entangled in the balloon's upper surface. Then, barrage balloon and bomber began sinking earthwards. "It only lasted a few seconds, though it felt like an hour," he remembered. "Then I notice[d] the British searchlights were shining from above — we had fallen off the balloon, and now we were upside down, with virtually no forward speed, and I was going down out of control." It felt "as if I was playing a piano which was falling from a fifth storey".[16] He ordered his crew to bale out. But then the bomber regained flying speed and with every gun in the sound bearing on him he completed his mine-laying mission, before heading thankfully for home.

The lull continued on the following day, 23 July. Two German bombers were shot down while following convoys, but Fighter Command suffered no combat losses. Although Wednesday 24 July started with only isolated reconnaissance sorties, the day would see the return of heavy formation attacks by the Luftwaffe. At about 8a.m., two *Staffeln* of Dorniers attacked a convoy in the Straits of Dover. Six Spitfires of No. 54 Squadron succeeded in disrupting their bombing runs but did not bring any of the enemy aircraft down. The squadron was scrambled again at 11.20a.m., after radar picked up a large force approaching a convoy leaving the mouth of the River Medway, Kent. When the fighters made visual contact over Margate, they reported 18 Dorniers flying in tight formation, with about 40 Me109s protecting them above. No. 65 Squadron was also scrambled to help, while nine Spitfires from No. 610 Squadron at Biggin Hill were vectored to patrol the Dover Straits area to cut off the German retreat.

Adolf Galland, newly promoted to major, was leading the Me109s, which now joined battle with the six Spitfires of 54 Squadron. Two of the German

169

aircraft were hit first, in both cases killing the pilots. Then, one of the victors, Sergeant George Collett, was himself hit and compelled to land. Almost immediately afterwards, Pilot Officer Johnny Allen, an accredited "ace" with eight victories to his credit, was also hit. According to his number two, Al Deere, who stuck with him as he went down, he "glided towards the coast. Just as he crossed his engine appeared to pick up again and turned towards Manston hoping, no doubt, to get it down safely there. The next moment fire broke out in the engine and at once the aircraft flicked on to its back and dived into the ground on the outskirts of Foreness." Allen did not survive.

In the meantime, the arriving No. 65 Squadron had gone after the Dorniers, but through accurate crossfire the British fighters were kept out of effective range by the tight formation. They did, however, manage to down a further Me109, before the Germans, low on fuel, dived for home. As they did so, a fresh *Jagdgeschwader* roared in to protect their withdrawal. But they were surprised by the lurking 610 Squadron, which shot down two aircraft straightaway and drove the rest back. One of the squadron's number was killed crash-landing back at Biggin Hill.

It had been a comparatively quiet day in the Channel, but nonetheless 17,000 tons of shipping from three convoys had been sunk, and other vessels were badly damaged. By now, the Germans had established radar installations on the cliffs at Wissant, on the Channel coast opposite Folkestone, from which to observe the movements of convoys.

Adolf Galland

Adolf Galland (1912–96) was, with Werner Mölders, one of the two most famous German pilots of 1940. As with many German airmen, Galland first took to the air in a glider, at one of the schools set up in the interwar years to get around the Versailles restrictions on the development of a German air force. As a boy he had read stories of the First World War aces Oswald Boelcke and "Red" Baron von Richthofen. In 1932, aged 20, he was accepted for pilot training at a commercial school. His talents were noticed and he was selected for secret military training, before joining the civil airline Lufthansa as a pilot, flying airliners to Barcelona.

In 1933, with Hitler in power, he switched to the air force, and in April 1937 went to Spain to fly biplane fighters in the Luftwaffe-directed Condor Legion in support of General Franco's nationalist rebels. By the middle of 1940, Galland was in what he felt was his element, emulating his childhood heroes in combat against the British.

Galland was a complex and deceptive personality. He seemed, at first glance, to fit one established image of the dashing aviator, with his love of wine, women and good times. He appeared good-humoured, unimpressed by authority

171

and relaxed about discipline. But Galland was also, like Richthofen before him, a calculating warrior who took a scientific approach to killing. Although indeed "one of the boys", Galland was also intimate with the top brass. Initially at least, he admired Goering, another First World War ace, and admitted to his biographer that, after leaving his first private meeting with Hitler, "he felt a mutual respect had been forged."

In 1941, Galland succeeded Mölders as *General der Jagdflieger*, responsible for tactical fighter planning, until he was relieved of the role in early 1945 and sent back to the frontline, having fallen out with Goering and other leading Nazis. A prisoner of war from 1945 to 1947, he spent his subsequent career in aviation, working in Argentina and Germany.

Galland's powerful, gregarious personality enabled him to play the part of the "Good German" in the forgiving atmosphere that prevailed among the rival airmen after the war. He and Douglas Bader were photographed together, and he met the British ace Bob Stanford-Tuck on a number of occasions.

Some of those whom Galland fought were never persuaded, however. In the blunt opinion of Christopher Foxley-Norris, "Galland was a shit."[17]

In fact, it had been a German, Heinrich Hertz, who in 1887 began experimenting with radio waves. He found that they could be transmitted through different types of materials, but were reflected by others. In 1904, another German, Christian Hülsmeyer, gave public demonstrations in Germany and the Netherlands of his patented *Telemobiloskop*, which used radio echoes to detect ships so that collisions could be avoided. This was the moment when, in essence, radar had been invented. But while French and American physicists then set to work developing the new technology, in Germany the invention was all but ignored for the next 30 years.

Eventually, in 1934, two German scientists, Hans Hollmann and Hans-Karl von Willisen, built the first commercial radar system for detecting ships. It could detect vessels up to 10 kilometres away, although it was unable to show range. It was the German navy, rather than the Luftwaffe, that took an interest. In the summer of 1935 a pulse radar was developed, which, in tests, was shown to be able to spot a large vessel 8 kilometres away, accurately enough for guns to be laid. The same system could also detect an aircraft at 500-metre altitude at a distance of 28 kilometres, and somewhat belatedly the Luftwaffe became interested in the technology, ordering a dozen sets of what became known as *Freya*. (The seaborne version was known as *Seetakt*.)

The German radar had little in common with the huge masts that rose along the English coast. *Freya* operated in the 1.2-metre wavelength (a tenth of that of the Chain Home system), and it was much smaller, with a better resolution. Yet by the start of the war only eight of these units were in operation, on Germany's border.

The Telefunken company developed a superior system, named *Würzburg*, for home defence; but radar was of limited use to the Germans while the Luftwaffe was engaged in its offensive role in the Battle of Britain, except for finding targets in the waters of the Channel. But this they could now do easily, and the grip on the Channel — as demanded by the *Kriegsmarine* — seemed ever tighter.

Early on Thursday 25 July, these new radar installations picked up a convoy of 21 merchant ships, codenamed CW8, with escorts off Southend, heading westwards. At first the Germans sent over only fighter sweeps. Shortly after midday, one of these was met by Spitfires from No. 65 Squadron, and an Me109 crashed into the sea during a low-level pursuit. Both sides threw more fighters into the combat. By 12.45p.m., 20 Hurricanes from Nos 32 and 615 Squadrons were engaged in a furious dogfight with 40 Me109s, which only came to an end when fuel ran low for both sides. At this moment, with the skies above the convoy empty, a mass attack of more than 60 Stukas swept in. Five vessels were sunk and a further five damaged. Nine Spitfires from No. 54 Squadron rushed to help, but they arrived just as German fighters appeared in huge numbers. Two of the British aircraft were shot down, with one pilot killed.

Thirty Ju88 bombers, together with more than fifty Me109s, launched a further attack on the beleaguered convoy at 2.30 in the afternoon. On guard over the vessels was a paltry force of just eight Spitfires from No. 64 Squadron. As the rest of the squadron was scrambled, along with 12 Hurricanes from 111 Squadron, the small force went in on the attack, outnumbered five to one. With the arrival of RAF reinforcements, the Junkers and their escort broke for home. But the convoy did not stay unmolested for long. As it passed Folkestone, it was strafed by Me109s, then pounded again by Ju88s, which managed to time their attack between fighter patrols. Two escorting destroyers, sent out from Dover, were badly damaged. No. 56 Squadron arrived as the bombing was under way, and soon Spitfires from Nos 64 and 54 Squadrons were also involved, taking on a huge swarm of Me109s. Both squadrons lost three aircraft each. The Germans also deployed their fast surface E-boats against the vessels, and by the time the convoy reached its destination at Portland — itself under attack this day from *Luftflotte 3* — only two of the original twenty-one coal transporters and coasters were undamaged.

No. 54 Squadron had lost five pilots killed and three wounded in the previous three weeks, including, said Al Deere, "two of our most experienced leaders". The squadron had, in the same time, flown 504 combat sorties and was exhausted. "The strain of long hours at readiness and repeated combats against overwhelming numbers was having a depressing effect on the more inexperienced squadron pilots," said Deere. Of the original seventeen pilots serving when the Dunkirk fighting opened, only five remained. These five, though rich in experience, "had reached the point of physical and mental tiredness beyond which lies the realm of fear", which, Deere said, could spread like a disease down through the squadron and even affect the groundcrews.[18] Now, the squadron was withdrawn from the frontline. As it moved north to Catterick, No. 41 took its place at Hornchurch.

Fear was only natural, and as the Battle of Britain ground on it did not diminish. A very small number of soldiers and airmen felt little of it and indeed enjoyed the war. But the vast majority faced a constant struggle between the impulse for self-preservation and the compulsion to follow orders and not to let comrades down. "When it comes to the point, a sincere desire to stay alive is all too likely to get the upper hand," wrote 616 Squadron's Hugh Dundas, who experienced a sickening panic during his first combat mission. "Certainly, that was the impulse which consumed me at that moment that day. And that was the emotion which I had to fight against, to try and try and try again to overcome, during the years that followed."[19]

Combat flying left pilots drenched in sweat. The grinding tension of constant readiness shredded nerves, and mental and physical exhaustion lowered their defences against fear. Al Deere explained that: "The dangerous state is reached in battle when one is so tired mentally and physically that the ever present urge of self-preservation overrules the more normal urge to do one's duty."[20] Most pilots leaned heavily on the support of their peers. In Fighter Command culture, anxiety was masked by banter and ironic humour and an admirable, but artificial, insouciance. What Pilot Officer James Goodson, an American flying with 43 Squadron, remembered was "the jokes, the fun in the mess, the camaraderie. If people were frightened, tired, neurotic, disillusioned and despondent there was an unwritten law in Fighter Command that you did anything rather than show it. Probably those cracking the jokes the most, who were making silly schoolboy pranks in the mess, they were probably the most frightened but they never, never showed it."[21]

Not everyone could prevail in the constant struggle with fear. Later on in the battle, Peter Brothers was posted to 257 Squadron and found a unit with its morale in tatters. On one occasion its pilots had been ordered to patrol Maidstone at 20,000 feet, when they saw a horde of German aircraft. The squadron piled in but the commanding officer remained behind, insisting that the orders were to patrol and he was sticking to them. "On the third occasion of this happening," said Brothers, "we decided that he just didn't like combat. He was avoiding it, I think."[22]

Sergeant Stanley Wright, an NCO at Manston, told the story of a Blenheim air gunner: "He went off one morning in one of twelve aircraft. He went off later that morning in one of the six that remained. In the afternoon, he was told to go up in one of the three that was left — and he said 'NO!' "[23]

It was impossible to maintain a constant *sang froid*. Tempers frayed and snapped. Brothers remembers a young pilot at Biggin Hill who lost his cool when his boiled egg was not properly cooked. He threw it at the

WAAF waitress. Some became emotionally numb, morose, withdrawn, and avoided companionship. Others became unusually animated, smoking incessantly, forcing themselves to laugh loudly, feigning high spirits. "You could sometimes see a deterioration in one of your pals," said Sergeant Maurice Leng of No. 73 Squadron. "They're not quite the same person that you knew. Morose, quiet, nontalkative — they're losing the motivation to carry on. Although they probably wouldn't know that themselves. And you'd think, 'Poor old George. I don't think he's going to last long.' And very often, he didn't."[24]

Many pilots had regular nightmares, and some developed physical symptoms, such as excessive sweating, shakes and facial twitches. Edith Kup, a WAAF plotter, remembered seeing a young pilot "out of the corner of my eye, and he sort of sagged down the wall. I said, 'Would you like to lie down? We have some beds in the Ops Room.' He said, 'Yes,' so I asked someone to keep an eye on him. The boy had cracked but nobody said anything. Later, I went back into the Ops Room, and he was asleep. We tried to wake him and we couldn't, so we rang the medical officer and asked him to come. And when they picked him up, he was stiff, from head to toe, you know, he didn't sag in the middle. And the medical officer said to me, 'You're looking at some one who's literally scared stiff.' Nobody saw him again — he was whisked off."[25]

The decision as to whether a crack-up was due to breakdown or cowardice was always complicated, as Al Deere explained:

In the case of fighter pilots, in particular, it presented squadron and flight commanders with a really difficult problem and one with which they were being continually faced. Up till the moment the air battle is joined, each pilot is a member of a team and should he be inclined to cowardice the presence of other aircraft serves as an antidote to his feelings, the more so when he knows that for the initial attack he is under the censorious eyes of the other pilots in the formation. It is immediately subsequent to this first attack that the opportunity occurs for the less courageous to make their get-away without seeming to avoid the issue.

Deere himself admitted that once, alone in the sky, "temporarily isolated from the main battle", he had to grimly "talk himself into going back". Deere was one of the most confident and aggressive pilots in Fighter Command; if he struggled, then certainly many others would have taken the opportunity to avoid further combat. As Deere explained, "under just such circumstances it is most difficult to prove that a particular pilot has not pulled his weight. After the initial attack it is almost impossible to observe the actions of any one pilot, and unless a watch has been set on a suspect — it has been done — there can be no positive proof of cowardice."[26]

The experienced "aces" themselves were not immune to nerves. "Ginger" Lacey, of 501 Squadron, recorded how:

179

Towards the end of the Battle I had just taken about as much as I could bear. My nerves were in ribbons and I was scared stiff that one day I would pull out and avoid combat. That frightened me more than the Germans and I pleaded with my C.O. for a rest. He was sympathetic but quite adamant that until he got replacements I would have to carry on. I am glad now that he was unable to let me go. If I had been allowed to leave the squadron, feeling as I did, I am sure that I would never have flown again."[27]

The RAF approached the issue with wartime ruthlessness. "We had one case who just refused to fly and he was stripped down to the lowest rank," said Sergeant Charlton Haw of 504 Squadron. "His wings were taken away from him and he was put on to cleaning latrines. He was taken out of the sergeants' mess so we didn't have any more contact with him and then he was posted away and I never heard of him again."[28] Such men were branded by the RAF as suffering from "LMF" (Lacking Moral Fibre). Officers deemed guilty of the condition were stripped of their rank, dismissed from the service and lost their flying wings. Because LMF was thought to be "dangerously contagious", such men would then be posted to menial jobs on other bases, where it was made sure that everybody knew what had happened.

In spite of atrocious flying weather on 26 July — low dark cloud and heavy rain all over Britain — the Luftwaffe still came, albeit in small numbers. In the early morning, Hurricanes from 601 Squadron at Tangmere were called to the assistance of a convoy south of the Isle of Wight under attack from *Fliegerkorps VIII* dive-bombers. The convoy was undamaged, but the squadron lost an aircraft and pilot to accompanying Me109s. Just before midday another convoy was raided, this time in Middle Wallop's part of the Channel. No. 238 Squadron intercepted and succeeded in shooting down one of the fighter escort, and for once all their aircraft and pilots returned unharmed. The Luftwaffe lost a further two reconnaissance bombers that afternoon, but isolated German raids dropped bombs on Hastings, Weymouth, Bristol and Aberdeen.

Heavy thunderstorms threatened the following morning, but as the clouds cleared, the two sides again joined battle for control of the Channel. At dawn the Germans spotted a large eastbound convoy, codenamed Bacon, off Portland, and at 8a.m. 30 Stukas took off from their base near Caen on the Normandy coast. Collecting a fighter escort of a *Jagdgeschwader* of Me109s, they met the convoy over Weymouth Bay. Three Hurricanes of 238 Squadron scrambled from Middle Wallop and intercepted the Stukas just as they were preparing to dive on the ships below. Flying Officer Charles Davis shot down one dive-bomber, but the rest were too well protected by their escort and they escaped unscathed.

In the meantime, a second wave of 20 more Stukas had taken off from Caen to attack the convoy near Swanage, Dorset. Although Hurricanes from 238

Squadron and six Spitfires from 609 Squadron were on patrol over the ships, they failed to get through the Me109s to the Stukas, and the Spitfire of James "Buck" Buchanan, John Bisdee's great friend in 609 Squadron, simply vanished. No-one saw him shot down and, once the attackers had departed, two of his fellow pilots searched out to sea for some sign of him, but without success. John Bisdee recalled his car, a small sports model: "It sat forlornly outside the dispersal hut for several days until someone could be found to take it away. The empty motor car definitely had an effect on me. I'd been in it on many occasions. I was quite pleased to see that little car go."[29] In the nine weeks since the start of Dunkirk, 609 Squadron, which prided itself on its dash and insouciance, had lost nine pilots, including seven of the twelve Auxiliary officers who had made up the squadron at the start of the war.

The Royal Navy was also having a bad day. Off the Suffolk coast, where convoys had come under sporadic attacks, He111s sank the destroyer HMS *Wren*. Then Dover was attacked twice, with Messerschmitt Me109s used as fighter-bombers for the first time. This tactic made them slow and vulnerable, and less able to carry sufficient fuel. It was a move understandably unpopular with their pilots. But it did mean, in theory, that Me109s could no longer be ignored by Fighter Command if flying on their own.

The second raid, by Ju88s and 87s as well as Dorniers, heavily escorted, succeeded in landing a bomb alongside the destroyer HMS *Codrington*. The explosion broke the back of the ship, which sank in two pieces, with the stern beached on the seafront by Dover's White Cliff Hotel, where it would lie for the remainder of the war. Two other vessels were severely damaged, and burning oil spread over the harbour. It was clear that Dover's anti-aircraft defences, crippled by pre-war austerity, were inadequate.

RAF reconnaissance had reported during the day that preparations were underway at Cap Gris Nez for a giant artillery position, of a size more than capable of landing shells on Dover. This, together with the success of the day's enemy attack, led to the abandonment by the Royal Navy of Dover as a destroyer base. The remaining warships there withdrew to the North Sea ports of Harwich and Sheerness. From there, destroyers could still be effective against an invasion force in the Dover Straits, but a frontline position had effectively been lost and the Royal Navy denied the freedom of the English Channel. It was a significant victory for the Luftwaffe.

In accordance with the preparations ordered for Operation Sea Lion, attacks on Dover now rose in frequency and strength. At noon on Sunday 28 July, radar stations at Dover, Rye and Pevensey picked up a large formation to the west of Calais, and then, soon after, another to the east of the city. Their progress was tracked to the mid-Channel, when, inexplicably, the bombers turned back. At 1.30p.m. though, the radar screens were again busy, with a formation heading for Dover. Eight squadrons from No. 11 Group had been moved to the forward airfields of Hawkinge, Manston

183

and Martlesham. As the attacking formation neared the English coast, the Observer Corps reported more than 60 Heinkel He111s along with 40-odd Messerschmitt Me109s. Spitfires from 74 and 41 Squadrons and Hurricanes from Nos 111 and 257 were ordered up to intercept, with instructions that the former handle the escort while the latter take on the bombers.

First to arrive was No. 74 Squadron from nearby Manston, led by the South African ace "Sailor" Malan. The squadron made a determined attack on the Me109s of *Jagdgeschwader 51* led by another ace — Major Werner Mölders, who had 25 kills to his name. Three Messerschmitts were shot down and two more damaged, for the loss of two Spitfires, with one pilot killed. No. 41 Squadron then arrived and had the biggest success of the day. Flight Lieutenant John Webster managed to hit Mölders' Me109. The German ace made it back to his base at Wissant, but he was severely wounded and therefore would play no part in the battle for the following month.

Werner Mölders

Serious and introverted, a devout Catholic with little apparent enthusiasm for the Nazis, Werner Mölders (1913–41) was Germany's best fighter pilot of the early years of the war, and arguably one of the greatest fighter pilots of all time. Although only 27 years old in 1940, he was known as *Vati* — "Daddy" — and was mentor to aces such as Adolf Galland and

Helmut Wick. He was commanding a *Staffel* (squadron) before the age of 22, a good teacher and an inspirational figure to other fighter pilots. Perhaps most importantly, he was the main architect of the tactics employed by the German fighter wings during the Battle of Britain.

Mölders' father had been killed in the First World War, but in 1931, aged 18, Mölders joined the German army before requesting transfer to the new Luftwaffe three years later. Initially rejected as an unsuitable fighter pilot, he overcame problems with nausea and vomiting to become a squadron leader and instructor. Like Galland and Wick, Mölders was inspired by the example of First World War aces such as Baron von Richthofen and Oswald Boelcke. Flying an Me109, he shot down 14 aircraft during the Condor Legion's intervention in the Spanish Civil War, where he was instrumental in developing the *Rotte/ Schwarm* type of fighter formation that became the German standard procedure.

During the Battle of France, Mölders claimed 25 kills, and he was rapidly promoted. He was shot down in early June 1940 and taken prisoner, but he was released less than three weeks later after the armistice between Germany and France. At the end of July he was put in charge of *Jagdgeschwader 51*. He was out of action for a month, after having been wounded on 28 July 1940, but by the end of the Battle of Britain he had 30 claimed kills to add to his tally, which continued to rise during 1941 as the RAF pursued its controversial policy of engaging the Luftwaffe over France and the Channel.

Action on the Eastern Front took Mölders' score of successes beyond the one hundred mark. In August 1941 he was made the Luftwaffe's *General der Jagdflieger* (fighter general), giving him responsibility for tactical planning. It all came to an end when he was killed on 22 November 1941, after the He111 carrying him from the Crimea to Berlin crash-landed during a thunderstorm.

After his death, his fighter wing, *Jagdgeschwader 51*, carried his name. Following the war, Mölders continued to be honoured by the Federal German military, with a destroyer, a battalion of signallers and a fighter *Geschwader* named after him. The last was, however, removed by the German parliament, the *Bundestag*, in 1998, a gesture for the 61st anniversary of the bombing of Guernica. Petitions of protest poured in, but the decision remained unchanged. The *Bundestag* decided that the Condor Legion "should not be honoured any more", and doubts were cast on Mölders' anti-Nazi credentials.

Fighter Command braced itself for heavy attacks on Monday 29 July, on account of the perfect flying weather that the day brought in. At 7a.m. the first enemy formations were detected crossing the Channel, heading for Dover. The Air Ministry had been pleading with Air Vice-Marshal Park to provide more protection for the port, and the 11 Group commander now obliged, sending 11 Spitfires of 41 Squadron from Manston to attack the formation's right flank and 12 Hurricanes of 501 Squadron from Hawkinge against its left. The Spitfires arrived first, to find that they were still massively outnumbered, facing 48 Stuka dive-bombers and, high and to the right, about 80 Me109s. No. 41 Squadron split into two, with one flight attacking the bombers, and the other engaging the fighters. But the Me109s had the advantage of height; straightaway Flying Officer D. R. Gamblen was shot down and killed. Four more of the squadron's Spitfires were hit and forced to crash-land, though the pilots survived unhurt. Those attacking the bombers had more success, shooting down two of them. As No. 501 Squadron arrived, followed by reinforcements in the shape of No. 56 Squadron Hurricanes, the sky above Dover became a mass of vapour trails, as a huge dogfight developed involving about 200 aircraft. As bombs fell in Dover harbour, so too did the bombers, with two further Stukas crashing into the sea along with a Hurricane from 56 Squadron.

Soon after, two convoys in the Channel were attacked, the first by Ju88s, which had flown in low enough to avoid radar detection. One bomber was downed by a barrage balloon and another by anti-aircraft fire from the ships, but the fighter cover from 610 Squadron arrived too late to help. An attack on the second convoy by Me110s was intercepted and driven away, but not without substantial damage to two Hurricanes from 151 Squadron.

In the east, three squadrons of fighters, Nos 66, 17 and 85, drove away a heavy raid on Harwich by He111s and Do17s, shooting down three of the Heinkels. Further west, the raiders were more successful. Again using the low-level approach to avoid radar detection, a lightning raid on shipping off Portland saw another precious British destroyer, HMS *Delight*, hit by a bomb and sunk.

Poor weather on the following day led to a much-reduced level of enemy activity, but the RAF still flew nearly 700 sorties, many in response to nuisance raids launched against Northeast Britain by bombers based in Norway. Two German raiders were shot down, and the RAF suffered no casualties.

In fact, the British had initiated a respite in the Channel Battle by sending through no convoys for a few days, which meant no patrolling Fighter Command aircraft were drawn unwillingly into battle over the Channel. German fighter sweeps went unchallenged, much to the frustration of Major Galland, who relished the pure combat that they entailed, redolent of the pioneering days of aerial warfare over the Western Front 25 years before. The Germans did all they could to tempt the British fighters into combat, sending weak bomber forces as decoys while strong fighter formations waited at high altitude, but at Fighter Command headquarters Dowding held back.

The month of July had cost Fighter Command dearly in pilots, and the Luftwaffe had yet to unleash its full force. By now, Dowding had lost 80 flight commanders and squadron leaders. Of the pilots left, only about half had any experience of combat. Those who had been involved in the fighting were approaching physical and mental exhaustion. On 27 July Dowding ordered that each should have a minimum of eight hours off duty in every twenty-four, and a continuous twenty-four hours off every week. To preserve their men, Dowding and Park limited the numbers they sent up, even if it meant they were hopelessly outnumbered at the point of interception.

Thus, German fighter sweeps continued to be ignored or intercepted late. Dowding knew that the Me109 could usually carry enough fuel for only 80 minutes' flying time, which meant, having crossed the Channel, a mere 20 minutes over England — less if involved in a high-speed combat. So, sector controllers would, if initiating action, attempt to intercept just as the Messerschmitts were heading home. Any delay to their journey home could be fatal for the Germans. The Me109 pilot Günther Büsgen remembers how much his colleagues feared the choppy waters of the Channel: "On one occasion the English drove the whole unit off course to the Isle of Wight. Six planes went down in the Channel because they had simply run out of fuel. They just fell into the sea and the pilots drowned. It's something you never forget."[30]

Many German pilots developed a gastric complaint they came to call "Channel Sickness". Some theorized that it was caused by looking at the waves. Others put it down to fear of ditching and an almost inevitable watery death. Ulrich Steinhilper, another Me109 pilot, described that "in the beginning, Channel sickness was just a funny expression, more or less a nickname, nobody ever thought it would occur. But after a while, some pilots really were vomiting before flight or in flight, some of them got ulcers and had real problems with the stomach. I too had a high temperature."[31]

On the morning of the last day of July, a thick haze blanketed the Channel. Nevertheless, German bombers probed the south coast from dawn. No. 111 Squadron, operating in dangerously bad visibility, found a Ju88 bomber over the Channel and sent it back heavily shot up and carrying a dead crew-member. "Sailor" Malan believed that the return of damaged aircraft could have a greater impact on the morale of the Luftwaffe than the non-appearance of a bomber that had been destroyed. Later in the battle, he told a doctor acquaintance how he had changed his tactics to cripple bombers rather than shoot them down outright. "If you shoot them down they don't get back and no-one in Germany is a whit the wiser," he said. "So I figure the right thing to do is to let them get back. With a dead rear gunner, a dead navigator and the pilot coughing his guts up as he lands . . . if you do that it has a better effect on their morale."[32]

The day saw an improvement in the defences over Dover, perched at the tip of Britain's frontline. Twenty-three balloons rose over the cliffs and town, attached to motor winches cemented in the ground. Beleaguered residents of the frontline town cheered their arrival.

Barrage balloons presented a surreal but comforting sight wallowing in the skies above Britain's towns. They loom large in many childhood memories of Britain during the Second World War, and they were simple but very effective, as the Luftwaffe knew well. The British Balloon Command had been established in 1938 under the leadership of Air Marshal Sir E. Leslie Gossage (1891–1949) to protect cities and other key targets. By the middle of 1940 there were 1,400 balloons, a third of them over the London area. The balloons were designed to deter low-level bombing attacks — at 5,000 feet or under — thus forcing raiders to go higher, from where accuracy was more difficult. This also assisted the efforts of anti-aircraft units, which could not traverse fast enough to attack aircraft flying at low altitude and high speed. Most balloons were a little over 29 feet (8.9 metres) long and 25 feet (7.6 metres) in diameter, and were connected to a ground site or a lorry by either a single steel cable or a series of cables. The balloons could float in the sky at up to about 4,925 feet (1,500 metres), the maximum height that the weight of their cables allowed.

The steel cable between a balloon and the ground could, like a cheese-wire, slice straight through the wing of an aircraft, dealing it a knockout blow. Some cables were designed to detach and become entangled in an aircraft's wing, whereupon small parachutes on the

191

cable would open, causing drag and, in theory, the plane to crash.

The deployment of balloons over Dover was followed by the appearance, at about 3.30p.m., of a large enemy formation, and 11 Group reacted vigorously, scrambling 30 Spitfires and 24 Hurricanes. But only No. 74 Squadron's 12 Spitfires, taking off from Manston, were over Dover in time to intercept the two *Staffeln* of Me109s, which had arrived, it appeared, intent on shooting up the new balloon barrage in preparation for a bombing raid.

As before, proximity to the attackers meant that the defenders intercepted quickly but lacked the time to gain height. "B" Flight of 74 Squadron was still climbing when it reached the German fighters, and it would suffer accordingly. Three of the six Spitfires were hit in the two minutes from 3.48p.m. to 3.50p.m. Two of the pilots were killed, but the third managed to steer his stricken aircraft back to Manston. The squadron succeeded in damaging one of the attackers, but the rest escaped before the other British fighters arrived.

As July drew to a close, both air forces could reflect on their material and human losses during the month. The numbers of German air force dead and missing, nearing 500, were much higher than those of the British of course, for each time a bomber went down it took with it several men in contrast to a single-piloted fighter plane. But those bombers were inflicting death and destruction on the ground and on the convoys.

In the eyes of US Ambassador Kennedy, Britain remained doomed. He was still reporting back to Washington that British surrender was "inevitable". But he did not represent a consensus opinion. The US defence attaché Raymond Lee took a more optimistic view. "What a wonderful thing it will be if these blokes do win the war!" he wrote. "They will be bankrupt but entitled to almost unlimited respect."[33]

Much depended on Hitler's next move. And the Battle of Britain was about to enter a new and more intense phase.

CHAPTER
SIX

Intensification

1 August to 17 August 1940

As the month of August 1940 opened, Adolf Hitler issued a new directive, No. 17, for the "final conquest of England". It announced his intention "to intensify air and sea warfare against the English homeland":

> The German Air Force is to overpower the English Air Force with all the forces at its command, in the shortest time possible. The attacks are to be directed primarily against flying units, their ground installations, and their supply organizations, but also against the aircraft industry, including that manufacturing anti-aircraft equipment.
>
> After achieving temporary or local air superiority the air war is to be continued against ports, in particular against stores of food, and also against stores of provisions in the interior of the country. Attacks on the south coast ports will be made on the smallest possible scale, in view of our own forthcoming operations.
>
> On the other hand, air attacks on enemy warships and merchant ships may be reduced except where

some particularly favourable target happens to present itself, where such attacks would lend additional effectiveness to those mentioned in Paragraph 2, or where such attacks are necessary for the training of air crews for further operations.

The intensified air warfare will be carried out in such a way that the Air Force can at any time be called upon to give adequate support to naval operations against suitable targets. It must also be ready to take part in full force in Operation Sea Lion.

I reserve to myself the right to decide on terror attacks as measures of reprisal.

The intensification of the air war may begin on or after 5 August.

The exact time is to be decided by the Air Force after completion of preparations and in the light of the weather.

The Navy is authorized to begin the proposed intensified naval war at the same time.

The next day, Goering laid out orders for an all-out assault. His aim was to overwhelm the RAF in the air and crush it on the ground in a concentrated series of massive raids. The operation was to be called *Adlerangriff* — Attack of the Eagle — and it would start on *Adlertag* (Eagle Day), whose date would be decided by meteorological forecasts of a spell of fair weather.

Goering intended to throw all the resources of *Luftflotten 2, 3* and *5* into the effort, bombing Fighter Command in its bases or luring its aircraft up to be destroyed in aerial combat. The attack would also be directed at the infrastructure that sustained Britain's air defence, including radar installations. With his customary optimism, Goering expected the RAF to survive only a few days under such an assault. All that was needed was a final period of preparation and then three consecutive days of good weather. Initially, *Adlertag* was set for 10 August, eight days after the orders had been given.

The decisiveness of the orders and the confidence with which they were issued suggests a unanimity of view among the Nazi hierarchy as to the wisdom and necessity of the invasion plan. But uncertainties still persisted, not least in the mind of Hitler himself. His attention was increasingly being drawn eastwards. On 31 July, he had scheduled the invasion of Britain for 15 September. But two days previously, he had announced to his military staff that he wanted to attack his real enemy and the focus of his ideological hatred — the Soviet Union — as soon as possible. The question of when to invade was taking on a new urgency. At the beginning of July, Sir Stafford Cripps, the British ambassador in Moscow, had handed Stalin a memorandum from Churchill urging him to break his pact with Hitler and turn against Germany. The communication soon found its way into the hands of the German Embassy in Moscow, and it supported the view that, by striking at Russia, Germany would also be effectively defusing the threat from Britain. Hitler now believed that "Russia is the factor by which England sets the greatest store. If Russia is beaten," he announced, "England's last hope is gone."

On the night of 1 August, bombers ranged all over Britain, carrying hundreds of thousands of leaflets with the translated text of Hitler's "Last Appeal to Reason" of the previous month, urging British surrender. Most of the leaflets fell among the sheep and cattle of East Anglia. The newspapers later carried jocular pictures of citizens cutting up the leaflets and fastening them to their privy doors, for use as lavatory paper. The prospect of a settlement had disappeared long before the paper fluttered to the ground, as Hitler himself recognized.

The propaganda effort, and Hitler's ruminations over Russia, did nothing to slow down the preparations for the *Adlerangriff*, which meant in the immediate term a lull in the fighting in order to muster strength. The first few days of August saw skirmishing but few major combats. The Luftwaffe's energies were spent, instead, in moving units to forward bases nearer the coast. Both sides intensified crew training. The flying conditions were often poor, with rain, cloud and fog, and for the first week of August more men and machines on both sides were lost through accident than enemy action.

The Luftwaffe nonetheless flew a number of minelaying and reconnaissance missions and attacked the few vessels that were now plying the Channel. On 3 August, a thick fog in the south of England gave way to cloud; the Channel remained empty of shipping, and there were only a few scattered bombing raids in the west. Sunday 4 August was cloudy and foggy, and, except for Luftwaffe reconnaissance over the Bristol Channel and the English south coast, was even quieter than the previous day. During the night, however, there were bombing raids in the north and west — on Bradford, Crewe, Liverpool, South Wales and the Firth of Forth.

The relative quiet only encouraged a feeling that a great storm was about to break. On 31 July, Churchill's secretary, Colville, had heard that the head of the Secret Service had "now received news of imminent invasion from over 260 sources. The main attack would be in the south, with diversions against Hull, Scotland and Ireland."[1] Ambassador Kennedy was reporting that the Luftwaffe must soon put the RAF "out of commission", and a few days later Britain's head of armament purchasing in the United States delivered worrying news that there was a growing doubt about "the capability of Britain to survive". America, he said, was becoming "shy of starting production of weapons for a country which might 'go under' at any moment".

By now, the English landscape itself had altered, reflecting the sense of drama and dread. Seaside towns that would, in a normal summer, be thronged with holidaymakers were full of men and women in uniform, and the beaches were forlorn and empty. In one of his regular BBC broadcasts, on 14 July, J. B. Priestley described the eerie silence that had descended on Margate.

Everything was there: bathing pools, bandstands, gardens blazing with flowers, lido, theatres, and the like; and miles of firm golden sands all spread out beneath the July sun. But no people — not a soul. Of all those hundreds of thousands of holidaymakers, of entertainers and hawkers and boatmen — not one. And no sound — not the very ghost of an echo of all that cheerful hullabaloo — children shouting and laughing, bands playing, concert parties singing, men selling ice-cream, whelks and peppermint rock, which I'd remembered hearing along this shore. No, not even an echo. Silence. It was as if an evil magician had whisked everybody away.

The psychological atmosphere was charged with fear and doubt, and the question of maintaining morale was of ever greater strategic significance to the government. The authorities regarded the strength of public resolve — the population's ability to absorb the physical and psychological pain of a protracted bombing campaign — as of equal importance to Britain's capacity to resist the Germans militarily. The people were bound more closely to this war than any in Britain's history, and it was a connection Churchill was determined to maintain. He had told the nation in July that "this is not a war of chieftains or of princes, of dynasties or national ambition. It is a war of people and of causes."

There was a correspondingly large campaign to maintain public morale. Bureaucrats pumped out a

stream of publicity material about security consciousness and the need for selflessness. Posters warned
citizens that "Careless Talk Costs Lives" and that it was
their duty to remain "cheerful" and "resolute".
Exhortation was reinforced with threats. On 11 June, it
had been made a criminal offence "to make or report
any statement likely to cause alarm and despondency".
Prosecutions soon followed. One man was imprisoned
for three months for telling two New Zealanders: "You
don't want to fight in this bloody war"; another who
supported Indian independence received a two-month
sentence.

Dark rumours nevertheless flourished. At the end of
May, the New York Times had reported a story,
emanating from Britain, that the Germans had reared a
voracious strain of grasshopper, which was to be
released in Britain to devastate crops and the food
supply. There was talk of poisoned chocolate or
cigarettes being distributed, and of frightening new
weapons the Germans were set to unleash. Above all,
fifth columnists were believed to be everywhere,
directing enemy aircraft or preparing the way for
parachutists.

The rumours filled the vacuum caused by official
censorship of the news. At the beginning of the war,
television broadcasts, which were in their infancy and
reached only a handful of people, were shut down "for
the duration". The radio, or "wireless", ruled the
airwaves, and there were six news bulletins a day on the
BBC Home Service. The reports of the fighting, as with
the content of The Times and other newspapers,

consisted largely of communiqués from the Air Ministry and the Ministry of Home Security. The tone was usually upbeat. "The superiority of our airmen and machines was most convincing," reported *The Times*, quoting an eyewitness to the fighting over the Channel on 10 July. "All day long the pilots' combat reports came in. Always they told the same story — victory against the odds," commented the paper the following day.

The unvaried diet of good news created an appetite for something different. The distinctive broadcasts of the man nicknamed "Lord Haw-Haw" filled that gap. Haw-Haw was in reality William Joyce, an American-born Irishman and supporter of Mosley's British Union of Fascists. Both a fervent anti-Semite and anti-communist, he slipped out of Britain in August 1939 when fascist sympathizers were starting to be rounded up. He was then installed in Berlin to broadcast to Britain. Sounding like an "old-fashioned schoolmaster, loaded with sarcasm,"[2] he warned the British of their impending defeat and derided their military efforts. It passed into legend that his bulletins were packed with details suggesting that German eyes were everywhere, such as the mention of a stopped clock on a village church. But there are no records of such details, and the stories of his alleged omniscience appear to have been spread by his British supporters. Joyce's nasal, jeering broadcasts amused more than they demoralized Britons in 1940. Nonetheless, he was hanged for treason after the war.

The job of sustaining morale was given to the Ministry of Information. At the outset it was amateurish, condescending and unpopular with press and Parliament alike. Facile suggestions emanated from the ministry, such as telling actors that they were "counted upon to keep people cheerful, lead singing etc." "Your Courage, Your Cheerfulness, Your Resolution Will Bring Us Victory," proclaimed one poster: the sentiments were denounced by *The Times* as "insipid and patronizing invocations", which caused nothing but "exasperation". A comedian, Tommy Handley, renamed the Ministry of Information the "Ministry of Aggravation and Mysteries".

The relationship of the population to the battle raging about them in the skies was symbolized by a continuing and highly successful campaign for communities and organizations to "buy" their own Spitfire. *The Times* from the summer of 1940 is full of reports of donations, big and small, to "Spitfire funds" to finance new aircraft. On 10 August, the paper reported, the Canadian biscuit baron and MP for Macclesfield, Garfield Weston, presented £100,000 to the fund. All over the country fundraisers were finding novel ways of attracting donations. A "Dorothy fund" was established, whereby the nation's Dorothys could make a contribution and see a fighter plane named after them. In Brighton, the paper wrote, a special dog-race meeting had raised £400. Lloyds Bank presented enough money for a Spitfire, which was to be called "Black Horse" after its trademark. Supporting the funds was good publicity.

On 7 August, *The Times* reported:

To celebrate the run of *Black Velvet*, now approaching its 550th performance at the London Hippodrome, George Black and Moss' Empires will give all the admission receipts from all performances for the next four weeks for the purchase of Spitfire fighters. George Black hopes to provide at least two Spitfires, to be named "Black Velvet" and "Black Vanities", the latter being the title of the new show which will succeed Black Velvet.

The fundraising effort also spread to the empire. Under the heading "Empire Gifts", *The Times* of 3 August reported that the contribution from the Gold Coast (modern-day Ghana) had reached £25,000 and that Trinidad had also contributed more than £10,000. These were very large sums for small, impoverished colonies. Based on average earnings, £10,000 in 1940 would be nearly £1.5 million today. On 6 August, *The Times* reported that an appeal in the *Madras Mail* had raised £22,500. This would pay for four Spitfires, which were to be named Kerala, Andhradesa, Tamilnad and Karnataka. In Jamaica, *The Gleaner* newspaper was also busy raising money, sending in £5,000.

The relative lull in operations in the first few days of August allowed Fighter Command to replenish its squadrons: 720 aircraft now became available compared with 587 on 30 July, and the numbers of aircrew grew to 1,465, compared with 1,200 at the end of July. New units came into existence too: on 2 August another Polish fighter squadron, No. 303, was created to join 302, which had been formed in mid-July.

With improving weather on 5 August, German aircraft patrolled the Channel in strength again, looking for shipping. At 8.30 in the morning, a patrol of six Spitfires from No. 64 Squadron was "bounced" by a *Staffel* of Messerschmitt Me109s from *Jagdgeschwader 54*. Lacking height, two of the British planes were downed, and one pilot, Sergeant Lewis Isaac, was killed; he had joined the squadron only a few days previously. Below the fight, a convoy chugged eastwards, left alone by the Luftwaffe, which was clearly saving its efforts for the big effort ahead. Only when the ships reached the Straits of Dover were the vessels attacked — this time by Ju88s, escorted by Me109s. Hurricanes from 151 Squadron successfully intervened, shooting down a fighter as well as damaging one of the bombers.

Both Tuesday 6 and Wednesday 7 August remained quiet. Ensconced at Carinhall, the Prussian estate Goering had named in memory of his sickly aristocratic wife, the *Reichsmarschall* outlined his plans to his *Luftflotte* commanders. In order to destroy the RAF, he said, "all fighter escorts will be doubled in number and will fly at staggering levels of height."

The reduced enemy activity prompted the British to restart shipping activity in the Channel on 7 August. In the evening, 20 ships lying in the mouths of the Medway and the Thames prepared for a dash through the Channel to deliver a cargo of coal to Dorset. The convoy was codenamed Peewit, and great care was taken to avoid a repeat of the devastation wrought on Convoy CW8 on 25 July. Peewit would have nine naval escorts, improved anti-aircraft cover and its own balloon barrage. Furthermore, it would be timed so that it passed through the Straits of Dover in darkness. The plan, however, took no account of the German *Freya* radar system recently installed on the heights of Cap Blanc Nez near Calais, which soon picked up the convoy and gave the Luftwaffe time to prepare their attack.

The ships that made up Peewit totalled about 70,000 tons. They moved out of the river mouths on the evening tide and met up with their escort. The convoy formed into two columns, each led by a balloon ship. Twenty-six-year-old Arthur Hague was captain of the *Borealis*, to which one of the balloons was tethered, and he recorded how:

> . . . night fell as we passed Dover and in a calm sea under a moonless sky we crept past Beachy Head . . . Some time in the middle watch I became aware of the powerful throb of engines and assumed this to come from enemy bombers crossing the Channel on a night raid. Suddenly a loud explosion lit the sky and I saw that the coaster immediately astern of Borealis had fallen out of line and was listing. In a flash, it occurred to me that the throbbing I had heard was not aircraft but German E-boats, and they were on the shoreward side of us, attacking from under the cliffs."[3]

The E-boats were fast, designed for the rough conditions of the North Sea and armed with four torpedoes each. They launched their weapons into the mass of shipping, and panic ensued. Tracer fire from the anti-aircraft ships lit up the sky, as every gun on the convoy opened fire. Two ships smashed into each other while taking evasive action, and the convoy scattered. The E-boats continued to harry the ships along the south coast, sinking two vessels and damaging a third.

Daylight the following morning saw the surviving ships of Peewit steaming close under the south coast cliffs for safety, as the Royal Naval vessels tried to shepherd them back into two columns. By 10.30a.m., they were on their way again, with a fighter escort from 145 Squadron overhead. The planes, together with the convoy's balloons, kept at bay sporadic raids by enemy dive-bombers.

Shortly after midday, when Peewit was about five miles south of St Catherine's Point, on the most southerly tip of the Isle of Wight, Me109s suddenly appeared and headed straight for the barrage balloons. The gasbags, wallowing in the wind, made easy targets. "Under a hail of incendiary bullets," recorded Arthur Hague, "the *Borealis*' balloon disintegrated in flames. Then, out of the sun, roared a flight of Ju87 dive-bombers."

Luftflotte 3 had sent 57 Stukas against the convoy, escorted by 20 Me110s and 30 Me109s. Arthur Hague remembered that:

I saw this W-shaped silhouette of the dive-bomber coming zooming down towards us. I saw the bomb leave the plane before it zoomed off upwards and a fraction of a second later there was a violent explosion on the foredeck. The foremast jack-knifed and everything movable on the bridge crashed around us. Then, within minutes, RAF Hurricanes fortuitously appeared overhead.

The radar at Ventnor, on the Isle of Wight, had picked up the large German formation, and Air Chief Marshal Dowding was ready with 18 Hurricanes from three squadrons, as well as the Spitfires of 609 Squadron at Warmwell. No. 145 Squadron from Tangmere was among the Hurricane interceptors. "Our first view of the convoy near St Catherine's Point was of Ju87s in their bombing dives," said 145 pilot Peter Parrot. "Above the Ju87s were the escorting Me109s and farther to the southeast were two more large formations of enemy aircraft approaching the convoy — a formidable sight. I had already taken part in the Battle for France, and patrolled over Dunkirk during the evacuation, but I had never before seen so many aircraft in the sky at once."[4] Parrot's squadron dived out of the sun at the flank of the formation, sliding through the fighter screen to shoot down two of the Stukas. But, despite the weight of numbers on the British side, many found themselves caught up in dogfights with the Messerschmitt escorts and were unable to prevent the Stukas plunging on the vessels below. Within minutes, four ships had been sunk and a further seven vessels badly damaged.

The dogfight, involving about 150 aircraft, lasted for 20 minutes, before dwindling fuel forced the raiders to turn home. Two Hurricanes from 238 Squadron had been shot down, and the Germans had lost three Ju87s, one Me110 and three Me109s, with similar numbers damaged. The scattered remnants of the convoy now reassembled. The *Borealis* had lost its steering and had to be taken under tow. But *Luftflotte 3*'s commander, Hugo Sperrle, was not finished with Peewit yet. At about 4p.m., over 80 Stukas attacked, escorted by 68 fighters. Two squadrons of Hurricanes, Nos 145 (in its third major combat of the day) and 43, dived out of the sun to hit the raiders. Three Stukas were shot down and five damaged by 145, while No. 43 engaged the Me109s, shooting down two. Each of the Hurricane squadrons lost three of their number in the Channel.

Of the 21 vessels that had left Southend, only 4 arrived undamaged at their destination of Swanage. The destruction of Peewit was to be the worst marine disaster in British waters during the entire war. But the significance of the fighting lay in the way the respective air forces had performed.

The scale of the combat on 8 August overshadowed anything that had come before. The American-born Conservative MP for Southend West, Henry "Chips" Channon, recorded in his diary "a great air battle over the Channel, and a vast number of German aeroplanes have been brought down over the coast! Our Air Force is sublime. 53 raiders, the newspapers announce, were brought down today."

In fact, thirteen Hurricanes had been lost, with four more damaged, as well as one Spitfire; twelve pilots had been killed and three wounded. The Luftwaffe had lost eight Me109s, one Me110, and seven Ju87s. Eighteen more German aircraft had been damaged, some past repair. For the Luftwaffe, Peewit had been a target of opportunity, not part of Goering's *Adlerangriff* plans. But the huge size of the attacking formations led Fighter Command to the conclusion that the all-out assault had started. The RAF order of the day, issued that night, read: "The Battle of Britain is about to begin. Members of the Royal Air Force, the fate of generations lies in your hands."

Fighter Command had, though, learned an encouraging lesson. The day's actions had shown Dowding and his commanders that mass attacks by the Germans could be picked up by the radar stations in enough time to scramble fighters so they were in the best position to confront the raid.

As it turned out, 9 August saw a relative drop in the tempo of fighting, as the Luftwaffe prepared for *Adlerangriff*, in theory to commence the following day. Nonetheless, they still flew several hundred sorties. Off the east coast, half a dozen He111s searched unsuccessfully for a convoy, and then dropped their bombs on coastal towns in Yorkshire and elsewhere in the north. Hurricanes from 79 Squadron at Acklington intercepted, shooting down a bomber that had just successfully hit Sunderland's shipyard. On the south coast there was a further attack by fighters on the Dover balloon barrage, and a Ju88 was found circling the remnants of convoy Peewit. Hurricanes from Nos 234 and 601 Squadrons brought it down at about 2.30 in the afternoon.

As the afternoon progressed, there was no sign of the clear weather predicted by the Luftwaffe's meteorologists. If anything, conditions seemed to be worsening. Goering decided to postpone his great assault for 24 hours. Saturday 10 August brought cloud, rain and thunderstorms over northern France, the Channel and southern England. A handful of scattered raids and reconnaissance sorties by the Luftwaffe either foundered in the poor weather or were driven away. For the last time for many weeks to come, there were no combat casualties on either side.

Sunday 11 August began promisingly for the Germans with fair weather, but then deteriorated. The meteorology reports said it might be two days before there was a sustained improvement. Luftwaffe weather-reconnaissance aircraft reported an area of high pressure approaching from the mid-Atlantic, which would deliver a few days of fine weather over the south of England and the Channel. Zero hour for *Adlertag* was now set for 05.30hrs on 13 August.

A higher number of attacks occurred on the Sunday, however, in what seemed like a dress rehearsal for Eagle Day. Early in the morning, No. 74 Squadron was patrolling the south coast when two formations of Me109s and Me110s swept across the Channel to

210

target, once more, the Dover barrage balloons. The 109s shot up three of the balloons, and then the Me110 heavy fighters, carrying small bombs, managed to hit the port, although they caused little serious damage. No. 74 Squadron arrived as the enemy planes were departing, but before the squadron could engage them properly it was intercepted by a *Staffel* of Me109s. The German forces shot down one British pilot, Pilot Officer Peter Stevenson. He was lucky to survive the onslaught and a bale-out into the treacherous waters of the Channel, as he recorded:

I climbed up to him. He must have thought I was an Me109 but when he suddenly dived away I followed him and gave him a two-second deflection burst. The enemy aircraft lurched slightly and went into a vertical dive. I kept my height at 15,000 feet and watched. I saw the enemy aircraft dive straight into the sea fifteen miles south-east of Dover and disappear in a big splash of water. I then climbed to 23,000 feet up-sun and saw a formation of twelve Me109s 2,000 feet beneath me, proceeding north of Dover. It was my intention to attach myself to the back of this formation from out of the sun, and spray the whole formation. As I was diving for them, a really large volume of cannon and machine-gun fire came from behind. There were about twelve Me109s diving at me from the sun and at least half of them must have been firing deflection shots at me. There was a popping noise and my control column became useless. I found myself doing a vertical dive, getting faster and faster. I pulled the hood back. I got my head out of the cockpit, and the slipstream tore the rest of me clean out of the machine. My trouser leg and both shoes were torn off. I saw my machine crash into the sea a mile off Deal. It took me twenty minutes to come down. I had been drifting eleven miles out to sea.

One string of my parachute did not come undone, and I was dragged along by my left leg at ten miles an hour with my head underneath the water. After three minutes I was almost unconscious; then the string came undone. I got my breath back and started swimming. There was a heavy sea running . . . After one-and-a-half hours, an MTB [motor torpedo boat] came to look for me. I fired my revolver at it. It went out of sight, but came back. I changed magazines and fired all my shots over it. It heard my shots and I kicked up a foam in the water, and it saw me. It then picked me up and took me to Dover.[5]

At the same time, German fighters were roaming along the southeast coastline in an attempt to lure their British counterparts to challenge them. A sweep over Sussex was intercepted by Spitfires from No. 64 Squadron, which shot down two Me109s. On the whole, though, Park avoided rising to the provocation, preserving his resources for the bomber fleets that would surely soon be on their way again. Just before 10a.m., the Isle of Wight radar station at Ventnor reported what looked like a heavy raid assembling over the Cherbourg peninsula. Park and the commander of 10 Group, Air Vice-Marshal Sir Quintin Brand, decided that this was probably the enemy's main effort of the day, and they began to organize a response. Spitfires from 609 Squadron at Warmwell were ordered up to patrol, while No. 1 Squadron was scrambled from Tangmere. Six other squadrons in the west were put at "readiness" level.

Quintin Brand

Of all the group commanders during the Battle of Britain, Sir Christopher Joseph Quintin Brand, in charge of 10 Group, had the most distinguished record as a fighter pilot. He was born in South Africa in 1893 and served in the local defence force during the first two years of the First World War. After that, he transferred to the Royal Flying Corps. In 1917, he was one of the three pilots who carried out the first ever night-time patrol by single-seater fighters, a mission over the Thames Estuary described as "perhaps the most important event in the history of air defence".

By May 1918, Brand was leader of 112 Squadron. In the last German air raid of the First World War, he brought down one of the three Gotha bombers destroyed that night, only narrowly escaping with his life as the flaming bomber plunged into the sea close by. This action won him the Distinguished Service Order (DSO). On 15 September 1918, he was attacking an enemy aircraft over France. His engine's sump was punctured, covering the

213

windscreen in oil. Despite this, he pursued his opponent, driving him down to 200 feet above ground, at which point he was forced to call off the attack. For this, he was awarded the Distinguished Flying Cross (DFC).

After the war, Quintin Brand and Pierre van Ryneveld, another ex-RFC South African, made one of the first flights from England to the South African Cape. Starting from Brooklands on 4 February 1920, they flew their Vickers Vimy bomber, named *Silver Queen*, to Cairo. On 11 February, they crashed, at night, near Egypt's Wadi Haifa. The two engines were saved, however, and fitted to a new air-frame, so the pilots were able to continue their journey and reached Pretoria on 5 March, where the aircraft was destroyed in a take-off accident. The South African air force supplied them with a de Havilland DH9 and they landed in Cape Town on 20 March. For their achievement, they were both knighted.

From 1925 to 1927, Brand was senior technical officer, then principal technical officer, at the Royal Aircraft Establishment at Farnborough. Between 1932 and 1936 he was director general of aviation in Egypt, before returning to England to take up the post of director of repair and maintenance at the Air Ministry. In July 1940, on the creation of 10 Group to defend Southwest England and South Wales, he was appointed its commander and promoted to the rank of air vice-marshal.

Brand enjoyed a good relationship with Park and

Dowding, frequently deploying his squadrons effectively to back up the efforts of 11 Group. He also supported their tactics of using small and rapidly deployed groups of fighters, rather than the "Big Wings" favoured by Leigh-Mallory and others. Thus he found himself in the wrong camp when Dowding and Park were moved from their commands, and he was posted in late 1940 to take over a training group. He retired from the RAF in 1943 and died in Rhodesia (Zimbabwe) in March 1968 at the age of 74.

Within a few minutes of the initial warning, it was clear that the formation was huge and that the raid was advancing rapidly. It appeared to be heading for the Royal Navy base at Portland in Dorset. Elements of six further squadrons — Nos 152, 145, 87, 213 and 238 — were scrambled. Although forewarned of the size of the force, the pilots were still taken aback at what they saw approaching. Rank after rank of small dark shapes were coming out of the west, a swarm of 54 Ju88s, 20 He111s, 61 Me110s and 30 Me109s — a total of 165 aircraft. It was the largest single raid launched against England so far. In the vanguard were the fighters, a mixture of Me109s and 110s, at various heights, circling and clearly aiming to distract intercepting fighters to give the bombers a clear run. The two sides clashed, just before 11a.m., in the skies above Dorset between Weymouth and Swanage.

The German tactics had some success, and the British fighters found themselves caught up in an enormous dogfight south of Portland, as planes swooped and turned, shooting and trying to avoid being shot. The bombers unloaded their cargoes, setting two oil tanks on fire. One of the Heinkels was pursued and shot down by Eric Bann and Sergeant Henry Marsh of 238 Squadron. It was a successful moment in an otherwise terrible day for the squadron. Five of their Hurricanes went down, with four of their pilots killed. The dead included Flight Lieutenant Stuart Walch, a 23-year-old Australian who transferred to the RAF in 1937 and was one of the most experienced pilots in the squadron. Another was Flying Officer Michal Steborowski, a 31-year-old veteran and one of the Polish airmen who had escaped to England to continue the fight against the Nazis. He had joined the squadron only six days before and had already shot down an Me110. The youngest of the victims was Flight Sergeant Geoffrey Gledhill, who had arrived at 238 Squadron a week before his death. He was 19 years old. No. 111 Squadron also lost four of its pilots that day, as did 601 Squadron, all shot down by Messerschmitts over Portland. The mess at the squadron's Tangmere base was a chilly place that evening.

After such a day it was hard not to come to the conclusion that survival was as much about luck as skill. The dead included highly experienced pre-war service officers, like Flying Officer James Gillan of 601 Squadron, as well as gifted amateurs and greenhorns.

The same rule of luck applied to squadrons as well as individuals. No. 609, in the same skies against the same enemy, had had a successful day and escaped virtually unscathed. After being scrambled from Warmwell, Squadron Leader George Darley led "B" Flight in an attack on a formation of Me110s. Flying straight across the top of the circle of twin-engine fighters, Darley almost collided with one of the Me110s as he shot it down, killing the pilot and wounding the gunner. Four more Me110s fell to the squadron in their first attack. John Bisdee was one of the intercepting pilots:

> I hit one of the Messerschmitt 110s and one of its engines started pouring smoke. It turned over on its back to try to evade but I was determined not to let the bugger go. I turned over as well and shot down after him. I lost him for an instant and the next thing I saw was a pile of burning wreckage down below just near the long man, the Cerne Abbas giant, who had a very rude male organ sticking up. I remember seeing a whole lot of farm labourers dancing around it waving pitchforks and that kind of thing. So I beat the thing up and did a victory roll and at that moment I looked up in the clouds and two parachutes appeared. The crew of this thing had got out. They landed safely a long way away from the farm labourers with their pitchforks, who might have given them a rather unpleasant reception.[6]

One of the men who had not flown that day watched the fighters of 609 return, noting "to my surprise nobody was missing. After such a fierce scrap it seemed too good to be true."[7]

In the afternoon of 11 August, a group of Dorniers and Me110s launched an unsuccessful attack on a convoy off Harwich. No. 74 Squadron, some of whose pilots had already flown three sorties before lunch, intercepted, together with sections from Nos 17 and 85 squadrons. Two fighters from 74 Squadron and one from 17 Squadron were shot down by the Me110s, and their pilots killed. As this German force retreated, another appeared, heading for the Thames Estuary. Again, 74 Squadron was in action, along with 111 Squadron. They drove the raid back, but by now the weather was deteriorating fast, with huge clouds forming over Southeast England. The rest of the afternoon was mercifully quiet.

It had been a day of terrible attrition. The Luftwaffe had lost just over 30 aircraft, but the RAF's losses were just as heavy. Twenty-seven fighters had gone down to the Luftwaffe's guns. More alarmingly, 25 British pilots had died. Fighter Command could not sustain such losses for long without suffering a serious decline in efficiency and morale.

By the Monday, 12 August, the Luftwaffe was ready to start executing the orders laid out by Goering in his *Adlerangriff* plan. On the urging of General Wolfgang Martini, head of the *Luftnachrichtentruppe* (the Luftwaffe signals branch), it was decided to turn the Luftwaffe's destructive power against one of the defenders' crucial resources. Coordinated attacks were ordered on every known radar installation on the south coast ahead of the great attack. Subsequent raids on RAF coastal stations would test out whether a "black-out" had been achieved.

At just after 7a.m., nine Me109s of *Jagdgeschwader* 52 sped across the coast at Dover and moved rapidly eastwards over Kent. Despite the strictures from HQ against being drawn into these provocations, 12 Spitfires from 610 Squadron, based at Biggin Hill, took up the chase. One Spitfire was shot down and four more damaged, though two of the Me109s also fell in the skies over New Romney.

Now that one squadron of defenders was successfully preoccupied with the diversion, the Luftwaffe launched its attack on the south coast radar stations.

Sixteen Me110s from the Luftwaffe's *Erprobungsgruppe* (Experimental Group) 210, led by Stuka ace Hauptmann Walter Rubensdörffer, attacked in four groups in a skilful manoeuvre, flying low and changing direction to fool the defences. First, the Home Chain Low station at Dover, for detecting low-flying aircraft, was hit by four of the Me110s, followed two minutes later by a strike on the station at Rye. Pevensey was next, where a bomb cut off the electricity supply. All three stations were now out of action. A fourth attack on the Chain Home High Station at Dunkirk, near Canterbury, caused no vital damage.

As emergency measures swung into place to restore radar coverage, a substantial German bomber force streamed through the gap to attack the RAF's forward stations. Lympne, near Folkestone, was the first to suffer, struck by 141 bombs from Ju88s. Fortunately for 11 Group, this was only an emergency satellite station, and the damage caused had little effect on the sectors' operations. The fact that this airfield was chosen gave an early hint that the Luftwaffe's intelligence about the workings of Fighter Command was far from complete. There was a more damaging attack on Hawkinge, a few miles away to the east, which blew up two hangars, destroyed four fighters on the ground and also damaged maintenance workshops. Work started immediately to fill the 28 craters on the airfield.

Meanwhile, over the French coast a substantial force of some 100 Ju88s (of *Kampfgeschwader* — Battle Wing — *51*), 120 Me110s (of *Zerstörergeschwader* — "Destroyer Wing" — *2*) and 25 Me110s (of *Zerstörergeschwader 53*) had taken advantage of the holes torn in the radar curtain to form up undetected. They were well on their way to their target before being spotted by Poling radar station, Kent, at 11.45a.m. But even then, no-one was sure where the aircraft were heading. For a time, it looked like they were aiming to cross the coast near Brighton, but then Observer Corps personnel reported the huge fleet veering westwards towards the Isle of Wight. Faced with such numbers, Park and Dowding once again committed relatively large forces, throwing 48 Hurricanes and 10 Spitfires against them. While the Me110s adopted their orbiting "circle of death" formation, trying to provoke the British fighters into a risky attack, about 70 Ju88s found a gap in the thicket of barrage balloons protecting Portsmouth and struck the town hard. The Royal Dockyards, the railway station and ships in the harbour all suffered, as well as shops and homes. Twenty-three people were killed and a hundred injured. The British fighters were kept back by the heavy flak being pumped into the air over the harbour. They waited for the bombers to leave before pouncing. The formation's lead bomber fell as it headed for home and plunged into the sea off Bognor Regis.

While the main German force was attacking Portsmouth, a smaller group of Ju88s swung in on the Isle of Wight and dived on the radar station at Ventnor, whose commanding position on the high ground behind the town made it of particular interest to the Luftwaffe. The attack was accurate and devastating. Fifteen 500 kg bombs demolished almost every structure in the compound. The aerial lattice between the transmitter towers was also severely damaged. The British moved a mobile unit to the area and broadcast dummy signals to try to fool the Germans into thinking that the station was still operational. It was not until 15 August that Ventnor was really functioning again, and then only partially so.

Spitfires of No. 609 Squadron arrived over the Isle of Wight to find about 200 German aircraft circling. Again, the German fighters waited on high, but as at Portsmouth they were ignored by 609 and its accompanying squadron, No. 152. The British fighters concentrated on the bombers, shooting down two of them. But the bombers' gunners were able to inflict equal damage, shooting down two of 152 Squadron's

Spitfires and killing their pilots. The German fighter escort descended to join the mêlée but was unable to chase away the British fighters, suffering the loss of four Me110s and two Me109s within the space of a few minutes.

Just before 1p.m., the Luftwaffe launched another airfield raid, the third of the day. Spitfires from No. 65 Squadron were about to take off on patrol from Manston, Kent, when a group of Me110s swooped in to bomb and strafe. At the same time, 18 Dorniers made a pass over the airfield, dropping 250 kg and fragmentation bombs. The airfield erupted into smoke, chalk dust and chaos. Jeffrey Quill, the legendary test pilot who was the second man to fly the Supermarine Spitfire and was now serving with 65 Squadron, described how:

> . . . we were just formed up on the ground and waiting Sam's signal to start rolling. I was therefore looking out to my left towards the leading section when I became aware of, rather than actually hearing, a sort of reverberating "crump" behind and to my right. I looked quickly over my right shoulder to see one of the hangar roofs close behind us ascending heavenwards . . . I caught a glimpse through smoke of what looked like a Bf 110 [Me110] pulling sharply out of a dive and immediately concluded that it was high time for Quill to be airborne."[8]

Manston was the most forward and exposed point in the Fighter Command network, stuck on the bare promontory of the North Foreland. Not only did its position make it particularly liable to attack, but its pilots also had little time to gain height before the raiders' arrival.

The pressure on the radar stations was maintained until the early evening, when Kesselring sent three small raids against Dover and Hastings. But the attacks were intercepted in good time. The defenders had learned another tactical lesson and were now ignoring the fighter escorts forming an umbrella overhead in favour of tearing into the ranks of the bombers. That night, Luftwaffe signals chief Martini assessed the damage done to the British radar. The reports were disappointing. From monitoring radio signals from the target stations it seemed that all of them were back in action by the afternoon. Assuming that their workings must be deep underground, Martini came to the conclusion that it was possible to shut down British radar cover for short periods only.

As the German pilots went to bed on the eve of what was to be their Eagle Day, the weather worsened. When dawn broke on 13 August it was no better. Fog clung to many of the Luftwaffe bases of northern France, and a thick blanket of cloud pressed down on the Channel.

The plan of attack, as set out by Goering, envisaged great fleets of bombers, protected by a swarm of escorts flying at maximum height so as to be able to swoop like raptors on the British fighters as they attacked. But in these weather conditions the Messerschmitts would be unable to see through the mattress of cloud, leaving Fighter Command to savage their charges.

Goering looked at the unrelieved grey overhead and hesitated. There was some hope that another humiliating postponement could be avoided, for the meteorology men claimed the situation would improve in the afternoon. So the *Reichsmarschall* ordered operations to be held back until 2p.m.

The message, though, was slow to filter down the line. Oberst Johannes Fink, the *Kanalkampfführer* himself, had already taken off in command of 74 Dorniers of *Kampfgeschwader 2*. He led the formation towards the French coast, where he was due, at 5.30a.m., to meet a fighter escort of 60 Me110s from *Zerstörergeschwader 26*. Then he was to proceed to targets on the Isle of Sheppey. News of the delay was signalled to him, but it never got through. Fink's radio was out of action and he pressed on, blithely unaware of the change of plan. The Messerschmitts were in place, but, as Fink said, "they kept coming up and diving down in the most peculiar way. I thought this was their way of saying they were ready. So I went on and found to my surprise that the fighters didn't follow." Clearly the fighters had, unlike Fink, received the postponement order, but with no radio link between the fighters and the bombers, the message could not be relayed.

The heavy cloud protected the bombers, and, as they crossed the North Foreland, their direction could not be accurately divined by the Observer Corps personnel straining to scan the murky skies. The radar cover was makeshift, provided by the emergency set installed after the preceding day's attacks. The result was that, of the five squadrons scrambled to intercept, only No. 74, led by "Sailor" Malan, succeeded in engaging the bombers before they reached the Isle of Sheppey.

"Sailor" Malan

In July 1940, Adolph Gysbert Malan (1910–63) was a flight lieutenant with No. 74 Squadron; by August, he was leading the squadron. Thirty years old, he had endured a tough upbringing in South Africa, where he had been a sea cadet (1924–6) under the brutal discipline of the training ship *General Botha* and endured a flogging that left him scarred for life. He served as an officer in the merchant navy, with the Union Castle line, and in 1932 joined Britain's Royal Naval Volunteer Reserve. It was the years of maritime experience that gave him his subsequent nickname, "Sailor".

Then, in 1935–6, he learned to fly and applied for an RAF short-service commission, rising to flight lieutenant by 1939. Seeing his first action — and his first kills — in late May 1940, Malan was to prove an exceptional pilot and an inspiration to others. He was brilliant, accurate and deadly: it was said of him that he could "spot a fly on the Great Wall of China at five miles".[9] In August 1940 he compiled his influential *aide-mémoire* "Ten of My Rules of Air Fighting"; by March 1941 he was wing

225

commander at Biggin Hill.

Older than most of the other Battle of Britain pilots, Malan was married, with a son (Jonathan) who had Winston Churchill as a godfather. Malan survived the war, leaving RAF service in 1946 for civilian life in a changing South Africa, where he remained an opponent of the developing apartheid policies until his death, from Parkinson's disease, in 1963. But by then his reputation had long been secure, as the RAF fighter pilot with the most "kills" to his name — 32 — over the course of the war.

TEN OF MY RULES FOR AIR FIGHTING

1. *Wait until you see the whites of his eyes. Fire short bursts of one to two seconds only when your sights are definitely "ON".*

2. *Whilst shooting think of nothing else, brace the whole of your body: have both hands on the stick; concentrate on your ring sight.*

3. *Always keep a sharp lookout. "Keep your finger out."*

4. *Height gives you the initiative.*

5. *Always turn and face the attack.*

6. *Make your decisions promptly. It is better to act quickly even though your tactics are not the best.*

7. *Never fly straight and level for more than 30 seconds in the combat area.*

8. *When diving to attack always leave a proportion of your formation above to act as a top guard.*

9. *INITIATIVE, AGGRES-SION, AIR DISCIPLINE, and TEAM WORK are words that MEAN something in Air Fighting.*

10. *Go in quickly — Punch hard — Get out!*

Fink's formation now split in two, with one *Gruppe* heading for the naval base at Sheerness and the other for Eastchurch air base. Like Lympne, which was attacked the day before, Eastchurch was not an important part of No. 11 Group's set-up. It was primarily a Coastal Command station, focused on German naval raiders rather than the vital air-to-air struggle. By chance, however, there was a squadron of Spitfires at the base, No. 266, which had just been moved south from the Midlands.

The first bomb landed soon after seven in the morning. No. 266 Squadron pilot Dennis Armitage remembered waking "to find my bed waltzing around the room, which seemed most unpleasant but was caused by what in reality was a blessing . . . the bogginess of the land. The whole place shook as if we were having a major earthquake, but the bombs . . . buried themselves deeply before exploding, leaving nothing but a little pile of earth." Nonetheless, the raid caused considerable damage. Five Coastal Command Blenheims were destroyed on the ground, as well as a hangar containing 266's ammunition and other important equipment. One of the groundcrew's huts

227

was also hit, killing 16 men and injuring more. But none of the fighter pilots was killed, and only one Spitfire was destroyed on the ground, the rest having been carefully dispersed around the airfield.

As Fink's bombers wheeled away from their target to race for the protection of the clouds, they were set upon by fighters from 111 and 151 squadrons. Flight Lieutenant Roddick Smith of No. 151 Squadron was flying the only Hurricane in the RAF that had cannon rather than machine-guns:

> I ordered the attack, telling my pilots to dive through the enemy formation and on into the clouds, as I assumed the rear formation were Messerschmitt 110s and three quarters of my pilots were new. I opened fire at about 300 yards with my cannon, firing into the general mass as the enemy were in exceptionally close formation. One immediately burst into flames and another started smoking when my windscreen front panel was completely shattered by enemy fire, and I broke away downwards and returned to North Weald."[10]

The Hurricanes of No. 111 Squadron launched another frontal attack, causing havoc. Five Dorniers were shot down and several more of them were damaged.

On his return, a furious Fink telephoned Generalfeldmarschall Kesselring "and shouted down the line exactly what I thought about it. I asked what

. . . the people at HQ thought they were doing to send us out unprotected."

Another German group had also failed to receive the delay message. At about 6.30a.m., radar picked up an enemy formation approaching the coast between Hastings and Bognor. Fighter Command sent up four squadrons, and No. 43 made contact first, with what turned out to be a fighter formation of Me109s and Me110s of *Jagdgeschwader 2*. As they raced westwards, a German fighter was shot down between Petworth and Shoreham. But more Me109s arrived to bolster the force. As 11 Group's fighters peeled off to return to base, ammunition exhausted, No. 238 Squadron from 10 Group rose up to meet the raiders, though the British pilots were heavily outnumbered.

"We had rather a shock," said pilot Gordon Batt. "We were instantly in a mass of aircraft." As always, with closing speeds of up to 600 miles an hour, everything happened in fractions of a second. "We were attacked first by Me109s from above, which chopped me off from the other five of the flight." Finding himself suddenly alone, Batt peered around the empty sky before spotting some eight or nine Me109s below him. "I started to dive to attack, when it suddenly felt as if a steam-roller had hit me. The aircraft bucked and jumped out of my control." Batt opened the hood to jump, but then changed his mind. Although his propeller had stopped and his machine was streaming engine coolant, he turned his stricken Hurricane north, breaking cloud at 2,000 feet. To his great relief, he was over land. "There was not a field bigger than a postage stamp, so I elected to force-land with the wheels up in a field near to a farmhouse, so that if I did get into difficulties the farmer would come to my aid." Pulling his straps tight, he prepared for a rough landing. "As I hit the field, the big air scoop under the Hurricane dug in and rocked me forward . . . eventually, having made a nasty groove in the farmer's crop, I came to a standstill. I rapidly released my safety straps and parachute harness, heaved myself out of the cockpit and ran along the wing, falling over backwards into the dusty barley and dry earth."[11]

High above, the raiders had turned for home, their fuel exhausted, but not before consigning another Hurricane to destruction. Eric Seabourne of 238 Squadron had experienced his first combat on 13 July and his first kill — an Me109 — on 8 August. But on 13 August his luck ran out. "I didn't see who it was but I got a cannon shell in the radiator. I watched the oil temperature just going up and up and up until all of a sudden there's a bang and the engine just stopped dead." But he was still under attack, and now bullets struck the gravity tank just in front of his cockpit, which started "burning quite happily. It got hotter and hotter, so I thought it was time to abandon ship." He unstrapped himself, but the cockpit hood was jammed. This was the nightmare that every pilot dreaded — slow death by burning. Already Seabourne's clothes were scorched, and his wrists and face burnt. His non-issue rubber goggles had melted onto his face. "All the time the three Me109s on my tail kept firing at me and then suddenly my port wing broke off. The aircraft turned over on its back." Loose in the cockpit, Seabourne's body crashed against the hood and it fell away at last. He was out: "The cold air revived me, I can tell you." Fearful of being strafed by the enemy fighters, he waited until he was in the cloud at 2,000 feet before pulling the ripcord on his parachute. "The only snag was that when the thing opened up two of the straps were crossed about my neck, so with my burnt hands I had to hold them to one side to ease the pressure on my neck. The next minute there was an almighty splash and I was in the water."

He had been told that it was imperative for pilots who landed in water to free themselves from their parachutes: "Well, I ignored that completely. I don't know why but I still kept my parachute, which billowed out all around me." He did, though, blow up his Mae West lifejacket and floated around in the Channel for about an hour, which "after the burning cockpit even seemed quite pleasant". As Seabourne drifted in and out of consciousness, he was suddenly alerted by a large bow wave that his rescue was imminent. It was a destroyer, the *Bulldog*, which was still in action, firing its anti-aircraft guns and keen to keep on the move. A scrambling net holding two seamen appeared over the side and Seabourne was firmly grabbed. "But I still had the parachute tied around my right leg so as he got under way of course there was a nasty crack and the leg snapped." Seabourne hardly felt it; the experience of being burned in his aircraft seemed to have extinguished his ability to feel pain. Once on board the vessel, he was pumped full of morphine and eventually delivered to the naval hospital in Portsmouth. There he lay next but one to an injured German pilot: "He was an English speaker and he was creating because he had been shot down by a Hurricane, which he thought was much below his dignity. If it had been a Spitfire it would have been OK, but not a Hurricane."[12]

The westward-headed free chases on 13 August had been designed to draw defending fighters away from a raid by Ju88s from *Kampfgeschwader 54* against an airfield at Odiham in Hampshire (again, one with little defensive importance) and the Royal Aircraft establishment at Farnborough. But the formation was spotted by "A" Flight of 601 Squadron, which was climbing towards the German fighter sweep. Harassed by the fighters, and struggling to fly and navigate in the poor weather, the Ju88s turned back when only ten miles inland.

Shortly before midday, a force from *Zerstörergeschwader 2* also jumped the gun. A group of 28 Me110s had been due to escort Ju88s of *Kampfgeschwader 54* on a diversion raid on Portland. This time the bombers received the postponement order but not the fighters, which set course for the naval base nonetheless. Two squadrons of British fighters — Nos 238, again, and 601 — were waiting for them, and before they could escape, one of the Me110s was shot down and two more badly damaged by 238 Squadron Hurricanes. But the beleaguered squadron, which had lost five aircraft and four pilots two days previously, saw two more of its fighters shot down, with one pilot, Sergeant Marsh, who had shared a victory with his number two Eric

Bann a few days previously, missing and presumed dead. Bann blamed himself, as he described in a letter home shortly afterwards (15 August): "Tony Marsh, my section leader, and I were the last two in action and I think I must have done too much flying for I fainted and I, poor Tony's guard, left him to the mercy of all. Oh dear, I did feel bad, when I learned he never came back."

As the confusion that muddled the opening of Eagle Day cleared, so did the skies. At 1p.m. the word went out that *Adlertag* was now definitely "on". The first attack of the afternoon formed up over Cherbourg and the Channel Islands. At 3.30p.m. it appeared on the radar screens across a 40-mile front. As Dowding at Fighter Command HQ watched the WAAF operators push the enemy markers across the board with their croupiers' rakes, he concluded that the Germans were heading for 10 Group in the west.

There was no doubting now that this was an all-out assault. It was the largest formation yet launched against England. On the eastern flank were 120 Ju88s of *Kampfgeschwader 54* and *Lehrgeschwader* (Teaching Wing) *1*, escorted by 30 Me110s of the latter. On the western flank were 27 Ju87 dive-bombers of *Sturzkampfgeschwader 2*. In the vanguard flew 30 Me109s of *Jagdgeschwader 53*, and behind them 52 Ju87s of *Sturzkampfgeschwader 77*, escorted by Me109s of *Jagdgeschwader 27*.

Feldwebel (Technical Sergeant) Karl Hoffmann of *Gruppe 1, Kampfgeschwader 30*, found himself awestruck at the size of the armada being gathered for the *Adlertag* onslaught.

We had been briefed the day previous to Adlertag that we would be going across the Channel in strong formations to attack England. At last, we would be concentrating in large bomber formations with a fighter escort. For so long, we had been flying our individual missions on simple operations like photographic reconnaissance or mine-laying duties. Some, like us, had not even seen a British fighter or even fired a shot in anger and it hardly seemed as if a war was on at all, Now, our airfields had many bombers at the ready, many had been flown in from inland airfields, and I could see that now our great Luftwaffe would be at last attacking England.[13]

Before the main thrust crossed the Channel, a free sweep by Me109s of *Jagdgeschwader 5* raced along the coast near Portland, attempting to draw defending fighters to the west. No. 152 Squadron's Spitfires took up the chase, but all the early attack had achieved was to bring more British fighters to readiness. Soon, just under 80 Hurricanes and Spitfires were airborne to take on the main formation.

Ploughing through by sheer weight of numbers, one German bomber group hit Southampton at about 4.05p.m., causing heavy damage to the port and to residential areas. Meanwhile, 40 Ju88s of *Kampfgeschwader 54* were now carrying out the raid on Portland from which they had been recalled in the morning. But an interception by fighters from Nos 152, 213 and 601 Squadrons drove them back, with 601 downing three of their Me110 escorts. At the same time, a force of Ju87s had managed to cross the coast undetected and wheeled northeast intent on bombing the important sector station at Middle Wallop. But the formation had taken a long route over the Channel, and by now the Stukas' fighter escorts' dwindling fuel reserves had forced them to turn back. No. 609 Squadron was scrambled in time to gain the height to make a devastating attack on a *Staffel* from *Sturzkampfgeschwader 2*. Weighed down by their bombs, the Stukas were even slower than usual and six of them were shot down. John Dundas, who was one of those claiming kills, wrote in the squadron's diary: "Thirteen Spitfires left Warmwell for a memorable tea-party over Lyme Bay, and an unlucky day for the species Ju87."[14] Returning back to base, one of the Ju87 survivors reported: "They ripped our backs open right up to the collar."[15]

Other Stuka formations crossed the coast unopposed, but, searching for the forward base at Warmwell, they got lost and ditched their bombs at random, before heading home. Yet more Ju87s had been ordered to target Middle Wallop, but they bombed the grass airstrip at Andover in error. Only one found Middle Wallop, but dropped its bombs on the village rather than the base.

As the attack in the west faded, Kesselring's *Luftflotte 2* began to launch raids in Southeast England. Two Stuka groups crossed the coast, one over

Dover, the other near Dungeness. No. 56 Squadron intercepted, but was soon involved in battles with escorting Me109s as the formation moved northwards. The Stukas never found whatever targets they were seeking, and so ended up jettisoning their bombs over Canterbury, Ashford and Ramsgate in Kent.

The other group of 40 Stukas of *Lehrgeschwader 1*, led by Hauptmann Berndt von Brauchitsch, son of the German army's commander-in-chief, had greater impact. Throughout the day the German tactic had been to use fighter sweeps in an attempt to divert the Fighter Command forces, while bombers arrived shortly afterwards to exploit the defensive gap. Often the bomber force had arrived too late, giving the British fighters time to engage the raiding fighters, return to base, refuel, rearm and get airborne again in time to meet the bombers. But this time, over Kent, the plan worked, and as a fighter sweep by Me109s of *Jagdgeschwader 26* drew Nos 56 and 65 squadrons away, shooting down four of 56's Hurricanes, von Brauchitsch's Stukas proceeded to Detling airfield, near Rochester.

The attack came as a complete surprise. No air-raid sirens were sounded, and the airfield defences were slow to react. The first many of the staff knew of the raid was the sight of Me109s racing in low with their cannons blazing. The dive-bombers followed. It was just after 5p.m., and the mess halls were full. All the hangars were hit, as well as the operations block where the commanding officer, Group Captain Edward Davis, was killed by falling concrete. The fuel dump was set ablaze, and the runways and hard standings were cratered. The raid killed 67 people and destroyed 22 aircraft. Despite the devastation, the operation had no effect on the efficiency of Dowding's defences, for Detling was a Coastal Command airfield.

During the night of 13/14 August, the Luftwaffe was busy again, hitting targets as disparate as Aberdeen, Norwich, Swansea, Liverpool and Belfast. In the last city, the Short's factory was hit, destroying five of the RAF's new groundbreaking four-engine Sterling bombers. The heaviest raid was on the new "shadow" Spitfire factory — at Castle Bromwich, near Birmingham, which was badly damaged.

The Shadow Factory Scheme was an example of British farsightedness that contrasted sharply with the surprisingly short-term approach taken by Germany towards waging aerial war. Long before the conflict began, British planners had understood the inevitability of aviation-industry factories becoming prime targets for enemy bombers. In April 1936, the government established a scheme to set up "shadow factories", which would provide alternative production capability for the military aircraft industry by using the enormous capacity of the motor-car industry. Arrangements were made for Austin, Rover, Humber, Standard and Daimler plants to produce parts for aircraft engines. Other factories started producing propellers and ammunition. The Rootes group factory at Speke, Liverpool, was equipped to produce Blenheims, and the Austin Motor Company in Oxford was adapted for manufacturing Fairey Battles. Rolls-Royce set up shadow factories in Crewe and Glasgow to manufacture Merlin engines, and by 1938 a wide network of subcontractors had come into existence at hundreds of sites around the country.

Spitfire production was ensured by Supermarine's shadow factories at Cosford in Shropshire and Desford in Leicestershire, should its Southampton works be knocked out. The Nuffield Group, which owned Morris Motors, also built the large Castle Bromwich factory, targeted on 13 August. Should — despite such precautions — Hurricane and Spitfire production be obliterated, there was a contingency plan for the rapid mass production of a basic, nimble eight-gun fighter, the Miles M20, which could be thrown into a last-ditch battle, should all else fail.

The last ditch had not yet been reached, but it had been a frenetic day. The MP "Chips" Channon noted in his diary: "Another big day along the Channel, with many planes down: shall we be invaded tomorrow? As I write, I hear the buzzing of planes on high, and think that London will certainly be raided soon. I feel that at long last we are entering upon a decisive phase of the war."[16] That evening, as both sides assessed the day's damage, it seemed to the Germans that they had destroyed 84 British fighters. The British reckoned they had knocked out 64 German aircraft. The true figures were closer to 47 German losses against 13 British fighters in the air, 3 of whose pilots were killed. The importance of the day lay in the fact that Goering's

Luftwaffe had failed to land anything like the sort of heavy blow on which his plan's success depended.

To the *Reichsmarschall's* frustration, the weather on 14 August was similar to that of the morning before, with thick clouds at 2,000 feet making large-scale operations impossible. Fighter Command had a morning's respite to rotate exhausted squadrons and repair damaged aircraft. No. 238 Squadron, which was one of the hardest-hit during the battle, was withdrawn from the frontline to rest and absorb replacement pilots. Most of its original pilots had been killed or injured. "We'd lost pilots and, of course, aircraft, in a devastating way," said Sergeant Gordon Batt. "I do wonder why I was spared." The next day, together with his commanding officer, he went to visit his friend Eric Seabourne at the naval hospital in Portsmouth, where, badly burned, he was recovering. Batt remembered sitting on Seabourne's bed and asking him how he slept without eyelids.[17] From their new temporary home at St Eval airfield in Cornwall, Eric Bann wrote to his parents: "I am afraid that our duty at the front line has told its tale upon our systems. Our engagements have been really hectic . . . we are all down with nerve trouble and have been sent to this rest camp . . . just Gordon Batt and I remain among the sergeants and many of our officers have gone."[18]

At around noon on 14 August, radar at Dover showed a substantial enemy force building up over Calais. Air Vice-Marshal Park ordered up 42 fighters from Nos 32, 65, 610 and 65 Squadrons. Over Dover they met three *Gruppen* — about 90 aircraft — of

Me109s from *Jagdgeschwader 26* along with 80 Stuka dive-bombers. One *Gruppe* of the Messerschmitts stayed with the Stukas, while the others successfully drew the intercepting British fighters into battle. Because they were operating close to their bases, the Me109s were able to remain in combat for longer than usual, and a huge 200-aircraft dogfight developed. A formation of the Me109s shot down eight of Dover's barrage balloons and Stukas sank the *Goodwin* lightship. Two Me109s were shot down, as well as three Stukas, and the RAF defenders lost seven fighters and two of its pilots.

While Park's forces were occupied, Manston airfield came under attack again from Me110s of the elite *Erprobungsgruppe 210*. They destroyed three Blenheims on the ground, and four hangars took direct hits. One raider was brought down by fire from a Bofors gun manned by aircrew from the Blenheim squadron. Manston's exposed position and proximity to the Luftwaffe bases made it particularly open to attack, and returning German aircraft with bombs still on board were now in the habit of dropping them on this convenient target of opportunity. The extreme vulnerability of the aerodrome created an atmosphere of danger in which death could come without warning, at any time of day.

Eric Clayton, an RAF fitter with No. 56 Squadron, travelled by car to Manston the next morning.

As we neared the airfield we encountered a great cloud of chalk dust; at the station barrier the MP [Military

Policeman] informed us that we had just missed a heavy bombing attack. As we entered the station (incredibly, a public road ran right through it), there was a scene of devastation; wrecked hangars, several damaged Blenheims and the airfield pitted with craters, including recently filled ones.

During this raid, two Bf 110s [Me110s] had been shot down by groundfire, one of which had crashed on to the tarmac apron in front of the hangars. Because of the haze we did not see these at the time. This was an appropriate baptism, for during our stay the airfield was subjected to almost daily attacks, mainly low level dive-bombing by Bf 110s and strafing by Bf 109s [Me109s]. A nerve wracking feature was the existence of a permanent yellow status, because Manston was on the coast and enemy aircraft could rapidly change from attacking coastal shipping to appear over the airfield.

This was reflected by a warning voice over the Tannoy urgently announcing a change in status to red (which meant attack imminent) and almost immediately to purple coinciding with the crump of exploding bombs. There was little time for us to dive for cover into a nearby shelter. It was considerably worse for the unfortunate airmen and soldiers who were detailed to fill in bomb craters immediately after a raid, in order to try and keep the base operational.

It was a lethal activity, for when a red was announced, they had to jump into a lorry and, from the middle of the airfield, hurtle to some distant cover. Inevitably there were casualties. The Hurricane we had come to repair had been pushed into a small Bellman hangar near the main road and on the opposite side of the airfield from the defending fighter squadrons, 32, 65 and 610. We set to work but found we had neglected to bring a particular spare part; we hoped the station stores would have it. Reluctantly, we set out next morning along the main road to reach the stores on the other side of the airfield. We passed an unoccupied gun emplacement from which, we were told, one of the Bf 110s had been shot down.

Shortly, we came upon the crashed aircraft and gingerly approached it. The body of the dead pilot could just be seen through a hole in the fuselage and from the point of impact there was a trail of wreckage and shreds of flesh — a grisly indicator of the air-gunner's dreadful end. Under the wing of the Me110, I noticed the magneto from one of its Daimler-Benz engines; it was quite different from that of the Merlin engine. Out of curiosity, I quite improperly kept it as a souvenir.

In the west, the weather brightened during the afternoon of the 14th, and Sperrle's *Luftflotte 3* began sending out small raiding formations, spread over a front of about 100 miles. Inevitably, some of the bombers got through 10 Group's stretched defences. Shortly before 6p.m., a lone Junkers Ju88 appeared suddenly out of the clouds above Middle Wallop, Dorset. Groundcrew rushed to close the heavy hangar doors to protect the Spitfires inside. But now the Ju88 had gone into its steep bombing dive. At 1,500 feet it released its 500 kg bombs, scoring a direct hit on Hangar No. 5. Three men struggling to close the door were crushed to death as the roof, walls and doors collapsed. A No. 609 Squadron pilot, Eugene "Red" Tobin was nearby:

> My head was spinning, it felt as though I had a permanent ringing in my ears, I felt the blast go over me as I lay there flattened on the ground. I got up and my instinct was to run towards the hangar. It was carnage, I saw one overalled person with his foot and half a leg blown off, another had a great red patch on his chest with a load of mess hanging from it, another was rolling in agony with one of his arms missing."[19]

As the bombs fell, a flight from 609 Squadron struggled to get airborne, dodging explosions and craters on the runway. David Crook recorded that:

> We sat in our aircraft and waited. A few minutes later we heard the unmistakable "ooma-ooma" of a German bomber above the clouds. I immediately signalled to my ground crew to stand by, as I did not intend to sit on the ground and be bombed. I kept my finger on the engine starter button and waited expectantly. Almost immediately the enemy bomber, a Junkers 88, broke out of the cloud to the north of the aerodrome, turned slightly to get on his course and then dived at very high speed towards the hangars. At about 1,500 feet he let go four bombs — we could see them very distinctly as they plunged down, and seconds later

there was an earth-shaking "whoom" and four great clouds of dust arose. All this happened in a matter of seconds only, but by this time, everybody had got their engines started and we all roared helter-skelter across the aerodrome. Why there were no collisions I don't know, but we got safely into the air and turned round to chase the enemy.[20]

A Spitfire on patrol above the airfield shot down the Ju88 as the bomber came out of its dive, but now the squadron encountered a small group of He111s from *Kampfgeschwader 55*. David Crook and John Dundas singled out the leader, and together they destroyed it. When the wreckage was examined later, it was found to contain the bodies of three senior Luftwaffe officers. "They had probably come over to see how the operations against England were progressing," wrote Crook. "I hope they were suitably impressed!"[21]

Another Heinkel group penetrated 10 Group's defences and bombed an airfield at Colerne in Wiltshire. The Luftwaffe had clearly spotted Hurricanes there (which were in fact inoperational while undergoing maintenance) and added Colerne to its target list. Little serious destruction resulted. A further group got as far as Sealand in Cheshire, home of No. 30 Maintenance Unit. The damage was more substantial but it was quickly repaired. On the coast, most of the small German raids were driven back, but Southampton was bombed, and its main railway line was blocked for a while. Bombs also fell on residential areas.

At the end of the day, assured that Middle Wallop was again operational and that Manston would be back in action in 12 hours, Park and Dowding were confident that when the weather improved enough to allow another all-out attack, Fighter Command would be ready.

Eugene "Red" Tobin, who narrowly escaped the Middle Wallop raid with his life, was distinctive in that he was one of a small group of US citizens who, impelled by ideology, chance or adventure, served in Fighter Command during the Battle of Britain. He and two other young aviators — Vernon Keogh and Andrew Mamedoff — had travelled from the United States together to fight the Germans. They started off in Finland, then moved on to France during the *Blitzkrieg* before ending up in 609 Squadron. They later became the first members of No. 71 Squadron, the first "Eagle Squadron" made up of American volunteers. All were subsequently killed in action. The best-known US volunteer, however, was Pilot Officer William "Billy" Fiske, a Cambridge graduate and US Olympic bobsleigh team member, who joined 601 Squadron at Tangmere in July 1940. He crash-landed there on 16 August, following a fight with a Ju87 over Bognor, and died of his wounds the next day. A memorial to him was unveiled in St Paul's Cathedral the following year, engraved with the words "An American Citizen who died that England might live."

The poor weather continued early the following day, 15 August. Goering took the opportunity to summon his

Luftflotte commanders and senior officers to his mansion at Carinhall to discuss the failures of the 13 August attack and to reassess tactics. Those present included Kesselring, Sperrle, General Bruno Lörzer of *Fliegerkorps II*, who had flown with Goering in the previous war, and Generalmajor Joachim Coler of *Fliegerdivision XI*. At the end of the meeting, Goering issued a directive that suggested growing disquiet at the top of the Luftwaffe. It identified Stukas and Me110s as vulnerable. Goering now ordered that three fighter *Gruppen* should accompany every Stuka *Gruppe*, one to go ahead and draw away intercepting fighters, the second to dive alongside the bombers, the third to give cover high above.

This was a highly impractical suggestion. It was not possible for the fighters to maintain the slower pace of the bombers without flying with their flaps down and weaving, which would waste fuel and severely limit their time over the target. Furthermore, the Me109 did not have the Stuka's air brakes, which extended below the wings outboard of the fixed undercarriage and enabled the bomber's steep but slow dive. The twin-engine Me110s, Goering declared, must be used more economically, "only where the range of other fighters is inadequate, or where it is for the purpose of assisting our single-engine aircraft to break off combat". He also ordered that there must be only one officer in any crew flying over Britain — a reflection of the losses of experienced personnel.

Goering judged the attack on radar stations to have been a waste of time, as the stations had been restored to service so swiftly. In other respects, the directive sought to focus the efforts of the Luftwaffe more closely on what Hitler had ordered as the prime goal — the destruction of the RAF. Secondary targets should be chosen more carefully and shipping ignored unless circumstances were exceptionally favourable.

While the discussions continued, the weather in northern France and southern England improved significantly. By 11a.m. there was only a light wind and a clear blue sky — ideal weather for a large attack. The chief of staff of *Fliegerkorps II*, whose massive force of 800 bombers and 1,000 fighters had been scheduled to lead the day's attack, was Oberst (Colonel) Paul Deichmann. Unable to contact his superiors, because Goering had ordered that his meeting with senior officers not be disturbed, Deichmann launched the attack on his own authority. Now the largest German aerial force mustered so far readied for take-off.

A few minutes after 11a.m., radar on the Kent coast picked up the first of the formations over Calais. There were two *Staffeln* of Stukas from *Lehrgeschwader 1*, which were soon joined by another 26 Ju87s from *Sturzkampfgeschwader 1* and dozens of Me109s. As the first wave advanced, a second appeared behind it. Soon there were too many plots on the radar to distinguish between formations as hundreds of German planes took to the air.

At Hawkinge forward airfield, near Folkestone, two squadrons were at readiness. At 11.10a.m., eleven Hurricanes of 501 Squadron were scrambled; eight minutes later, twelve Spitfires of 54 Squadron were sent up. It was good timing for Fighter Command. Fifteen minutes later, the first wave of Ju87s — lavishly protected by Me109s — was overhead. But, thanks to the radar warning, the British fighters were in the air, and with plenty of height to manoeuvre. By this stage of the battle, the division of labour was well established. The Hurricanes pursued the bombers, while the Spitfires took on their high-flying escorts. Two Spitfires were shot down engaging the top cover. Then, to protect the now dive-bombing Stukas, the Me109s swooped on the Hurricanes.

Pilot John Gibson of 501 Squadron had shot down a Stuka and damaged another one before he felt the sickening jolt of Me109 cannon-fire hitting his aircraft. As he went through the familiar preparations to bale out — he had been shot down twice before — he realized that his Hurricane was heading directly for a built-up area of Folkestone. Steering his stricken fighter towards the sea, he baled out at just 1,000 feet. Still over land, he had the presence of mind to take off his new shoes as he descended, dropping them in a field before his parachute followed his aircraft into the Channel. "I had a brand-new pair of shoes handmade at Duke Street in London. We used to fly in a jacket, collar and tie, because we were gentlemen," he later laughed. "I thought I was going to get these shoes wet in the Channel so I took them off while I was still in the parachute."[22] On his return to Hawkinge, Gibson was awarded the Distinguished Flying Cross (DFC), but he was also reunited with his precious shoes, sent in by a farmer on the off-chance that they belonged to one of the local pilots.

Mrs Joanna Thompson, a Kent housewife, witnessed the aerial dramas unfold from her garden:

> The sound was unthinkable, you never heard anything like it, and there, out of the sky planes were falling blazing to the ground, parachutes with little men hanging helplessly underneath drifted towards earth, even flying boots and pieces of aircraft came down hitting the tin shelter with a terrific thud. I think it was now that this war was so close to home, that we suddenly became proud of these pilots, men and young men, who we didn't even know, yet we cheered them on in every dogfight that we saw.

While the British fighters struggled with hugely superior numbers of Me109s, Stukas had succeeded in diving on Hawkinge to drop fifteen 250 kg and 50 kg fragmentation bombs on the airfield. Direct hits destroyed a hangar and pulverized one end of a barrack block. But the intention had been to destroy fighters on the ground, and the early warning meant that the targets were already airborne.

Meanwhile, other parts of the giant formation had wheeled away to pound nearby Lympne once more. Unopposed by British fighters, Ju87s battered the base's infrastructure. Both Hawkinge and Lympne would be out of action for several crucial days.

As the decisions reached at Carinhall had yet to be communicated to the Luftwaffe units, radar targets had been included in their orders. A group of Stukas from the Hawkinge raid peeled away, still carrying their bombs, to strike at the Chain Home Low station at Foreness and the Chain Home High stations at Dover and Rye. This time, the Germans had more luck: bombs falling outside the compounds cut power to all three, putting them out of action for the rest of the day. The destruction increased the already heavy burden on the shoulders of the Observer Corps.

The consequent radar blind spot meant that a midday raid by Me110s of *Zerstörergeschwader 76* arrived over hard-pressed Manston unopposed. Fortunately, No. 54 Squadron had just taken off again, after refuelling; but two Spitfires from 66 Squadron were destroyed on the ground and sixteen groundcrew were killed as the twin-engine fighters strafed the base with cannon and machine-gun fire.

As the raids in the south progressed, at the opposite end of the country the Luftwaffe made its boldest move of the day. After Norway had fallen, Dowding knew his northern flank was vulnerable. The Germans were convinced that northern Britain had been stripped of fighter defences to feed the heavy combat in the south. Fighter Command forces were indeed spread thinly, and many of the squadrons were unblooded, but Dowding also had a couple of battle-tested fighter squadrons "resting" in Air Vice-Marshal Richard Saul's 13 Group.

The attack on what the Luftwaffe imagined was a vulnerable point got underway at 9.30a.m., when a *Staffel* of Heinkel He115 seaplanes took off from their base in Norway and set course across the North Sea towards Dundee. The move was designed to lure defending fighters away to the north, while the main attack hit airfields at Usworth, near Newcastle, and Dishforth, north of Leeds. Half an hour later, 72 He111s of *Kampfgeschwader 26*, each loaded with 3,000 pounds of bombs, left their bases at Stavanger and Sola. They were joined 20 minutes later by 21 Me110 heavy fighters of *Zerstörergeschwader 76* as their escort. The long distances involved meant the mission was beyond the range of the single-engine Me109s of *Luftflotte 5*. The Messerschmitt Me110s carried long-range fuel tanks, with some stripped of their rear gunners to lessen the load and reduce fuel consumption.

Richard Saul

Richard Saul (1891–1965) commanded 13 Group during the Battle of Britain, where he was responsible for 200-odd aircraft and the sector stations defending the north of England, Scotland and the strategically important base at Scapa Flow.

During the First World War Saul had served in the Royal Flying Corps as an Observer and was awarded the Distinguished Flying Cross (DFC). He spent part of the 1920s and 1930s stationed in Iraq, and by 1933 he was commanding 203 Squadron. He was an exceptional sportsman, and during the 1920s he represented the RAF at rugby and hockey; he also won the RAF tennis championship twice (1928 and 1932). Saul was a fine organizer, and during the 1930s he helped devise the structure of Fighter Command. He was Senior Air Staff Officer at Fighter Command HQ before eventually becoming the commander of No. 13 Group in July 1939, with his headquarters at Newcastle.

Saul moved on to command 12 Group in December 1940; two years later he was in charge of air defences in the eastern Mediterranean. His RAF retirement came in 1944. But later his organizational abilities were put at the service of the United Nations Relief and Rehabilitation Administration (UNRRA), attempting to ensure effective relief supplies in the former Axis-occupied Balkans. After the war, he served for a time as Vice-Chairman of the International Transport Commission, based in Rome, before moving to Canada in the 1950s, where he took up a rather different occupation — managing a university bookshop.

The "decoy" He115 seaplanes did their job well, appearing on the Anstruther Chain Home High radar shortly after midday, heading for the Firth of Forth before turning back some 40 miles from the Scottish coast. But from then on, the plan started to unravel with disastrous consequences for the Germans. Because of a navigational error, the He111 and Me110 formation — minus nine Heinkels that had turned back with mechanical trouble — found itself also heading for the Firth of Forth only a few miles south of the diversionary thrust. The ruse had backfired.

Realizing their mistake, the bombers turned south, but this took them directly into the path of eleven Spitfires from No. 72 Squadron, scrambled from Acklington, Northumberland, and now heading north. The squadron, veterans of France and Dunkirk, made contact off the Farne Islands to find they were facing not thirty raiders, as had been reported, but over a hundred. "None of us had ever seen so many aircraft in the sky at one time," said Pilot Officer Robert Elliott. But the Spitfires had been given plenty of time to gain height, and now found themselves 3,000 feet above the enemy formation. Wheeling to the seaward side of the Germans, they dived down out of the sun. "There was a gap between the lines of bombers and the Me110s coming up in the rear, so in there we went," wrote Elliott. "I do not think they saw us to begin with. When they did, the number of bombs rapidly jettisoned was fantastic. You could see them falling away from the aircraft and dropping into the sea, literally by the hundreds. The formation became a shambles."[23]

In the first attack, two Me110s and one bomber were hit, generating panic. Some of the Me110s formed a defensive circle, others dived low and headed for home. No. 72 Squadron fought for five minutes, and then, just north of Blyth, its place was taken by the Hurricanes of No. 605 Squadron, scrambled from Drem, southeast of Edinburgh, at 12.25p.m. The Luftwaffe lost four more bombers shot down and then, as the formation approached Newcastle, it was attacked by No. 41 Squadron from Catterick and No. 79 from Acklington, the latter, like No. 72 Squadron, an experienced unit.

Pilot Officer E. A. Shipman, of No. 41 Squadron, was one of those in action. He made a confirmed "kill":

We were ordered to attack Me110 fighters escorting He111s at 18,000ft in the Durham area. Leading Green Section, I attacked the section of Me110s on the left of the formation, but before getting into range my target turned about and offered a brief opportunity to fire a two-second burst, without result. I then picked another target and managed to get in a series of deflection shots while the enemy aircraft was evading quite violently. Finally at 200 yards range I put the starboard engine out of action. The 110 made an erratic turn to port, emitting clouds of smoke, and disappeared into the cloud below, apparently out of control. This was the only occasion when my camera gun worked and the film clearly showed all that had happened, confirming my claim.[24]

By 12.45p.m., almost all the Messerschmitts and many of the Heinkels had retreated across the North Sea. A few pressed on, scattering bombs in the Newcastle area. Several Heinkels did not survive the long journey back to their Scandinavian bases. Eight bombers and seven Me110s had been shot down, for the loss of only one British aircraft.

★ ★ ★

The same morning *Luftflotte 5* mounted another, even riskier, attack. Around 50 Junkers Ju88 bombers from *Kampfgeschwader 30* in Denmark set off to bomb fighter airfields at Church Fenton and Leconfield in Yorkshire. They were unaccompanied by escorts, relying instead on speed, surprise and the belief that there would be few fighters around to oppose them.

Shortly after 1p.m., the raid was plotted approaching Staxton Wold radar station, overlooking the North Yorkshire coast, from the northeast. The commander of 12 Group, Air Vice-Marshal Trafford Leigh-Mallory, scrambled elements of four squadrons, but it was No. 616 and a flight of No. 73 that made the interception as the Ju88s crossed the coast at Flamborough Head. Six bombers were shot down straight away, but the rest pressed on, swinging south to attack the airfield at Driffield. They dropped 169 bombs, which destroyed four hangars. Six RAF personnel were killed and a further twenty wounded. Ten aircraft were destroyed on the ground, but they were Whitley bombers rather than the all-important Hurricanes and Spitfires. Apart from a hit on an ammunition dump at Bridlington, the raid had no other successes.

Oberleutnant Rudolf Kratz was one of those who flew in *Kampfgeschwader 30*'s unescorted attack. He recorded his heady experience of the raid:

The coast. The initial point. No time left for thinking — there lay England, the lion's den. But the eagles were going to attack the lion in his lair and wound him grievously.

"Fighters to starboard . . ." Three specks overflew us, disappeared to the rear, and after a diving turn, hung behind us. "Your turn now." The words disappeared in the rattle of our machine guns. In short bursts the volleys flew towards the first fighter. He turned away and the second one took his place. This one's fire is ineffective as well and both passed below and were shot at by our ventral gunner. Like hornets they swooshed through our formation, the roundels on their fuselage looking like eyes.

"Five fighters to port above," reported the wireless operator calmly. "Dammit," the pilot said, but did not get agitated. We kept on flying towards our target. Staring before us we tried to locate the airfield amidst the ragged clouds. "There, the field, below us."

The target at last — the fighters were beginning to be a real nuisance. The time had come now. I did not give a single Pfennig [penny] for the life of those below — drop the HEs [high explosives], away with the blessing! The aircraft went into a dive, speed rapidly building up, and the wind roared and howled around us. The hangars grew and grew. They were still standing. The AA guns were firing away at us, but they were too late.

A jolt — the bombs were free, the steel bodies out whistling down. Below all hell was let loose. Like an inferno, steel hit steel, and stones. Bomb upon bomb exploded, destroying and tearing apart what they hit. Hangar walls and roofs crumpled like tin sheets, pieces flying through the air. Aircraft were shattered by a hail of splinters. Barracks tumbled down, enormous smoke and dust clouds rose like mushrooms. Here and there explosions and flames shot up. The airfield and the hangars were already badly hit but bombs kept falling from the bombers that followed us, kept raining down in a horrible shower. Fire from exploding ammunition burst upwards like torches. The English AA artillery had been eliminated, their firing positions turned into craters.

The sun shone into our cabin. The enemy fighters had been got rid of. Below us lay the wide sea. How beautiful the Earth can be. Hands loosened their grip on the machine guns. What happened just a few minutes ago lay behind us and we relaxed. The engines were running evenly, we were flying home. The airfield didn't exist any more; that was the result.[25]

Kratz's sense of elation bore little relation to the tangible results of the two *Luftflotte 5* attacks. The Luftwaffe had lost 20 per cent of the aircraft deployed, with more than 80 aircrew dead or missing. The attack had been a disaster for the air fleet, which would carry out no further major daylight operations.

In the south, the RAF was under more pressure than ever before. During the afternoon, there were so many raids it was almost impossible to establish where they were heading. A *Daily Express* reporter, watching from the coast, wrote that the mass of hostile incoming aircraft was so dense that they appeared "to make an aluminium ceiling to the sky".

At 2.15p.m., Kent and Essex stations of the Chain Home radar network started picking up large concentrations of aircraft over Calais and Belgium. The sheer volume of incoming aircraft and the gaps in the radar cover made it very difficult to get a sense of the shape and size of the attacks. In fact, the raiders were three *Gruppen* of Dorniers from *Kampfgeschwader 3*. They were heading for the north Kent airfields, together with a swarm of escort fighters from bases in the Pas de Calais.

While attention was focused on this huge armada, a lightning raid on the fighter station at Martlesham Heath, Suffolk, was executed by sixteen Me110s and nine Me109s of *Erprobungsgruppe 210*. The formation passed undetected only some 20 miles away from Foreness Chain Home Low radar station, "blinded" in the morning's attacks. Only three pilots of No. 17 Squadron, which had moved to the airfield for the day, managed to get airborne. The attackers' bombs smashed equipment stores and damaged two hangars, the station workshops, the officers' mess, and water and telephone connections, putting the base out of action for two days. Nine Hurricanes from No. 1 Squadron managed to catch the raid, but were set on by the Me109s. The German planes claimed three British fighters shot down, and the raiders escaped unharmed.

Eighty-eight Dorniers, the entire available strength of *Kampfgeschwader 3*, together with 130 Me109s from *Jagdgeschwader 51, 52* and *54*, approached the coast at

Deal at 3.30p.m. At the same time, a further 60 Me109s from *Jagdgeschwader 26* crossed the Kent coast either side of Dover. No. 11 Group could counter at first with only 12 Hurricanes of Nos 111 and 151 squadrons apiece and 12 Spitfires of 64 Squadron. Four more squadrons quickly scrambled: Nos 1, 17, 32 and 501. The Dorniers proceeded almost unmolested as far as Faversham, Kent, where they split, one group heading for Rochester, the other towards Eastchurch.

At Rochester, nearly 300 bombs fell, destroying hangars, workshops, storage sheds and six Sterling bombers under construction at the nearby Short Brothers factory. Eastchurch also received a battering. While 11 Group's fighters were tied up in a huge mêlée with Me109s, further raids hit Maidstone, Hawkinge airfield, Dover, Rye and the radar station (again) at Foreness.

In the west, Sperrle's *Luftflotte 3* forces were also on the move. At about 5.20p.m., a force of some 60 Ju88s of *Lehrgeschwader 1* and 40 Messerschmitt Me110s of *Zerstörergeschwader 2* was intercepted by 43 Squadron southeast of the Isle of Wight. As the formation proceeded over Southampton and the Solent, three more squadrons — 249, 601 and 609 — tried to drive it back, but the Ju88s broke through, with half of them heading for Middle Wallop and the other half for Worthy Down, near Winchester. However, little damage was done in either place and the raiders suffered heavily, with 601 Squadron downing four of the bombers.

David Crook was one of the 609 Squadron pilots in action when his efforts took an unexpected turn:

We got off the ground only a few minutes before they arrived at the aerodrome, and were unable to intercept them, or even to see them until they were practically over the aerodrome [Middle Wallop] as they [Ju88s] dived out of the sun, dropped their bombs, and then streamed back towards the coast as hard as they could go. But we were attacking them the whole time and shot down at least five . . . There was a Blenheim fighter squadron stationed with us; they are not fast enough for day fighting but are used a lot for night work. Incidentally, they are twin-engined machines and very similar in appearance to the Junkers 88. One of these Blenheims happened to be doing some practice flying near the aerodrome when the attack started, and in a fit of rather misguided valour he fastened himself on to the German formation as it ran for the coast and started attacking the rear machines. We were rapidly overhauling the German formation, and when I was in range I opened fire at the nearest machine, which happened to be the Blenheim. Quite naturally, it never occurred to me that it could be anything else but a Ju 88. I hit both engines and the fuselage, and he fell away to the right with one engine smoking furiously. I saw him sliding down and noticed a gun turret on the fuselage which rather shook me, as I knew the Ju 88 did not have this. Fortunately the pilot had been saved by the armour plating behind him, and he managed to make a crash landing on the aerodrome and was quite

O.K., though the Blenheim was full of bullet holes and looked rather like a kitchen sieve. The rear gunner was not quite so lucky, for he got a bullet through his bottom which doubtless caused him considerable discomfort and annoyance, but was not serious. Nothing was said about this mistake . . . [26]

Fighter Command's 10 Group was now thinly stretched, and when a heavily escorted raid of Ju87s from *Sturzkampfgeschwader 1* threatened Portland, Air Vice-Marshal Brand had to call on two Hurricane squadrons — Nos 87 and 213 — from Exeter to intercept. They met the enemy aircraft well south of Portland, but, seeing that the formation contained around 60 Me109s and 20 Me110s, as well as 40 Stukas, they called for reinforcements. The Spitfires of 234 Squadron went in, and while they engaged the German fighters, the Hurricanes attempted to down the slower Stukas and Me110s. Several enemy planes were destroyed, but, outnumbered five to one, the British fighters suffered, too.

On the same day, the progress of the raids was followed by Winston Churchill during a visit to Fighter Command Headquarters at Bentley Priory. Guided by Dowding, he watched the huge map board below them in the operations room showing squadrons in action, refuelling and rearming and then taking off again. Dowding's anxieties were soothed by the apparent weakness of the Luftwaffe's intelligence picture, which led it to waste its efforts on bomber bases that were irrelevant to the survival of its real target, Fighter Command.

But the Luftwaffe had not yet finished for the day. At about 6.20p.m., while free chases of Me109s from *Jagdgeschwader 26* distracted the radar stations still in operation, a formation of Dorniers crossed the southeast coast unchecked. To the north of this formation, *Erprobungsgruppe 210* was in action again, with 15 Me110s and 8 Me109s. This time the targets were Biggin Hill and Kenley, two vital 11 Group sector stations guarding the skies around London. Unlike the establishments at Bentley Priory and Uxbridge, the control rooms for the sector stations were housed in flimsy buildings above ground. A direct hit on one could paralyse the whole sector. From Biggin Hill, Nos 610 and 32 Squadrons were scrambled and met the Dorniers about ten miles southeast of the airfield. Two of the bombers were shot down, but then the British fighters became embroiled in the escort and the Dorniers ploughed on. This time, however, they missed their target, bombing West Malling aerodrome instead, a base not yet fully operational.

Meanwhile, *Erprobungsgruppe 210*, having failed to rendezvous with an escort of Me109s as planned, pressed on towards Kenley, taking a roundabout route in the hope of fooling the defences and hitting the airfield from the north. Suddenly, a gap in the clouds showed an airfield below and they dived to attack. Their bombing was fearsomely accurate, smashing into buildings and wrecking the airfield. Some bombs overshot the base, hitting three small factories, where workers were just starting the night shift. No air-raid warning had sounded: 62 people were killed and a further 172 were injured. But again the Luftwaffe had missed its primary target. It was Croydon, rather than the much more important Kenley, that lay charred and smoking. Furthermore, Croydon, unlike Kenley, was within the boundaries of Greater London, which Hitler had ordered should not be bombed. Pilot Officer Ronald Brown, of 111 Squadron, remembered of the Croydon raid that:

> . . . they killed the old squadron pet. He was a Staffordshire bull terrier called Butcher. He was badly injured and we couldn't get him out from under the stonework. I'll always remember Johnnie Walker, a Canadian, had the unfortunate job of crawling underneath and shooting him to put him out of his misery. There were also two or three chaps killed and a young telephonist who was lying there with half her head blown off.[27]

As the Messerschmitt Me110s turned for home, they were intercepted by No. 111 Squadron, which had scrambled from Croydon just in time to avoid destruction. The pilots now took revenge, shooting down four of the Experimental Group's Me110s, including that of the formation leader, Hauptmann Walter Rubensdörffer, who was killed. A further three Messerschmitts fell to No. 32 Squadron.

At 7.30p.m., a raid on Dover was driven back by 54 Squadron: it was the final action of what had been the most momentous day yet of the Battle of Britain. The Luftwaffe had flown over 2,000 sorties, as compared to Fighter Command's 974. At one point, the sheer weight of the onslaught had forced Dowding to put 130 fighters in the air at the same time, multiplying the risk to his precious assets and magnifying the chances of a catastrophic loss that would prise open Britain's air defences. As it was, 11 Group just about held its own, with every pilot either in combat or at readiness or standby, waiting in their cockpits or next to their aircraft for the scramble call that would throw them back into combat.

The Luftwaffe had caused considerable damage, although in many cases the targets hit were irrelevant to the crucial work of crushing Fighter Command. The German air force had also, on occasions during the day, shown considerable tactical skill, using feint attacks and altering direction to confuse the defenders. But often the complicated procedures had broken down, and fighter escorts had missed meeting their charges or been forced to turn back through lack of fuel. The effort had also cost them dearly. Seventy-five German aircraft had been shot down — and 15 August became known in the Luftwaffe as *der schwarze Donnerstag* ("Black Thursday"). Fighter Command had lost 30 aircraft, with 17 pilots killed. The day had been an epic effort. Prime Minister Winston Churchill, leaving Dowding's HQ that evening, was moved to describe it as "one of the greatest days in history".

★   ★   ★

Given the previous day's disasters, the Luftwaffe showed extraordinary resilience when it returned to the attack on Friday 16 August. At 10.45a.m., after the early mist had cleared, the defenders tracked three small raids approaching Kent from the south and east. Believing it to be a feint, Park committed only limited forces, of which even fewer managed to intercept. Two *Staffeln* of the attacking Dorniers broke through and dropped almost 80 bombs on West Malling aerodrome, where personnel had been busy repairing the damage of the day before. This time the airfield was put out of action for four days.

Shortly before noon, radar showed three large formations heading for the southeast. This time Park sent up 86 fighters to intercept. A formation of 24 Dorniers of *Kampfgeschwader 2*, together with Me109s in escort, were heading up the Thames Estuary apparently on the way to attack Hornchurch. At 12.25p.m., nine Spitfires of No. 54 Squadron descended on the bombers and forced them to turn back. The British fighters were joined by two more squadrons, which harassed the bombers as they headed back across Kent.

For Heinz Möllenbrook, piloting a Do17-Z of *Gruppe 3*, luck ran out when at 12.22p.m. he was shot down over Kent:

On our return flight I was in the last wave of three aircraft. We were attacked a number of times. On the first attack the plane to the left of us was hit and veered off past us. We got hit in an engine so were flying on just one. Soon we were on our own. Keeping the plane in trim was taking up all my concentration. During the second and third attacks my radio operator and mechanic were both wounded. On the fourth attack my right arm was shattered but I was still able to fly the plane. Then a Hurricane [piloted by John Thompson of 111 Squadron] attacked us from the front . . . The frontal attack wounded my left shoulder and probably also damaged our steering. The steering column fell from my hand. I baled out with my observer who thought the other two, already badly wounded, were both out of the plane. They were subsequently found dead. I don't know how they got out. We too, however, were in grave danger. The plane was spiralling down and we were caught in its centrifugal force. The observer, in extreme panic, let out the oxygen from his life-jacket kit and it caught fire. Then, suddenly there was peace.

Anyway I was lucky. My legs had been shot up but I was caught up with my parachute in a tree hanging fifty centimetres above the ground.

Möllenbrook was freed from the tree by two farm workers. "Then they took me into their kitchen and the grandmother bound my arm, and by doing so saved it. She gave me a whisky, or perhaps two, against the pain."[28]

To the west, 150 enemy aircraft had crossed the coast between Brighton and Folkestone. While 30 Spitfires from Nos 64, 65 and 266 Squadrons engaged the escorting Me109 fighters, 21 Hurricanes of Nos

111 and 32 Squadrons attacked the bombers head on. During the engagement, Flying Officer Henry Ferriss from 111 Squadron collided with a Dornier and was killed. Another casualty was 266's new squadron leader, Rodney Wilkinson. "I shan't forget his engaging charm, his curious shuffle and infectious gaiety," wrote MP "Chips" Channon in his diary two days later. "He had a natural elegance, but seemed fated to die: indeed, he always said so . . . He was typical of the type which is serving and saving England and there will be many aching hearts when the news of his death comes out."[29]

Some of the bombers turned for home, but others split up into smaller formations and spread out to the north and northwest. Bombs were dropped at Farnborough and over the South London suburbs and the London docks, causing 66 civilian deaths.

The third German formation, consisting of more than 100 aircraft from the Cherbourg area, appeared to be heading for Portsmouth or Southampton. At 1p.m., on a signal from the lead aircraft, the formation split into four, with the largest group heading directly for the sector station at Tangmere. Two squadrons from the base had been scrambled as well as six others from airfields to the west, but they were unable to prevent the Stukas from carrying out a textbook dive-bombing attack. Explosives fell on the quarters, the workshops and the cookhouse. In a quarter of an hour, every hangar was damaged. Seventeen planes had been caught on the ground and wrecked, including all four of the new radar-equipped night-fighting Blenheims and seven Hurricanes under repair. Fourteen service-men and six civilians were killed.

When the survivors at Tangmere emerged from the shelters, they were greeted by the macabre sight of a body hanging from a tree. Only the operations room had survived untouched; everywhere else was shattered by bombs, and the runways were heavily cratered. Anne Lowe, a WAAF, survived the raid, as did her sister, who was asleep after a night shift:

> The sinister sound of the air-raid warning started and loudspeakers over the airfield said, "Take cover, take cover, Stukas sighted over Selsey coming towards Tangmere, take cover, take cover." The warning got louder and louder and then you could hear the approaching aircraft.
>
> I rushed to her [her sister's] quarters, hauled her out of bed and began to run with her. She could run faster than me and she got ahead. The next thing, they were coming down — phrommmmm. Then the first bomb fell nearby and I was flung about thirty feet in the air, coming down with my stomach on a brick. But I staggered on into the trenches.

Meanwhile, a small group of Ju87s had swung to the west and now descended on Ventnor radar station on the Isle of Wight, restored since the attack of 12 August. Twenty-two bombs landed on target, putting the station out of action until 23 September. The Luftwaffe seemed to have forgotten or ignored

Goering's directive that bombing radar stations was a waste of time.

Other elements of the formation attacked the anti-aircraft defences of Portsmouth harbour, while Ju88s and Me110s struck at the naval establishments of Gosport and Lee-on-Solent, where six naval aircraft were destroyed and three hangars damaged. The Gosport raid was sighted by three patrolling Hurricanes from 249 Squadron, only recently moved down from the north. It was Flight Lieutenant James Nicolson's first combat. Leading his section against a pair of Ju88s, Nicolson was hit from behind by the powerful forward guns of an Me110 and wounded:

The first shell tore through the hood over my cockpit and sent splinters into my left eye. One splinter, I discovered later, nearly severed my eyelid. I couldn't see through that eye for blood. The second cannon shell struck my spare petrol tank and set it on fire. The third shell crashed into the cockpit and tore off my right trouser leg. The fourth shell struck the back of my left shoe. It shattered the heel of the shoe and made quite a mess of my left foot. I was just thinking of jumping out when suddenly a Messerschmitt 110 whizzed under me and got right in my gun-sight . . . I pressed the gun button for the Messerschmitt was in nice range; I plugged him first time and could see my tracer bullets entering the German machine.[30]

Nicolson, ignoring his pain, the smoke and extreme heat, and with his instrument panel "dripping like

269

treacle", shot down the Me110. The next moment, he dived head first out of his cockpit. Blinded in his left eye by blood and with his hands terribly burned, he fell 500 feet before he succeeded in pulling his ripcord. As he drifted down, he then came under fire from members of the Home Guard on the ground, who shot him in the buttocks. Three months later, having recovered from his wounds, Nicolson was awarded the only Victoria Cross earned by a fighter pilot during the battle.

There were more raids during the late afternoon, preceded by German fighter sweeps designed to drag the exhausted Fighter Command pilots into the air, so that they would be back refuelling when the bombers arrived. One sweep descended on Manston, strafing the airfield buildings and destroying a Spitfire and a Blenheim on the ground. Meanwhile, Nos 1, 610 and 615 Squadrons engaged a formation of Heinkel He111 bombers, escorted by Me110s, over the Sussex — Surrey border. Hurricanes of Nos 32, 56 and 501 Squadrons took on another enemy raid, which appeared to be heading for Biggin Hill, successfully driving it back, while Spitfires from 610 Squadron engaged the fighter escort.

Following their visit to Bentley Priory the previous day, Churchill and his chief of staff, Hastings Ismay, were now at 11 Group's headquarters at Uxbridge. Smoking was strictly forbidden in the Group's underground operations room, but an exception was made for the prime minister's ever-present cigar. "There had been heavy fighting throughout the afternoon," Ismay later wrote. "At one moment every single squadron in the Group was engaged; there was nothing in reserve, and the map table showed new waves of attackers crossing the coast. I felt sick with fear."

Fighter Command was now fighting on a front from Harwich to Portsmouth, and it was inevitable that some bombers would get through. Two Ju88s penetrated all the way to Brize Norton airfield in Oxfordshire. Approaching the runway, they lowered their landing gear in the hope that they would be mistaken for Blenheims. The ruse worked, and as they crossed the perimeter the wheels went up and 32 bombs were released. Inside one of the hangars was a large number of fuelled-up aircraft. A bomb set off an enormous explosion, destroying 46 planes, the majority of them training aircraft, but also including 11 Hurricanes undergoing repairs.

As on the previous day, the Luftwaffe's target had been planes on the ground, and as before there had been much effort wasted on attacking non-Fighter Command airfields. But the strain of opposing them had been exhausting and costly. Many of the RAF pilots flew four or five combat sorties, and 20 aircraft were shot down.

At the end of the day, Churchill, still at Uxbridge, was told that a hundred of the enemy had been shot down, though the real figure was nearer fifty. The inaccuracy was inevitable in the swirling confusion of aerial combat. Churchill was once again deeply impressed by what he had seen. The experience seems to have inspired perhaps his most famous phrase. "As evening closed in and the fighting died down," wrote Ismay, "we left for Chequers. Churchill's first words were, 'Don't speak to me; I have never been so moved.' After about five minutes he leaned forward and said, 'Never in the field of human conflict has so much been owed by so many to so few.' The words burned into my brain."[31]

Saturday 17 August at last brought some relief, both for defenders and attackers. The sky was so empty of raiders that some radar operators thought that their equipment had malfunctioned. At Biggin Hill, No. 32 Squadron's pilots caught their breath, having spent the last two days at almost constant readiness, dossing down under the wings of their aircraft. "Not a single sausage, scare, flap or diversion of any description today. Amazing. Heavenly day too," wrote Squadron Leader Michael Crossley in the unit's unofficial diary.

The day's lull was a sign that the Luftwaffe, too, was desperate for a respite. Pilots were nearing exhaustion, and aircraft had to be repaired and patched up, a process that often involved sending the machine on a train or lorry all the way back to the Reich.

In England the work of fixing the damage of the day before continued. At Tangmere, shot-down German airmen were pressed into helping fill the airfield's numerous craters, often by hand as no bulldozers were available. Electricity supplies, crucial to the base's communications, were quickly restored; water and accommodation took longer — latrines now consisted of a plank over a ditch, and WAAFs had to sleep on benches at nearby Goodwood racetrack.

Fighter Command had lost 78 pilots killed in the last eight days, with a further 27 badly wounded. The majority of them were experienced men. Since 1 August only 70 new pilots had joined Fighter Command, many of them greenhorns, fresh from the accelerated courses that the operational training units were now having to run. Dowding was forced to fill the gaps with volunteers from Bomber and Coastal Command, the units that would be needed to repel any invasion. There was no other choice. Everything was being gambled on the survival of Fighter Command.

As the summer dusk fell, though, everyone felt thankful for a day of relative quiet. The lull would only be fleeting. The Luftwaffe was licking its wounds, but it was also gathering its strength for the next great effort. The following days were to be among the most desperate of the battle.

CHAPTER
SEVEN

Hardest Days

18 August to 6 September 1940

Fighter Command was now engaged in a desperate fight to survive as a serious deterrent force. Sunday 18 August would become known in Battle of Britain legend as "The Hardest Day". That morning the Luftwaffe had at its disposal 276 Junkers Ju87 Stukas; 768 twin-engine Heinkel He111, Dornier Do17 and Junkers Ju88 bombers; 194 Messerschmitt Me110s; and 745 Messerschmitt Me109s, as well as reconnaissance aircraft. Against them, Fighter Command could muster 419 Hurricanes and 211 Spitfires, as well as small numbers of the much less effective and now obsolescent Blenheim, Gladiator and Defiant fighters. The single-engine fighter forces were fairly evenly balanced. However, Fighter Command had the double task of shooting down bombers and fighting off their escorts. The German fighter pilots could concentrate on the single task of destroying their counterparts. The defenders had to cover a large number of potential targets. More than ever, it was vital that the RAF fighters were in the right place at the right time, and at the right height.

There was mist on the Channel as the first, by now routine, German reconnaissance aircraft appeared high over the south coast, tracking the movement of aircraft to the RAF's forward bases. By noon it was clear that the day was going to be a dramatic one. High-level radar around Dover reported the largest build-up yet of enemy aircraft, and every 11 Group fighter was brought to readiness. No. 501 Squadron, already in the air, was now ordered to patrol above Canterbury. Four more squadrons were sent to cover the line between Canterbury and Margate to protect the docks, the Thames Estuary and Gravesend and Hornchurch airfields. A further four squadrons, numbering twenty-three Spitfires and twenty-seven Hurricanes, were ordered to guard Kenley and Biggin Hill.

Before the Hurricanes of 501 Squadron could engage any enemy aircraft, they were ambushed by a high-altitude fighter sweep of Me109s from *Jagdgeschwader 26*, led by Major Gerhard Schöpfel, which shot down four Hurricanes within moments over Canterbury. Schöpfel himself sent Pilot Officer John Bland down in flames to his death:

> Suddenly I found a squadron of Hurricanes below me in the usual British formation of tight threes, which were climbing in a spiral. I circled about 3,300ft above them. Then I saw a pair of Hurricanes weaving behind the formation, on guard against attack from astern. I

waited until they were curving north-westwards from Folkestone, then attacked out of the sun and below.

Schöpfel claimed that he shot down both weavers without the main body of the squadron realizing.

Now I was beneath a third machine. I fired a short burst. This aircraft likewise fell apart. The British flew on, having noticed nothing. I positioned myself under a fourth machine. This time I had to get closer. When I pressed the firing button the Hurricane was so close to me that fragments from it hit my aircraft. Oil covered my cockpit so thickly that I couldn't see, and after two minutes of action had to break off. After I had broken off, Oberleutnant Sprick led No. 8 *Staffel* in an attack on the British, who were now aware that Germans were right behind them and dived. However, Sprick managed to shoot down two more. I think this was the first time in this war that a pilot shot down four British aircraft on the same sortie. Looking back at those anxious moments, it was not very difficult. My shots must have hit the right place, so that there was no time for the others to be warned.[1]

Two other Fighter Command pilots were badly wounded in the encounter, and one escaped unharmed. Meanwhile, some of the bombers were approaching their targets.

First on the target list was Kenley. Kesselring's plan was that high-level bombers, in two waves, would pound the airfield, and then a low-level attack by nine

Dorniers of *Kampfgeschwader 76* would deliver the *coup de grâce*. The latter crossed the Channel at only 100 feet, avoiding high-level fighters and radar detection. They then raced northwards, following railway lines and hugging the valleys.

Betty McNabb was taking a cliff walk near Beachy Head when the Dorniers crossed the coast. She remembered that:

> It had been a beautiful morning, peaceful and quiet, and as we strolled enjoying the tranquillity of the morning, we both spoke and agreed that it was a shame that there had to be a war on, on such a tremendous day as this. I can remember the gentle breeze, so gentle it hardly rustled the leaves on the trees, and all the birds seemed to be singing quite oblivious to our presence, when suddenly we heard a heavy rumbling sound, almost the sound of a strong wind coming towards us. We could see nothing, but the sound got louder it was so strange.
>
> Then suddenly, and it gave us both a fright really, these huge dark shapes appeared over the cliffs almost as if they had come right out of the sea. The noise was now deafening as what must have been six or seven huge bombers disappeared as soon as they had appeared and all was peaceful again. My God it was scary.[2]

On their approach, the Dorniers flashed through Burgess Hill in Sussex, strafing as they went, at alarmingly low altitude. From the third floor of a hospital in the Luftwaffe's path, a bewildered patient found himself looking directly into the cockpit of the leading bomber.

The German crews had been briefed to expect a mass of smoke at the target following the earlier high-level bombing. But they arrived over a peaceful, intact Kenley, for the high-level bombers had been delayed by heavy cloud over their airfields in France. As they released their bombs, the Dorniers came under fire from the airfield's anti-aircraft guns, which succeeded in bringing down the German commander, Oberleutnant Rudolf Lamberty. Coming down in a field near the airfield, he struggled free of his burning cockpit to face a troop of Home Guard, guns pointed. Lamberty raised his hands in surrender, and when the Home Guarders saw burned shreds of flesh falling from them, they lowered their rifles.

In the later stages of the Battle of Britain, when the Blitz was wrecking London, some German airmen who parachuted onto English soil were handled roughly. But for the most part, those Luftwaffe personnel who escaped alive from their aircraft were treated humanely. Christabel Leighton-Porter, who modelled for the *Daily Mirror* cartoon character Jane, was in Lyme Regis, Dorset, when there was a raid over the sea. "They shot down a German plane and I remember all the people on the beach getting in a circle and then a boat brought in the Germans that had baled out. Everybody was shouting. Even the little kiddies were encouraged to join in and boo. But when the Germans got out of the boat, people saw that these were very frightened young blond boys and everybody went very quiet."[3]

For most people, such an episode was the first time they had seen a real German. A. G. Street, a Home Guarder, chased through the Wiltshire countryside trying to find an enemy airman who had been seen baling out. When captured, "he seemed a very ordinary, decent-looking lad," Street commented. "As I was driving home, I realized that I, a civilian, had just experienced my first taste of war, and that I disliked it intensely. I was dead keen to hunt that fellow, felt the same exhilaration as I did when hounds were running, and would have shot him on the instant if need be. But, somehow, when he was caught I had no further quarrel with him."[4]

For Lamberty, danger was not quite over. Moments after his capture, another wave of German raiders arrived and the British and Germans together threw themselves to the ground. Then he was led, together with his crew, along a road to the base. On the way they met a group of civilians, to whom Lamberty offered his parachute. In return he asked for help getting his cigarettes out of his pocket as his hands were too burned to function, a request which was granted. From the base he was taken to a hospital where his burns were treated.

Over Kenley, with Nos 111 and 615 Squadrons successfully distracted by the higher-level bombers, the Dorniers' bombs had rippled across the base, destroying all ten hangars, the stores building and six Hurricanes. All communications and electricity and water supplies were cut. One bomb landed directly on a shelter trench, killing twelve and injuring twenty. The returning RAF Kenley squadrons looked down on smoke-hazed devastation. They landed on a strip of ground that threaded between the craters, marked out with white flags. Lillias Barr, a WAAF officer stationed at Kenley, experienced the mayhem:

> Someone called out that the sick quarters had a direct hit, so I sped in that direction. I remember running over the hummocky grass. There were lots of people badly shaken sitting about. The doctor had been killed, and Mary Coulthard, one of the two WAAF sickbay attendants, was badly injured. She had the most enormous cut in her thigh. I had never seen anything like it, she had been thrown on to a steel helmet which had sliced through her leg. She and the other attendant were smiling though, because they had applied a tourniquet which had worked; and I smiled too — I, who under normal circumstances could faint at the sight of someone's cut finger! We tied a label on to her before she was taken to hospital.[5]

Work began immediately to get Kenley operational again using an emergency plan. A new operations room was set up in a disused butcher's shop in nearby Caterham High Street. Restoring all the vital telephone links took more time, however, and it was two hours before 11 Group HQ at Uxbridge was back in contact with all its sector stations.

High-level bombers arrived at Biggin Hill, too, but their bombs dropped to the east of the airfield, doing little damage.

The Luftwaffe attacks now swung westwards. At about 2p.m., four formations were mapped approaching the Isle of Wight. It was the largest Stuka strike yet — though it was fated to be the last. Over a hundred Ju87s — the whole of *Stukageschwader 77* — each with a 550-pound bomb under its fuselage and four 110-pounders under its wings, were heading in a four-pronged formation to attack the airfields at Gosport, Thorney Island and Ford, and Poling radar station. The Luftwaffe's reconnaissance flights had led it to believe that the airfields were used by Fighter Command. In fact, Gosport was primarily a torpedo development unit, Thorney Island was the base of two Coastal Command Blenheim squadrons, and Ford was a naval air station. The bombers were protected by nearly 160 Me109s. "It was a magnificent sight," said one of the Stuka pilots, as the giant formation assembled. "Cherbourg lay in the sunshine below us, with the breakers visible along the coast. The sky had a light blue tint while over the Channel there was a light haze."[6]

When the attackers reached the Isle of Wight, a formation of 22 Stukas peeled away to the west, heading towards Gosport. Before they reached their target, their top cover of Me109s came under attack from the Spitfires of 234 Squadron, which shot down three of them. But the lower-level formation ploughed on to attack Gosport unmolested, and they succeeded in damaging two hangars and wrecking four aircraft.

Near Bognor Regis, Sussex, the formation had split again, with two *Gruppen* heading to the east against Ford and Poling, while one *Gruppe* turned northwest to attack Thorney Island. At Ford, there was no warning for personnel to get to the shelters and an anti-aircraft complement of only six guns. Bombs hit the barracks hut, the hangars and the airfield's fuel storage, killing twenty-eight and wounding a further seventy-five. Fourteen aircraft on the ground were destroyed.

"Jock" Colville, Churchill's assistant private secretary, was observing the action overhead:

We were sitting on the terrace looking towards Thorney Island . . . Suddenly we heard the sound of AA [anti-aircraft] fire and saw puffs of white smoke as the shells burst over Portsmouth. Then to our left, from the direction of Chichester and Tangmere, came the roar of engines, then the noise of machine-gun fire . . . shading our eyes to escape the glare of this August day, we saw not far in front of us about twenty machines engaged in a fight. Soon a German bomber came hurtling towards us with smoke pouring from its tail and we lost sight of it behind the trees . . . Out of the melee came a dive-bomber, hovered like a bird of prey and then sped steeply down on Thorney Island. There were vast explosions as another and another followed, and my attention was diverted from the fight as clouds of smoke rose from the burning hangars of Thorney aerodrome. In all, the battle only lasted about two minutes and then moved seawards, with at least two German aircraft left smouldering on the ground.[7]

At Thorney Island, airfield hangars and a fuel dump were hit, as well as more naval aircraft. The largest force of 31 Stukas now dived down on Poling. Radar operator Avis Parsons was working on a switchboard there, feeding the information from Poling and nearby Truleigh Hill through to the filter room at Fighter Command.

"There was a scream," Parsons recalled later, "as the Stukas dived and then the noise of the explosions was terrific." Parsons continued working for 15 minutes and then the lines went dead. Five minutes later, the Stukas had finished. They had dropped 87 bombs. In "R" Block, where Parsons was working, all the windows were smashed and the doors blown in. Outside, cars were ablaze, huge craters had been gouged everywhere, and chunks of metal from the aerial mast littered the ground.

But the Stukas had suffered as well. At the start of the attack they had been intercepted by Hurricanes of 43 Squadron, which had caught them at their most vulnerable moment, when they were committed to their dives. Five were shot down and another two badly damaged before the high-level escort came to the rescue. The other *Gruppen* now also started to come under fierce RAF attack. While 234 Squadron Spitfires held the Messerschmitt escort from *Jagdgeschwader 27*

283

at bay, fighters from Nos 152, 601 and 602 Squadrons completed the massacre started by 43 Squadron. In all, the British fighters shot down sixteen Stukas, with two crashing on their return to France. A further four were badly damaged.

It was a decisive defeat for the Junkers Ju87, the aircraft that had been the terror of Europe. After 18 August, Stukas would be used no more in the Battle of Britain.

By 5p.m., the aircraft of *Luftflotte 2* had returned, refuelled and rearmed, and were massing again over the Calais area. Radar accurately estimated the formation at about 250 aircraft. The Luftwaffe's aim was now improving, and the targets this time were the important sector stations of Hornchurch — which protected the London docks, the Thames Estuary and the industrial-commercial centres of Dagenham and Tilbury — and North Weald, which backed up Hornchurch as well as protecting the Home Counties.

The German plan was for 52 Heinkels of *Kampfgeschwader 53* to take off first and cross the Essex coast north of Foulness before heading inland to North Weald. Fifteen minutes after the Heinkels, fifty-eight Dorniers of *Kampfgeschwader 2* would take off in the direction of Deal, Kent, so that both attacks would cross the coast at the same time. The Dorniers would then follow the Thames Estuary in the direction of Hornchurch. Both bomber groups were to be protected by 140 Me109s and Me110s.

Air Vice-Marshal Park reacted quickly to the threat to his northern sector stations, ordering 13 squadrons to readiness or into the air. Following an agreement made the previous day, 12 Group put four squadrons in the air to cover the airfields, which meant that 140 fighters were being deployed. Four squadrons — Nos 32, 54, 56 and 72 — were sent forward to engage the enemy before they neared the targets. The 12 Hurricanes of 56 Squadron glimpsed the Heinkel group just off the Essex coast. "We had to go up through a bit of cloud and suddenly we saw them," said Flying Officer Innes Westmacott. "I must say I gulped a bit! It looked an enormous raid."[8]

As a section of the squadron targeted the bombers, the close German escort of Me110s moved to block the attack, desperately accelerating from the 180mph they had been forced to maintain to stay with the Heinkels. At such slow speeds the Me110s were sitting ducks. Five were shot down by 56 Squadron, which also managed to fatally damage one of the He111s. Soon they were joined by No. 54 Squadron Spitfires, which shot down two further Me110s and damaged several more. Now out of ammunition, the two British squadrons peeled away, unharmed, but having failed to turn back the bombers. The Luftwaffe's intentions had been revealed, however, so Park sent up Nos 85, 151, 257 and 310 Squadrons, a total of 61 Hurricanes.

Squadron Leader Peter Townsend led No. 85 into action against the immense incoming formations:

The squadron was flying well together as we entered cloud at ten thousand feet, heading straight towards "a hundred plus". We emerged from clouds

285

somewhere over the Thames Estuary and there advancing towards us was a massive column about a mile and a half high, stepped up wave upon wave. At the base were Ju87s, above them Heinkels, then Dorniers and Ju88s, then a layer of Me110s, and above, at about twenty thousand feet, a swarm of Me109s . . . When they saw the British fighters KG2 [*Kampfgeschwader* 2] closed in tight. This gave them a formidable concentration of fire especially now that they had an extra MG15 on each side . . . As we closed in on the bombers, the Ju87s and Heinkels turned away seawards. A dozen Me110s cut across us and immediately formed a defensive circle. "In we go," I called over the R/T, and a moment later an Me110 had banked clumsily across my bows. In its vain attempt to escape, the machine I was bent on destroying suddenly looked pathetically human. It was an easy shot — too easy. For a few more seconds we milled around with the Me110s. Then down came a little shower of Me109s. Out of the corner of my eye I saw one diving for me, pumping shells. A quick turn toward it shook it off, and it slid by below, then reared up in a wide left hand turn in front of me. It was a fatal move. My Hurricane climbed round easily inside its turn. When I fired the Me109 flicked over and a sudden spurt of white vapour from its belly turned into flame. Down came another. Again a steep turn and I was on its tail. He seemed to know I was there, but he did the wrong thing. He kept on turning. When I fired, bits flew off, the hood came away and then the pilot baled out. He looked incongruous hanging there, a wingless body in the midst of this duel of winged machines.[9]

To the south, 32 and 501 Squadrons clashed with the Dornier formation, but they were hit hard by the escorting Me109s, losing four fighters and failing to deflect the raid. But then, as both formations closed on the airfields, the weather intervened. Thick cloud was now forming and, with the strict order still in place that no bombs should be dropped on London, the Luftwaffe crews had no option but to turn back. As they headed for home, the strong RAF forces near North Weald brought down more of the unwieldy Me110s.

Oberst Josef Priller, a fighter pilot with *Jagdgeschwader 26*, described the difficulty of calculating how long fuel would last, especially given the vagaries of the weather.

It often happened, particularly over the Channel, that the unpredictable weather cooked up some nasty surprise. Fighter aircraft had a relatively short range and sometimes had barely enough fuel left to get them home. In settled weather, one could calculate with reasonable accuracy how much to keep in hand for the return leg, but those conditions seldom prevailed in the operational zone. Sometimes, it would be fair over England, but thickly clouded over France.

A *Gruppe* in our *Geschwader* experienced an example of this one day when tricky weather during the morning enforced an urgent change in the planned operations . . . In the afternoon the sun came out and this *Gruppe* was ordered to take off. It penetrated about thirty or forty miles deep into England, "free hunting", which meant looking for enemy aircraft, and low-level attack. On the way back they found that suddenly the whole French coast had become covered with cloud and fog. No fewer than eleven machines were reported missing. During the course of the evening ten others turned up one at a time. They had had to go separately far inland to look for somewhere to put down. Most of them had eventually found an airfield but one had had to make a belly landing.[10]

After operations concluded on 18 August, British propaganda declared a great victory, claiming it was Fighter Command together with the anti-aircraft batteries that had turned back the early evening raids. The headline in *The Times* the next day read: "Germany's Heaviest Air Defeat", followed by the claim that 140 Luftwaffe planes had been shot down, at least twice the actual number. The *Daily Mirror's* story was headed "140–16: R.A.F.'s Biggest Victory". Fighter Command admitted to just over 20 fighter losses. The real figure, though, was 39, including the 6 Hurricanes destroyed on the ground at Kenley.

The afternoon's action, like that of the morning, had been a blow to the Luftwaffe's resources and morale. By now, the disparity was clear between what the Luftwaffe crews had been told of Britain's fighter defences and what they had themselves seen in the skies over Kent. For once, the RAF put up enough aircraft to make the fighter ratio very nearly one-to-one. "Only a few of us have not yet had to ditch in the Channel with a badly damaged aircraft or a dead engine," said Oberleutnant Hahn of *Gruppe 1, Jagdgeschwader 3.* "Utter exhaustion had set in. For the first time pilots discussed the prospects of posting to a quieter sector."[11]

After the attrition of 18 August, poor weather would limit activity for the next five days, allowing both sides to rest, repair their forces and take stock. At a meeting at his Carinhall estate on 19 August, Goering took out his frustrations on his men. He blamed the fighter pilots for the losses affecting his bomber fleets, and he replaced several commanders with others considered more aggressive. He ordered closer escorting, even though an examination of the statistics would have revealed that it was when the Me109s were engaged in free hunts that they inflicted the most losses. Goering also decreed that the Me110 "Destroyer" would itself now fly with Me109 escorts. The Ju87 "Stuka", it was confirmed, would take no further part in the battle other than in exceptional circumstances. He also decreed his immediate aims:

We have reached the decisive period of the air war against England. The vital task is to turn all means at our disposal to the defeat of the enemy Air Force. Our first aim is the destruction of the enemy's fighters. If they no longer take to the air, we shall attack them on the ground, or force them into battle by directing bomber attacks against targets within the range of our fighters. At the same time, and on a growing scale, we must continue our activities against the ground organisation of the enemy bomber units. Surprise attacks on the enemy aircraft industry must be made by day and by night. Once the enemy Air Force has been annihilated, our attacks will be directed as ordered against other vital targets.[12]

Fighter Command also analysed the heavy fighting of the previous six days. The strength in depth that had been created by pre-war planning was beginning to tell. Supplies of fighters, either new or patched up by the efficient Civilian Repair Organization, were steady. In fact, the numbers available were set to increase. The problem, though, was pilots. Since 8 August, 90 pilots had been killed and another 50 injured badly enough to be *hors de combat*. In the same period, only 65 novices had arrived from the operational training units. It was vital that each squadron retain at least a core of experienced men to provide guidance and leadership. A high proportion of enemy "kills" was achieved by a small number of the most aggressive and skilful pilots.

New orders were given to try and minimize losses. Pilots were discouraged from engaging over the sea, where so many of them had perished after having baled out safely. Sector-station controllers were again urged to avoid combat with free sweeps of Me109s, however glaring the provocation.

Dowding's other great concern was his 11 Group sector stations — Northolt, Tangmere, Kenley, Biggin Hill, Hornchurch, North Weald and Debden. Much effort by the Luftwaffe had been wasted on other, less important, aerodromes, but now these vital nodes of Fighter Command's system were coming under heavy attack.

After a quiet morning on 19 August, a build-up of aircraft was spotted over Calais. Then, for about an hour after midday, about 100 Me109s sped over Dover and the south coast, trying to lure British fighters into the sky but encountering only rain and cloud. To the west, about 30 Ju88s were sent in the direction of Portsmouth and Southampton. Several were driven back after interception by 602 Squadron Spitfires from Westhampnett, but others pressed on as far as South Wales. Here they hit oil storage tanks at Pembroke Dock. A couple of the Ju88s also penetrated to the airfield at Bibury, which was used by a night-fighting detachment of Spitfires from No. 92 Squadron. One fighter was destroyed on the ground and three others damaged, but two of the squadron's planes got airborne and chased the raiders, downing one of the Ju88s.

That night, German bombers criss-crossed the country as far north as Liverpool. They inflicted over 100 civilian casualties, but the raiders failed to locate their fighter airfield and factory targets.

The following day, Tuesday 20 August, started cloudy, but the morning still saw heavy German reconnaissance over the Thames Estuary and the airfields of Southeast England. A characteristic lightning raid was carried out by the *Erprobungsgruppe 210*, but its target — Martlesham Heath airfield in

291

Suffolk — escaped major damage. In the afternoon, there was only one major raid, by 27 Dorniers escorted by 30 Messerschmitt Me109s. Their target was Eastchurch, but the formation was turned back by No. 615 Squadron, which shot down two of the bombers and one fighter with the assistance of Spitfires from No. 65 Squadron.

That day, and having been deeply stirred by the tenacious efforts of the RAF in recent days, Winston Churchill addressed the House of Commons. His speech, with its nod to the St Crispin's Day speech in Shakespeare's *Henry V*, immortalized the epic feats being fought in the skies by "the few" — the laconic description that would enduringly define the men of Fighter Command:

> The gratitude of every home in our Island, in our
> Empire, and indeed throughout the world, except in
> the abodes of the guilty, goes out to the British airmen
> who, undaunted by odds, unwearied in their constant
> challenge and mortal danger, are turning the tide of the
> war by their prowess and by their devotion. Never in
> the field of human conflict was so much owed by so
> many to so few.

The relative lull in operations continued on Wednesday. In addition, a reorganization of the German fighter wings — whereby more Me109s were to be concentrated in the Pas de Calais — meant that the Luftwaffe launched only light raids. Nevertheless, attempting to prevent Fighter Command from having time to rest and recuperate, Kesselring and Sperrle ordered pairs or trios of aircraft to probe all along the front, from Cornwall to Skegness. Several raiders were shot down, but bombs hit St Eval airfield, Cornwall, disturbing the recuperation of No. 238 Squadron, hitting a hangar, and destroying four Blenheims as well as damaging a further four.

Thursday 22 August followed a similar pattern, with most Luftwaffe units grounded by poor weather. As if to compensate, the early morning saw the first outbreak of shelling by the heavy artillery units now established at Cape Gris Nez. Some hundred shells were fired at a convoy passing through the Straits of Dover between 8a.m. and 9am. No vessels were hit, so *Erprobungsgruppe 210* went on the attack soon after midday, protected by Me109 fighter sweeps on its flanks. As the bomb-carrying Me110s approached the ships, Spitfires from Nos 54 and 610 Squadrons swung into action, and during a fierce dogfight two of the British fighters were shot down, with one pilot, Sergeant G. R. Collett, killed. But the convoy survived undamaged, and most of the rest of the afternoon saw only limited enemy incursions, by fighters.

The only other heavy raid of the day was once again carried out by aircraft of *Erprobungsgruppe 210*. It was just after 7p.m., and at Manston aerodrome the redeployment of No. 600 Blenheim Squadron away from this exposed position was almost complete, with the last of the supplies and equipment being loaded onto lorries. Suddenly the Me110s swept in from the sea and dropped some thirty bombs, destroying two

Blenheims as well as hangars, offices and storehouses. Remarkably, there were no casualties on the ground.

Sporadic Luftwaffe raids continued across the country on 23 August, including on some BBC wireless stations. Fighter Command claimed a Ju88 and a Heinkel 111 shot down while losing none of its own planes or men, either in the air or on the ground. But more than 30 civilians died as a result of air raids.

Saturday 24 August brought perfect weather, with the skies bright and clear, and with it an inevitable upsurge. From 8.30a.m. the day would see six major attacks over ten hours, carried out by a total of more than 500 bombers and fighters. This would be the first day of two weeks of sustained air offensives on a massive scale.

At 8.30a.m., Pevensey radar picked up German aircraft across a broad front. Fifteen minutes later, the enemy forces had organized themselves into a close-flying formation of 40 Do17s and Ju88s, protected by 66 Me109 fighters. Twelve Fighter Command squadrons were scrambled in response, with Spitfires of No. 610 Squadron, from Biggin Hill, making the first contact. With the advantage of height and the sun behind them, they succeeded in breaking up the raid, which retired to the southeast and then split up, though some bombs fell on the streets of Dover. Spitfires of No. 54 Squadron, from Hornchurch, shot down three Me109s as they turned for home.

Shortly after the disappearance of this raid from the radar screens, another was detected crossing the Channel from Cap Gris Nez. No. 610 Squadron had only just returned to Biggin Hill when it was scrambled again, along with Nos 151 from North Weald and 501 from Gravesend, against an incoming formation of Ju88s and Me109s. No. 264 Squadron at Hornchurch, equipped with its Boulton Paul Defiants, was also ordered up. This move was a sign of Fighter Command's stretched resources, for a month earlier the massacre of No. 141 Squadron, which flew Defiants, had demonstrated painfully the aircraft's weaknesses.

The defenders managed to break up this raid too and return to their bases. For the Defiant squadron, this meant the forward base at Manston, by now the RAF's least popular airfield. Some of the squadron were still refuelling when, shortly after 1p.m., a raid warning sounded. Most of the Defiants got airborne, taking off as bombs started to hit the base, but they were unable to gain height fast enough to avoid being pounced on by German fighters. Three were shot down, including that of the commander, Squadron Leader Philip Hunter, and all six men inside the three aircraft were killed. The remainder returned to Hornchurch, only to be forced to scramble again amid falling bombs at just after 3.30p.m., when the airfield came under attack. Two of the Defiants collided as they raced to take off, and another was shot down shortly afterwards.

At the same time as the Hornchurch attack, a force of 46 Dornier Do17s and Heinkel He111s attacked North Weald. The raid was met by two British squadrons. Intercepting pilots often had to run the gauntlet of German fighters lurking high above them, ready to pounce. As David Crook described:

> It was always a rather tricky and unpleasant business attacking the bombers while their fighter escort were still in position above. Often it was almost impossible to see them because of the blinding sun, but you always knew they were there, and as soon as they saw a favourable opportunity, they would dive down and attack. Generally, therefore, we had to try to get in one very quick attack on the bombers and then turn round before the fighters arrived on the scene.[13]

On this occasion, though, the Me109 cover was too high to provide swift protection, and 151 Squadron's Hurricanes succeeded in attacking the Heinkels, while 111 Squadron adopted its head-on charge against the Dorniers. About 20 bombers struggled through and inflicted substantial damage. Nevertheless, after these assaults both Hornchurch and North Weald were still able to function.

For the Germans, attacking to the north of London was highly risky as they were operating at the very limit of the range of their Me109s. And, as the North Weald bombers headed for home, their Me109 escort long departed, they were only rescued from annihilation by the clever defence of accompanying Me110s.

Poor, battered Manston was once again in the firing line. Seventeen men were killed, the runway badly cratered and the telephone lines destroyed. The decision was taken to abandon the base except for emergency deployments or refuelling.

By 4p.m., Air Vice-Marshal Park had committed almost all of his 11 Group fighters, and he called on 12 Group commander Leigh-Mallory to provide cover for his northern airfields. Leigh-Mallory seized on the chance to demonstrate the "Big Wing" approach, which was being championed by the air vice-marshal and his subordinate, Acting Squadron Leader Douglas Bader.

At the heart of the "Big Wing" tactical concept was the belief that large formations of attackers were best opposed with large numbers of defenders. It was partly born out of the genuine belief that wing-sized formations of three to five squadrons stood a better chance of defeating the Luftwaffe than the one or two squadrons that Park preferred to send up. But it was also driven by service politics. The brunt of the fighting was being borne by Park's men in the southeast. No. 12 Group, based in the Midlands, was at one remove from the frontline, and Leigh-Mallory and Bader — both ambitious men — felt themselves on the sidelines. When they were called on to support 11 Group, it was often too late to make a difference. On several occasions, Park requested their help for the subsidiary role of guarding No. 11 Group airfields.

Park himself offered practical objections to the Big Wing tactic. Radio communications were not good enough, he argued, to be able to control more than one squadron in the air. Operating more than a dozen aircraft increased the risk of collisions and "friendly fire" tragedies, and anyway the German raids were too widespread to make a Big Wing practicable. The short time between the detection of an attacking force and its arrival meant there was not enough time to assemble a large force before the raiders had crossed the Channel.

Dowding supported his protégé Park, maintaining that the more aircraft sent into battle the greater the risk of drastic losses of machines and pilots. But the argument was sharpened by a deep animosity between Park and Leigh-Mallory. It has been counted as a failure of Dowding's that he did not crush the time-wasting dispute between his two key subordinates.

Much of the resistance to the Big Wing theory turned out to be justified by events. Of the 32 occasions that a Big Wing was ordered up by Leigh-Mallory, only 7 resulted in combat, and only once were the Big Wing fighters the first to intercept. But at the time the pilots of the wings returned to their bases with impressive claims for the number of enemy aircraft downed. These turned out to be exaggerated. There was little doubt, however, that better use could have been made of 12 Group to strengthen the overall defensive strategy. And in time, when Fighter Command could concentrate on inflicting losses rather than protecting its airfields and resources, the switch to Big Wing tactics became much more feasible and gathered pace.

On 24 August, Leigh-Mallory sent up three squadrons to form up over Duxford before heading *en masse* to the rescue of North Weald and Hornchurch. The experiment was, though, a *débâcle*. The last planes to take off, No. 19's Spitfires, never met up with the other two squadrons, though they were the only fighters to make a proper interception.

No. 10 Group was also drawn into the day's fighting. At 3.40p.m. a large formation was spotted on radar approaching the Isle of Wight. Expecting Ju87 dive-bombers and another feast of kills, the intercepting fighters were positioned too low for the incoming Ju88s and Me110s. Several squadrons had been scrambled, but only No. 609 made contact, close to Portsmouth, and in the worst possible position. The raid appeared earlier than expected and 609 Squadron found itself 5,000 feet directly below the formation. They were lucky to escape with only one Spitfire shot down, and they were unable to turn the raid back. Two hundred 250 kg bombs fell on Portsmouth, hitting shops, factories, houses and the naval dockyards. The raid inflicted more casualties on the ground than any single attack so far, with 104 killed and 237 injured.

David Crook, of 609 Squadron, recorded feelings of impotence in the face of the attack:

At about 4p.m. we took off with orders to patrol Portsmouth at 10,000 feet . . . on this occasion we were the luckless ones sent low down to deal with any possible dive-bombers. We hated this — it's a much more comforting and reassuring feeling to be on top of everything than right underneath. Superior height is the whole secret of success in air fighting. However, "orders is orders" and so we patrolled Portsmouth. Very soon a terrific A. A. [anti-aircraft] barrage sprang

299

up ahead of us, looking exactly like a large number of dirty cotton-wool puffs in the sky. It was a most impressive barrage; besides all the guns at Portsmouth, all the warships in the harbour and dockyard were firing hard. A moment later, through the barrage and well above us, we saw a large German formation wheeling above Portsmouth. We were too low to be able to do anything about it . . . They were now releasing their bombs, and I cannot imagine a more flagrant case of indiscriminate bombing. The whole salvo fell right into the middle of Portsmouth, and I could see great spurts of flame and smoke springing up all over the place. We spent a very unpleasant few minutes right underneath the German formation, praying hard that their fighters would not come down on us. However, the danger passed and a very disgruntled squadron returned home, having seen so many Huns and yet not having fired a single round.[14]

Although the Luftwaffe had lost over 30 aircraft during the day's attacks, it had reasons to believe its fortunes were improving. The day had shown that, unencumbered by Stukas, its attacks had been numerous and fast enough to penetrate almost anywhere in Southeast England. Unlike on 18 August, when the weather had come to the rescue, the bombers had got through, even to targets north of London, as the smoking wreckage at North Weald and Hornchurch testified.

Fighter Command was having to contend with new problems and challenges. Its radar network, weakened by damage, had been tested to the limit by the sheer numbers of incoming hostile aircraft. In addition, the controllers' finely balanced decision-making had been complicated by the clever new Luftwaffe tactic of maintaining a constant stream of aircraft flying parallel to the Sussex coast about 20 miles out to sea, occasionally feinting towards land.

With the fall of darkness, there was no respite. From just before 11p.m., nearly 200 more German bombers streamed across the Channel, this time with only searchlights and anti-aircraft guns to take them on. There was a successful interception by a Blenheim night-fighter, but mostly the bombers ranged freely over Kent, Sussex and Surrey. Bombs meant for the Thameshaven oil storage depot and Short's aircraft factory in Rochester fell on the City of London and at least nine other London districts. In Bethnal Green the bombs ignited fires, the destruction witnessed by the young Ron Harvey, who was among the very first to be "bombed out":

When the warning sounded I was woken up by Mum or Dad and I went downstairs through the kitchen into the back yard to the shelter where there were already some neighbours . . . I remember it was a bright moonlit night. Being twelve years old, I wasn't taking notice of the grown-ups. I was just at the door of the shelter and I heard this German plane come over and I knew it was German because of the drone of the engine. A few seconds passed and then there was a whistle of a bomb coming down. I was just by the

301

door. Someone shouted "There's something coming down. Duck!" and I ducked and I must have had my face to the right because I saw the two black balls fall on the house. The bombs exploded and it wasn't like a "boom" or a blast, more like the crack of a thunderbolt, which echoed through the street for a few seconds and that was that. The shelter was full of dust and someone said, "Gas!" but I knew it wasn't, it was brick dust. The next thing I remember is being out of the shelter . . . and there was all this activity going on — I suppose it was rescue work. And there were lots of people digging out my sister and her boyfriend. They were roughed up a bit, a few bruises; all the chimneys had come down. There was no damage for miles and miles around before that. I was going to school just round the corner, it was as if there wasn't a war on. That was the beginning of the war for me, when things started happening.[15]

St Giles' Church in Cripplegate was damaged too in the attack, and bombs landed on Oxford Street department stores. Nine people were killed and fifty-eight injured.

When Goering found out that Central London had been hit, in contravention of the strict rules laid down by the *Führer*, he was furious, demanding the names of the guilty aircrafts' captains and threatening them with transfer to the infantry. But there was no calling the bombs back, and now the nature of the wider struggle was irreversibly altered. Within 24 hours, Bomber

Command launched its first raid on Berlin. Flying Officer Wilf Burnett piloted a four-man Hampden bomber during the attack on the German capital: "We had expected Berlin to be one of our targets at one time or another once the hours of darkness allowed us to cross the coast in safety. The orders came through on 25 August. We were given industrial targets in Berlin. All the crews wanted to have a go, purely and simply for no other reason than to refute Goering's boast that Berlin would never be bombed."[16] Flying at 10,000 feet, together with another 80 Hampdens and Wellingtons, the British bombers followed the Dutch coastline and then headed inland, guided by moonlight falling on rivers and canals below. But as they approached Berlin, after about four hours' flying time, thick cloud descended. The bombers' principal target was the Siemens-Halske factory, but the anti-aircraft fire kept them too high to allow them to aim their bombs accurately, so they landed on fields and woods and also on some residential areas of the city.

No-one was killed in the Berlin raid, but its occurrence was an embarrassment to Goering, given his declarations regarding the city's safety. "Berliners are stunned," wrote the German-based US correspondent William Shirer in his diary. "They did not think it could ever happen." Churchill was delighted though, writing the next day to his chief of the air staff: "I want you to hit them hard and Berlin is the place to hit them." The prime minister ordered further raids for 28, 30 and 31 August.

★　★　★

On the morning of 25 August, in spite of fine weather, the Luftwaffe continued flying just *Staffel*-strength formations up and down the Channel in an effort to exhaust the British defenders and lure Fighter Command away from its bases. However, neither Air Vice-Marshal Park nor Brand at 10 Group was inclined to take the bait. Then, in the late afternoon, Ventnor radar station picked up several enemy formations to the west of the Cherbourg peninsula. Soon they grouped together and began to approach Weymouth Bay. There were more than 300 aircraft, made up of nearly 100 Ju88 bombers (of *Kampfgeschwader 51* and *54*), 120 Me110 heavy fighters (of *Zerstörergeschwader 2* and *3* and *Lehrgeschwader 1*) and, following behind and above, a *Gruppe* of Me109s from *Jagdgeschwader 53*.

As the formation approached the coast, it split into three, targeting Portland, Weymouth and Warmwell. All the Middle Wallop, Exeter and Warmwell squadrons had been scrambled, with the Hurricanes of No. 17 ordered to defend Warmwell. One No. 17 Squadron pilot, Flying Officer Count Manfred Czernin, a naturalized Englishman of East European descent, attacked head on and then from the rear, shooting down three Me110s in quick succession. He recorded the day's successful duelling in a crisp summary:

One broke. Chased and fired from above. Nose went down, EA [enemy aircraft] burst into flames and crashed straight into the sea. Climbed and resumed attack. Beam attack and 110 broke away pouring smoke and went into a vertical dive, burst into flames and crashed into the sea. Resumed attack and had to break off as Spitfire on its tail firing at him. Shook him off and attacked 110 and after long burst from quarter astern, nose dropped and it lost height . . . and glided down with both engines out. Broke off as obviously it was going to crash and saw two Spitfires attack it again. One baled out and then EA nose dived into a wood two miles SE of Dorchester and burst into flames.[17]

Two more Me110s fell to other pilots of 17 Squadron. But the squadron's leader, Cedric Williams, was himself downed by return fire from one of the twin-engine fighters, which severed his port wing and almost certainly killed the pilot. Swooping Me109s accounted for another Hurricane, but its pilot was rescued safely from the sea after baling out. One of the Me109s was shot down by the squadron in return.

All but seven of the forty-odd bombers that No. 17 Squadron encountered were turned back, but those few had a lucky strike on Warmwell. The station's sick bay and two hangars were hit, but, more importantly, a bomb that landed outside the airfield cut the station's telephone and teleprinter cables.

Meanwhile, 87 Squadron's twelve Hurricanes from Exeter went in against the Ju88s heading for Portland, while 609 Squadron's Spitfires from Middle Wallop targeted the Me110s. "My mouth feels hellishly dry," No. 87's Ian "Widge" Gleed later wrote of the encounter. "There is a strong sinking feeling in my breast. Thank God a doctor isn't listening to my heart. It's absolutely banging away."[18] Laurence "Rubber" Thoroughgood shot down one of the bombers — his first and only kill of the battle — and No. 609 Squadron, with the crucial advantage of height, accounted for two of the Me110s and another five damaged. The Spitfires of Pilot Officer David Crook and Flying Officer Piotr Ostaszewski-Ostoja were hit, but both safely returned to Middle Wallop. Cook's excitement had got the better of him, as he remembered:

We sighted a very big German formation coming over the coast below us, and the C.O. swung us into line astern and manoeuvred into a good position for the attack. Then, down we went. I happened to be almost last on the line, and I shall never forget seeing the long line of Spitfires ahead, sweeping down and curling round at terrific speed to strike right into the middle of the German formation. It was superb!

The great weight and fierceness of this onslaught split up the Huns immediately and they scattered all over the place, with Spitfires chasing them right and left. I saw an Me110 below me and dived down on him going very fast indeed. Unfortunately I was going too fast and in the heat of the moment I forgot to throttle back with the result that I came up behind him at terrific speed and overshot him badly. I got a good burst of fire at practically point blank range as he flashed by and then I had to turn away very violently or I should have collided with him. His rear gunner took advantage of my mistake and fired a short burst at me, and put several bullets through my wing, very close to the fuselage and only a few inches from my leg.

When I turned round to look for the Hun he had disappeared. Though there was a lot of fighting in progress and machines were turning and diving all over the sky, I had dived down below them all and couldn't do much about it . . . I returned to base absolutely furious with myself for having missed that Me110. He was right in front of me, and if only I had not gone at him so wildly I should have had him easily. Anyway, it taught me to be a little more cool in future. One lives and one learns — if lucky.[19]

Messerschmitt Me109s then dived on the *mêlée*, forcing the British fighters to break off from the vulnerable bombers and Me110s. No. 87 Squadron pilot Sid Wakeling was turning to face the new threat when a cannon shell ripped into his cockpit. His comrades heard him over the R/T saying that his hand had been blown off, but that he was going to try to land his Hurricane. But the aircraft was now on fire and spiralling down towards the Dorset countryside. At the last moment Wakeling was seen jumping clear, but his parachute failed to open and he died as he hit the ground, the day's sole casualty from 87 Squadron. Three days previously he had written chirpily to his girlfriend, Daphne:

My darling,

Many thanks for your long letter but I am sorry that our first letters crossed. Well dear, I have at last got my own machine. It is brand new and will be super when I have flown it for a few hours. At the moment I am having a "Felix the Cat" painted on it. My pal Rubber [Thoroughgood] also has his own machine now so the "Heavenly Twins" are quite happy . . . I have been shifted back to my old flight again so I am still in the same flight as Rubber. Well dear please give my regards to everyone and I hope you are feeling fit.

So, Cheerio Darling

Yours as Ever

Sid xxxxxxx

The squadron's countermeasures managed to down three of the Me109s, accounting for a further two as the raiders turned for home. Other squadrons, arriving as the dogfight drifted west of Portland, were less successful, and a further six British fighters were lost.

Laurence Thoroughgood later summed up the spirit of the pilots at this time: "We were fighting over our home ground and this had a great bearing on our morale. The Luftwaffe certainly had the numbers but this only seemed to spur us on. We certainly got tired but were fit and young."[20] But some squadrons were reaching the end of their physical and mental reserves. No. 54 Squadron, down to only seven serviceable Spitfires, was desperately tired and in need of a rest. For now, though, they would have to fight on.

No. 32 Squadron, based at Biggin Hill, had been in combat since May. At 6.30p.m. on 25 August they were in the forefront of an interception over Dover. Kesselring had sent over a raid of more than 100 aircraft, and Park had responded with six squadrons. No. 32 Squadron dived on the bombers — Dornier Do17s — shooting down one, but was in turn pounced on by Me109s, which shot down two of its number, killing a pilot. This meant that the squadron now had hardly enough pilots for a full flight. Two days later, No. 32 was withdrawn to Northumberland. "We were down to seven pilots," said pilot Peter Brothers. "Funnily enough, of the original pre-war squadron, many had been shot down, wounded, some burned, but nobody had been killed. It was only the new boys who had died."[21] The vulnerability of inexperienced fighter pilots would be gruesomely demonstrated as Dowding was now forced to move untried squadrons to the frontline.

From first light on Monday 26 August, high-level Luftwaffe reconnaissance planes criss-crossed the skies over 11 Group's area, looking for concentrations of fighters on the ground. By late morning, more than 150 German aircraft were approaching from the direction of Lille, crossing the coast near Deal in Kent. Most of them headed west, while some Me109s went on a shooting spree across the Kent countryside, and a number of Heinkels turned for Folkestone, which was bombed. No. 616 Squadron, only recently moved south from Church Fenton, was vectored from Kenley to intercept, but it arrived too late to catch the bombers, encountering instead a great mass of about 50 Me109s over Dungeness. As the Spitfires desperately climbed in an effort to get the sun behind them, they were "bounced" by a further 30 Me109s, which, in 30 seconds, shot down four of them, with two pilots killed and two wounded. A further two Spitfires force-landed after being hit.

The main German formation, ploughing on over Canterbury and then Maidstone, was now involved in a long dogfight with some 40 Hurricanes and 30 Spitfires. Again, Park sent up the Defiants of 264 Squadron from Hornchurch. This time they succeeded in downing one Dornier and damaging another, but they were then jumped by two *Gruppen* of Me109s. Three of the Defiants were shot down, completing the almost total destruction of the squadron's fighting ability. As the Me109s chased the survivors away, using up precious fuel, No. 1 (Canadian) Squadron rushed at the Dorniers, only to be caught in a crossfire that downed three of their Hurricanes. Three more fighter squadrons joined in and the Me109s started deserting their bombers as their fuel supplies dwindled. In the end, only a handful of Dorniers got through to bomb Biggin Hill and Kenley, where little damage was caused.

By 1p.m., the raiders were flying back over the Channel. They were quickly replaced by fighter sweeps and a dummy raid north of the Thames Estuary. This consisted of Dorniers empty of bombs, but with a swarm of Me109s lurking above. No. 85 Squadron was scrambled and managed to attack the Dorniers of *Kampfgeschwader 3* in a head-on charge without falling prey to the Me109s. Squadron Leader Peter Townsend led the charge:

> There was one way to get at the bombers without get-
> ting mixed up with the fighter escort. "Stand by for
> head-on attack and watch out for those little fellows
> above," I called. Then I brought the squadron round
> steadily in a wide turn, moving into echelon as we
> levelled out about two miles ahead on a collision
> course. Ease the throttle to reduce the closing speed
> — which anyway allowed only a few seconds' fire. Get
> a bead on them right away, hold it, and never mind
> the streams of tracer darting overhead. Just keep on
> pressing on the button until you think you're going to
> collide — then stick hard forward. Under the shock of
> "negative G" your stomach jumps into your mouth,
> dust and muck fly up from the cockpit floor into your
> eyes and your head cracks on the roof as you break
> away below.[22]

Several of the bombers were damaged for the loss of one British aircraft, whose pilot baled out safely.

A new enemy raid was detected at 2p.m. off the coast of Belgium. This, too, headed towards the Thames Estuary, closely watched by Park, who surmised that it was aimed at Hornchurch, North Weald or London itself. This time, with the radar picture confused, the size of the German raid was overestimated, leading Park to put ten squadrons into action against what turned out to be about 80 Dorniers of *Kampfgeschwader*

2 and *3*, escorted by 40 Me109s and the same number of Me110s.

South of Clacton, part of the German force — including about half of the bombers — swung east and appeared to be heading directly for Central London. Park ordered up almost all of the rest of his forces and also called on 12 Group to defend his northern airfields.

Meanwhile, the northerly thrust of 40 Dorniers crossed the coast just south of Colchester, where it encountered heavy flak. Most of the bombers turned back, but half a dozen Dorniers pressed on, bombing Debden. Three airmen were killed, buildings destroyed and an aircraft on the ground badly damaged. There was no sign of the promised cover from 12 Group. No. 19 Squadron, from Duxford, just ten miles away, arrived only after the bombers had departed.

The six Dorniers escaped, but the main home-bound formation was now intercepted by 310 Squadron from Duxford. It was the first combat for the Free Czech squadron. Although plagued by problems with their radio transmitters, the Czechs showed impressive determination. Their squadron leader, G. D. M. Blackwood, had to bale out, but some of the Czech pilots had better luck, as Blackwood recorded:

The Czechs really did a fine job despite their aggressive attitude. I think their only problem was that as soon as they saw an enemy that would make for a possible target, nothing else mattered. On that day, I picked out a Dornier that was not in formation and made him my target. I fired a short burst, then another, and the bomber started to wobble a bit. Just then, I smelt burning, and it wasn't long before the starboard fuel tank burst into flame. I undid my harness and the oxygen tube, opened the hood and turned the aircraft upside down and fell out.

One of the Czechs, Emil Fechtner, managed to get in one of our first successes of the day. By all accounts he started his firing way too early, but kept his finger on the button, and at about 100 yards a [Messerschmitt] 110 belched smoke from one of its engines. But then he was jumped on by half a dozen 109s, so discretion being better than valour, he went up into the cloud cover and disappeared from sight.[23]

One of the pilots, Sergeant Edward Prchal, chased a Dornier for 30 miles before shooting it down, only to be set upon by an Me109, which hit his Hurricane in the wing and forced an emergency landing near Upminster. Another Dornier and the Me110 were also shot down by 310 Squadron, for the loss of three Hurricanes, with all the Czech pilots baling out safely. Then, No. 111 Hurricane Squadron arrived from Martlesham, along with 56 Squadron from North Weald. Five further Luftwaffe aircraft were shot down, although both squadrons lost two fighters each.

The other part of the raid — heading, it seemed, for London — was met by a large force of fighters just north of Southend. Once again, the Me109s' dwindling fuel reserves forced them to leave the bombers to their fate. Several Dorniers and Me110s were shot down,

313

and a signal flare from the leading aircraft aborted the raid. The German formation turned south, dropping its bombs at random over Kent, on Rochester, Maidstone, Ashford, Canterbury and Dungeness.

Following a pattern now established, the afternoon saw Generalfeldmarschall Sperrle throw his forces from *Luftflotte 3* into the battle. At around 4p.m., some 50 He111s (of *Kampfgeschwader 5*) with 107 Me109s and Me110s set off across the Channel heading towards Portsmouth and Southampton. Eight squadrons were sent up in response, but only Nos 43, 615 and 602 succeeded in intercepting, shooting down four He111s and four Me109s for the loss of two Hurricanes and two Spitfires.

Pilot Officer Harold North of 43 Squadron was one of three Fighter Command pilots wounded. Having led his Yellow Section in a head-on attack on the Heinkels, he dived down, almost being hit by the bombs being jettisoned hastily by the enemy. He then climbed back into the attack, hitting a Heinkel, which started belching smoke. At that moment he was wounded in the shoulder by cannon fire, but continued firing the rest of his ammunition into a straggling Heinkel before baling out.

Flight Lieutenant Charles MacLean, of 602 Squadron, also survived the encounter, but not without consequences:

I followed the formation back over the Channel and was engaged in doing head-on attacks on the leading aircraft of this big wave of bombers . . . on the second one, I'd slowed down to about 160mph to increase the

amount of time for shooting. Suddenly there was a
frightful bang and a searing pain in my right leg about
six inches above the ankle. I looked down to find my
right foot hanging loose, all messed up with blood and
sinews. I was at 16,000 feet, the pain was fiendish and
I thought I'd have to bail out. I threw back the hood,
took off my mask and looked down at the sea. It
looked beautiful — blue and inviting. Then I tried my
throttle and the engine was answering . . . I flew back
to Tangmere as fast as I could. I was worried about
the amount of blood that I was losing but it didn't
seem to be coming out very fast and I thought there'd
be enough to last. Indeed there was and I landed back
at Tangmere with the wheels up . . . I retired to
hospital where it was the usual old story. They tried to
pretend that they hadn't taken the leg off but it was
pretty obvious that they had.[24]

Most of the Heinkels dumped their bombs into the
sea, and there was only light damage to the coastal
towns. It was to be the last major raid from Sperrle's
Luftflotte for three weeks, as his bomber force was
redirected to night attacks on industrial targets in the
English Midlands.

It had been a hard day for both sides. The Luftwaffe
had lost 41 aircraft more than the RAF. But Fighter
Command had suffered badly too, with 26 fighters
destroyed and 3 very badly damaged, against a total loss
of only 17 Luftwaffe fighters. Air Vice-Marshal Park's
greatest concern that evening, however, was the failure
of 12 Group to protect Debden, which placed a further

strain on his working relationship with Leigh-Mallory. The next day he reported: "Thanks to the friendly co-operation afforded by 10 Group they are always prepared to detail two to four squadrons to engage from the West mass attacks . . . Up to date 12 Group . . . have not shown the same desire to co-operate by dispatching their squadrons to the places requested . . . When 12 Group offered assistance and were requested by us to patrol our aerodromes, their squadrons did not in fact patrol over our aerodromes."[25] Park was already inclined to blame Leigh-Mallory for the attack on North Weald on 24 August. Now Debden was added to his list of grievances.

During the night of 26/27 August, more than 200 bombers raided Bournemouth, Plymouth, Coventry and Birmingham. But bad weather on the Tuesday morning brought a respite, and the Germans flew only reconnaissance sorties. Meanwhile, at the Luftwaffe bases in northern France and the Low Countries, plans were being drawn up for ever tighter escorts for the bomber fleets. It was apparent that British fighters had struggled to get at the bombers when they were surrounded on all sides by Me109s. However, Luftwaffe fighter pilots vigorously protested that this policy meant that they would never surprise Fighter Command's Spitfires and Hurricanes. Instead of going after them, they would have to wait for the enemy to come to them. The policy confirmed that the destruction of RAF airfields and planes on the ground had taken priority over destroying Fighter Command's planes in the air.

Trafford Leigh-Mallory

The Battle of Britain would probably have been fought very differently if Air Vice-Marshal Trafford Leigh-Mallory had been in charge of Fighter Command in 1940 (as he would be two years later), or even if he had been given Park's job as 11 Group commander at the beginning of the year (as he felt he ought to have been).

Born in Cheshire in 1892, Leigh-Mallory joined a Territorial Regiment at the outbreak of the First World War, and shortly afterwards he received a commission in the Lancashire Fusiliers. He was wounded during the Second Battle of Ypres. In July 1916, he was seconded to the Royal Flying Corps, where he flew reconnaissance and bombing missions. He stayed on after 1918 in the Royal Air Force, and in 1937, after service at the Air Ministry and overseas, he was given command of 12 Group, responsible for the fighter cover over Central England.

Leigh-Mallory was intelligent and well educated, and those who worked with him found him industrious, loyal to his friends, caring of his pilots and willing to take advice. But he was also openly ambitious and prone to pomposity, characteristics that some explained by his need to escape from the shadow of his famous older brother, George Mallory, the mountaineer who had perished on Mount Everest in 1924. The appointment of Keith Park, junior to him in rank, to the command of the frontline No. 11 Group clearly rankled.

Strongly influenced by Douglas Bader, who served under him, Leigh-Mallory's advocacy of the "Big Wing" deployment of fighters in large numbers was closer to Air Ministry opinion than to the Dowding and Park system of immediate forward response with small numbers. Leigh-Mallory's vigorous campaigning and intriguing during the Battle of Britain for the adoption of the tactic created strong tensions with both his superior and his opposite number at 11 Group.

With the sidelining of Dowding and Park after the Battle of Britain, Leigh-Mallory's star rose. He took over 11 Group command, where he initiated offensive and aggressive, but ultimately wasteful, fighter sweeps over France. In November 1942, he was promoted to the rank of air marshal and appointed to lead Fighter Command. He went on to play a key role in the planning and execution of air cover for the Normandy landings.

Leigh-Mallory was killed in November 1944, when the plane taking him and his wife to his next appointment as air commander-in-chief, South-East Asia Command, crashed en route in the French Alps during bad weather.

Dowding took the opportunity of the lull to rotate some of his squadrons. No. 65, down to 12 pilots and only 9 aircraft, was moved from Hornchurch, Essex, to Church Fenton in Yorkshire; it was replaced by 603 Squadron, currently at Turnhouse in Scotland. No. 54 Squadron looked on enviously, but instead of being moved it was supplied with fresh aircraft, bringing its number back up to 12 Spitfires. The next day would be very busy for its exhausted pilots.

The cloud and drizzle of the previous day had cleared, and at first light on 28 August came the now familiar reconnaissance sorties. At 8a.m. a raid was plotted building up over the Pas de Calais. Thirty-two Hurricanes from Nos 79, 85, 501 and 615 Squadrons were sent up to intercept, along with 12 Defiants from No. 264 Squadron. All made contact as two heavily escorted formations — one of Heinkels and one of Dorniers — crossed the coast northwest of Dover. Twenty-three Dorniers of *Kampfgeschwader 3* made for Eastchurch, Kent, while twenty-seven Heinkels from *Kampfgeschwader 53* headed for Rochford in Essex.

No. 79 Squadron attacked the Heinkels but was engaged by the escorting fighters. In the meantime, No. 264's pilots went in on the attack against the bombers, claiming one shot down and another damaged; but they were pounced on by Me109s lurking above. Their Boulton Paul Defiants were slow and vulnerable, and their gun turrets could not fire forwards, rendering the aircraft vulnerable in daytime action. Four of them were downed, and a further three damaged. It was the end of the road for the Defiant.

After today's events, the aircraft was withdrawn from daylight duties.

One of 264's pilot officers, Jim Bailey, aged 21, had a lucky escape when the Me109s "bounced us from behind. My engine stopped and I had to dive for the ground whilst pretending to be in a spin . . . I had to crash land. As this was August the ground was hard and the field I chose had a double hedge. The fields of Kent were obstructed by wooden poles to prevent German glider troops landing, so I had to weave my way between (them) before hitting the hedge. As I climbed from the cockpit, my super air gunner Sgt Oswald Hardy said to me 'Did you see this?' He pointed out that a number of the poles had connecting electric cables. I had flown underneath without even having noticed!"[26]

The Heinkels ploughed on to the Rochford area, but heavy flak disrupted their bombing runs and they inflicted little damage. The Dorniers got through to Eastchurch, protected from the attacks of 501 and 605 Squadrons by their escort of about 60 Me109s from *Jagdgeschwader 1* and *51*. Several RAF bombers were hit on the ground and buildings destroyed, but the airfield, which was primarily used by Coastal Command, would remain operational.

A few hours later, bombers were back over Rochford. A mass of Dorniers of *Kampfgeschwader* 3, heavily escorted by Me109s and Me110s, had approached from the Thames Estuary. No. 54 Squadron was scrambled, as well as No. 1 Squadron. "They covered the whole sky ahead," said 54 Squadron's Al Deere, "a solid mass of aircraft from about 15,000ft up to 32,000ft at which height a dozen or so 109s weaved along in the wake of hundreds of escort fighters below."[27]

By now, Deere was well used to the frantic routines of scrambling, "the usual mad rush to cockpits; a feverish pushing of starter buttons; a roar as twelve Merlins sprang into life; a jostling for places at the take-off end; and the squadron was airborne for another combat." But this time the flight experience was different: "Up and up we climbed; first Gravesend was left behind, then Chatham, then Canterbury, and finally Dover, plainly visible to twelve pairs of eyes which gazed down as it passed below the squadron, now at 33,000ft. This was the highest we had been and, in the jargon of the fighter pilots, 'we were hanging on our air-screws'. It was cold, extremely cold; my feet were like lumps of ice and tiny prickles of cold stabbed at my legs, just above the knees."[28] One of the Me109s was shot down, and the airfield again escaped serious damage, although Deere himself was shot down for the third time — this time, he believed, by a Spitfire.

At around 4p.m., radar plotters tracked a third incoming raid and, with several flights protecting the sector stations, Nos 85, 54, 56, 151 and 603 Squadrons were vectored to intercept near the coast. But this time there were no bombers to be found. Instead, the raid consisted of five *Gruppen* of Me110s and six of Me109s. It was the sort of fighter-to-fighter combat that the controllers were anxious to avoid. The defenders, though, were in an advantageous position.

No. 85 Squadron, led by Peter Townsend, was at 18,000 feet above Dungeness when they saw Me109s below them. Although ordered to ignore fighters and go for the bombers, they had height and the sun behind them. The temptation was too strong. Townsend called out "Down we go! Pick your own." "It was as if we had flushed a covey of partridges," he later wrote. "One pulled across me in a steep left hand turn, giving me a perfect shot. It rolled over belching white smoke — a hit in the cooling system." He fastened onto another Me109, but it dived and the Hurricane could not keep up even at full boost. Townsend followed, firing short bursts in the hope of slowing the Me109 down. "But in the heat of the chase I forgot the basic rules, until suddenly, wham! A bullet splintered in the cockpit. Never did I get out of anybody's way so fast. Stick forward, bottom rudder, engine cuts, clouds of black smoke." Townsend made it back to his base at Croydon.[29]

Sam Allard, another 85 Squadron pilot, shot down an Me109 about three miles off Folkestone. As the Me109s raced for home, the squadron followed, shooting down three more into the sea. The action, 85 Squadron's most successful of the Battle of Britain, was watched from below by Winston Churchill, who was visiting Dover.

The other intercepting squadrons were less fortunate. No. 603, in action on the very day of its arrival in the south, lost three of its Spitfires, with two pilots killed. Richard Hillary, who would later write *The Last Enemy* about life and death as a fighter pilot, was one of three of the squadron who arrived late to the fight after repairs to his aircraft. "We landed at Hornchurch at about seven o'clock to receive our first shock," he wrote. "Instead of one section there were four Squadrons at readiness; 603 were already in action. They started coming in about half an hour after we landed, smoke stains along the leading edges of the wings showing that all the guns had been fired. They had acquitted themselves well although caught at a disadvantage of height." In all, the day's combat had cost Fighter Command 17 aircraft.

That night saw the first mass raid of about 150 bombers by the Luftwaffe. The target was the port of Liverpool, where vital supplies from the United States were being unloaded. The bombing was inaccurate, falling on a wide area and doing little damage to the docks but causing casualties. Smaller forces hit Birmingham, Bristol, Bournemouth, Coventry, Derby, Manchester and Sheffield. Civilian deaths and injuries were mounting. All over the country air-raid sirens dragged people out of bed and into the shelters, and shut down factories and workshops. The raiders had little to fear from night-fighters. Blenheims were sent up, but only one enemy bomber was sighted.

The morning of Thursday 29 August began with blank radar screens everywhere. The survivors of 264 Squadron flew their Defiants out of Hornchurch, to be replaced by No. 222 Squadron from Kirton-in-Lindsey. The newcomers had much to learn. They parked their Spitfires wingtip to wingtip, peacetime style, and had to be told that this was inadvisable in the current circumstances. At Kenley, 615 Squadron left and 253 Squadron arrived with 18 Hurricanes from Turnhouse.

It was not until about 3p.m. that the first large build-up of enemy aircraft was plotted over the French coast. Park reacted forcefully, sending up nine squadrons to join the four already patrolling in the air. The pilots were under instructions to avoid the attritional fighter-versus-fighter combat of the day before. But the radar picture was deceptive. There was actually only a small number of bombers among the mass of German aircraft; it was mainly composed of fighters — more than 500 Me109s of *Jagdgeschwader 3, 26, 51, 52* and *54*, together with 150 Me110s from *Zerstörergeschwader 26* and *76*.

No. 85 Squadron spotted the enemy formation as it crossed the coast just before 4p.m. "I had sighted eighteen Heinkels coming in over Beachy Head several thousand feet above us," wrote Squadron Leader Townsend. "As we climbed, hanging on our propellers, the blue above glinted with little silver flashes. Me109s! As I watched, they grew in number until there were myriads of them — we thought some two hundred in all . . . Labouring up painfully beneath the Heinkels, our twelve Hurricanes were sitting ducks . . . Then the inevitable — down came the Me109s and it was each one for himself. When my Me109 came, firing, I whipped round and caught him doing that fatal turn across my sights. Tighten the turn, nose up a little, and I had him. The Me109 staggered, like a pheasant shot on the wing. A big piece flew off, maybe the hood. A plume of white smoke trailed. I had a split-second impression of the pilot, seemingly inert during those last dramatic moments. Then the aircraft stalled and dived to earth near Hastings."[30] Another Me109 was shot down, but 85 Squadron lost two aircraft itself. The other squadrons were quickly ordered to avoid combat.

The standard gunsight available to Townsend and the other Fighter Command pilots was the reflector sight, which projected an illuminated ring, usually with a central cross, onto an oval glass behind the windscreen. The pilot adjusted the ring to fit the target size. However, from the 1930s the Royal Aircraft Establishment at Farnborough, Surrey, had been working to devise a gunsight that would automatically aim the fighter's guns at a point ahead of the enemy so that the rounds and the target would arrive at the same place at the same time. In 1937, the design of the Gyro gunsight (GGS) was completed. A rapidly spinning mirror was mounted on a Hooke's universal joint, which connected it to a hemisphere of thin copper rotating between the poles of two powerful magnets. Although the GGS was used to great effect during the Battle of Britain, there were only a few of them available.

Early in the evening of 29 August, Kesselring sent over several fighter sweeps, but it was clear that Park was not to be drawn into a pointless fight. One *Staffel* of Me109s did, however, catch 501 Squadron patrolling near Hawkinge airfield. The squadron had been in action since 10 May, and its pilots included flying ace "Ginger" Lacey and experienced men such as John Gibson. But previous heavy losses meant that it also

325

included its fair share of novice fighter pilots. Bill Green, who described himself as "probably the most inexperienced pilot in the RAF", did not even see the enemy before his aircraft was hit:

> There was a crash of glass, and a hole appeared in the middle of the supposedly bullet-proof windscreen about the size of a tennis ball, or a little larger. I heard bits falling into the cockpit and I was immediately covered in glycol liquid coolant. The aircraft was finished, the stick was just like any old bit of stick. I realised I had to get out and I already had the hood back and I got as far as just taking the weight on my feet and I was gone. I think my head must have been exposed to the wind and I was just sucked out. I found myself in space and I started to roll around trying to find the parachute release and thought to myself, I'm never going to find this ripcord.

Green eventually located the cord and pulled it, but nothing happened. "I was going through the air at one hundred and forty miles per hour, terminal velocity, and the wind noise was quite terrific . . . I really thought my number was up." His parachute pack was trapped between his legs. Suddenly, at just 300 feet above the ground, a gust of wind opened the parachute folds:

> There was a jolt when the parachute kicked me backwards . . . after the noise of the freefall, I was struck by the sudden quiet. It made more impact on

me than any noise I'd ever heard. I thought, Gosh, I'm all right.

I'd picked up some cannon splinters in my leg, and it was swollen and in the centre there was a hole, just as though you'd stuck a pencil right through it. When I got back to Hawkinge I went to sick quarters and the doctor laid me out and started probing around with what looked like a steel knitting needle. I fainted. That really put me out of action then for the rest of the Battle of Britain.[31]

Gibson was shot down too, but it was his fifth time baling out, and he was by now well used to parachuting. He shared a lift back to Hawkinge with Green. Lacey downed one of the Me109s and another was damaged.

On the night of 29/30 August the bombers were back over Merseyside to unload more explosives on the docks area, still smouldering from the night before. But this time the activity did not lead to a falling off of raids the next morning. The coming days looked ominous for the defenders. An extensive anticyclone covering northwestern Europe promised several days of fine weather. The Battle of Britain was now entering a decisive phase, in which the Luftwaffe would have to break the power and the will of Fighter Command or accept that it was never going to create the conditions of air superiority that would allow an invasion to take place. The clock was ticking, as the date set for Operation Sea Lion hurried closer. It was the time for

Goering to muster all the forces at his disposal and to attempt to crush the British air defences by concentrated and relentless assaults.

On Friday 30 August, for the first time, the Luftwaffe attacked with everything it had. Soon after dawn the first of several probing moves began. No. 111 Squadron's Hurricanes ran into a *Gruppe* of Dorniers, near Manston, escorted by about 30 Me110s of *Zerstörergeschwader 75*. They reported the formation and then went into the attack, damaging one of the heavy fighters. The Hurricanes were quickly joined by three of No. 54 Squadron's Spitfires, which managed to hit (but not shoot down) two of the bombers.

At about 10.30a.m., the first sizeable formation rolled towards the Kent coast. It was the vanguard of three waves, spaced at only half-hourly intervals. Low cloud made the job of the Observer Corps watchers especially difficult, but they identified the force correctly as consisting of 60 Me109s. Park declined the challenge, but put his fighters at readiness — at Kenley, Biggin Hill, Northolt, Croydon, North Weald, Rochford and Hornchurch airfields — in the expectation that bombers would follow.

Sure enough, at 11a.m. Observer Corps posts reported 40 He111s, 30 Do17s, 60 Me109s and 30 Me110s approaching the Kent coast at three different points. Nine squadrons were scrambled. No. 85 Squadron had been sent to patrol over Dungeness at 18,000 feet. "I could see the enemy circling at Cap Gris Nez like a swarm of gnats," wrote Peter Townsend. "We waited up-sun in the English sky — eleven Hurricanes ready to pounce . . . Escorted by scores of Me109s and Me110s, a score of Heinkels advanced further towards the English coast." As the Heinkels and Me110s crossed the shoreline, Townsend ordered a head-on attack. "I took my little band of Hurricanes down in a shallow dive, slipped them into echelon and turned in well ahead of the Heinkels, heading straight at them. Our attack, I wrote later in my combat report, 'had the desired effect'."[32]

The German formation was scattered, and two Me110s were shot down for the loss of one Hurricane, although the pilot baled out unhurt. Elements of the formation pushed on towards Ashford, Kent, where they were intercepted by Nos 43, 79 and 603 Squadrons, and a huge dogfight developed. While it raged, another enemy wave was crossing the skies over the Channel. The radar screens were showing something that had never been seen before. They were clogged with a continuous flow of white blips, bombers and fighters streaming in an unbroken line towards England.

All of 11 Group's squadrons were now at readiness or in the air. Among them were the new boys from 222 Squadron, and 30 August would prove a bad day for them. Patrolling over Gravesend at about 11.25a.m., they were bounced by ten Me109s. One Spitfire was shot down, but the wounded pilot managed to put down at Hornchurch. It appeared that the squadron was still flying in the regulation "vic" formation, which had long been abandoned by frontline squadrons in favour of looser tactics that allowed quick responses to ambushes. "Flying in threes turned out to be crazy," said George Unwin of No. 19 Squadron. "If you're flying in threes and you want to turn quickly you can't without running into the other fellow. The Germans knew this and they flew in twos. We had to pick this up and reorganise our tactics accordingly."[33] Formation attacks were time-consuming to set up, and because the wingmen of the "vic" were concentrating on the target and on staying in position relative to the leader's plane, the fighters were vulnerable to being "bounced" from above, just as 22 Squadron was. Nevertheless, the outmoded tactics had a surprisingly long official life. Even in 1941 formation attacks were still being taught to fighter pilots.

From Kenley, the other "green" squadron, No. 253, was scrambled when it seemed the airfield was about to be attacked. The attack failed to materialize, and the fighters were instead vectored south to take on the third wave of bombers, which was crossing the coast near Hove and already being harried by No. 43 Squadron from Tangmere. Three of the 253 Squadron Hurricanes got separated from the rest and were sent east and told to climb as fast as they could.

Just south of Maidstone, Squadron Leader Tom Gleave saw that "stretching as far as the eye could see were rows of Me109s riding above the haze . . . it was a fantastic sight". Gleave led his three Hurricanes into their flank. "I turned with the tide and took a bead on the nearest Me109," he wrote later. On a slight right-hand turn he shot from 175 yards, hitting the engine cowling and cockpit. "The hiss of pneumatics, the smell of cordite in the cockpit and the feel of the nose dipping slightly under the recoil all lent excitement to the first real combat in my short-lived career at Kenley." After firing for about four seconds, he saw "sunlit pieces of the shattered Perspex spiralling after like a shower of tracer. The Hun slewed slightly on while on his back, his nose dropped and he dived beneath out of my sight — going straight down."[34] By now, Gleave's two wingmen had disappeared — both had been quickly shot down — and Gleave had an Me109 on his tail. He dipped to the right and then pulled up in a sharp climb to his left, which brought him back into the centre of the formation. Another Me109 appeared in his sights, and he fired, seeing the German fighter dive spewing black smoke.

As he looked down, he almost collided with another Me109, which streaked past his nose, but then turned into his sights. Gleave fired again, and once more saw his bullets hit home. "I seemed now to be in the midst of a mass of 109s. They were all over the place but still trying to keep some semblance of a formation. Tracers passed above and below, curling downwards and giving the impression of flying in a gigantic cage of gilt wire." Yet another Me109 passed in front of him, and Gleave fired from only 75 yards (67 metres). After only a few seconds he heard a series of "feeble clicks" as his ammunition supply expired; but it was another "kill", his fourth in a matter of minutes. As three further Me109s attached themselves to his tail he made his exit, "flicking the Hurricane on its side at the same time sticking the nose well and truly down, skidding and turning until I was going flat out".

It was an extraordinary feat given the supposed inferiority of the Hurricane to the Me109. But Peter Townsend, himself flying Hurricanes, pointed out that the Hurricane had a trick or two when in a tight spot:

> The Me109. It had the legs of the Hurricane and, thanks to fuel-injection, could jump straight into a dive without the engine cutting, as did our carburettor-fed Merlins. But we had one great advantage: we were more nimble in a turn. So everyone knew what to do: "If the Me109s interfere and it's each one for himself — never climb, never dive. Just turn. Since you haven't got eyes in the back of your head, keep weaving and bear in mind: you're always in danger. Attack from the sun if possible, but never forget to 'beware the Hun in the sun'."[35]

Elsewhere, ten squadrons from 11 Group were in combat over Kent, with the remainder of Gleave's 253 Squadron losing another Hurricane over the Isle of Sheppey. By 11.45a.m., sector controllers were confronted with a picture of whirling confusion, with 48 Observer Corps posts reporting combat overhead.

With almost all his forces now in the air, Park called on 12 Group to defend Kenley and Biggin Hill. Once again, the group's response was to create controversy and bad feeling. Instead of guarding the airfields, the 12 Group pilots went looking for the enemy, missing a *Staffel* of Ju88s, which detached itself from the third

332

bomber wave coming over at midday to attack Biggin Hill. More than thirty 250 kg delayed action bombs were dropped from 18,000 feet, most of them falling on neighbouring villages. At the same time, nearby Kenley was also hit, with buildings destroyed and aircraft on the ground crippled. Croydon and Detling suffered minor damage.

For the first time, there was no precious pause in which to refuel, reflect and recuperate between raids. Shortly after 1p.m., three more waves of attacks by bombers, Me110s and Me109s poured across the Channel at 20-minute intervals. A lucky strike on the main electricity grid shut down the radar stations at Rye, Pevensey, Foreness, Dover, Fairlight, Beachy Head and Whitstable, knocking them out for three hours. The loss of cover meant that only five Squadrons succeeded in intercepting the next raid. One of these was No. 222 Squadron, in the air again and learning once more the harsh lessons of combat. Another Spitfire was lost and two more badly damaged. Kenley, Tangmere and Shoreham were all hit.

At around 4p.m., the defenders were starting to hope that the German effort would now slacken. But the worst was still waiting. For the next two hours, nineteen *Gruppen* of enemy aircraft crossed the Channel, racing to Biggin Hill, Kenley and North Weald as well as to aircraft and component factories at Oxford, Luton and Slough. Although they had been in almost continuous combat since 10.30a.m., Nos 1, 56, 79, 222, 253, 501 and 603 Squadrons were sent up again to intercept. The Oxford raid was turned back, but a formation of

30 Heinkels from *Kampfgeschwader 1*, escorted by Me110s, had crossed the coast north of the Thames at about 5p.m. and broke through to Luton. There it hit the Vauxhall works, killing fifty-three people on the ground and injuring another sixty. Bombers that had missed their primary targets struck Detling airfield, setting oil tanks ablaze, damaging hangars and runways and cutting electricity and telephone lines.

For one squadron, technically not yet operational, the day would produce a baptism of fire. At 4.15p.m., Polish 303 Squadron, which had been formed on 2 August, left Northolt for a training flight. It was due to meet up with a squadron of Blenheims to practise dummy attacks on them north of St Albans, Hertfordshire. As the Hurricanes circled above the Blenheims, a large group of German planes came into view, having penetrated 11 Group's forward defences. Ludwik Paszkiewicz — "Green 1" — spotted the enemy aircraft first and reported over the radio to his squadron leader, Ronald Kellett, that he wanted to attack. But Kellett was keen to get his Hurricanes and the vulnerable Blenheims out of danger, and he made no reply. Paszkiewicz then saw a lone Dornier, which was below the formation, banking towards him. "When enemy aircraft was almost head on," reads the Squadron's intelligence report:

> . . . he saw the Hurricane and dived steeply, followed
> by Green I. When enemy aircraft straightened out,
> Green I closed and fired a burst at 250 yards at the

fuselage from dead astern — no effect apparent. Green I closed to 100 yards and, getting under the enemy aircraft, fired a long burst at the starboard engine, closing to point blank range. Engine stopped and caught fire. Green I broke away . . . Enemy aircraft crashed and exploded.

Paszkiewicz then returned to Northolt, where the rest of the squadron had already landed. In front of his fellow pilots he was given a severe reprimand for leaving the formation without authorization. But Kellett privately congratulated Paszkiewicz for his skilful and deadly attack, and he announced that on his personal recommendation the squadron was fully operational. There was wild applause.

Paszkiewicz's action was typical of the dash and determination exhibited by the Polish airmen in Fighter Command. They had shown extraordinary determination in escaping after the fall of Poland, making their way via Romania and, by a variety of routes, to France. There, many of them had taken part in the air battles of the *Blitzkrieg*, before escaping again to Britain.

Initially, the Polish pilots had been distributed around Fighter Command. On 13 July, however, they had got a squadron of their own, No. 302 (City of Poznan), equipped with Hurricanes, and it became operational in late August, arriving on the frontline in October to take part in the last phase of the Battle of Britain. It was overshadowed, though, by No. 303 (Kosciuśzko). The unit was the descendant of the squadron that had fought against the Soviet armies in

Poland's war with her Russian and Ukrainian neighbours in 1920. It took its name from the Polish military hero Tadeusz Kosciuśzko, who had led an uprising against Russia in 1794.

The experiences of seeing their homelands at the mercy of the Germans had hardened the Poles — and the Czechs — and they were regarded by their fellow pilots as more than usually concentrated and aggressive. Stories circulated of Polish pilots shooting baled-out German aircrew as they dangled on their parachutes. There is little evidence that this was a regular practice, but the historian Adam Zamoyski records that "it is true that some pilots . . . finished off parachuting Germans by flying directly over them; the slipstream would cause the parachute to cannon and the man would fall to the ground like a stone."

Despite arriving late to the battle, 303 Squadron went on to destroy more German aircraft than any other Hurricane squadron and was the fourth-highest scorer of all the fighter units. (303 also included the Czech pilot Josef František, who is credited in some lists as the highest scoring pilot on the British side during the battle.) In all, 139 Polish pilots flew sorties in the battle, with 30 losing their lives. They accounted for nearly 20 per cent of enemy kills.

As afternoon moved into evening on 30 August, ten Ju88s, flying low at under 1,000 feet, feinted towards the Thames Estuary at about 6p.m. before heading directly for Biggin Hill. The attack achieved almost total surprise. No. 79 Squadron was on the ground, with No. 610 patrolling too far away to help. As the pilots of 79 Squadron rushed to get airborne, the station's personnel hurried to the shelter trenches. Sixteen 500 kg bombs fell with devastating accuracy. One landed on an airmen's shelter trench, killing everyone huddled inside. Another buried a dozen airwomen in their trench. One of the four remaining hangars was smashed, along with barracks, storehouses, the armoury and workshops. Three Spitfires were destroyed on the ground and a further two were badly damaged. Thirty-nine ground staff died, twenty-six were wounded, and telephone, electricity, water and gas lines were cut. Hornchurch sector station was forced to take over control of the Biggin Hill sector while Post Office engineers worked frantically to reconnect the base's communications.

Felicity Peake, aged 26 and already a war widow, commanded the 25 WAAFs at Biggin Hill. She described how "the storm broke" as sirens sounded and she ran to the shelter trench, which rapidly filled with people "packed like sardines". Soon she could hear bombs falling:

. . . at the far side of the aerodrome, each one seeming to come nearer until one fell just outside our trench. I remember thinking, I suppose one feels like this in an earthquake. The vibration and blast were such that one felt that one's limbs must surely come apart. Bombs fell pretty continuously, the noise was indescribable.

As soon as the bombing finished, she:

. . . climbed over the earth and rubble that had been blown into our trench and out into that lovely summer day. All was strangely quiet. I wound my way back the way I'd come towards the WAAF guard room. As I approached I saw a woman lying on the ground on the other side of the road into the station. When I started to walk across a voice said to me, "Don't bother, she's dead." I distinctly remember saying to myself and thinking to myself, This is the first dead person I have ever seen. I've got to get used to this. So I made a point of standing and looking at her and then I did find that my feelings were at least controllable. When I arrived at the guard room, or what was left of it, I found that the airwomen's trench had had a direct hit . . . Many airmen were already digging to reach the airwomen who had been trapped in their trench. The dry summer had made the ground unusually hard and their task was no light one. As the work went on, we must all have had the same thought: What shall we find when we reach them? Ambulance and stretcher parties were standing by, a way was cleared, and gradually, one by one, the airwomen were brought out.[36]

Miraculously, although many of the twelve airwomen buried were badly injured, only one, New Zealander Corporal Lena Button, had been killed.

Night closed on a day of desperate fighting. Fighter Command had flown 1,054 sorties, an unprecedented number that would remain the highest daily tally for the entire battle. Twenty-two squadrons had been in action, many up to four times. One squadron, No. 56, went up seven times. The Germans had also had an exhausting day. The crews of Kesselring's *Luftflotte 2* flew 1,310 sorties. As darkness fell, Sperrle's *Luftflotte 3* took over, sending 130 bombers to Liverpool and South Wales, as well as single-bomber sorties against North Weald, Debden, Biggin Hill, Hornchurch, Detling, Eastchurch, Thorney Island, Calshot, Rochford, Broxbourne, Derby, Norwich and Peterborough. Damage to the airfields was light, but the constant alarms and alerts wore down civilian and Fighter Command personnel alike. And the German assault was far from spent.

At 8a.m. on the last day of August, reports from the now-restored radar stations signalled four waves of enemy aircraft forming up, one on the way to Dover and the other three heading up the Thames Estuary. The Dover raid turned out to be Me109s only, flying at 25,000 feet, where they were more than a match for the British fighters. When they were identified by the Observer Corps, Park hurriedly recalled the two squadrons — Nos 501 and 1 (Canadian) — which had been sent to intercept. The order, however, came too late for the Canadians, who were jumped by the Messerschmitts and lost three fighters, with two of the pilots receiving serious burns to face and hands. With no other opposition in the sky, the Me109s set about the Dover balloon barrage.

339

Meanwhile, the formation racing up the Thames Estuary had been confirmed as a mixture of He111s, Do17s and Me110s. Park ordered up 13 squadrons from 7 airfields around London, leaving himself very little in reserve. As the British fighters closed on the raiders, the latter broke into several groups, each targeting, again, the Fighter Command airfields. Near Clacton in Essex, 12 Hurricanes from 257 Squadron at Martlesham engaged 50 Me110s. Two of the raiders were shot down, but the Me110s also took down two British fighters, killing a pilot.

As other raiders approached North Weald, they were met by No. 56 Squadron near Colchester. The Me109 escort shot down four of the squadron, killing one pilot and wounding two more. The Hurricane pilots, exhausted after their exertions the previous day, retreated and the bombers ploughed on to North Weald, where they caused considerable damage.

While North Weald was under bombardment, another formation of 40 Dorniers, with a heavy Me110 escort, was heading further north, making for 12 Group's sector station at Duxford. The attack came as a surprise, and having no fighters at readiness Leigh-Mallory was forced to call on 11 Group for assistance. Fortunately for the airfield, Park had 111 Squadron on patrol nearby. Speeding northeast, the squadron succeeded in manoeuvring into a position to launch another head-on attack. The Luftwaffe formation scattered, and the Me110s went into a defensive circle. Abandoned by their escort, the Dorniers jettisoned their load over the fields and turned for home. One bomber and one Me110 were shot down for the loss of one of 111 Squadron's Hurricanes.

Aircraftman Charles Cooper, a 111 Squadron armourer, witnessed an incident testifying to the pilots' utter fatigue: ". . . we noticed one aircraft [had] landed and taxied a short distance only to stop some way off with the engine still turning over. Thinking the pilot had been wounded, we dashed over to the aircraft, only to find the pilot, Johnny Walker DFC, a Canadian, was leaning forward with his body held by the Sutton harness, head on his chest and asleep with exhaustion."[37]

Duxford had been spared, but bombers made their way unchecked to Debden. There they dropped a hundred 250 kg bombs, causing eighteen casualties, destroying three barrack blocks and the sick bay, and severely damaging four Hurricanes caught on the ground. No. 19 Squadron's Spitfires from Fowlmere had been scrambled shortly after 8a.m. to intercept this raid, but they caught up with the bombers only after the damage was done. Over Little Shelford, they spotted the retreating formation of about 20 Dorniers and some 50 Me110s. The Spitfires went into the attack, but the Me110s had the advantage of height.

The experienced No. 19 Squadron was, at this stage of the battle, unique, in that its Spitfires had been fitted out with cannon to test their operational use. It was the latest development in a long effort, since the mid-1930s, to improve the punch of Fighter Command's weaponry. The challenge in terms of a single-engine fighter was to maximize firepower while minimizing the weight of guns and ammunition.

A special Air Ministry meeting on armaments in July 1934 had decided that the high speeds of the new generation of monoplane fighters would mean that they would only be able to hold an enemy bomber in their sights for two seconds. For such a brief attack to be decisive, argued ballistics expert Captain F. W. Hill, the fighter would need at least eight guns firing 1,000 rounds per minute. Despite opposition from older officers used to two or four guns, in 1935 specification F.5/34 was issued, which included instructions to the designers of the Spitfire and Hurricane that both should carry eight Browning machine-guns with 300 rounds each — enough for about 14 seconds' firing.

The American-manufactured Browning, which dated from the First World War, was an excellent weapon, reliable and fast-firing, capable of up to 1,260 rounds per minute. At first the guns were imported, but soon manufacturing rights were acquired by the Vickers Company to make them in Britain. For the sturdy Hurricane, these instructions presented no difficulties, and the guns were mounted in the wings in four-gun batteries. But the Spitfire had much thinner wings, and it proved impossible to group the guns in a single gun bay. Instead, two two-gun batteries were installed, which made for slower rearming. For both fighters, Dunlop developed and supplied electrically controlled pneumatic cocking and firing systems. It also proved necessary to provide hot-air ducts to prevent the gun lubricant from freezing at the unprecedented heights at which these new fighters could operate.

The bullets were 0.303 inches in calibre, the same as standard-issue rifles. It became clear in the early stages of the Battle of Britain that these were not always able to penetrate the armour installed in German bombers and fighters. Fighter Command armourers started introducing De Wilde incendiaries and armour-piercing bullets, which increased effectiveness, but they still required a "lucky hit" — on an engine, a vital control, or the pilot — to bring an enemy aircraft down.

By contrast, the Luftwaffe's Me109s were armed with two wing-mounted Oerlikon 20mm cannon and two 7.9mm-calibre machine-guns in the nose. In the small-framed Messerschmitt there was room for only 60 cannon rounds per gun, and the rate of fire at 520 rounds per minute was under half that of the British fighters' machine-guns. But the Me109 still carried a heavier punch — a three-second burst from an RAF fighter weighed about 13 pounds (almost 6 kg); the same burst from an Me109 delivered 18 pounds (over 8 kg). The cannon shells of a Messerschmitt exploded on impact, which meant that one or two hits could bring down a metal-skinned Spitfire. Me109 pilot Hans-Ekkehard Bob summarized the differences: "In a fraction of a second, I could bring down a Spitfire. If I could hit it twice, I could destroy it. The English had to score a great many hits with their machine-guns to bring a plane down but they didn't need to shoot as accurately."[38]

343

To make up the gap, the minister for aircraft production, Lord Beaverbrook, advocated introducing the cannon and pushed for conversion. A suitable weapon seemed to be available — the 20mm cannon that Hispano-Suiza had been manufacturing in Britain since 1937. Beaverbrook argued successfully for Fighter Command's most experienced squadron, No. 19, to try it out in battle, even though tests were far from being completed. At the beginning of July, the first of the Mark 1B Spitfires had been delivered to the squadron at Fowlmere, armed with a Hispano-Suiza cannon in each wing.

The squadron soon discovered that the guns provided great accuracy, destructive power and range. But the feed mechanism was unreliable and the ejector caused repeated jamming of spent cases and stoppages. If one gun stopped, the asymmetric recoil made it impossible to fire the other one accurately. It was also prone to icing up at heights above 20,000 feet, and the small amount of ammunition — 6 seconds' worth — was deemed insufficient. But Beaverbrook was not deterred and the squadron, with its new armament, was sent into battle.

In time the gremlins were shaken out, and in 1941 Hurricanes were armed with four Hispano Mark II guns; but continuing difficulties with the Spitfires meant that most carried only two cannon, alongside six machine-guns.

Those technical difficulties were not solved as No. 19 went into action on 31 August; it would prove a bad day for the squadron. Flying Officer James Coward, Green Section leader, was on the point of firing when he was hit in the leg by a cannon shell. He felt little but, looking down, "I could see my foot hanging loose on the pedal, but you thought you were invincible and I still went in to open fire." However, the recently fitted cannon in his wings jammed. Still heading directly for the Dornier, Coward ducked as the top of his Spitfire grazed the underside of the bomber. The hood of his plane was ripped off and the Spitfire spiralled downwards, out of control and spraying its pilot with petrol. "I baled out at 22,000 feet," said Coward, "and got caught on the back of the cockpit as I went." Thrashing about on top of his aircraft, he was suddenly free:

I was going to free-fall for a bit in case they shot up my parachute, but my foot was thrashing around up by my thigh and the pain was too much. I pulled the ripcord and I swung there in a great figure of eight. The blood was pumping out of my leg — it was amazing how bright it was so high up. I thought I'd bleed to death so I used the radio wire from my helmet to put a tourniquet round my thigh. After that, I felt no pain, apart from the petrol that had drenched me and was stinging my armpits and crotch. I drifted across Duxford towards Fowlmere and then the wind took me back again.[39]

Luckily for Coward, a doctor was at hand when he landed painfully in a field. He was taken to

345

Addenbrooke's Hospital, where his leg was amputated below the knee.

One other No. 19 pilot who had been shot down baled out unhurt. The Spitfire of young Pilot Officer Ray Aeberhardt had also been hit, but he attempted to get his struggling aircraft back to ground at Fowlmere. Armourer Fred Roberts was watching: "He went up on his nose on landing and the plane caught fire, we were there and we watched him burning, we couldn't do anything, we couldn't get near him. We hadn't got the fire-fighting facilities at Fowlmere and that sort of thing, you know."[40] Aeberhardt, at 19, had been the youngest man in the squadron. No. 19 had lost four aircraft shot down, for only one Me110 in return.

Shortly after 9a.m., two more Luftwaffe groups, one of about 20 Dorniers escorted by fighters, the other of Me109s and Me110s, swept up the Thames Estuary. The Dorniers dropped 80 bombs on Eastchurch airfield, causing limited damage, while the fighters strafed Detling.

Further waves of Me109s over Kent were ignored by Park, but when two new formations of bombers — Heinkels and Dorniers — were mapped heading for Croydon and Biggin Hill, he had to react quickly. No. 85 Squadron's pilots at Croydon were sent to their aircraft, whose engines had already been started. Leading the squadron, Peter Townsend glanced back at his men, whose fighters had formed up behind him. "They looked superb, all those Hurricanes," he later wrote, "straining against the brakes with their long, eager noses tilted skywards and the sun glinting on their whirling propellers. Every pilot was watching me, waiting for the signal. At last it came: 'Off you go,' called Kenley, and we were racing forward with a bellow of twelve thousand horsepower." It was the last time Townsend would lead his squadron into battle by day. "The bombs were already on their way down. I had just moved the lever to raise the undercarriage, when my engine faltered, faded, and picked up again. Blast had struck the motor like a punch in the wind. Turning in the cockpit, I saw the rest of the squadron emerging from a vast eruption of smoke and debris." Overhead, thousands of feet above, Me110s were "wheeling in the blue, with Me 109s swarming above."[41]

At a severe height disadvantage, No. 85 Squadron did well, "flogging their Hurricanes mercilessly during the climb" and shooting down at least two Me110s, but losing three aircraft in the process, including the squadron leader's. "A blast of shot suddenly splattered my Hurricane," recalled Townsend, "my left foot was kicked off the rudder-bar, petrol gushed into the cockpit. The shock was so terrific that for a few instants I lost control and went into a steep dive . . . then I straightened out. By some miracle, my Hurricane had not burst into flames . . . My windscreen was starred with bullets . . . I baled out and watched my poor Hurricane dive into the trees and blow up." Injured in the foot, Townsend would be out of action for weeks, one of several highly experienced pilots lost from the frontline on 31 August.

There was some damage to Croydon, but it was Biggin Hill that was worst hit. Two *Staffeln* of He111s broke through to bomb from 12,000 feet, hitting two Spitfires on the ground, as well as two of the remaining hangars and other buildings. Most serious was a further hit on the vital operations room, severing the communications and power lines again, thus undoing all the hard work since the raid of the previous day. Sergeant Gunner Ben Elswood was one of those manning the sector station's anti-aircraft battery at the time:

Anyone would think that we were the only important aerodrome protecting London. Day after day, raid after raid. As soon as the bombers come over and make bloody holes in the ground, we go out and fill 'em up again. Everything is in poor shape, but Jerry hadn't broken our spirit. Hangars continued to operate even with no roofs on. There was always a steady stream of ambulances to take the injured to hospital, in fact it got to a bloody state where they queued up waiting for the next raid. If there were heroes though, then it had to be the women. They just don't know how to bow to defeat. Bloody marvellous they were, stuck to their posts like glue, each one deserved a medal.[42]

As they left Biggin Hill, the Heinkels were attacked by 253 Squadron, which shot down two of their number. But Squadron Leader Tom Gleave, the destroyer of four Me109s the previous day, was hit by fire from his blind spots behind and below him. His reserve fuel tank, between the instrument panel and the engine, burst into flames, splashing Gleave with burning fuel. With the cockpit on fire, he struggled to bale out. He groped among the flames in front of him to disconnect his radio lead and oxygen tube, but in vain. As his clothes and hair caught fire, he squirmed out of his harness, yanked open the hood, and wrenched off his helmet. He shot from the cockpit like a projectile and then steeled himself to pull the ripcord with his blistered hands.

Landing in a field, Gleave surveyed his legs and arms, on which the flesh now hung in charred strips. He had feared being burned more than anything. As well as his legs and arms, his hair, eyelids and nose had also been consumed by the heat of the burning cockpit. A WAAF, Igraine Hamilton, who worked at Orpington Hospital remembered: "When Tom Gleave's wife came to see him for the first time after his crash, she said, 'I don't know! Playing with matches again?' Anyone who had a wife like that was very lucky."[43]

Ten minutes earlier, the sector station at Hornchurch had also come under attack. The Luftwaffe had learned to focus and coordinate their attacks with devastating effect. There was little warning. No. 54 Squadron's Al Deere was lined up with his comrades on the runway, when "a wildly gesticulating voice" started shouting over the radio telephone, "Hornet aircraft get airborne as quickly as you can, enemy in the immediate vicinity."[44] Below, Richard Hillary of 603 Squadron was watching. "I looked up again, and this time I saw them — about a dozen slugs, shining in the bright sun and coming straight on," he wrote. "At the rising scream of the first bomb I instinctively shrugged up my shoulders and ducked my head."[45]

"I was not quite airborne, when a bomb burst on the airfield, ahead of me and to my left," wrote Deere. For a moment, he thought he had made it. Then "a tremendous blast of air, carrying showers of earth, struck me in the face and the next moment [I was] thinking vaguely that I was upside down." "I saw the three Spitfires," wrote Hillary. "One moment they were about twenty feet up in close formation; the next catapulted apart as though on elastic. The leader [Deere] went over on his back and ploughed along the runway with a rending crash of tearing fabric; No. 2 put a wing in and spun round on his airscrew, while the plane on the left was blasted wingless into the next field." Hillary saw no more as he dashed for the shelter.[46]

Deere's Spitfire had indeed hurtled down the runway on its back. "Finally the aircraft stopped its mad upside-down dash leaving me trapped in the cockpit, in almost total darkness, and breathing petrol fumes, the smell of which was overpowering," wrote Deere. "Bombs were still exploding outside, but this was not as frightening as the thought of fire from the petrol now seeping into the ground around my head. One spark and I would be engulfed in flames." Miraculously, none of the three pilots had been killed, and one now came to the aid of Deere, freeing him from the cockpit. They helped each other across the airfield to the shelter as machine-gun bullets hit the ground around them.

350

When the pilots and airmen and women emerged from the shelter, they found that "Gaping holes and great gobbets of earth were everywhere," Hillary wrote, "the runways were in something of a mess." Six airmen had been killed and many more wounded. "Sick quarters bore all the signs of a casualty clearing station, a queue of injured airmen and stretcher cases filling the passageway," wrote Deere. Sixty bombs had been dropped in a line across the airfield, from just outside the perimeter through the 54 Squadron dispersal area and beyond into a housing estate. Hangars and the operations room, however, had not been hit. The station commander ordered that every available man and woman, including officers, should immediately repair the aerodrome surface, and by 4p.m., says Hillary, "there was not a hole to be seen".

At Biggin Hill, too, furious work was under way to restore communications, infrastructure and runways. But both sector stations would be hit again before the end of the day. At about 5.50p.m., Ju88s and Me110s of *Erprobungsgruppe 210* dropped thirty bombs each on Biggin Hill and Hornchurch, where two Spitfires were destroyed on the ground. The Biggin Hill raiders were engaged by the Hornchurch squadrons, Nos 222 and 54, with losses on both sides.

It was now clear that the Luftwaffe's tactics had changed from mass attacks across a wide front to incessant, concentrated assaults on the approaches to London held by 11 Group. The last two days had seen 2,800 enemy sorties against the sector stations, hitting the vital organs of Fighter Command. Without the

351

incalculable benefit of radar and the early warning system in operation, Fighter Command would have been overwhelmed.

As it was, it had still been a grim day. Most of the Fighter Command losses were the result of fighter-versus-fighter combat. With the concentration of Me109s in the Pas de Calais, the enemy bombers now had a thick phalanx of escorts, which the Hurricanes and Spitfires were having great difficulty penetrating. And that night, the bombers were over England again, with most of the force concentrated, once more, against Liverpool. At the same time, the invasion itself was taking visible shape in the form of the huge build-up of shipping gathering in the French Channel ports.

Today, Fighter Command had suffered 37 aircraft destroyed, 9 pilots killed and 18 others badly wounded. Fighters had also been destroyed on the ground. The Luftwaffe had lost 39 aircraft in combat. The margins were shrinking to nothing.

The intensive fighting and attrition were also having a more subtle effect on the make-up of Fighter Command, altering the deep sense of hierarchy that normally pervaded it. Before the Second World War, there were sharp distinctions among the ranks. In October 1936, Peter Brothers had arrived at his squadron as a pilot officer. "Back then you were a 'bog rat', just a pilot officer, lowest of the low, unwanted, and underpaid," he remembered. "Nobody spoke to you except when a flying officer or a flight lieutenant would tell you to go and press the bell so a waiter would come in to get him a drink."[47]

Between officers and other ranks, there was an even sharper divide, which had persisted even when the fighting started — when officers and sergeant pilots were doing the same job and sharing the same dangers. "There was no familiarity or anything like that," said Flight Sergeant George Unwin of No. 19 Squadron. "You never mixed at all, you were trained like that, the RAF built it into you."[48] This was partly a hangover from before the war, when the majority of sergeant pilots were ex-apprentices who had been accepted for flying training but might at any stage be required to return to their old trades.

Unwin remembered that by an unspoken agreement the officers and NCOs drank in different pubs. This was not the case in every squadron, but all units had different messes, with the officers' one superior in comfort to that of the NCOs. Officers also had a smarter, more comfortable uniform, and a batman or orderly to make their tea and clean and maintain their uniforms. NCOs had to polish their own buttons. Nearly a third of the "fighter boys" in the summer of 1940 were NCOs and almost all those who survived would eventually be given commissions. But, to begin with, in order to become an officer it helped greatly to have gone to the right school, or to have the bearing of an officer and gentleman.

This culture of division could lead to practical inefficiencies. "When I became an officer," said Cyril "Bam" Bamberger of 610 Squadron, "the controller and the wing commander would drop into our mess and we were up to date with what was going on. We were very well briefed. But the sergeant didn't know what was going on. This separation was a big weakness."[49] Even among the sergeants there was a pecking order, with those from the RAF Volunteer Reserve looked down on by the regulars who had come up through apprenticeships. That men who were doing the same job should have such different levels of status and privilege was unremarkable at the time.

As the battle wore on, many of the distinctions were eroded by the challenges and consequences of the fighting and by the shared danger. Also, the technical nature of a pilot's job meant that the RAF had to become more meritocratic — and thus more socially egalitarian — than the other services, and the culture of mickey-taking, along with the consciousness that all pilots by the very nature of their job belonged to an elite, helped blur the internal distinctions. Auxiliary squadrons lost their exclusive character as the original men were killed, wounded or posted away, and as more NCOs arrived at squadrons, so the social mix was also diluted. Before 1940 was over, even the squadrons that, pre-war, had been the most exclusive contained men from every conceivable background.

On the evening of 31 August, Dowding went to dinner at the prime minister's country retreat, Chequers. "Jock" Colville recalled the robust conversation:

Dowding is splendid. He stands up to the P.M., refuses
to be particularly unpleasant about the Germans, and
is the very antithesis of the complacency with which
so many Englishmen are afflicted. He told him that he
could not understand why the Germans kept on
coming in waves instead of concentrating on one mass
raid a day which could not be effectively parried.
Ismay suggested that they might be short of planes
and have to use bombers twice daily. There was a
great discussion about the ethics of shooting down
enemy pilots landing by parachute, Dowding maintaining it should be done and the P.M. saying that an
escaping pilot was like a drowning sailor.[50]

The next morning, assuming that the Luftwaffe would
be exhausted after the efforts of the previous two days,
Dowding took the opportunity to pull two shattered
squadrons out of the frontline. No. 151, with only ten
aircraft and twelve pilots left, moved from Stapleford to
Digby and was replaced by 46 Squadron, rebuilt since
its destruction in the Norwegian campaign. No. 56
Squadron, leaderless and down to seven aircraft, retired
to the comparative calm of Boscombe Down, with 249
Squadron taking over its duties at North Weald. Biggin
Hill was battered and only semi-functioning, now able
to accommodate only one squadron rather than the
four it had housed previously. So, No. 72 moved to
Croydon, while 79 Squadron alone remained at Biggin
Hill to provide airfield defence.

At 10.20a.m. on 1 September, the first raid was
reported assembling over France. Half an hour later,

the German aircraft were advancing towards Dover on a five-mile front. Fourteen squadrons were scrambled, intercepting the raiders as they crossed the coast between Dungeness and Margate. On reaching land, the force split into two groups, each of about thirty bombers and fighters, with one formation heading for the Thames Estuary.

A fierce dogfight now developed over northeastern Kent. No. 85 Squadron had been in action the evening before, shooting down four Me109s over the Channel. It was now back in combat, downing two more of the single-engine Messerschmitts. No. 1 Squadron from Northolt and No. 54 from Hornchurch joined the combat, while No. 72 Squadron was sent up from Croydon. The latter lost three Spitfires when it was jumped by Me109s.

While the defenders were engaged by the Me109s, however, the bombers got through, hitting Detling, Eastchurch and the London docks. At Biggin Hill, 79 Squadron was caught on the ground, and at least one Hurricane was destroyed.

The defending fighters hardly had time to refuel before the aircraft of Nos 1, 54, 72, 85 and 616 squadrons were scrambled again, as 170 Luftwaffe planes crossed the Kent coast shortly after 1.30p.m. Three squadrons — Nos 72, 253 and 616 — engaged the attackers over Folkestone and Hastings, and No. 85 Squadron ran into them near Lympne. One of 85's Hurricanes developed engine trouble and the pilot landed at Lympne airfield, only to see his aircraft wrecked when bombs started falling on the runways and hangars.

No. 85 Squadron stayed with the Luftwaffe formation as it ploughed north, but the Hurricanes could not penetrate the escort to break up the bombers, which stayed on a course for Biggin Hill and Kenley. As the fighting moved closer to London, the defenders started to suffer badly. Four Hurricanes were shot down. One of the pilots was killed in his cockpit, a second died when his parachute failed to open, and a third, already badly burned, suffered a broken back, leg and arm when his parachute only partially opened. Sergeant Glendon Booth would die of his injuries five months later, aged only twenty.

No. 85 Squadron had now been in action seven times in four days and had lost its wounded commander, Peter Townsend, and a total of nine aircraft. As its diary lamented, "only six Hurricanes, all that remained of the squadron, landed at Croydon, with one landing wheels up." Two days later, the squadron was withdrawn from the frontline.

As the German formation neared the sector stations, the aircraft remaining there for airfield defence were sent up, including No. 79 Squadron from Biggin Hill. But they were unable to turn back the raid, and three 79 Squadron aircraft were shot down. The bombers arrived at Biggin Hill while a funeral service was underway for those killed in previous raids. First, the twin-engine Me110s came in low, bombing with great accuracy and destroying buildings and infrastructure; then, Dorniers dropped high explosives from on high.

Kenley suffered as well, with Do17s bombing during a low-level run over the airfield.

At 5.30p.m. came the last wave of attacks, as seven distinct formations were plotted approaching across the Channel. Most of these turned out to be fighters, which raced across the southern part of Kent, strafing balloon barrages and other targets of opportunity. With the defences distracted, a formation of bombers and Me110s hit the forward airfields of Hawkinge and Lympne, and then moved on to Biggin Hill. It was the third attack of the day, and the worst. A direct hit wrecked the operations room, forcing its move to a shop in the village, and four Spitfires were destroyed on the ground. Biggin Hill's last remaining squadron, No. 79, was moved to Croydon.

As daylight operations ended on 1 September, the Luftwaffe had flown only half the number of sorties it had flown the day before; but the German planes had still succeeded in hitting vital airfields. Fighter Command had failed to stop them and had suffered 16 fighters shot down and 4 damaged. The Germans had suffered similar losses, but they must have felt they were at last making headway in their plan to wreck the infrastructure of Fighter Command and destroy its ability to defend the British homeland.

That night, 120 German bombers ranged across England against scattered targets. The morning light of 2 September saw an attack at 7a.m., when a *Gruppe* of Dorniers from *Kampfgeschwader 3* and one *Geschwader* of Me109s assembled over Calais. Sixty fighters were scrambled in response, as the raid approached Deal, but only twenty of them made contact; the others were kept back to patrol over the vulnerable airfields.

Above Maidstone the formation split up and fanned out to attack Biggin Hill, Rochford, Eastchurch and North Weald. The latter was saved from damage by the intervention of 222 Squadron from Hornchurch and 249 Squadron from North Weald. No. 249 lost three aircraft, but managed to break up the bomber formation sufficiently to disrupt the targeting of the airfield. But the raids on Eastchurch and Rochford were more successful for the Germans. At Rochford, an ammunition dump was hit and five planes destroyed on the ground. Spitfires of 72 Squadron managed to intercept the Biggin Hill raid, having recently arrived south from Acklington. While they were at 13,000 feet and tussling with Me110s, Me109s and Dorniers, nine bombers flew in at low level, causing further damage.

No. 603 Squadron from Hornchurch had been scrambled when it looked, for a moment, as if their airfield were about to come under attack. As the bombers headed away, 603 was ordered to give chase and succeeded in downing three Me109s over the sea. One fell to the guns of Richard Hillary.

By noon, another large formation was approaching Dover. This time, Park sent up his fighters earlier, ordering them to hit the main formation before it split up into groups heading for individual targets. No. 72 Squadron, flying from Croydon, sighted and engaged the 250-strong body of planes to the north of Rochester, and No. 603 Squadron joined the mêlée just east of Sheerness. Three of the 603 pilots were shot down, but all of them survived. The German formation did succeed in breaking into separate attacks, and once again a huge dogfight broke out over the Kent countryside, involving 70 Fighter Command aircraft. Nos 111 and 222 Squadrons both sustained losses, while above Ashford No. 43 Squadron shot down two Me109s but lost three aircraft itself. Pilot Officer Tony Woods-Scawen had successfully baled out on four previous occasions, but now he found himself in a stricken Hurricane only 1,000 feet above the ground. He jumped nonetheless, but at that moment his aircraft exploded above him, killing him. His brother Patrick, a pilot in No. 85 Squadron, had been lost the previous day. As before, the Hurricanes and Spitfires found themselves dragged away in a high-altitude fight while the bombers ploughed on unmolested beneath. Bombs targeted Biggin Hill, Kenley and Hornchurch, where a successful last-ditch defence by No. 603 Squadron saw many of the bombers driven to jettison their loads wide of the aerodrome.

Then, at 5.30p.m., 250 more enemy aircraft were over Kent, leading to another huge fracas between 160 Me109s on the one side and fighters from Nos 46, 72, 111, 222, 501, 603 and 616 Squadrons on the other. No 501 was hit hard, losing four Hurricanes, with two pilots wounded and one killed. One squadron member, Peter Morfill, remembered the occasion with a laconic matter-of-factness that suggested just how accustomed the squadrons were becoming to transient mortality:

One lunchtime, at Gravesend, a chap came in a beautiful Riley car and as it stopped, we looked in and saw squash rackets, tennis rackets and golf clubs, I think. The CO asked the newcomer, "Where have you come from?" He replied, "So-and-so Spitfires."

"Hurricanes here," said the CO. "Same thing, anyway. Grab yourself some food but forget sleeping quarters at the moment, we'll do that later on. We're on readiness in quarter of an hour so you've just got time to grab something. We lost three blokes today, so you're on."

"Yes, sir!" he replied. I will always remember his face. Anyway, we took off at about two o'clock and he was dead at quarter past. So after the day was over, the CO phoned his mother, and she didn't want to know anything, not the car, nothing, so now we had a squadron car. We used to go from Gravesend down the hill to the pub down the bottom there and could get seven people in this car.[51]

The early evening Luftwaffe raids targeted Detling and Eastchurch, where the bomb dump was hit. Everything within 400 yards (365 metres) — buildings, drainage pipes, power and telephone cables and five aircraft — was destroyed. It was the final straw for Eastchurch; like Manston before it, the airfield was declared non-operational.

The most worrying development was that bombers were now reaching aircraft factories. At Brooklands the Vickers works that produced Wellington bombers was struck, and at Rochester the Short Brothers factory was hit, with civilians killed and buildings demolished. Fortunately for Fighter Command, the raiders missed the Hawker factory at Brooklands, which had been their primary target.

It had been another gruelling day for Fighter Command. Over 700 sorties had been flown and 25 fighters had been destroyed, with another 4 badly damaged. Seven airfields had been hit, for which effort the Luftwaffe had lost 22 planes shot down and nine damaged.

Once again, Dowding was forced to shuffle his forces. At Croydon, No. 111 Squadron from Debden took the place of 85 Squadron. The replacements were hardly rested and fresh. The pilots had been averaging four hours' sleep a night and they were down to seven aircraft. At Hornchurch, No. 54 Squadron was reaching the end of its endurance. Even Al Deere, famously calm, found himself twitching and snapping. One pilot fell asleep into his breakfast plate. The next day, 3 September, the squadron was replaced by No. 41 Squadron, which had been re-forming at Catterick. The new squadron commander had a shock. "We were amazed at the eagerness of you chaps to get away from Hornchurch, but we soon learned why," he said. "None of you looked as if you had slept for a week." Al Deere calculated that during August his squadron had received 18 replacements, but now only 16 pilots remained for the transfer north. No. 66 Squadron arrived at Kenley from Coltishall. Both Nos 41 and 66 Squadrons would suffer a painful first few days in the south. "After the hard lessons of the first two days, we became more canny and determined not to let ourselves be caught from above," wrote Richard Hillary, whose 603 Squadron had suffered over the previous few days.

Tuesday 3 September was, of course, the first anniversary of the start of the war, and Britain found herself in a grim situation. Across the Channel, nearly 2,000 barges, 1,600 escort vessels, 419 tugs and 168 transports had been assembled. On the same day, Generalfeldmarschall Wilhelm Keitel ordered the embarkation of invasion materials to begin in eight days' time, on 11 September, the date set for Invasion Day minus ten.

In the meantime, Fighter Command's sector stations were targeted once again. The largest raid on 3 September started appearing on British radar at around 8.30a.m.. Three squadrons went to meet the attackers, but they were ordered to disengage once it was realized that the enemy formation consisted almost entirely of fighters. However, by 9.30a.m. a large formation of 54 Do17s, 80 Me110s and 40 Me109s was flying up the Thames, heading, it seemed, for North Weald or Debden, or perhaps even London itself. Park scrambled No. 249 Squadron from North Weald, No. 17 from Debden and No. 603 from Hornchurch, and they joined battle.

No. 603 Squadron climbed to meet the raiders. As its pilots moved into line astern, Me109s dived on top of them. The Spitfires turned to meet them, and a fierce dogfight ensued. Richard Hillary managed to fire two bursts at an Me109, seeing smoke start to appear, but was then shaken as his aircraft was struck. Within seconds, the cockpit was on fire. Hillary wrenched at the hood, but it stuck fast. He undid his harness to free his arms, but now the flames were licking around him and he passed out. Then, the Spitfire flicked into a spin and rolled onto its back, at which point Hillary, still unconscious, fell from the plane. The cold air brought him round. He grabbed at his ripcord, the canopy blossomed overhead and he drifted down into the sea off Margate. It was three hours before he was picked up and taken to hospital to be treated for serious burns to his face and hands.

No. 603 Squadron lost one other Spitfire, with another wounded pilot, and No. 17 suffered as well. One of its pilots, Sergeant Desmond Fopp, was badly burned but managed to bale out after being hit by an Me110. As he recalled:

We were scrambled late and did not get sufficient altitude to achieve a favourable attacking position from above, with the result that we had to attack head-on at about 20,000 feet, and hope to break up the large formation of Do17s, with guns blazing which did separate them considerably. I had just put a Dornier's engine out and he was smoking badly when I saw three Me110s coming in behind me in line astern. By this time I had run out of ammunition but decided that as I could not match them for speed I would turn into them and simulate an attack. This I did and to my astonishment and joy they broke all round me so I immediately half rolled and dived for the deck. Unfortunately for me one of them was also below and behind out of sight and managed to put a cannon shell into the radiator, with the result that all I heard was a thump and the next second I was sitting in a ball of fire.[52]

Flying Officer David Hanson shot down a Dornier but was struck by return fire. By the time he had struggled free of his cockpit, he was only a hundred feet off the ground and was killed when he plunged to earth. A third No. 17 pilot managed to force-land his stricken aircraft at North Weald.

The efforts of the pilots could not prevent an attack on North Weald, where 200 bombs, many delayed-action, were dropped. Four of the base personnel were killed on the ground and the runways were cratered. Hornchurch and Debden were also hit, but both remained operational.

As the bombers departed, Hurricanes from six squadrons attacked in waves. A number of Me110s were shot down, with successes for Nos 46 and 303 Squadrons. But the former accidentally shot down two Blenheims near North Weald (as well as losing three of its Hurricanes), and the latter, for all its aggression, saw one aircraft lost and one damaged for its one kill. In other squadrons, losses were surprisingly high against the retreating formation of Dorniers and Me110s. Four aircraft of 257 Squadron were shot down, with one flight commander killed and another very badly burned.

Two squadrons from 12 Group's Duxford sector were also called on, and having had a longer time to climb they found themselves in a better attacking position. No. 310 Czech Squadron fell on the Me110s, shooting down four of them, and Spitfires of 19 Squadron hit a further three. The latter were hampered, though, by continuing problems with their experimental cannons.

The afternoon of 3 September would see only one half-hearted raid, as the Luftwaffe drew breath for the next phase. In The Hague, Goering and his senior commanders debated the next move. Goering sensed that Hitler was losing faith in the invasion plan. It would require a huge new effort by the Luftwaffe to restore confidence. Intelligence reports suggested that Fighter Command was running out of aircraft and that its bases around London were in ruins. What better way to lure the rest of Dowding's forces into the air than to attack London itself? Otherwise, Dowding could simply move his forces north, out of range of Me109s, to preserve them for deployment against an invasion. Hitler, furious with the continued Bomber Command attacks on Berlin, was ready now to countenance such a move.

Sperrle was more cautious and distrusted the optimistic assessments of Fighter Command's supposedly paltry resources. But Kesselring, who spoke with the authority of having overseen the aerial destruction of Warsaw and Rotterdam, pressed for an all-out offensive on the British capital. "If you can pull off these attacks," he told the Luftwaffe commanders, the invasion would become unnecessary and "you will have saved the lives of 100,000 German soldiers."

Perennially self-confident, Goering went on to address his senior lieutenants:

My fellow commanders, we are now on the brink of victory. An assault and an invasion of England is now more promising than ever before. Our intelligence has now informed us that the RAF is now down to less than a hundred fighter aircraft, the airfields protecting London are out of action because of the superb and accurate bombing of our bomber forces, their communications are in disarray, and now we are told, their air commanders are arguing with each other.

Gentlemen, another phase is now almost complete. The RAF is now no longer the great threat that it used to be, and we can now draw every available fighter plane that the RAF has into the air, because the next target must be London itself.

On Wednesday 4 September, Hitler announced the change of German strategy in a speech at the Berlin *Sportpalast*, which was later broadcast. "Just now . . . Mr Churchill is demonstrating his new brainchild, the night air raid," he said. "When they declare that they will increase their attacks on our cities, then we will raze their cities to the ground . . . We will stop the handiwork of these night air pirates, so help us God!"[53]

Bombs had been falling on British civilians for three months. Over a thousand people had been killed by the end of August, and as many again injured. But to switch the whole weight of the German bombers against London, rather than the RAF airfields, was a decisive change of strategy by the Luftwaffe.

London was an obvious strategic target. Heavily populated, it was the hub of national road, rail and water transport and of the country's commerce, industry and finance. It was the nation's biggest port and the centre of the government, legislature and judiciary. Primary targets would still be industrial and commercial, in particular the docks. But the Luftwaffe command was fully aware that many civilians would be killed. It was part of the plan to cause terror and chaos and create pressure from a panic-stricken public on Britain's rulers to seek terms with Hitler. The threat of invasion loomed in the background. During his speech, Hitler made a menacing joke. "In England they're filled with curiosity and keep asking 'Why doesn't he come?' Be calm. Be calm. He's coming! He's coming!"

For three more days, though, the attacks on Fighter Command would press on relentlessly. The weather stayed bright and fair, ideal conditions for the attackers. As on the preceding days, RAF losses were equal to, or greater than, the Luftwaffe's.

On the morning of 4 September, 70 He111s and Do17s with 200 Me109s approached the Kent coast between Dover and Hastings, then split up to attack Eastchurch and Lympne. Just after midday a formation of 300 aircraft approached Folkestone, while another raid homed in on the Poling radar station and yet another formation approached Brighton. Park put up 14 squadrons, including newly arrived No. 66 and two borrowed from other sectors. During fierce fighting, 66 Squadron lost five Spitfires. Apart from one formation that got through to damage the Short Brothers factory in Rochester, the raids were driven back.

Under cover of the larger raids, 20 bomb-carrying Me110s had crossed the coast near Littlehampton and were flying northwards at low altitude, following the railway lines. At 1.15p.m. they were spotted 6,000 feet over Guildford, Surrey, by the Observer Corps. No. 253 Squadron, patrolling from Kenley, was alerted and intercepted them, diving on the low-flying Messerschmitts, shooting down five and leaving a trail of wreckage across the Surrey countryside. But some of the heavy fighters made it to their target, Brooklands, where they again hit the Vickers works rather than the Hurricane-producing Hawker factory. The raid was still devastating. Six 500 kg bombs landed on the machine shops and assembly sheds for Wellington bombers, killing eighty-eight people and wounding many more. The factory was wrecked, and it was four days before bomber production restarted.

On Thursday 5 September, No. 66 Squadron lost a further three aircraft. The day saw Kesselring abandon his established pattern and instead launch smaller raids, over a period of eight hours starting at 10a.m. The first formations were intercepted by four squadrons, including the newly arrived No. 41 Squadron, which engaged Dorniers and Me109s over the Thames Estuary, shooting down two of the fighters and damaging two bombers for the loss of one Spitfire. At the same time, No. 79 Squadron was scrambling to defend its Biggin Hill base, while eight Hurricanes of 111 Squadron took on a hundred enemy aircraft just north of Dungeness.

Soon afterwards, No. 19 Squadron, now back in standard Spitfires armed with machine-guns, hit a raid of more than 100 aircraft heading for Hornchurch. The formation was turned back, but the squadron lost its commanding officer, shot down and killed, and had two other Spitfires badly damaged.

Lympne and Eastchurch airfields suffered some minor damage, and at about 3.30p.m. a raid was plotted again over the Thames Estuary. No. 73 Squadron had landed at Debden from the north only at 11.05a.m., but it was ordered up against the formation of He111s and Ju88s. After damaging one Heinkel, the squadron was "bounced" by Me109s, and within moments had lost four Hurricanes shot down, with one pilot killed and another wounded. But then the Me109s were themselves "bounced" by Hurricanes from the Polish 303 Squadron, which accounted for three of them. While the fighters slugged it out, the bombers hit oil-storage facilities at Thameshaven, starting an immense blaze.

This raid turned out to be the Germans' most successful of the day, and once more Fighter Command lost as many aircraft as the Luftwaffe. No. 41 Squadron did not repeat its success of the morning. During the afternoon it lost four aircraft, and the squadron commander and a flight commander were killed. The deaths of senior men were particularly alarming for the inexperienced pilots. Peter Brothers, veteran of No. 32 Squadron, was one of those selected from "resting" squadrons to bolster "green" units, and on 5 September he arrived at 257 Squadron. Two of the squadron's flight commanders had been killed the previous day. "The squadron morale was absolutely zilch," said Brothers. "Obviously the young chaps thought, well, if the flight commanders can get shot down, what chance have we got?"[54]

On the morning of 6 September Kesselring reverted to staggered raids, sending over substantial formations from first light. Early in the morning, No. 303 Polish Squadron was hit while trying to disrupt a bomber formation over Kent. Five of its aircraft were shot down, and both squadron commanders were wounded.

There were further attacks on Thameshaven, still burning from the day before, and Brooklands was raided again. This time, the Hawker factory was bombed, but the damage was slight. Throughout the day, squadrons were kept busy just defending their home aerodromes, and losses were again steady. No. 601 had four of its pilots shot down, with two killed, and in all twenty-three RAF fighters were destroyed during the day. The Luftwaffe also sustained similar losses.

Amidst the aerial killing and bombing of that day, there yet remained instances of chivalry. Flight Lieutenant Michael Robinson of 601 Squadron recorded how:

Having attacked two Me109s at the mouth of the Thames Estuary, I saw a third Me109 flying past me. I followed him down to ground level and chased him southwards. He never rose above 100 feet until well south of Maidstone and then throttled back. I overtook him and formated [flew at a fixed distance] on him, pointing downwards for him to land. He turned away so I carried out a dummy quarter attack, breaking very close to him. After this he landed his Me in a field at about 140mph some 25 miles south-east of Maidstone. The pilot got out apparently unhurt and held up his hands above his head. I circled around and waved to him, and as he waved back I returned and threw a packet of twenty Players at him and returned to base. He picked up his cigarettes.[55]

Gentlemanly conduct could not, though, conceal the fact that Fighter Command was approaching a crisis. During the previous two weeks it had seen 295 of its fighters destroyed and 171 seriously damaged. Even with the improvements in production, the aero factories were struggling to keep up with the rate of attrition. Workers were tiring and productivity was slowing. Six of the seven sector stations of 11 Group were now bombed almost to the point of collapse. Five of its advanced airfields were seriously damaged. During August, just over 300 pilots had been lost and only 260 had arrived to replace them, many inadequately prepared by the shortened training time now in operation. To Squadron Leader A. V. R. "Sandy"

Johnstone, of 602 Squadron, it seemed "a funny way to run a war":

> Two further pilots have come to us straight from a Lysander squadron with no experience whatsoever on fighter aircraft. Apparently demand has now outstripped supply and there are no trained pilots available in the Training Units, which means that we will just have to train them ourselves. However, it remains to be seen whether we can spare the hours, as we are already short of aircraft for our own operational needs.

The failure of supply to match demand, in terms of pilots, demonstrated amply the fact that the airmen lived with the daily prospect of death. Flying, even outside of war, was a dangerous business: the prospect of death from error, weather conditions or mechanical failure was close from the moment a would-be pilot took his first flight. Combat multiplied both the opportunities for, and the means of, dying: so the pilots perished from bullets and cannon shells, from burning — or from being dragged down into the depths of the sea by the weight of their heavy boots, parachutes or jackets if they managed to bale out and were not entombed in their aircraft.

The truth revealing itself was that the average life expectancy of a Fighter Command pilot was 87 hours' flying time. Of the 2,917 pilots who flew combat missions during the Battle of Britain, almost 20 per cent — 544 — were killed. It became natural to regard death in action less as a possibility and more as an inevitability. "I thought, I am going to die," recalled 32 Squadron's Peter Brothers. "If it doesn't happen today, it'll happen tomorrow."[56]

In most of the pilots' accounts, death is expressed in understated, euphemistic ways: smashing into the sea or ground was called "going in". Death was "the chop". So-and-so was "lost" or "went west". The levity was designed to rob death of its power, but it did not always work. Richard Hillary used the same expression, "failed to return", for all his squadron's losses; but however euphemistic, the phrase ends up ringing through his book *The Last Enemy* like a funeral bell. There were few bodies to deal with in aerial warfare. But every pilot could imagine the horror as he saw a comrade go down in a burning cockpit, particularly as sometimes cries, prayers and screams could be heard over the radio-telephone.

The tradition of insouciance in the face of death had been established by the aviators of the previous war. "In such an atmosphere," wrote Cecil Lewis, a veteran of the skies over the trenches, "you grew fatalistic, and as time went by and left you unscathed, like a batsman who has played himself in, you began to take liberties with the bowling. You took unnecessary risks, you volunteered for dangerous jobs, you provoked enemy aircraft to attack you. You were invulnerable: nothing could touch you. Then, when one of the old hands, as seemingly invulnerable as yourself, went West, you suddenly got cold feet. It wasn't possible to be sure — even of yourself. At this stage it required most courage to go on — a sort of plodding fatalism, a determination, a cold-blooded effort of will. And always alone! No friends right and left, no crowd morale!"[57]

At the beginning of the war, many units were close-knit, bonded by shared training and — in the case of the Auxiliary squadrons — place and family friendships. It was the early losses in the spring of 1940 that hit squadrons hardest. By late August and early September, the original social cohesion had loosened, and among relative strangers losses were easier to bear. There was, anyway, no time for grieving. "You didn't spend days moping around," said No. 19 Squadron's George Unwin. "You just said, 'Poor old so-and-so's bought it,' and that was it."[58]

But the death of a close friend was still felt intensely. Gordon Batt of 238 Squadron was already depressed at the unit's losses when, towards the end of September, his best friend, Eric Bann, was killed when his parachute failed to open. "When Bann disappeared, I was even worse," said Batt. "I didn't make friends at all. You do get to a point where you do not wish to be hurt any more. I just did my job, to the best of my ability, had jovial off-duty parties, but no friends, no more [of] that. I do not even know the names of many of the people I later flew with and were killed. I just blotted that out of my mind. I just concentrated hard on doing my job, and staying alive. Otherwise you'd go barmy, I think."[59]

With the first week of September drawing to a close, Dowding began to consider withdrawing the remainder

375

of his battered forces to northern England to be thrown into the fight when the actual invasion began. The British Army was tensing for action, in the belief that command of the air was about to be lost and invasion was imminent.

But then, just as it seemed the final blows were about to fall, the Luftwaffe changed direction.

CHAPTER
EIGHT

Culmination

7 September to 31 October 1940

Hermann Goering was confident that 7 September 1940 would be one of the greatest days of his life. During the previous afternoon, his special train, *Asia*, complete with private bedroom, study and cinema, had carried him across Germany and the Low Countries towards the northern French coast. He was eager to be present for the final phase of the great battle, and he spent the morning of 7 September touring airfields in the Pas de Calais before proceeding to Cap Gris Nez, from where the White Cliffs of Dover could be seen clearly across the sparkling waves of the English Channel. The *Reichsmarschall* had dressed for the occasion in his comic-opera powder-blue uniform encrusted with yards of gold braid. A lavish picnic was laid out to sustain him while he watched the show, and photographers were on hand to record his moment of triumph.

Across the water, the defenders looked up at the clear skies with heavy hearts and prepared themselves for another desperate day. After days of relentless pounding, the fabric of Fighter Command was battered and torn. Its pilots were strung out with fatigue and strain, and the replacements coming to fill the gaps caused by losses and exhaustion were novices flying into an intensely lethal environment where inexperience most commonly equalled death.

Park wrote later that the damage to 11 Group's airfields was now so bad that it "greatly reduced the defensive power of our fighter squadrons. The destruction of numerous telephone lines . . . using emergency sector Ops. Rooms . . . and an almost complete disorganization of the defence system made the control of our fighter squadrons extremely difficult . . . had the enemy continued his heavy attacks against Biggin Hill and the adjacent sectors . . . the fighter defences of London would have been in a perilous state."[1]

But following Goering's meeting with his commanders four days before, and unbeknownst to Fighter Command, the Luftwaffe's tactics were about to change radically. On 7 September the target would be *Loge*, the German codeword for London. Goering's decision to shift the weight of the attack to the capital was driven by his natural impatience rather than rational calculation. The primary aim of the Luftwaffe was to achieve air superiority. In the preceding days it had undoubtedly done great damage to bases and infrastructure, but there were still many aircraft coming up to oppose the raids. Rather than accept that this was evidence that its intelligence services had underestimated the strength of Fighter Command, the German leadership chose to regard each robust response as the last rally before collapse. Once London was threatened directly, the RAF would have to put "the last fifty Spitfires" into the fight, which Kesselring confidently assessed were all that were left, and the German fighters could dispose of them in one final action.

There were also now good political reasons for attacking London. Hitler had made his wishes clear in his 4 September speech. Britain's gall in bombing Berlin would have to be avenged, and Goering was anxious to please his master.

Although the morning of Saturday 7 September dawned sunny, clear and hot — perfect bombing weather — the drama was slow to begin. A German reconnaissance plane checking on bomb damage to Liverpool was intercepted and shot down, after a long chase. Just before midday, radar picked up a small formation just off the coast. Spitfires of No. 66 Squadron on a routine patrol were vectored to intercept, but they broke off when it turned out the intruders were only Me109s trying to provoke a fight. Otherwise, there was an ominous quietness. Squadrons were stood down, and pilots dozed in the sunshine. It was hard, though, to relax. It seemed clear that the lull was only a pause for breath, and the longer the wait, the more time the Luftwaffe had to assemble its forces.

Across the Channel, Luftwaffe airfields were busy arming and fuelling an enormous host of aircraft for the great assault to come. Just before 4p.m., the quiet spell over southern England was broken as the first radar reports were processed at Bentley Priory and counters started appearing on the situation map. All over the south, fighter squadrons were brought to readiness.

An air armada of nearly 1,000 Luftwaffe aircraft was building up over the French coast. It was the greatest collection of aircraft ever seen. There were 348 bombers in the fleet, stacked up in towering layers from 14,000 to 20,000 feet, while above and behind them, outnumbering them almost two to one, buzzed 617 fighters, charged with protecting the formations and intent on destroying every Hurricane or Spitfire that attempted to penetrate the ranks. The vast aerial formation rolled across the Channel on a front that was 20 miles wide.

The first Observer Corps reports of the enemy's massed ranks reached the Maidstone centre at 4.16p.m., "many hundreds of aircraft" having been sighted approaching the coast between Deal and North Foreland. At 4.17p.m., eleven Fighter Command squadrons were ordered to scramble, and six minutes later all the remaining fighter squadrons in 11 Group were brought to readiness. Calls went out to 10 Group and 12 Group to stand by to help.

Air Vice-Marshal Park was away from 11 Group's Uxbridge headquarters, so decision-making fell elsewhere. It was judged that the assault must be another attack on the hard-pressed sector stations, on the oil terminal at Thameshaven, or on the aircraft factories. Squadrons now raced to guard these locations.

Once across the coast, the Luftwaffe force split up, and, at varying altitudes, changed direction, criss-crossing the flight paths of the formations above and below them. For the British, tracking the huge number of aircraft was extremely difficult, but it was clear that one large group was heading north towards the Essex coast, threatening North Weald, while another, made up of more than 200 bombers, was veering west towards Biggin Hill and Kenley. But when the northerly group reached the Thames Estuary, it suddenly swung to the west and headed directly up the river. The westerly group, meanwhile, had bypassed the sector stations, passed over Central London and then turned towards the East End and the docks. When a third group, following behind, headed on a direct line from the coast to the East End of London, the target was at last clear.

The convergence on the capital was a surprise. Frantically, the order went out to the squadrons in the air to leave their airfield and factory patrols and rush to the capital. Although Dowding had 23 squadrons airborne by the time the first bombs started to fall, only a few were able to intercept the bombers before they struck the city.

The first four squadrons to be scrambled — Nos 1 and 303 (Polish) from Northolt, 504 from Hendon, and 501 from Gravesend — were in the air by 4.20p.m., but were sent to patrol airfields and the oil depot at Thameshaven. Joined in the air by No. 249 Squadron from North Weald five minutes later, they now hurtled towards the stream of enemy aircraft, to be confronted with an awesome sight. In the words of Francis K. Mason, the great chronicler of the Battle of Britain, they "found themselves on the edge of a tidal wave of aircraft, towering above them, rank upon rank, more than a mile and a half high . . . covering the sky like some vast irresistible migration".[2]

No. 249 Squadron intercepted a forward part of the enemy force over Maidstone, but was hugely outnumbered by the escorting fighters and soon found itself surrounded by more than 60 Messerschmitt Me109s. During a fifteen-minute dogfight, six of No. 249 Squadron's Hurricanes were lost, one pilot (Pilot Officer R. D. S. Fleming) was killed and three were wounded, and all without having any impact on the enemy armada — there was not a single "kill".

No. 303 Squadron ran into a layer of the bomber stream over Loughton in Essex — 40 Dorniers at 20,000 feet, with a formation of Me110s above and behind, and above them, at about 25,000 feet, the Me109s. The Polish squadron was about 4,000 feet above the bombers and dived, turning its whole force broadside. "We gave them all we'd got," said their English squadron leader, Ronald Kellett, "opening fire at 450 yards and only breaking away when we could see the enemy completely filling the gunsight. That means we finished the attack at point-blank range. We went in practically in one straight line, all of us blazing away."[3]

The squadron claimed ten bombers destroyed or damaged, for the loss of two aircraft. It was a sweet revenge for men who had been driven from their Polish homes and loved ones by the German invasion. Nos 1 and 63 Squadrons also had early successes, sending several bombers tumbling away from their formations. But the German fighter screen proved very hard to penetrate.

In the city, the sirens had sounded at 4.43p.m. Londoners were used to alarms by now and ambled rather than ran to the shelters. At Upton Park football ground, West Ham fans enjoying a 4–1 lead over Tottenham Hotspur grumbled as they trooped out of the ground. Eighteen-year-old Betty Roper was in the East End, near Victoria Park: "We heard the sirens. Nobody went into the shelters at first." But the sky was clear, and soon fingers were pointing upwards at the ominous black dots approaching from the east. "There were hundreds of them," said Betty. "The sky was black and you could see the bombs falling. They were like silver. Soon the docks were alight."[4]

Eighteen-year-old Fire Watcher Robert Barltrop was on the flat roof of Sainsbury's grocery in Walthamstow. Shoppers ignored the air raid warning, but "this time the all-clear didn't come . . . I had a view across to the east and I saw the planes coming from the Dagenham and Barking directions. They were following the Thames like a little swarm of flies. They puffed some anti-aircraft fire all around them and as I sat there watching, the planes got more and more numerous. Then clouds of smoke began to rise from the East End. Then the clouds gradually became one huge cloud."[5]

For the young Horace Davy, the war now truly came home to him:

The sirens went and we went to a local air raid wardens' post to shelter. I can remember looking up in the sky to see the German bombers and seeing some of our aircraft, the puffs of smoke from the anti-aircraft guns and the barrage balloons which seemed to be pretty useless. I climbed up an exterior fire escape to get a better view and I clearly remember some pinging noises. It was the shrapnel from exploding shells that was beginning to fly around. Then my father shouted at me to get down.[6]

The first wave of bombers included more than 150 He111s and Do17s, flying three miles high. An onlooker from below couldn't help admiring the "majestic orderliness" of the fleet. At about 5p.m., the aircraft arrived over the docks, warehouses and crowded terraces of the East End. Incendiaries fell, and within moments huge fires sprang up and a massive pall of smoke climbed upwards, blinding the anti-aircraft gunners and acting as a beacon for the bombers following.

Oberstleutnant Paul Weitkus, commanding a *Gruppe* of *Kampfgeschwader 2*, had orders to attack the docks near Tower Bridge. "We all had sketches of our targets," he said. "When we reached [the] Docks there were not many fighters but the guns seemed quite good." They "placed the bombs very well and large fires started."[7] To Helmut Staal, in the leading flight of bombers:

It had been an easy flight up from the Thames Estuary and along the Thames. There was no opposition and we felt that we had the whole sky to ourselves. We were at 5,000 feet. The docks at Woolwich stood out almost as if beckoning for us to release our bomb load. Through the glass canopy I could see tall cranes and the long square shape of the three main docks. I lined them up carefully, and as I pressed the release button I looked elsewhere at the huge mass of buildings and warehouses below, then just caught a glimpse of the sticks of bombs as they kinked from side to side as they fell towards earth.[8]

But now Fighter Command forces were at last arriving in strength, over London, the Thames Estuary and the Isle of Sheppey, attacking both incoming and returning bombers. "They dived through the bomber formation from a terrific height," remembered 45-year-old veteran Johannes Fink, the commander of *Kampfgeschwader 2*. "We had the impression that each fighter had chosen one bomber and was diving to attack it . . . It was a horrible feeling when they came down on you." Fink's Dornier Do17 was hit. He was the only one of the four-man crew to escape unhurt, and it was a tribute to the sturdiness of their aircraft that it managed to struggle back to the base at Arras.

By 5p.m., Dowding had 23 squadrons in the air, all racing towards the Thames Estuary. Soon an epic dogfight involving over 1,000 aircraft developed over London and the estuary, criss-crossing the sky with "contrails" and the sinister glitter of tracer bullets. Squadron Leader "Sandy" Johnstone of No. 602

Squadron experienced vividly the sheer confusion of the mass of aircraft:

All we could see was row upon row of German raiders, all heading for London. I have never seen so many aircraft in the air all at the same time . . . The escorting fighters saw us at once and came down like a ton of bricks, when the squadron split up and the sky became a seething cauldron of aeroplanes, swooping and swerving in and out of the vapour trails and tracer smoke. A Hurricane on fire spun out of control ahead of me while, above to my right, a 110 flashed across my vision and disappeared into the fog of battle before I could draw a bead on it. Everyone was shouting at once and the earphones became filled with a meaningless cacophony of jumbled noises. Everything became a maelstrom of jumbled impression — a Dornier spinning wildly with part of its port mainplane missing; black streaks of tracer ahead, when I instinctively put my arm up to shield my face; taking a breather when the haze absorbed me for a moment . . . [9]

Now and then an aircraft would dissolve into flames and slide earthwards, trailing smoke. Sometimes parachutes would appear and sway down through the chaos and the smoke rising from the fallen bombs. Sometimes they would not, and a stricken machine would glide to its doom, accelerating — it seemed to watchers — as it went, to erupt with a flash followed by a deep, final boom.

"You couldn't tell a 109 from a Spitfire in the chaos of diving machines and bursting flak," Paul Weitkus remembered (in a letter). "Whoever saw who first was the victor." No. 41 Squadron, scrambled from Hornchurch, hit the northern flank, but lost three aircraft. No. 43 Squadron, scrambled from Tangmere at 4.40p.m., came across a formation of 30 Dorniers over the Thames, guarded by 80 Me109s. In command was Squadron Leader Caesar Hull, a popular South African who had won the DFC in Norway. He ordered one section, under Flight Lieutenant John "Killy" Kilmartin — a handsome and enigmatic Irishman who had been fighting since the Battle of France — to engage the escort. Hull joined the other section under Flight Lieutenant Richard Reynell, a Hawker test pilot before the war, in attacking the bombers. They climbed until they were about 1,500 feet above the Dorniers, then attacked from astern. The bombers took evasive action, and each Hurricane picked out its own target. Several of the bombers were hit, but Kilmartin's section, hopelessly outnumbered, could not keep the Me109s away. One dived down on the squadron leader, whose Hurricane took a hit and went out of control, spiralling earthwards with no sign of Hull escaping. Man and machine together hit the earth in the grounds of Purley High School. Dick Reynell was hit as well. With his Hurricane trailing smoke, he succeeded in getting out of the cockpit and jumping moments before the fighter exploded into flames, but his parachute failed to open. His body hit the ground at Blackheath.

No. 234 Squadron, from 10 Group, was ordered up from Middle Wallop at 5p.m. It lost its CO, Joe O'Brien, over Biggin Hill, as well as its senior flight lieutenant, Pat Hughes, five minutes later over South London. Hughes had been attacking a Dornier when its wing ripped off and smashed into his Spitfire, causing him to crash. An Australian who had claimed 16 victories over the past two months, he was a severe loss. His aggression and cheerfulness had made him an inspiration for the rest of the squadron. As 609 Squadron's David Crook later wrote:

However many fighters we lost or damaged, replacements always turned up immediately. This must have demanded the most terrific efforts from both the factories and the ground crews, and though we couldn't see the efforts we did appreciate the results. But experienced pilots could never be replaced. You could only train the new ones as best you could, keep them out of trouble as much as possible in the air, and hope they would live long enough to gain some experience. Sometimes they did.

Crook's squadron, also racing from Middle Wallop, had more success. Its Spitfires caught a formation of bombers as they turned southwest of London, and they claimed the destruction of three Me110s, two Do17s and one Me109, all without loss. Flight Lieutenant J.H.G. McArthur accounted for one of their kills:

I went for the nearest bomber and opened fire from about 400 yards, meanwhile experiencing heavy return cross fire from the bomber formation. After about twelve seconds smoke started to come from the port motor and it left the formation. I then waited for it to go down to 3,000 feet and then dived vertically on to it and fired off the rest of my ammunition. It kept on going down seemingly still under some sort of control, until it hit the water about ten miles out from the centre of the Thames Estuary.[10]

A large number of the escorting Me109s had by now been forced to turn back for lack of fuel, and British fighters harassed the bombers as they returned home, many of the Luftwaffe pilots nursing damaged aircraft and wounded crew. But although their formations were ragged, they still held together, and many of the RAF's fighters were now also short of fuel following the dogfights of the twenty minutes after 5p.m.

A call had gone out to 12 Group, which sent into action a "Big Wing" comprising Nos 19, 242 and 310 Squadrons. But, again, they had taken so long to assemble that they had failed to intercept over Maidstone as planned. Some made their way independently towards the Isle of Sheppey, with the Spitfires of 19 Squadron about 3,000 feet above the two Hurricane squadrons. While still climbing, 242 Squadron was "bounced" by about 60 Me109s and lost 2 aircraft, with 1 pilot, Flying Officer John Benzie, killed. The fighters at last made contact with some bombers over the Thames Estuary. Later they claimed to have shot down 11 aircraft, although this turned out to be a gross overestimation of their impact.

By 5.45p.m., the whole Luftwaffe formation had turned south, and the "all clear" sounded in London at 6.15p.m. In just over half an hour of bombing, immense destruction had been inflicted on the city. The first wave had, with great accuracy, bombed Woolwich Arsenal on the south side of the River Thames as well as the entrance to London's dockland. The gunpowder storage bins at the Woolwich munitions factory were hit, sending great sheets of flame hundreds of feet into the air. Soon the whine and crash of high explosive and incendiary bombs shook the docks at Rotherhithe, Millwall and Limehouse. The gas works at Beckton was hit, then the West Ham power station. The cheaply built working-class terraces huddled between the docks and factories were pounded to dust and rubble, and whole streets were obliterated.

On the Surrey Docks 1.5 million tons of timber were set alight. The warehouses and stores around the Port of London had been stacked with combustible goods. The flames bloomed as the bombs landed, then leaped hungrily from each dry, flammable structure to the next. The Thameside Tate and Lyle refinery disgorged a torrent of molten sugar that covered the river in burning sheets. A rum store caught fire, the barrels exploding like bombs, and the streets ran with blazing spirit. The air was choked with soot, oil, chemicals, burning paint and rubber, bound together into a slimy, viscous vapour by the water of hundreds of hoses, which played on the inferno as ineffectually as a shower of rain on a volcanic eruption. Firemen found themselves surrounded, cut off, suffocated and vaporized by the superheated oxygen. Whole areas of the docks were abandoned to burn themselves out.

Bert Martin, then 16 years old, had joined his Civil Defence unit in Homerton, East London. That afternoon he was working the stirrup pumps and handling the hoses with their 14-pound brass nozzles. "I was terrified and resigned," he said. "I would be holding a hose amid burning buildings — I couldn't touch the buttons on my tunic because they were so hot. My face blistered. I don't think you ever get immune to it — the wreckage, the dead bodies. It was a kaleidoscope of hell."[11] Every available fire engine was in action. Fireboats, three hundred yards away on the opposite side of the river, found their paint blistering from the heat of the inferno, the massive conflagration now extending all along the riverside. George Wilkins, serving with the Auxiliary Fire Service, was on one of the fireboats:

At 4p.m., we on our Emergency Fireboat were ordered down to Tilbury. As we approached Tower Bridge we saw vast volumes of smoke on its eastward side rising white into the sunlight. We passed under Tower Bridge and soon were on the edge of an inferno. Everything was alight, tugs and barges were flaming and sinking in the river. All the timber of Surrey Commercial Docks was blazing furiously.

The sun had disappeared and darkness was as of night. A strong wind was whipped up by the great fire heat which caused small flaming planks of wood to be blown about like matchsticks, and the river itself was as turbulent as a whipped-up small sea. Small crowds of people were here and there at the water's edge crying out for rescue. Warehouses and all sorts of buildings were burning on both sides of the river. Not until we were near Greenwich did we see the sun again and then only as a pale disc through the great ceiling of smoke. There I saw a gasometer alight. To my surprise it did not explode but went as one great blue flame, like an enormous gas jet lasting only a minute.[12]

The worst-hit areas were the working-class districts of West Ham, Bermondsey, Stepney, Poplar, Bow, Shoreditch and Whitechapel. At Silvertown, bordered by the Thames, the River Lea and the docks, over 13,000 people were trapped. The City, where banks and businesses abutted the East End, also suffered.

When the "all clear" sounded, the fires were still raging, with nine miles of waterfront ablaze. Fire crews were summoned from as far away as Coventry. Auxiliary Fireman George Wheeler was called to a brick-built shelter in Wick Road, Hackney, at around 7p.m., which had received a direct hit. "The bomb had blown out a wall and the concrete roof had come down on the people inside. There were men, women, children; some alive, most dead. Everything was covered in this thick grey dust . . . I think there were about thirty dead. It was a terrible sight. As darkness came the whole of the skyline on the river as far as you can see was one big, red glow."[13]

The raids went on and on. In the fading light, guided by the firestorm, came the night-bombers of Sperrle's *Luftflotte 3*, more than 200 of them, unescorted and relying on the darkness for protection. From 8p.m. to nearly 5a.m. the next morning, an almost continuous stream of He111s, Ju88s and Do17s dropped high explosive and incendiary canisters into the dockland fires. By midnight, nine huge conflagrations, each three times the size of the biggest blaze seen in peacetime, were raging across the East End.

American journalist Ben Robertson, watching from high ground south of the city, reported "the most appalling and depressing sight any of us had ever seen . . . It almost made us physically ill to see the enormity of the flames that lit the entire western sky. The London that we knew was burning — the London which had taken thirty generations of men a thousand years to build — and the Nazis had done that in thirty seconds."[14]

One Mr Kyle, of West Ham, remembered how "Our brave warden, who for months had been swaggering about in his uniform, tin helmet cocked to one side, was cringing against the wall under the concrete steps, sobbing. I never saw him again."[15] After months of practice and false alarms, ARP wardens, firefighters, medics and other officials were now on the frontline. So too was the civilian population. In the crypt of a church in Bow, "people were kneeling and crying and praying. It was a most terrible night. I became unconscious," remembered Gladys Strelitz, from East Ham. The shelters provided for civilians proved at once to be totally inadequate. Near Liverpool Street, a goods station covered by flimsy railway arches was supposed to shelter 3,000. Soon there were 14,000 inside, with only basic sanitation. In Victoria Park, 1,450 people crammed into a shelter and had to stand shoulder to shoulder all night as water lapped around their ankles.

None of the shelters was capable of withstanding a direct hit. During the afternoon attack, Civil Defence Volunteer Emma Fredericks had been called out to help at a shelter in Limehouse that had become engulfed in flames, but could do little while the raid was still in progress. The Volunteers returned at about four o'clock the next morning to be told that there were still people alive inside. They started pulling away the collapsed roof of heavy beams, but had to stop while an unexploded bomb was defused by the Royal Engineers. "It was about midday before we again went in and tried to excavate the area around the shelter," said Fredericks. "We knew that there was now no hope of finding anybody alive, but one never knows. Stranger things have happened. When we finally got down to the shelter, we found body over body, people almost burnt to a cinder, the air smelt of burning flesh that had gone rotten, I could take no more and had to get out. I was proud of the job I was doing, but on this occasion I was not afraid to call myself a coward, I just could not do it, but like so many others I plucked up courage to go back later. But the situation was absolutely shocking."[16]

Just as the first wave of bombers had turned home, Britain's senior militarymen, the joint chiefs of staff, were meeting, at 5.20p.m. Together, they surveyed the situation facing the country. Photographic evidence showed a huge build-up of barges at Ostend and all along the continental Channel coast. Radio decrypts indicated that all German army leave had been cancelled from 8 September. Dive-bombers had now been moved to the Pas de Calais to cover the Straits of Dover. The chiefs also heard that the tides in the Channel would be "particularly favourable" for shipping between 8 and 10 September. The conclusion was that invasion was "imminent", and all forces in the UK were now ordered to "stand by at immediate notice". The General Headquarters Home Forces, on their own initiative, issued at 8.07p.m. the codeword "Cromwell", to bring all their forces to "immediate action". Many thought that this meant that the invasion was already under way. Church bells were rung, and several bridges blown up as the Home Guard dragged itself out of bed to man checkpoints all over southern England.

The night of 7/8 September was, for much of the country, a miserable, sleepless one. "At six o'clock the next morning, the sun tried to come out but it couldn't," remembered Walter Marshall, a Reserve Policeman. "The intensity of the smoke over the docks wouldn't allow it. It was the nearest I'd ever seen to hell."[17] Fires were still raging around the warehouses in

395

North Woolwich, the Royal Albert Docks, Queen Victoria Dock and George V Dock.

The East End was wrecked. Telephone and electricity lines had been cut, gas, water and sewage pipes ruptured. Streets were choked with debris and burnt-out vehicles. Unexploded and delayed-action bombs were everywhere. Some 430 civilians had been killed. Another 1,600 were seriously injured. Thousands were homeless. Many greeted the dawn staring, bewildered and desolate, at the wreckage of what had once been their homes. Unknown to them, this was just the beginning of what would become known as the "Blitz". With one night's exception due to bad weather, the bombers would return for seventy-six consecutive nights.

But after that first day and night, for all the terrors and losses, there was still a fragile consensus that it could have been worse. Interwar theories and popular fears had suggested that an attack on London would result in thousands of deaths, mass panic and civil breakdown. None of this had happened. There had been no terrible new weapon. None of the bombs had produced poison gas, apart from the fumes from the fires. Many bombs had failed to explode. Casualties had been significantly fewer than expected.

There was no mass hysteria among the working class, as had been feared. "People gathered their possessions together and piled them into perambulators. With children in their arms, they started their walk to friends or relatives," a *Daily Telegraph* journalist reported on the Monday. "Their morale was astonishing. As they were walking to their new homes many were laughing and joking among themselves . . . they have taken it on the chin." In the Monday morning's *Times*, a special correspondent reflected that, "Because of the dogged spirit of those manning our defences, Service and civilian, the Germans failed on Saturday to perpetrate a second Rotterdam in London. It was not for want of trying on their part . . ."

There was refuge in humour, as there would be in every bombed city of the war. In Chelsea on the Sunday morning, the pubs were packed. "Jokes were made to relieve the tension," wrote Theodora FitzGibbon, "beer mugs were put down more noisily to shut out other sounds. We were glued together by dread. All our eyes were rounder, the pupils enlarged, and although we laughed, our lips twitched with alarm."[18]

Churchill visited the City during the morning of 8 September, cheered on all sides, according to his account, with cries of "Good old Winston", "Good Luck" and shouts of "Are we downhearted?", eliciting the loud response from all sides: "No!" Whatever the inner feelings, the collective outward display was one of defiance, unity and resolution.

Soon afterwards 11 Group's commander, Keith Park, flew over London in his personal Hurricane. "It was burning all down the river. It was a horrid sight," he said. "But I looked down and said, 'Thank God for that,' because I realized that the methodical Germans had at last switched their attack from my vital aerodromes on to cities."[19]

Park's relief was justified. The decision by Goering to alter strategy and bomb London would be one of the most decisive of the war. The change of tactics granted a reprieve to Fighter Command, which, if the attacks on its bases had continued, might at last have been forced to retreat and regroup beyond the reach of German bombers and fighters. As it was, with London taking the force of the Luftwaffe's attacks, stations and infrastructure could be repaired. The frantic tempo of the preceding days, when pilots were fighting out of airfields that were simultaneously under attack, slackened slightly.

Satisfaction at the turn of events was tempered by the fact that the fighters had been unable to shield London. They had inflicted only 38 losses on the Luftwaffe, a small total considering the huge number of aircraft deployed. Fighter Command had seen 28 of its aircraft shot down, 19 pilots killed, and the capital battered. By contrast, Luftwaffe crews could see the huge pall of smoke over London all the way from their bases in northern France. To them it looked like a great victory. "I personally have taken over the leadership of the attacks against England," Goering announced in a radio broadcast on 8 September. "For the first time we have struck at England's heart . . . this is an historic hour."

The Saturday had been as exhausting for the Germans as for the British. The Luftwaffe had to pause before it could strike again. On Sunday 8 September, the fine weather faded and the clouds rolled in, to the huge relief of the defenders. "The weather was bad today, thank goodness, so we had a reasonable rest," reported Richard Barclay (in his diary), whose Squadron, No. 249, had been mauled the previous day. "I think we are all still a bit shaken after yesterday."

Dowding took advantage of the lull to rotate some of his most battered units. Exhausted and now leaderless, No. 43 Squadron retired to Usworth and was replaced by No. 607 Squadron, which had seen little action since France, apart from the abortive attack on the north by *Luftflotte 5*. No. 111 Hurricane Squadron was moved from Croydon to the relative safety of Drem, in Scotland; No. 79 Squadron was relocated from Biggin Hill to the South Wales airfield of Pembrey, from where 92 Squadron re-entered the fray, eager for more action.

Until about 11.30a.m. on 8 September, there was little enemy activity. But the quiet was followed by two hours of sustained attacks. Spitfires of No. 41 Squadron were on a routine patrol when they were vectored towards Dover, where they encountered a formation of Dorniers, heavily escorted. Severely outnumbered, the British fighters struggled against the Me109s. The aircraft of Flying Officer William Scott was seen trailing smoke and diving away from the battle. Neither pilot nor machine was seen again.

The Spitfires were reinforced by Hurricanes of 46 Squadron, and others, and soon the German formations began to break up. This success was partly the result of two new tactics on the part of Park. First, he deployed several fighter squadrons in pairs, which gave them a better chance of breaking into the bomber

399

ranks. Second, he had ordered that the chain of command follow rigidly their orders as far as height was concerned. Park was well aware that in order to avoid being "bounced" from above, sector controllers had been adding a few thousand feet to their ordered altitude. The squadron leader would then add a few more thousand for safety. The result was that the intercepting fighters were arriving among the high-flying Me109s, leading to fighter-versus-fighter combat of the type that Park was determined to avoid, while the bombers sailed on below. With Park's new discipline, the Hurricanes and Spitfires were arriving at the level of the bombers and were able to down several of them before the Me109s could dive to defend them.

Some elements of the German armada pressed on to London, where three bombers were downed by flak, and the attack was blunted. Bombers ditched their loads over Gravesend, Dover and Sevenoaks before turning back over the coast. The airfields were mostly left alone, giving 11 Group another priceless day in which to repair facilities and replenish supplies and aircraft.

During the daylight tussle, the RAF lost four fighters, with two pilots killed and two wounded. The Luftwaffe lost seven to combat, three of which were Me109s. The fact that only eleven squadrons had been used, and only just over a quarter of the sorties flown as compared to the previous day, gave many of Fighter Command's pilots a welcome day of rest. It had been the first time in ten days that Park's 11 Group squadrons were not at readiness the whole day.

400

There would, though, be no respite for the people of London that night. The sirens sounded at 7.30p.m., and soon afterwards the bombers were overhead. This time, many civilians spurned the crowded and unsanitary public shelters, instead heading for Liverpool Street, which was the nearest Underground station to the East End in 1940. After being barred from entry at first, they spent the night on the platforms and in a tunnel that was under construction.

The authorities had feared that the use of the Underground might lead to a "deep shelter mentality", that people would be reluctant to re-emerge and that vital war work would be neglected. But they were forced to relent, and by the end of the month more than 150,000 people were using the Underground network as shelter. The live rail was switched off and people found space wherever they could, accepting the stench caused by the absence of sanitation as the price of safety.

Nevertheless, 400 civilians were killed on the night of 8/9 September, as 200 bombers dropped 1,700 high-explosive bombs and countless incendiaries. By morning, 12 new areas of fire were blazing out of control. Six hospitals were damaged as well as docks, railways and warehouses. In one block of flats, 50 people died as a result of one bomb. A direct hit on the Columbia Market shelter also caused very heavy casualties. The next day, there were no trains running in or out of South London.

★ ★ ★

For Fighter Command, Monday 9 September began quietly. Apart from a couple of nuisance raids and the customary reconnaissance flights, there was little activity in the morning. Park had noticed that attacks on aerodromes had usually taken place before noon, and he guessed correctly during that morning's lull that the Luftwaffe would continue to ignore his sector stations in favour of metropolitan targets, which — the pattern so far suggested — they preferred to attack later in the day. He nevertheless took the precaution of lining up fighters from Nos 12 and 10 Groups to protect airfields and aircraft factories, and moved some of his forces forward to prepare for the expected afternoon attack.

The first signs of a big raid were picked up after 4p.m. Formations were massing over Calais and Boulogne. They reached the coast between the North Foreland and Dover just before 5p.m. The raid was led by Me109s, a tactic designed to lure up the British fighters early, so that they would be short of fuel when the bombers arrived. Park did not take the bait, but when the 109s were followed by large groups of bombers, Fighter Command rose to meet them. Over Surrey, No. 607 Squadron from Tangmere intercepted a formation of He111s and Do17s and, with the help of 605 Squadron, drove back the attack, although at the cost of six of their Hurricanes shot down and three pilots killed. No. 605 Squadron lost two aircraft, with one pilot killed. To the east, a raid approaching London was intercepted over Dartford by Spitfires of No. 222 Squadron.

402

The Coltishall and Fowlmere squadrons of Group 12, which had been detailed to guard North Weald and Hornchurch, now arrived, having taken the unilateral decision that they were needed further south. The "Wing" (consisting of Nos 19, 242 and 310 Squadrons) reached the battle in some disarray and short on fuel, but, if its pilots' claims are to be believed, it had a huge impact, shooting down 21 aircraft. (German records for the day are incomplete, and nothing like the wreckage of 21 aircraft was ever found.) Certainly, the mass of fighters caused a scene of utter confusion in the air, with pilots having to avoid friendly fire as well as the enemy's bullets and cannon shells. Douglas Bader, leading 242 Squadron, reported that he was chasing a Dornier when suddenly two Hurricanes dived down from each side in front of him. So intent were the Czech pilots of 310 Squadron on their target that they collided, the left wing of the Hurricane on the right folding and ripping away, sending the aircraft into an instant spin.

Douglas Bader

Several of the most successful, top-scoring Battle of Britain pilots became instant celebrities through exposure in the press and on the BBC. The most prominent was Douglas Bader (1910–82), whose determination to fly and fight despite the handicap of being a double amputee seemed a symbol of national resolve. His ebullience and love of the limelight, however, sometimes seemed at odds with the propaganda effort to present the pilots as ordinary young men and reluctant warriors to whom fighting did not come naturally.

Bader was born in London in 1910, the son of a soldier who died in 1922 of shrapnel wounds received in the First World War. His childhood heroes were the fighter aces of the Royal Flying Corps, and he was determined to become a pilot himself.

He won a scholarship to St Edward's School in Oxford, where he excelled at sports, then qualified as a cadet at RAF Cranwell. Finishing very close to the top of his class, he was commissioned into No. 23 Squadron RAF in July 1930. A year later he was selected to fly in the elite RAF aerobatic team. Its precision stunts and choreographed displays were a highlight of the June 1931 Hendon air show, with the press describing Bader's performance as "the day's best event". But Bader had a strong streak of disobedience and repeatedly ignored orders forbidding low flying.

On 14 December 1931, while visiting Reading Aero Club, he attempted one of his specialities — slow rolls at very low altitude — in his Bristol Bulldog fighter.

Regulations forbade this manoeuvre below 1,000 feet; Bader attempted it, apparently on a dare, below 30 feet. His left wing clipped the ground and he crashed, suffering appalling injuries. Both legs were amputated, one above the knee and one below. Bader later recorded the incident in laconic style in his logbook: "Crashed slow-rolling near ground. Bad show." He was still only 21.

In 1932, after a long convalescence, he was fitted with a pair of artificial legs and, through remarkable determination and persistence, he learned to walk again. In time, he was able to drive a specially modified car, play golf and even dance. His comeback instilled in him an unshakeable self-confidence. "Don't listen to anyone who tells you that you can't do this or that," he said. "Never, never let them persuade you that things are too difficult or impossible."[20] In the short term, however, his efforts to remain an RAF pilot were unsuccessful.

After the outbreak of war in 1939, things changed. A long campaign overcame official resistance and Bader was recalled to service. In February 1940, he was posted to No. 19 Squadron, based at RAF Duxford. George Unwin, who shared a room with him, put up with the scraping and squeaking as Bader adjusted his legs with a file and a tin of oil.

In April 1940, Bader left 19 Squadron to become a flight commander with No. 222 Squadron, also based at Duxford, and while patrolling the coast near Dunkirk in his Spitfire he shot down an Me109. A day or two later he bagged a Dornier Do17. His confidence and aggression brought him the command of 242 Squadron at the end of June 1940. This was a Hurricane unit based at Coltishall, made up mainly of Canadians who had suffered high losses in the Battle of France. Despite their initial resistance to the new commanding officer, the pilots were won over by Bader's strong personality and perseverance.

On 11 July 1940, Bader scored his first kill with his new squadron. "I am not one of those who see war as a cricket match where you first give anything to defeat the opponent and then shake hands," he said. "You knew you were flying with an ace in every sense of the word," commented fellow pilot Alan Smith. "A bloke who knew exactly what he was doing, who was on the ball, was afraid of nothing, and a great leader."[21] But Bader's bombastic nature and tendency to dramatize was in many ways the antithesis of the "fighter boy" ethos of ironic understatement. Many found him easier to admire than to like. His forceful character inevitably attracted criticism, and he was not universally popular with his comrades. "He made me sick," said John Freeborn, who flew with No. 74 Squadron. "I've never met such a self-opinionated fool in all my life."

But for everyone who hated him, there was another who adored him. "I never met anyone with such charisma," said Max Williams, one of the groundcrew for Bader's squadron. "He was awesome, marvellous."[22]

As a leading advocate, along with Air Vice-Marshal Leigh-Mallory, of the Big Wing tactic, Bader was able to put his theory into practice in the last phases of the Battle of Britain. In 1941, he was promoted to wing commander. Stationed at Tangmere, Bader led his wing of Spitfires on sweeps over northwestern Europe throughout the summer campaign.

By August 1941, Bader had claimed 22 German aircraft shot down; but that month his Spitfire was hit, and he was forced to bale out over occupied France, where he entered German captivity.

His captors treated him with great respect. General Adolf Galland, the German flying ace, offered the RAF safe passage to drop off replacements for Bader's damaged "tin leg".

Nevertheless, Bader tried to escape from the hospital where he was recovering, and over the next few years he made so many attempts at escape that the Germans threatened to take away his legs. In August 1942, he was finally dispatched to Colditz Castle, where guards outnumbered prisoners. Liberated in April 1945, he requested a return to action but was turned down.

Bader was given the honour of leading a victory fly-past of 300 aircraft over London in June 1945. He left the RAF soon afterwards and died in 1982.

Nine fighter squadrons, attacking simultaneously in pairs, met one of the biggest raiding groups over South London. The twenty or so Me110s immediately adopted their defensive circle, and many bombers dumped their loads and turned for home. But most of

407

them found themselves swept into a nearby battle, where 40 Ju88s were being ruthlessly and successfully attacked by 9 Hurricanes of No. 253 Squadron and 12 aircraft of 303 (Polish) Squadron.

Unteroffizier Peter Stahl was an experienced pilot, having flown as a civilian weather forecaster before the war. But 9 September was his first flight over England, and he recorded his heady experience:

Over Lille is our agreed meeting point with units from other *Geschwader*. Eventually there is an assembly of at least 200 bombers that gathers into some sort of order and sets course for London. Soon afterwards we are joined by an escort of Me109s and Me110s. There were 500–600 aircraft with me in tight formation. Wherever one looked, one saw our aircraft, all around, a marvellous sight. Among us we estimate that the total load destined to fall on London soon afterwards amounts to at least 200,000 kg. And this had been going on for some days already. Poor London!

Guided to its target by "black smoke pillars" from fires still burning in the capital, his formation released its first bombs.

Then it is my turn to press the red release button . . . The aircraft makes its usual jump of relief and we look down. The Thames bends, the docks and the whole colossal city lie spread out before us like a giant map. Then come the explosions of our bombs which we observe while banking in a wide turn eastwards, then

south . . . the effect of our attack is an enormous
cloud of smoke and dust that shoots up into the sky.
One cannot imagine that a town or a people could
endure this continuous crushing burden for long.

But then Stahl's formation started to break up as
British fighters appeared on the scene.

At first I take them for our own escorts and wonder
about their tactics, twisting around among bombers in
such a foolhardy way. Then I realize that they are British . . . there is tracer all around us, and a wild
twisting turning air combat has broken out between
our 109s and the Spitfires and Hurricanes. Now
everything is happening right underneath us! I get
away to hide in the thickest bunch of our bombers I
can spot nearby.[23]

For Stahl, the day proved lucky: one of his Ju88's
engines was hit and it started leaking oil, but he
managed to get back to his airfield near Amiens.

For many of the Luftwaffe pilots, who had been led
to believe that Fighter Command was all but finished,
the strength of the opposition was a shock. Far from
weakening, the British resistance seemed to have
stiffened. One large raid did manage to penetrate
Central London, but most bombers were blocked from
reaching their targets and ended up dropping their
loads on the residential areas of Purley, Norbiton,
Surbiton and Kingston-upon-Thames, as well as over
Canterbury.

Twenty-eight German aircraft were shot down, compared to Fighter Command losses of twenty-one aircraft (with six pilots killed and several severely wounded). Yet the day's fighting had been a tactical victory for the British, who managed to drive back most of the raiders short of their targets, and a blow to the morale of the Luftwaffe.

The events of Monday night, though, showed once again that Fighter Command was all but powerless to stop the bombers in the darkness. The sorties flown by British pilots were more of a risk to themselves than the enemy. Another 370 people were killed on the ground and 1,400 injured, as 170 bombers from *Luftflotte 3* showered explosives and incendiaries over a large area. The bombardment was moving westwards. In Central London, Somerset House by the side of the Thames and the Royal Courts of Justice were both bombed. Madame Tussaud's waxwork museum was hit and set on fire, as was the Natural History Museum in South Kensington. (During the firefighting at the museum, some of the seeds in the herbarium were soaked and would later begin to germinate, including samples collected nearly 150 years earlier.) A school in Bethnal Green, East London, which was being used as a shelter, took a direct hit.

The following day, Tuesday 10 September, saw poor weather, with rain and storms keeping Luftwaffe activity to a minimum. Until about 5p.m., there were only reconnaissance and weather sorties by the Germans. Then, small numbers of single aircraft or small formations, using the clouds as cover, carried out a series of nuisance raids on Tangmere, West Malling, Poling and Portsmouth. The only interception of note was by No. 72 Squadron, which caught a small number of Ju88s and shot down two of them over East Grinstead, Sussex. For the first time in two weeks, Fighter Command suffered no combat losses, though two pilots of No. 602 Squadron crashed at Tangmere that night after a patrol. In both cases, the men had no experience of night flying.

At this stage, the darkness presented far more difficulties for the RAF pilots than it did for the incoming Germans. Night-flying was dangerous and it was almost impossible for the British fighters to make the visual contact necessary to attack the bombers. "I flew a number of night sorties from Biggin Hill," said No. 501 Squadron pilot John Bisdee. "Of course it was awful to see, particularly the dockland area and the East End of London, absolutely in flames . . . the trouble was that it was practically impossible to locate a German bomber at night if you didn't have radar."[24] A handful of Blenheims and Bristol Beaufighters had been equipped with the new airborne radar, but they were too few in number and the equipment was far from reliable.

The ineffectiveness of night-time fighter interception threw the onus for counter-measures onto the guns of the Anti-Aircraft Command. Its pre-war history was not long — the formation of an anti-aircraft corps had been announced in June 1938, and it became operational in April 1939. By that time, the stimulus provided by the 1938 Munich crisis over Czechoslovakia had ensured that guns to supply it were rolling off the production lines. Even so, at the beginning of the war Anti-Aircraft Command remained one of the worst-equipped branches of the forces, with only 4,000 heavy and light guns and the same number of searchlights at its disposal.

The quality of its personnel was also questionable. Its leader, Sir Frederick Pile, complained that "AA Command were to get the leavings of the Army intake after every other branch of the Services had had their pick." During the winter of 1939–40, out of the twenty-five who arrived at a fairly representative battery, wrote Pile, "one had a withered arm, one was mentally deficient, one had no thumbs, one had a glass eye which fell out whenever he doubled to the guns, and two were in the advanced and more obvious states of venereal disease".

Pile was also exasperated by the selfish public reaction to the positioning of new batteries. "It was only necessary to suggest siting a gun anywhere near a golf-course, a building-estate, a park, on a farm, or even close to a polo-ground for everyone to demand through their M.P. that the guns be removed at once from that neighbourhood and put in some other neighbourhood," Pile wrote. "In nearly all the cases the protests were entirely successful." Pile admitted that "London was inadequately defended" and his guns "technically entirely unfitted for dealing with any but the bomber of twenty years earlier". In theory the guns, and the search-lights, were aimed by a system that found a target through sound location, but it was slow and inaccurate and many batteries simply blazed away at the skies. The sound of the guns was welcome, though, giving at least the illusion of defence.

The majority of the gun sites, wrote Pile, "were several feet deep in mud, and the gunners lived in crude dug-outs built by themselves by the emplacements. Blast from the guns . . . soon caused these hastily constructed living quarters to collapse, and nearly all of them became so warped from bombs and gunfire that it was futile to bale out the rain-water."[25]

The heavy anti-aircraft guns consisted mostly of 3.7-inch and 4.5-inch pieces that were fixed in place. Light, moveable guns included 40mm Bofors, Vickers Mark VIII 2-pounder and 3-inch guns. Machine-guns included the 0.303-inch Lewis, 0.303-inch Bren and 20mm Hispano. While high-flying bombers were almost impossible to hit, at lower levels "light flak" was very effective, but weapons were in short supply. Bofors guns were slow, loaded by hand and could get off only a few rounds against fast, low-flying enemy aircraft. Britain had no equivalent of the deadly light-flak batteries that travelled with the German army, the twin-37mm and quad-20mm guns.

The response of the anti-aircraft batteries to the night-time raids so far had been unimpressive. In part this was because they were holding their fire to leave the skies clear for RAF fighters. But after the destruction that occurred on 7 September, Pile ordered every available gun to London and decreed that "every gun was to fire every possible round". On the night of

10 September, the raiders were met by more than twice the previous amount of firepower, and the attackers were forced to fly higher. The resulting inaccuracy of the falling bombs meant more damage to residential areas, but the noise of the British guns raised civilian spirits. As the US military attaché Raymond Lee mused that night, "It is a pleasure to reflect that so much metal is going up instead of coming down."[26]

The night of 10/11 September saw the worst fire yet. At St Katharine Docks, paraffin, wax and animal skins were set ablaze. Flames shot 200 feet into the air. Soon the whole area was without gas, electricity or water. In one shelter nearby, 300 people huddled for most of the night, with only two buckets for sanitation. "People are tight-lipped and strained," wrote a teacher to a friend the next day, "no longer ashamed of their fear, and the shelters are full to suffocation."[27]

Despite the spectacle and the destruction, the bombing of London was doing little to bring the goal of German air superiority closer. The orders for the launching of Operation Sea Lion had been due to be given on 11 September. They were to be followed by a ten-day period of mine laying and embarkation, with the landing assault scheduled for 21 September. There were now more than 2,000 barges assembled to carry the attacking force to the British coast, and Grossadmiral Raeder informed Hitler that the invasion fleet would be ready on 15 September. But the unexpectedly strong British resistance during the daytime fighting of recent days had forced a pause for thought. Hitler told Raeder that although the Luftwaffe had achieved "tremendous success", the crucial condition for invasion — daylight air superiority — had not been met. His view was backed up by a report in the German Naval Staff Diary for 10 September: "There is no sign of the defeat of the enemy's Air Force over southern England and in the Channel area," it stated. "We have not yet attained the operational conditions which the Naval Staff stipulated to the Supreme Command as being essential for the enterprise, namely, undisputed air superiority in the Channel area and the elimination of the enemy's air activity in the assembly area of the German naval forces and ancillary shipping." The *Kriegsmarine* could not understand how the focus on London was helping the cause of the invasion: "It would be in conformity with the timetable preparations for Sea Lion, if the Luftwaffe now concentrated less on London and more on Portsmouth and Dover, as well as on the naval ports in and near the operational area."

The date on which the decision would be made was moved to 14 September. But time was slipping away. The longer the invasion was delayed, the greater the risk of bad weather and difficult sailing conditions in the Channel. The fate of the German operation now depended on the Luftwaffe delivering a devastating and decisive attack.

Unaware of the equivocation among the Nazi political and military hierarchy, Britain was now gripped by the sense that the climax to a historic crisis was approaching. The population braced itself for a landing that surely was only days away. On Wednesday 11 September Churchill made a patriotic broadcast to the nation:

We cannot tell when they will try to come. We cannot be sure that in fact they will try at all, but no one should blind himself to the fact that a heavy, full-scale invasion of this Island is being prepared with all the usual German thoroughness and method, and that it may be launched at any time now . . . We must regard the next week or so as a very important week for us in our history. It ranks with the days when the Spanish Armada was approaching the Channel and Drake was finishing his game of bowls or when Nelson stood between us and Napoleon's Grand Army at Boulogne. Every man and every woman will therefore prepare himself to do his duty, whatever it may be, with special pride and care . . . These cruel and indiscriminate bombings of London are, of course, part of Hitler's invasion plans. He hopes, by killing large numbers of civilians, women and children, that he will terrorise and cow the people of this mighty imperial city, and make them a burden and anxiety to the Government . . . Little does he know the spirit of the British nation, or the tough fibre of Londoners, whose forebears played a leading part in the establishment of parliamentary institutions.

There was a sense of imminence. "The invasion is expected at any moment now," wrote "Chips" Channon

416

in his diary the next day, "probably some time during the weekend."

Poor weather on the morning of 11 September limited the Luftwaffe to tactical reconnaissance. But by the afternoon the skies had cleared. A small German force approached the English coast near Dover at 3.05p.m. and then headed north. Accurate reports from the Observer Corps meant that Park was able to react proportionately, allowing him to have assets available when the main attack came in half an hour later. Most of the bombers were He111s from *Kampfgeschwader 1* and *26*, escorted by about 200 Me109 and Me110 fighters. By the time they crossed the coast at Folkestone and headed northwest towards Maidstone, Park had almost all of his 11 Group squadrons in the air, as well as support from Nos 10 and 12 Groups.

Over Kent, No. 1 (Canadian) Squadron from Northolt, No. 222 from Hornchurch and No. 238 from Middle Wallop swooped to attack. By now a standard technique had evolved, with the Spitfires clashing with the enemy fighters while the Hurricanes went for the bombers. But the British fighters were too few and, having been scrambled late, too low. Five were lost, and the bombers and their escorts ploughed onwards, turning into the Thames Estuary, bound, surely, for the capital once again. But as they realigned over the broad mouth of the River Thames, they were met by a massed force of six squadrons (Nos 17, 46, 72, 73, 249 and 266). Over the estuary between Herne Bay and Shoeburyness, and between Gravesend and Tilbury, a huge, swirling high-altitude battle developed. Two of the 12 Group squadrons — Nos 19 and 74 — also threw themselves into the *mêlée*, even though they had been detailed as usual to protect Hornchurch and North Weald. The Me109s, many at the limit of their fuel, were mostly checked by the fighters, but the bomber formations butted through the defenders and pressed on for London.

Meanwhile, a second wave of bombers and escorts had crossed the coast between Dungeness and Dover and was also heading up the Thames to London. Park had further squadrons in the air patrolling over sector stations and aircraft factories, which he now vectored to intercept. They swept into the edges of the Luftwaffe formation, whittling at its flanks, but still it ploughed on.

At about 4.20p.m. the raiders reached London, and high explosive and incendiaries started raining on the East End. As the bombers did their work, the Me110s that were still with them retreated to the south and formed a defensive circle, waiting to help them home. But that was all the protection the Heinkels could hope for. The Me109s were either still engaged or had headed back across the Channel before their fuel ran out. As the bombers sought to link up with the Me110s, the defenders saw their chance and took it. Sixty fighters from Nos 17, 56, 73, 222, 249 and 303 Squadrons fell on the as yet unprotected Heinkels of *Kampfgeschwader 26*. No. 303 (Polish) Squadron, which had just seen two of its aircraft shot down by Me109s over Kent, once more demonstrated its aggression, downing three of the He111s in ten minutes. Before the bombers could reach their escorts, the Me110s were attacked by Nos 17 and 73 Squadrons, which shot down four of them. Five more bombers were downed, and many more damaged. In the clashes of the afternoon, *Kampfgeschwader 26* lost more than 50 aircrew.

The Germans suffered, but the defenders paid a high price, too, in men and machines. Despite claims that 80 enemy aircraft had been destroyed, the figure was actually closer to 25. Fighter Command had lost 29, with 17 pilots killed.

Across the Channel there was nothing to suggest that the German timetable was slipping. Aerial reconnaissance was showing a continual build-up of invasion shipping in the ports. That night, Bomber and Coastal commands put up every available aircraft to attack Calais, Dunkirk, Le Havre and Boulogne. For over three hours, more than a hundred aircraft dropped eighty tons of bombs, destroying at least a hundred barges, but losing fifteen machines in the process. The RAF bombers were, on the whole, five years out of date, slow and lacking in armour compared with their Luftwaffe equivalents. Six further *Staffeln* of Me109s had recently been withdrawn from offensive action to guard the invasion preparations, and effective German flak units were now thick on the ground.

That night, 200 German bombers pounded London, and Merseyside was also hit hard. Throughout the hours of darkness, there were harassing raids over Scotland, Bristol, Lincolnshire and Norfolk, while along the east and south coasts mines cascaded into the sea to hamper the Royal Navy's ability to block the invasion.

Deteriorating weather the next day, Thursday 12 September, relieved the pressure on Fighter Command. The skies over the Channel were a solid mass of cloud as heavy rain swept over Southeast England. During the morning, radar picked up only isolated aircraft high above the seas off Britain's east and south coasts. Fighter Command left them alone. It was not worth the risk of attempting to intercept single intruders in such poor flying weather.

Around noon, small incoming formations were detected. They broke up into dispersed raids, sometimes of only one or two aircraft each, and none of them close to London. The weather made both interception and accurate bombing extremely difficult, but in several places cat-and-mouse games took place among the clouds. In the west, No. 152 Squadron was sent up from Warmwell and the pilots briefly sighted a Ju88, but before they could attack it vanished back into the murk. No. 238 Squadron had more luck, damaging another Ju88 and in the process killing one and wounding two of its crew. Another raider off the coast of Scotland was shot down, while at the other extreme of the country a squadron from Exeter claimed another lone enemy aircraft.

The Luftwaffe's night raids of 12 September were much smaller, with only 54 bombers over London and single aircraft scattered over the rest of the country. By the standards of the developing Blitz it was a night of comparative calm in the capital. Bombs fell on the City, in Aldgate, Mansion House and Holborn. An 800-pound bomb landed right in front of the steps of St Paul's Cathedral, and penetrated 26 feet into the ground. It took three days to dig it out. When it emerged, looking, in the words of one newspaper report, "like a vast hog about 8 feet long", it was driven by lorry to Hackney Marshes. When detonated, it blasted a crater a hundred feet across, an explosion that would have been powerful enough to reduce the façade of Sir Christopher Wren's masterpiece to rubble. It was Lieutenant Robert Davies of the Royal Engineers, the bomb disposal officer, and his assistant, Sapper George Wyllie, who neutralized the bomb. They became the first recipients of the new George Cross award for "acts of the greatest heroism or the most conspicuous courage in circumstances of extreme danger", which could be awarded to civilians as well as soldiers.

On the same night, Bomber Command hit the German invasion ports again. Seventy barges were reported destroyed, with two British aircraft lost to flak. Concentrations of German troops around the Channel ports, massing for the invasion, were also targeted, causing heavy casualties.

Hitler met with his senior army and air force commanders on Friday 13 September to review the invasion preparations. The results of the fighting on 11 September gave grounds for optimism. There was a feeling that the air assault could be on the brink of success. The commander-in-chief of the army, Walther von Brauchitsch, even suggested that the invasion might be unnecessary, and that the air campaign alone would be enough to bring about victory. Hitler himself remained oddly detached from events, sometimes seeming to accept Goering's glowing accounts of progress and predictions of impending victory, sometimes appearing doubtful and sceptical of Sea Lion's feasibility. He allowed the planning to continue at the same intense pace, however. There was no indication that the go-ahead would not be given the next day as planned.

In the meantime, it was another relatively quiet day in the cloudy and unsettled skies over Britain. Early-morning reconnaissance planes, reporting back on the weather and on Fighter Command dispositions, were left alone. Then, from 9.30a.m. to 11.30a.m., there was a stream of single aircraft crossing the coast near Hastings at the rate of about one every eight minutes. Most headed for London on a variety of different courses. Cloud and the high altitude of the raiders made interception almost impossible. The bombs were landing in the centre now, amid the symbols of British power, in Downing Street, Whitehall and Trafalgar Square. Buckingham Palace was bombed for the third time, and the royal chapel wrecked. The cloud allowed these single aircraft to penetrate deep inland, bombing an aluminium factory in Banbury, Oxfordshire, a railway junction outside Reading and buildings requisitioned by the Air Ministry in Harrogate.

Soon after midday, radio intercepts from German weather reconnaissance aircraft warned of further attacks. Park ordered key airfields to put at least one squadron at readiness. Soon, radar reported intruders heading towards mid-Kent, aiming, it seemed, for Biggin Hill, Kenley or London. Hurricanes from No. 501 Squadron were scrambled from Kenley, and they intercepted a small force of He111 bombers from *Kampfgeschwader 27*. "Ginger" Lacey shot one down before being hit by return fire. He baled out unhurt as most of the bombers turned back, having aborted their mission. Three small raids around Tangmere to the west were also driven away.

That night, the raids were heavier. At 8.45p.m. aircraft were reported building up over the Cherbourg area, and for the next three hours bombers streamed in from Cherbourg, Dieppe, Calais and Boulogne. The main target was London, but East Anglia was also hit. Four raids were flown from the Channel Islands to the Bristol Channel and South Wales.

There was a lull after midnight, but around 2a.m. a wave of aircraft, which had taken off from the Dutch islands, approached London from the northeast and pounded the capital until just before dawn. Only two of the attackers were shot down, one by a night-fighting Blenheim, the other by anti-aircraft fire.

The pattern of damage was becoming depressingly familiar. There was widespread destruction of the rail network, of the gas, electricity and water supply, and of houses and offices. In West Ham, Ravenshill School, which was occupied by families evacuated from their

423

homes, was demolished by high-explosive bombs, killing and injuring more than 50 people.

Hitler and many of his military men believed that such incidents would produce a clamour among civilians that would force Britain's politicians to seek negotiations. Credence was given to reports reaching Berlin from, among other sources, US Ambassador Kennedy in London that British morale was crumbling. In the imagination of the German press, social cohesion was dissolving: in London, the rich were avoiding their military duties and living in luxury while ordinary women and children went unprotected. In East London, the main target of the bombs, anti-war feeling ran through the rhetoric of the two most vociferous political groups, the Communists and the British Union of Fascists. On 11 September, the political insider Harold Nicolson, then working as parliamentary secretary to the Ministry of Information, wrote in his diary: "The people in the East End are still frightened and angry." But the intervention of the weather, which reduced visibility, and the technological inability to land bombs efficiently had made the Blitz a communal experience. Instead of hitting only the docks and industrial targets and, inevitably, the poor quarters that surrounded them, the circle of destruction widened to include the smart, western parts of London, including the seat of the king and queen. The rich and the poor were suffering alike. Eastenders who had flocked westwards to avoid the attacks on the docks now returned home. Queen Elizabeth declared, now that her own home had been bombed, that she "could look the

East End in the eye." Rather than deepening class faultlines, the bombing was creating, at least temporarily, a feeling of solidarity.

The hoped-for political effects of the bombing were, though, a subsidiary part of the German purpose. The main aim remained to destroy Fighter Command, and the attacks on the capital were intended to hasten that end by drawing the British fighters into a defensive war of attrition that would end with German control of the skies. Only then could the invasion safely go ahead.

On Saturday 14 September, Hitler held another meeting with his senior military commanders in Berlin. It was, in theory, the day of decision, the date on which Operation Sea Lion would be launched, to strike before the late-autumn weather in the Channel made an amphibious landing too perilous to attempt.

Hitler accepted, however, that daylight air superiority had not been achieved, and he delayed the decision once more. Now orders would be issued on 17 September, with the operation starting ten days later. In spite of the delay, he was full of praise for the Luftwaffe and his mood towards the operation had swung back to optimism. Bad weather was blamed for the slackening of progress. In an echo of Goering's predictions of the *Adlertag* offensive, Hitler declared that all that was required was five days' good flying weather to complete the elimination of Fighter Command. The Luftwaffe was primed for another maximum effort.

But throughout the morning the weather continued to thwart the German plans. The dense, murky cloud of the previous two days continued, restricting the

Luftwaffe to a few minor raids. However, Ju88 bombers from *Kampfgeschwader 1* attacked south coast radar stations and caused enough disruption to allow raids to arrive over Brighton and Eastbourne almost unopposed. A combination of small groups of He111s and Do17s killed or injured 60 people and caused substantial damage.

In the afternoon, and with no change in the weather, the Luftwaffe decided to risk the elements and mount two sizeable raids, and aircraft approached London from Kent and the Thames Estuary. The poor conditions hampered the defenders as much as the attackers. Twenty-two squadrons from 11 Group were sent up and five squadrons from 12 Group, but most failed to locate the raiders. Those that did came off worst in clashes with the escorts. Four of 73 Squadron's Hurricanes were shot down by Me109s and two damaged, one of them a victim of misidentification by a Spitfire. The thick cloud made accurate bombing impossible. Explosives were scattered over the suburbs, killing 49 people in the Richmond and Wimbledon areas of Southwest London.

A second attack began after 6p.m., with seven formations, each comprising between twelve and thirty aircraft. They crossed the coast at Dover and Lympne, heading for London and, it appeared, the fighter bases that had been providentially left largely alone since the attacks on the capital began. But ten fighter squadrons were in the air when the lead German aircraft crossed the coast, and the bombers were headed off. There were more scattered raids along the coast and inland later in the evening.

Fourteen British fighters had been shot down during the day, while the Luftwaffe had lost only half as many. To the Germans, looking for positive signs, it appeared that the British defences had been scrappy and disorganized. The message passed up the line to Goering was that the RAF seemed close to defeat.

The following day, Sunday 15 September, presented an opportunity to test out the truth of the claims about Fighter Command's weakness. Orders were issued for a massive Luftwaffe attack on London. But the piecemeal and rather chaotic response of Fighter Command the previous day was misleading.

Contrary to appearances, the German bomber crews and fighter pilots were going into battle against a force that was in considerably better shape than it had been just one week before. By switching the weight of their attacks away from the airfields and onto London, the Germans had achieved the opposite effect from the one they sought. The new circumstances reduced the time the British pilots had to spend in the air. In the six days before the start of the Blitz, Fighter Command had flown 4,667 sorties. In the six days after, it flew only 2,159. The decision to move the airfields and sector stations down the target list and concentrate on London resulted in two highly beneficial consequences for the RAF. It allowed Fighter Command not only to repair its infrastructure, but also to refresh and restore its pilots. The business of defending London was

427

intense, but the danger periods were short and intermittent. It was less exhausting and required less effort than the constant activity of the preceding period.

The result was that by 15 September Fighter Command had remustered its strength. New Polish pilots brought a valuable injection of aggressive and skilful personnel, while combat experience made veterans of pilots who were novices only weeks before. At the beginning of the Battle of Britain, a Luftwaffe that was combat-hardened from fighting on the Continent faced a largely "green" collection of British squadrons. But during the fighting the experience gap closed. In the words of 609 Squadron's David Crook:

> We had now learnt our lessons, though the price for this experience had been the death of several members of the squadron. We realized now the vital importance of getting above the enemy before going into action; we knew that cool thinking and the element of surprise can more than compensate for inferior numbers, and can sometimes produce astonishing results. We knew . . . that if you attack out of the sun the enemy will hardly ever see you until the last moment; and vice versa, how essential it is to maintain the most intense vigilance always in order to prevent being surprised oneself.[28]

Heroic effort had now returned all but the hardest-hit Fighter Command bases to something close to full operational efficiency. Since 7 September,

Dowding had been able to rotate his battered squadrons and introduce new pilots to those outfits worst hit by losses. A large number had enjoyed whole days of rest without being called to readiness. New pilots had even been able to fly a few training sorties before going into action. Fighter Command met the dawn of 15 September with high spirits and renewed energy.

It was the Luftwaffe crews that were now tired from incessant attacks and who, as the days passed and the defenders unfailingly came up to meet them, began to doubt their mission. As Adolf Galland recorded: "Failure to achieve any notable success, constantly changing orders betraying lack of purpose and obvious misjudgment of the situation by the Command, and unjustified accusation had a most demoralizing effect on us fighter pilots, who were already overtaxed by physical and mental strain."[29]

The night of 14/15 September was ominously quiet. Although the weather had cleared, only 50 bombers appeared over London. At bases on either side of the Channel, the airmen tried to sleep as groundcrew repaired, refitted and rearmed the aircraft. They could not know it, but the dawning day would pose the supreme test of their skill, their courage and their aggression.

Park was ready. Radio intercepts and reconnaissance had indicated that a very heavy attack was imminent. When the morning of 15 September dawned clear and bright, he knew that in all probability this was to be a crucial day. Yet he remained almost superstitiously disinclined to dramatize. He had important visitors at his headquarters in Uxbridge, the prime minister and his wife. "I do not know if anything will happen today," he told them as they looked down from the control room gallery at the map tables, which showed only a few counters indicating aircraft in the air.

The clear dawn had ripened into a glorious late summer day. The conditions were perfect for the Luftwaffe to finish its task. Yet they were taking their time in coming. From first light, Park had a full squadron at each sector station kept at readiness, while small patrols were mounted along the east and south coasts from Harwich to Land's End. Occasional Luftwaffe reconnaissance flights were shot down or chased away. Near Exeter, a lone He111 on a weather patrol was destroyed by Hurricanes from No. 87 Squadron.

Soon after 10.30a.m., unambiguous reports began to arrive of a massive build-up of aircraft over the Pas de Calais. Preparing a huge air armada was a slow and laborious process. While it went on, the Me109s wasted fuel buzzing in attendance and the British gained precious time to organize their defences.

The bomber force was made up of about a hundred Do17s from *Kampfgeschwader 3* and *76*. They were escorted by twice as many Me109s. When formed up, the fleet was almost 2 miles wide, and stacked up in layers between 15,000 and 26,000 feet. Shortly after 11a.m., the aircraft started crossing the coast near Dungeness. They flew in "vic" formations of three, five

430

and seven aircraft each, making a giant herringbone pattern in the sky.

Watching the build-up and trying to guess the Germans' intent, Park ruled out a decoy or airfield attack and decided that the enemy target was London. It seemed clear that this was a repeat of the great attack of 7 September. He knew that such a powerful force could not be turned back altogether. But if the escort could be held and engaged in fuel-sapping combat on the way to the capital, and the formation disrupted, it would become progressively less and less able to defend itself and the conditions would be created for his fighters to wreak heavy punishment on the raiders. But his plan required the most acutely judged timing if he was to provide a continuous defence and avoid his squadrons being caught on the ground.

By 10.55a.m., all of 11 Group's squadrons had been put at readiness. Park had also alerted Nos 12 and 10 Groups and requested reinforcements. Aircraft on patrol were ordered to return to base for refuelling. As the horde of German aircraft crossed the coast, Spitfires of 92 and 72 Squadrons from Biggin Hill raced to meet them, making the first interception between Dungeness and Canterbury. Park waited ten minutes and then sent up his second wave, consisting of nine more squadrons from bases around London: Nos 229 and 303 from Northolt, 253 and 501 from Kenley, 17 and 73 from Debden, 504 from Hendon, 257 from Martlesham, and 603 from Hornchurch. Five minutes later, No. 609 Squadron took off from Warmwell to guard the southwestern approaches to the city, while from 12 Group the Duxford Wing, now bolstered to five squadrons, prepared for action. Just over ten minutes later a further ten squadrons were ordered up into defensive positions above London.

The Spitfires in the vanguard, some 20 aircraft, swung into the giant formation over Maidstone just after 11.30a.m. Some of the German escort peeled off to engage. Moments later, No. 603 Squadron arrived to hit them while they were still trying to deal with the initial assault, quickly shooting down two Me109s. While more of their escorts were dragged into the dogfights, the Dorniers flew on, straight into the path of Nos 501 and 253 Squadrons from Kenley. No. 501 shot down two of the bombers, but lost two of its own in the fight. The giant formation, its shape more ragged now, rumbled on through the brilliant Kent skies. At every stage of the journey more fighters were closing to meet it — a clutch of Hurricanes from Nos 303 and 229 Squadrons, then three more Spitfire squadrons, which intercepted over the Medway, then another four squadrons of Hurricanes.

With his usual instinct for locating the dramatic centre of events, Churchill at Uxbridge was able to observe the action unfold during the crucial hours of the battle that day. He recorded how:

Presently the red bulbs showed that the majority of our
squadrons were engaged . . . A subdued hum arose
from the floor, where the busy plotters pushed their
discs to and fro in accordance with the swiftly changing situation . . . The Air Marshal himself [Park] walked

up and down behind, watching with a vigilant eye every move in the game, supervising his junior executive hand, and only occasionally intervening with some decisive order, usually to reinforce a threatened area. In a little while all our squadrons were fighting and some had already begun to return for fuel. All were in the air. The lower line of bulbs was out. There was not one squadron left in reserve.[30]

By the time the Luftwaffe armada had London in sight, just before midday, 15 Hurricane squadrons and 8 Spitfire squadrons were in the air, a force of over 250 fighters. All over northern Kent spectators looked up in awe and fascination at the chalky vapour trails being scribbled in the perfect blue by the rolling and tumbling dogfights. Above the southern suburbs of the city, the German aircrews found, for the first time, that they were outnumbered. As they set course for their targets, scanning the homely Victorian terraces, the parks, commons and railway lines, fixing on the river to lead them in, six squadrons of 11 Group were waiting for them and the Duxford Wing was on its way. No. 504 Squadron had been scrambled from Hendon at 11.20a.m. Just before that, two US Army Air Corps generals and a US rear-admiral had arrived at the airfield to see "the life of a fighter squadron". The visitors noted that the time taken from the order to all 12 Hurricanes being airborne was 4 minutes and 50 seconds.

South of Fulham, 504 Squadron saw hostile aircraft. "The bombers were coming in towards London from the southeast and at first we could not tell how many there were," said Squadron Leader John Sample. "We opened our throttles and started to climb up towards them, aiming for a point well ahead, where we expected to contact them at their own height. As we converged, I saw that there were about twenty of them, and it looked as though it was going to be a nice party, for the other squadrons of Hurricanes and Spitfires also turned to join in. By the time we reached a position near the bombers, we were over London — Central London, I should say. We had gained a little height on them, too, so when I gave the order to attack we were able to dive on them from their right." The first attack "broke them up pretty nicely," said Sample. "The Dorniers didn't fly particularly tight which was to their disadvantage," reported 504 pilot Sergeant Ray Holmes. "If they had done, they'd have had better firepower to beat off the fighters. But our CO went at them in a quarter attack and more or less went through them and spread them out a bit."[31]

Holmes spotted three Dorniers in "vic" formation, separated from their fellows but still stubbornly pressing on to the centre of London. Choosing the nearest of the three, he dived on it:

I made my attack on this bomber and he spurted out a lot of oil, just a great stream over my aeroplane, blotting out my windscreen. Then as the windscreen cleared, I suddenly found myself going straight into his tail. So I stuck my stick forward and went under him, practically grazing my head on his belly.

434

He saw the Dornier fall away, and then went in from the stern on a second bomber:

> I was shooting at him when suddenly something white came out of the aircraft. I thought that a part of his wing had come away but in actual fact it turned out to be a man with a parachute coming out. I was travelling at 250 miles per hour, it all happened so quickly, but before I knew what had happened this bloody parachute was draped over my starboard wing. There was this poor devil on his parachute hanging straight out behind me, and my aeroplane was being dragged. All I could do was swing the aeroplane left and then right to try to get rid of this man. Fortunately his parachute slid off my wing and down he went".[32]

Holmes attacked the third Dornier, colliding with its tail. He lost control of his Hurricane, but baled out safely to arrive to a hero's welcome on the streets below.

Douglas Bader, with five squadrons of the Duxford Wing, arrived with the sun behind him. From an ideal tactical position, 3,000 feet above the bombers, the wing smashed into the flank of the formation just as the bombers released their loads and turned for home. The bombers scattered in all directions, making it impossible for the dwindling number of Me109s to protect them.

The British pilots were cheered on in the streets below, where thousands were watching, enthralled by the twisting evasions and pursuits. The diarist of 609

Squadron recorded that one piece of a Dornier they had destroyed "reached the ground just outside a Pimlico public house to the great comfort and joy of the patrons".

Luftwaffe pilots were taken aback by the numbers of aircraft ranged against them, as Hans Zonderlind, a front gunner in a Dornier Do17, remembered:

From the time that we had been over Maidstone until reaching the outskirts of London, we had been under extreme pressure. The British fighters had been with us since we had first crossed the English coast and had gathered in intensity all the time. Our escort had been doing a grand job with the Spitfires at keeping them away from us, and we thought that should things remain like this, then this bombing run would be made easy . . .

We saw the Hurricanes coming towards us and it seemed that the whole of the RAF was there, we had never seen so many British fighters coming at us at once. I saw a couple of our comrades go down, and we got hit once but it did no great damage. All around us were dogfights as the fighters went after each other, then as we were getting ready for our approach to the target, we saw what must have been a hundred RAF fighters coming at us . . . where were they coming from? — we had been told that the RAF fighters were very close to extinction. We could not keep our present course, we turned to starboard [doing] all that we could to avoid the fighters and after a while I am sure we had lost our bearings, so we just dropped our bombs and made our retreat.[33]

The Germans had no chance to aim accurately. They scattered their bombs over South and Central London — over Beckenham, Westminster, Lambeth, Lewisham, Battersea, Camberwell, Crystal Palace, Clapham, Tooting and Wandsworth. Then the bombers wheeled sharply to the east or west, desperate to get away. Those fleeing westwards were caught first over Weybridge, then again further south. Those heading for the Thames Estuary were picked up by a swarm of four squadrons and harassed and hounded every mile of the way. The few Me109s left over England could offer little protection. Their fuel warning lights were glowing, and they too were heading homewards.

Luftwaffe pilots who became detached from their formations felt acutely vulnerable. Oberst Josef Priller, a fighter pilot with *Jagdgeschwader 26*, remembered that:

It was no easy task over England in September 1940. Sometimes the youngsters were the victims of their inexperience and over-enthusiasm. There were times when we heard a plea from someone who was confused and disoriented, and nothing could be done about it. I remember one occasion when a lad who hadn't, as we used to say, tasted much English air, lost sight of our formation after some frenzied twisting and turning about the sky. But we could see him: he had dived steeply and was over the outskirts of London. He should have stayed with the *Staffel* instead of chasing off on his own. When he grasped the situation he called for help: "Come quickly! I'm on my own over London."[34]

As the bullet-riddled Dorniers limped to earth at their bases around Antwerp, and the British fighters returned to their airfields to refuel and rearm, another force was assembling over northern France. At 1.30p.m. radar reported German bombers massing west of Calais. The formation took shape more quickly than the morning air fleet, and half an hour later it was crossing the Channel. This time there was a huge phalanx of 400 German fighters to protect 150 bombers. The force was staggered in three waves.

On airfields across Southeast England, pilots bolted down sandwiches and drained cups of tea, while the armourers, fitters and riggers worked frantically on their machines. Goering had hoped that his afternoon attack would catch Fighter Command on the ground, but the speed of the turnaround meant that all the squadrons involved in the actions of the morning were at readiness when the assault began. At 2p.m., Park scrambled eight squadrons to patrol in pairs above Sheerness, Chelmsford, Kenley and Hornchurch. Five minutes later he ordered up four more squadrons, then a further eight, and reinforcements were called in from 12 Group.

At 2.15p.m., the first German wave crossed the coast, again near Dungeness. Two more followed, separated by ten minutes. The force advanced on

London across a ten-mile front. Park and his controllers hoped to engage the German fighters early, luring them away from their charges, gradually stripping the bombers of their bodyguards, and opening them up to the attentions of the squadrons that would be waiting for them around and above London. As the German aircraft arrived over Romney Marsh, Spitfires from Nos 41 and 603 Squadrons (from Hornchurch) dived into the mass, shooting down two Dorniers before being jumped by the escorting Me109s. Just south of Maidstone, No. 73 Squadron ran into a group of unescorted bombers and destroyed three of them. Over Dartford, Spitfires of No. 66 and No. 72 Squadrons fastened onto a large body of bombers, and fierce dogfights broke out with the escorts. Four more squadrons arrived to join in. The formation wavered. Some of the pilots banked off to the right or left to try to escape the attacks or to turn back.

No. 303 (Polish) Squadron had been ordered up from Northolt and sent to cover the Kent coast along the Thames. Soon afterwards, the nine Hurricanes led by Squadron Leader Kellett came across a large formation over Gravesend. In the fight that followed, two Hurricanes were shot down, but the Poles managed to destroy at least two Me110s and a number of bombers. The squadron's intelligence report summarized the action:

S/L Kellett was ordered to patrol Northolt at 20,000ft. and took off with the nine serviceable machines. The other squadrons had left sometime previously and 303 operated throughout alone . . . when still 2,000ft below their patrol level, they sighted coming head on from the southeast a very large formation of bombers and fighters. The bombers were in vics of three sections line astern with Me110s in sq formation between the vics of bombers. To the flanks and stepped up above to 25,000ft. were many formations of Me109s. Blue Section had got rather in front of the others, and wheeling round to let them come up. S/L Kellett had to deliver a quarter frontal attack instead of head on. This he did initially with only the other two members of Blue Section — Sgt. Wojciechowski and P/O Zak. Probably as there were a lot of clouds about, the enemy imagined that this was the advance guard of a large force and began to wheel towards the east, and when the other two sections came in they turned completely to the east. After the first rush the Me110s and the 109s fell upon the nine Hurricanes which were compelled to defend themselves individually as best they could, and escaped destruction in the clouds. As it was, four of the aircraft which returned were slightly damaged by enemy fire, one, Sgt Adruszkow's, was destroyed, the pilot baling out unhurt at Dartford, and Sgt Brzezowski is missing.

From the west, a force of about 80 bombers was heading across the outskirts of Surrey towards Central London. They were met by Hurricanes from Tangmere — 213 and 607 Squadrons — which tore into them, shooting several down and throwing more off course.

The size and fierceness of the defending force continued to dismay the Luftwaffe crews, who had been told that Fighter Command was in its death throes. Over Kent they had been assailed by a total of 170 fighters, and 50 bombers had lost heart and turned back before reaching Chatham. But the huge numbers of escorting Me109s were fighting hard, too, and doing their job of fending off the full weight of the British fighters.

On reaching the outskirts of London, the German aircraft came under heavy anti-aircraft fire from the new batteries that had been brought in from elsewhere to defend the city. As the planes emerged from this barrage, they were faced with the biggest concentration of British aircraft they had yet encountered. There were fifteen squadrons facing them — ten from 11 Group and five from the Duxford Wing. For the second time that day, German aircrew were confronted by the alarming sight of a mass of British fighters, aggressive, determined and well organized.

Bader later complained that his force had been scrambled too late. The Spitfire squadrons, although flying above the Hurricanes, came in too low and had to climb to drive off the Me109s. But the sheer weight of his wing's charge still had the desired effect, forcing the enemy out of formation so that its defensive arcs dissolved into small desperate groups, whose concern was no longer to attack but to survive. "This time, for a change, we outnumbered the Hun, and believe me, no more than eight got home from that party," Bader later declared. "At one time you could see planes going

441

down on fire all over the place, and the sky seemed full of parachutes. It was sudden death that day, for our fighters shot them to blazes."[35]

It was not always, though, the Luftwaffe pilots who found themselves outnumbered, as No. 19 Squadron's Sergeant George Unwin discovered:

I got lost from my squadron and when I looked, there was not a soul in the sky. Then in the distance, I saw some ack-ack and I went towards it and I saw these waves upon waves of German bombers coming in. It was a fascinating sight. There seemed to be hundreds of them and I forgot about anything else. Suddenly, I found aeroplanes whizzing all around me. I'd flown smack into the middle of the fighter escort. Without thinking. Damn fool. I went into a tight turn and shot at several 109s as they went through my sights — and I actually shot two of them down. I got the first one and he bailed out. When I went to sight the next one, the light in my reflector sight failed. The bloody bulb failed. I was still in a tight turn and I shot the second one down without a sight. His petrol tank went up. It was probably the turn that saved me — the Messerschmitt couldn't turn like a Spitfire. It frightened me — I was all on my own in the middle of I don't know how many Messerschmitts but I didn't get a hole in me. I must have had a guardian angel with me.[36]

Thickening cloud and the relentless fighter assault spared the German target for the day — the Royal Victoria and Surrey Commercial Docks — from serious damage. Instead, the bombs fell over a wide area, on Hammersmith in West London, on Islington and Kilburn in the north, in the very centre on the Strand, and as far south as Croydon and Mitcham. This broad spread was testimony to how widely the formation was scattered and contrasted tellingly with the concentrated destruction the Germans had achieved eight days before.

The attacks on bombers continued relentlessly all the way to the coast, with three or more British fighters sometimes raking a single stricken bomber. Over Kent, a force of 50 Me109s arrived to shepherd the bombers home, but by then the damage had been done. For Pilot Officer Thomas Neil, of No. 249 Squadron, his second sortie of the day provided an unforgettable chase:

September 15 was a very special day. 249 Squadron, North Weald, had taken off in the morning and we'd intercepted about 30 Dorniers over Maidstone but we hadn't done very well. I shot at something but nothing happened. Then at about three o'clock in the afternoon, we were sent off again. We intercepted another group of Dorniers over Maidstone and this time everything went swimmingly. I found myself behind a Dornier and as I was firing at it, the crew suddenly bailed out. I was so close behind it that as one of the bodies came out, I ducked in the aeroplane, thinking, "My God, he's going to hit me." Their parachutes were undeveloped, they fell out. And then I remember breaking away and being attacked by some

German fighters. They set about me furiously and I defended myself. And then, as so often happened in combat, you're surrounded by aeroplanes like bees round a honey pot, and suddenly everything is quiet and there are no aeroplanes. It happens instantaneously. Then I saw another Dornier flying across my bows, about a mile away, which I immediately followed. It was going down the estuary, by this time we'd got up roughly over Gravesend. It took some time for me to catch it up because it was going in a slight dive. Eventually I caught it up and I suddenly found that a Spitfire was to my left. And thereafter it was fairly straightforward, a single aeroplane, on its own, two of us, we took it in turns to fire, it went down and down and down, out to sea, across a convoy of ships . . . I thought, "Oh God, we're going to lose this one, he's going to get home." The Spitfire and I had run out of ammunition but we flew alongside it. I could read all the letters on the cockpit, and I could see the damage that had been done. And then it got slower and slower and slower and the nose came up and up and up, and suddenly the tail hit the sea and it splashed down. I felt satisfaction — total satisfaction. The pair of us flew around and usually when an aeroplane hits the sea, it goes down and then comes to the surface. We flew around and nobody surfaced. As we flew back over the convoy the ships all blew their whistles.[37]

Long before nightfall it was clear that a great battle had been won, perhaps the decisive encounter of the summer air war. The Air Ministry announced that 183 enemy aircraft had been shot down. The real figure was 56, considerably fewer but still the heaviest daily loss the Luftwaffe had suffered so far in the campaign and a severe blow to its strength and morale. The German air force was fighting a war of attrition, but its enemy's numbers seemed to be growing. In the space of 90 minutes, 28 squadrons had been in action and the skies had been filled with more than 250 British fighters. Goering's claim that Fighter Command was down to its "last fifty Spitfires" was now a sour joke.

In contrast, the pilots of Fighter Command ended the day filled with elation. Their losses had been much lighter than the Luftwaffe's — 26 aircraft downed, with 13 pilots killed. For the first time they began to feel that they were controlling events. "What about the RAF yesterday?" Sergeant Eric Bann wrote to his parents the next day. "My gosh, for every bomb dropped upon the King and Queen old 238 gave them hell. We got 12 Huns in one scrap. We just went in as one man and held our fire until very close range and then blew them right out of their cockpits."

For Fighter Command, almost everything had gone right — detection, interception and destruction. The whole intricate organization, from radar station to Observer Corps look-out post, to group and sector station commands, to the "sharp end" of a pilot with his thumb on the fire button, and the entire communications infrastructure linking them — all had functioned exactly as they should. All but one of the squadrons sent up had made contact in the morning, and all 28 had tangled with the enemy in the afternoon, Fighter Command's best "hit" rate of the Battle of Britain. Improved coordination with Anti-Aircraft Command, and Park's masterful depletion of the enemy fighter force and careful management of his assets, had made the skies over London a place of doom for the German air force.

The RAF had been helped, too, by the Luftwaffe's poor performance. The first offensive was slow and predictable. After the early morning, there were fewer feints or dummy raids to confuse the defenders, and the huge attack had been made across a relatively narrow corridor, making effective interception easier. The second attack had allowed crucial time for Fighter Command to get back to readiness, and both raids had demonstrated the Me109's debilitating lack of fuel-carrying capacity. The main clash, in the skies over London, had been in a place of Park's choosing too, at the extreme limit of the German fighters' range.

The British press seized on the erroneous but irresistible claim of 183 enemy aircraft shot down. The *Daily Express* crowed that "Goering may reflect that this is no way to run an invasion". Churchill, though, had become concerned at the inflation of the figures. He wanted the Americans to believe Britain was winning the battle, but it was also important that the figures remained credible and backed up by evidence. But for once the hyperbole, if inaccurate in terms of the numbers, was right in its tone. The fine flying weather, longed for by the Germans to deliver their final blow, had ended up benefiting the RAF's fighter interceptors

446

more than the Luftwaffe. Wreckage of German aircraft was lying smashed in fields, lanes and streets all over Southeast England. "We must take September 15 as the culminating date," Churchill later wrote in his account of the battle. Indeed, it was the decisive day and has since been observed as "Battle of Britain Day". As the government's Official History of the battle noted, if 15 August had shown the Germans that air superiority was not to be won quickly or easily, then 15 September showed them that it could not be won at all. The Luftwaffe's attempt to assert daylight superiority, essential for invasion, had failed.

No-one, neither the pilots heading to the pubs in a mood of jubilation and hilarity born of relief, nor the earthbound civilians who had cheered them on, dared yet hope that the ordeal was over. And nor was it, for the fighting and dying would continue for some time yet. But on 15 September the moment of greatest danger passed. Though it was far from obvious at the time, the Battle of Britain was won.

When the men of Fighter Command awoke on the morning of 16 September and looked up, they saw the blessed sight of a carpet of thick rain clouds obscuring the sun. The German bombers stayed away for most of the day, and the Luftwaffe licked its wounds. It seemed, though, like a short respite rather than the beginning of the end, and in the days that followed few of the "fighter boys" felt that the end was in sight.

Despite the Luftwaffe's daytime losses, London had been hit hard again on the night of Sunday 15

September, with bombs falling on Hammersmith, the Strand, Westminster and the East End. Diarist "Chips" Channon recorded the following day that he "drove back to London via the East End, which is a scene of desolation. House after house had been wrecked, debris falls from the remaining floors, windows are gone, heaps of rubbish lie in the pavements. A large hospital and a synagogue still stand, but they are windowless. Some streets are roped off because of time-bombs. The damage is immense, yet the people, mostly Jewish, seemed courageous."[38]

Reconnaissance of the continental Channel ports showed a continuing build-up of German barges, despite the now nightly bombardments by Bomber and Coastal commands. That build-up led some in the British High Command to believe that invasion was still imminent. The prime minister was more sceptical, and he even introduced a note of cautious optimism into his rhetoric. On 17 September, Churchill told Parliament that "Sunday's action was the most brilliant and fruitful of any fought up to that date by the fighters of the Royal Air Force . . . We may await the decision of this long air battle with sober but increasing confidence."[39]

Goering now summoned his *Luftflotten* and *Fliegerkorps* commanders for a dissection of the action of 15 September. It was clear, at last, that Dowding was not down to his "last fifty Spitfires", and Goering reverted to his original plan. Fighter Command airfields and aircraft factories were to be targeted once again, while attacks on London continued. The big losses of 15 September forced a change in tactics. Large formations of bombers would no longer be deployed, unless circumstances were exceptional. The new approach would team bomber groups with huge fighter escorts. Bitter experience could not, though, quench Goering's taste for hyperbole. Fighter Command could still be destroyed in "four or five days", he predicted. His claim was based on another greatly inflated battle-damage assessment. The Germans believed they had destroyed 79 Fighter Command aircraft on 15 September, rather than the real figure of 26. In fact, Fighter Command numbers were on the increase. At the beginning of July, Dowding had been able to deploy 44 Hurricane and Spitfire squadrons. By the end of the year, there would be 71, many equipped with more powerful Mark 2 Spitfires and Hurricanes.

The Luftwaffe compensated for the relative daytime inactivity of 16 September with a vigorous effort overnight. The attacks continued until 5.30a.m. the next morning. In all, 170 aircraft dropped 200 tons of bombs, and much of the population was forced into air-raid shelters for another exhausting and fearful night.

While the night-time alarms were now becoming routine, the daylight action, in its new phase, locked Kesselring and Park in a tactical battle of bluff and counter-bluff. As the weather brightened during the afternoon of 17 September, waves of Luftwaffe fighters roared in from the Channel. Park was informed that few, if any, bombers were among them, and so he was inclined to ignore the incursions as the Me109s could cause little damage except to other fighters.

Nevertheless, No. 501 Squadron did clash with fighters from *Jagdgeschwader 53* near Ashford, Kent, losing two of its Hurricanes. Spitfires of 41 Squadron were then pulled into the combat over East Kent, followed by the Duxford Wing, whose 19 and 303 Squadrons both had successes. As would often be the case in the weeks ahead, British and German fighter losses were roughly equal, on this occasion about five each.

One of 501's pilots, Sergeant Edward Egan, was killed on 16 September when he failed to escape from his burning cockpit. Of all the fates that might befall a pilot, this was the worst nightmare. Some pilots reportedly even carried revolvers with them to end the agony in such circumstances. "I always wore goggles and gloves," said 249 Squadron's Thomas Neil. "The Hurricane got to two to three thousand degrees centigrade in a matter of seconds after being set on fire and that's why so many people were terribly burned."[40]

Sergeant Ralph Carnall of 111 Squadron had been shot down in flames on 16 August. Another burns victim, No. 41 Squadron's George Bennions, a schoolfriend of Carnall's, found himself in the same hospital. "His hair was burnt off," said Bennions, "his eyebrows were burnt off, his eyelids were burnt off. You could just see his staring eyes. His nose was burnt, there were just two holes in his face. His lips were badly burnt. Then, when I looked down, his hands were burnt. I looked down at his feet also. His feet were

450

burnt . . . I thought, 'What have I got to complain about?' "[41]

A special burns unit had opened at the RAF hospital at Halton, Buckinghamshire, to deal with the large number of cases. Alongside this facility was the civilian special burns unit at the Queen Victoria Hospital in East Grinstead, Sussex, led by Sir Archibald McIndoe. A New Zealander, McIndoe had started out specializing in tropical diseases and liver complaints but had become a plastic surgeon under the patronage of his cousin, Sir Harold Gillies. McIndoe was a highly skilful and imaginative surgeon, developing new techniques for treating badly burned faces and hands. From observing airmen shot down into the sea, he discovered that immersion in saline would promote healing as well as improving survival rates for victims with extensive burns.

Crucially, McIndoe also recognized the terrible psychological effects of disfigurement and did what he could to ameliorate them, hand-picking the prettiest nurses for the wards, abandoning rules about "lying to attention" and, above all, exuding confidence and calmness. He also understood the importance of social reintegration back into normal life, and encouraged locals in the hospital vicinity to invite the patients to their homes.

Hitler had, on 14 September, postponed making up his mind about launching the invasion until 17 September. But now that the day had arrived, he once more delayed the decision. The reason, according to the entry

451

for the day in the War Diary of the German Naval Staff, was that the RAF "was by no means defeated".[42] Hitler nonetheless insisted on the maintenance of a high state of preparedness.

On the night of 17/18 September, 268 bombers streamed in over Dungeness and Selsey Bill to hit London. The John Lewis department store on Oxford Street was all but burned down. Merseyside also suffered. At the same time, Bomber and Coastal commands took advantage of the full moon to attack enemy shipping concentrations, and at Dunkirk 500 tons of ammunition for the invasion armies were blown up.

Some domestic commentators were beginning to feel that social cohesion was now being threatened. Diarist Harold Nicolson noted on 17 September that: "Everybody is worried about the feeling in the East End, where there is much bitterness. It is said that even the King and Queen were booed the other day when they visited the destroyed areas." In partial compensation was the fact that Luftwaffe bombs had been encompassing a widening social mix: "Clem [Attlee, Labour Party leader in the Coalition government] says that if only the Germans had had the sense not to bomb west of London Bridge there might have been a revolution in this country. As it is, they have smashed about Bond Street and Park Lane and readjusted the balance."[43]

Daylight on 18 September saw a continuation of the cat-and-mouse game between Kesselring and Park. The weather was unsettled, relieved by bright intervals. At around 9a.m., radar reported considerable numbers coming in fast between Folkestone and North Foreland. Park ordered up 15 squadrons, but such was the speed of the attack that only six of them, from Biggin Hill and Hornchurch, intercepted. They found a swarm of fighters, with no bombers to target. Those that could followed their orders to avoid fighter-to-fighter combat and disengaged, but five Fighter Command aircraft were shot down.

Two hours later, another large attack was mapped. Fearing a repeat of the earlier action, Park held back. This time, though, Kesselring had added a small contingent of bombers to the formations, and they were free to pound Chatham and Rochester unopposed. Over Tilbury, two Ju88 bombers from *Kampfgeschwader 77* were shot down after the belated intervention of No. 19 Squadron's Spitfires from Fowlmere, and No. 41 Squadron caught two of the Me109s as they sped back over Maidstone.

After this miscalculation, Park put up a strong force against the next raid, which arrived mid-afternoon. This time, it was the right call. The formation contained a number of Ju88s, the Luftwaffe's fastest bomber, and as it approached Gravesend more than 100 British fighters attacked in waves. Nos 92 and 302 Squadrons came in first with a head-on attack, and then, over the Thames Estuary, the Duxford Wing swept down in an almost vertical dive. The wing's claim of thirty aircraft destroyed was a wild overestimation, the real figure being nearer four. But the spectacle was further evidence for the hard-pressed Luftwaffe bomber crews that the RAF was neither depleted nor demoralized.

During the day's fighting, Fighter Command lost 12 aircraft, but with only 3 pilots killed. About half of the pilots shot down would be back flying with their squadrons within 24 hours. On the same day, the Luftwaffe lost 15 aircraft and more than 50 airmen killed or taken prisoner.

Thursday 19 September was wet and the skies were quiet, with only 70 intruders crossing the coast, most of them flying singly. But on the ground a momentous decision was taken. The previous night, nearly 200 British bombers had pounded the German invasion fleet and its nearby troop concentrations. In the morning, Hitler ordered that the build-up of shipping, which had accelerated over the previous week, should be halted. The invasion barges were now to be dispersed to prevent losses, and the soldiers moved away from the coast. The decision marked the effective end of Operation Sea Lion. There would now no longer be time to assemble an invasion force in what remained of the year. The order was swiftly implemented by seamen eager to escape the nightly attacks by British bombers. A week later, reconnaissance photos showed a 40 per cent reduction in vessels in the Channel ports.

The suspension of the German invasion plan did not, however, lead to the diminution of the air campaign. The dim hope remained that the Luftwaffe could force victory either through the destruction of Fighter Command or by its new strategy of bombing the cities. The morning of 20 September saw another dangerous attack by waves of Me109s. This time Park responded with only four squadrons, and the British came off worst. Nos 92 and 72 Squadrons from Biggin Hill intercepted between Ashford and the coast and engaged the first formation. The Hornchurch squadrons, Nos 41 and 222, rushed to assist but were bounced by the second German wave and badly mauled. In all, the RAF lost seven Spitfires, with four pilots killed, while only two Me109s were hit.

Shorn of its escort duties, and thus freed from the frustration of wasting time and fuel by endlessly throttling back or weaving, the Me109 was now a very dangerous enemy. Above 25,000 feet the Me109's two-stage supercharger gave it a better performance than the Mark 2 Hurricanes and Spitfires coming into service. Dowding and Park had decided as early as July that German fighter forces were best left alone. But radar could not tell the type of aircraft producing a blip on its screens. The Observer Corps also had difficulty in identifying whether enemy formations contained bombers. Identification was made particularly difficult by hazy conditions or when the intruders were at a great height, a tactic used increasingly by the Luftwaffe.

On Saturday 21 September, the Luftwaffe began implementing Goering's order of 16 September to concentrate the offensive again on Fighter Command, and in particular the aircraft plants, now humming with activity. The effort, though, was scattered and half-hearted. The most significant sortie was against the Brooklands aircraft factory in Surrey, which was targeted by a lone Ju88 raider flying in low at treetop height, having followed the railway north from Guildford. Three of its bombs fell harmlessly, but the fourth, a delayed-action 250 kg high explosive, landed on the main Hurricane assembly shop. A courageous Canadian engineer, Lieutenant J. M. S. Patton, loaded the unexploded bomb onto a hastily cobbled-together sled and tipped it into a crater made by one of the other bombs, where it blew up harmlessly.

As the days went by, worsening autumn weather was beginning to come to the relief of the RAF. On 22 September, fog blunted the Luftwaffe attack, requiring Fighter Command to mount only 158 sorties in response, the smallest number since the beginning of the battle on 10 July. When, during the night, one of Churchill's private secretaries was woken to receive a message from President Roosevelt expressing concern that the invasion was imminent, it was not thought necessary to wake the prime minister.

Monday 23 September dawned bright and clear, though, and by 9a.m. there was a large build-up of German aircraft over Calais. Park reacted vigorously, sending up 24 squadrons. But the raiders were all Me109 fighters, and few British aircraft were able to gain enough height in time to intercept. Just after 10a.m., as the raiders crossed the coast and fanned out, they were intercepted by Spitfires from Nos 72 and 92 Squadrons from Biggin Hill and No. 73 Squadron's Hurricanes from Debden. In a torrid eight minutes, four of the Hurricanes, caught still climbing, were shot down. All four pilots were wounded, two of them suffering bad burns, but all survived. The Spitfire squadrons fared better, losing two machines and no pilots and downing three of the German fighters. Only seven other squadrons made contact, and, in all, eleven British fighters were shot down, with similar losses on the German side. The night, though, witnessed the heaviest raid yet on London, by over 250 bombers. Blenheims and Defiants were sent up to try to intercept, but without success.

On Tuesday 24 September, calmer weather in the English Channel once again raised fears of invasion — worries exacerbated by the heavy raids of the night before. During the day a force of 200 aircraft was successfully repulsed 20 miles short of London. *Erprobungsgruppe 210* also raided the Supermarine Spitfire works at Woolston, Southampton. The factory sat right on the waterfront, making it an easily identifiable target. Two *Staffeln* of Me110s dived on the factory, scoring five direct hits. The works itself sustained minor damage, but one of the bombs hit a shelter, killing almost 100 of the company's personnel. The whole attack lasted only eight minutes, but there was no Fighter Command interception. The force of Me110s had been flying too low or too fast for detection and interception. In the absence of friendly fighters, the local anti-aircraft forces had blazed away furiously, shooting down one raider and damaging two others.

German attacks focused once more on aircraft factories on Wednesday 25 September. At 11.20a.m., a

457

large force crossed the Channel. While fighter bombers carried out diversionary attacks on coastal towns, 60 He111s of *Kampfgeschwader 55*, with Me110s of *Zerstörergeschwader 26* and *Erprobungsgruppe 210*, crossed the coast at 11.15a.m. and headed northwards. Air Vice-Marshal Brand, 10 Group's commander, judged that the raid was heading for the Westland works at Yeovil, Somerset, and put up three squadrons to protect it. In fact it was heading for the aeronautical factory at Filton, near Bristol, and reached it unopposed. This factory produced Blenheims as well as aero engines for several other aircraft. Once the leading Me110s had marked the factory site, the Heinkels followed. Damage was extensive. More than 250 people were killed or injured, 8 completed aircraft were badly damaged, and production was severely curtailed. Belatedly, Nos 238 and 152 Squadrons arrived and downed five of the bombers as they retreated back across the Channel.

On 25 September, Unteroffizier Peter Stahl, of *Gruppe 2, Kampfgeschwader 30*, was sent on a lone raid in his Ju88. His earlier confidence had by now waned:

We're a bit more modest. It's not so much a matter of achieving some kind of success, but mainly to ensure there's at least an air-raid warning in London. However, for us poor sausages it is anything but easy. During the previous large-scale raids one could to some extent hide inside the large formations, but flying alone one is always exposed like a practice target to a well-coordinated defence organization.

All four of us are anxiously searching the sky around us for Spitfires. Sure enough, exactly at the spot where we could assume the sirens would begin announcing an approach raid on London, we see them: four fighters below us in a steady climb in our direction. It does not take us long to decide that there is nothing to be done here now. I break off our approach, tipping the aircraft on a wing and whipping round in the fastest turn of my life.[44]

Following the attacks of 25 September, No. 504 Squadron was moved from Hendon to Filton on 26 September. But now the Heinkels of *Kampfgeschwader 55* had another target, the Supermarine works at Woolston, which had been only slightly damaged by the attack two days previously. The raid arrived at 5.45p.m., and 70 tons of bombs hit the factory. Thirty people were killed, and production was completely stopped. Three completed Spitfires were destroyed and over twenty damaged. Six squadrons engaged the raiders, though only after the bombing, shooting down three aircraft but losing six fighters themselves. Had this attack on the key Spitfire factory occurred earlier during the battle, it might have had a severe impact. But the "shadow" factories at Cosford, Desford and Castle Bromwich were now on stream to make up the lost capacity.

The Luftwaffe turned again to Filton on Friday 27 September. This time, Brand was ready. Five squadrons met the formation of Heinkels from *Kampfgeschwader 55*, which were preceded by Me110s from *Erprobungsgruppe 210* and further protected by more Me110s from *Zerstörergeschwader 26*. Over Yeovil, the British fighters swept down on the bombers, breaking up the formation and forcing them to ditch their bombs before they reached the target. The Heinkels hurried for the protection of the Me110s of *Zerstörergeschwader 26*, which were waiting over Swanage to shepherd them home, but they themselves had come under fierce attack from No. 609 Squadron (from Middle Wallop) and others. The Me110s of *Erprobungsgruppe 210* pressed on to Bristol, but then lost four of their nineteen aircraft, including that of their commanding officer.

Pilot Officer David Crook was one of those taking part in 609's attack, and in his view:

. . . this was the first time in this war that we had met the enemy on even terms. Generally we were outnumbered by anything from three to one up to ten to one. But on this glorious occasion there were fifteen of them and twelve of us, and we made the most of it.

We were close to them now and we started to dive. I think that these moments just before the clash are the most gloriously exciting moments of life. You sit there behind a great engine that seems as vibrant and alive as you are yourself, your thumb waits expectantly on the trigger, and your eyes watch the gun sights through which in a few seconds an enemy will be flying in a veritable ball of fire.

All around you, in front and behind, there are your
friends too, all eager and excited, all thundering down
together into the attack! The memory of such
moments is burnt on my mind for ever.[45]

It had been a punishing day for the Luftwaffe. It was
about to get worse in the London area, where
Kesselring launched one of his last great daylight
offensives on the capital. At 8a.m., the first raid had
appeared on the plotting tables, and soon the radar
screens along the southeast coast showed a number of
aircraft approaching on a 50-mile front. These turned
out to be bomb-carrying Me110s, escorted by Me109s.
They were hit by pairs of squadrons and driven back
from London, scattering their bombs haphazardly.

Some of the Me109s remained in the London area to
protect a following wave of 55 Ju88s of *Kampfgeschwader*
77. But the bombers had been late forming up, and
before they could make the rendezvous they were
intercepted by a strong force of over 100 British
fighters. The formations were shattered and the
bombers forced to ditch their loads and turn back. In
the meantime, the Me109s had taken a mauling and
now dived low to race for home.

Fighter Command sustained losses as well. Nos 72,
73, 92 and 303 Squadrons all suffered. In a huge
dogfight over East Sussex, No. 249 Squadron lost three
aircraft. Sergeant George Palliser witnessed the demise
of South African Pilot Officer Percival Burton: "I saw
his contortions," he later wrote, "then I saw him
straighten and fly straight into the German aircraft.

461

Both crashed and Percy was killed. I was close enough to see his letters, as other pilots must have been and who also confirmed this incident, which in itself caused me to realize my young life and its future, if any, had jumped into another dimension."[46]

Just before midday, another 300-strong German force approached London. Most were turned back by intercepting fighters, and only about 20 bombers succeeded in reaching the centre. By the end of the day, 28 Fighter Command aircraft had been shot down, but the Luftwaffe had lost 54, with all crews killed or captured. Churchill was delighted with the day's results, declaring that "the heavy losses of the enemy . . . make 27th September rank with 15 September and 15 August, as the third great and victorious day of the Fighter Command during the course of the Battle of Britain."[47]

On Saturday 28 September 1940, Kesselring changed his tactics, sending smaller formations against London and Portsmouth. Their escorts included Me109s flying at heights of up to 30,000 feet. Here, only Spitfires could touch them, and even then at a performance disadvantage. The Hurricanes, particularly the older Mark 1 Models, were unable to operate effectively at such heights, to the worry and frustration of their pilots. Hurricane pilot Richard Barclay, of No. 249 Squadron, noted in his diary two days later: "We had hundreds of 109s above us. We were too high for the Hurricane anyway . . . an awful trip as we were quite helpless, just waiting to be attacked."

Both of the Luftwaffe raids were beaten back, but with severe losses. Sixteen British fighters were shot down and nine pilots killed, all for a return of only three German planes. Kesselring's use of his *Luftflotte 2* bombers as "bait" to bring up Fighter Command against his Me109s had worked well.

★ ★ ★

Saturday 28 September was also the last day of action for Eric Bann. After a much-needed rest at the quiet posting of St Eval in Cornwall, his No. 238 Squadron had returned to the fray at Middle Wallop on 16 September. On 28 September, the Macclesfield-born pilot did not return from his mission over the Isle of Wight. His parents, to whom he had written regularly, spent months trying to find out the circumstances of his end. Eventually, they received a letter from W. Butcher of the Isle of Wight constabulary:

The machine your son was piloting was seen flying at great speed towards Portsmouth, probably hoping to regain its base as I believe that it was on fire although not to any great extent. When at a good height over Brading Marshes your son was seen to bale out quite safely but watchers who saw him come down say that his parachute did not open and this was found to be correct when Police and Military recovered his body shortly after . . . As far as I could see your son was not wounded by the enemy as no gunshot wounds could be found on him at all but it was perfectly obvious that he died from a fractured skull. There was no

463

chance of life when found I am sorry to say. Had there
been I would have worked hours as also would my
men to have brought him round, but, under the
circumstances, I could see that it was perfectly hopeless from the start . . . I agree with you that at that
time these gallant men must have been very much
overworked but they have performed a most marvellous feat against overwhelming odds and have earned
the gratitude of all the civilised world and such is the
spirit of the British RAF that their names will live for
ever as the saviours of our country of which we are all
so proud.

After Saturday's mauling, fine weather on Sunday
29 September seemed to threaten more damaging
attacks for Fighter Command. Luckily for the
defenders, that was not to be. Cloud accumulated as
time wore on, and the day witnessed only nuisance
assaults on convoys and several high-flying sorties over
Southeast England. But the last day of September
dawned very bright. At 609 Squadron's base at Middle
Wallop "the weather was brilliantly clear", remembered
David Crook, "and when we got up we shook our heads
dismally, as we knew there would be a lot of trouble".

Sure enough, the Luftwaffe was mounting a big
effort. Soon after 9a.m., 200 aircraft crossed the coast
in two waves. Twelve squadrons went up to meet them,
and most of the bombers were turned back over
Maidstone. While dogfights continued over the Thames
Estuary, a free chase of Me109s and Me110s was
plotted near Weymouth. David Crook's 609 Squadron

was among the squadrons vectored to intercept. They were at 27,000 feet over Swanage, Dorset, when they saw their prey. The squadron flew over Weymouth Bay and then in towards land to approach the enemy out of the sun. When six Me109s appeared in front of them, the British fighters latched onto their tails and followed them down as they tried to plunge away. "God, what a dive that was!" Crook wrote. "I have a sort of dim recollection of the sea coming up towards me at an incredible rate and also feeling an awful pain in my ears . . . I pulled out of the dive as gently as I could, but the strain was terrific and there was a sort of black mist in front of my eyes . . . the Messerschmitt was now just ahead of me. I came up behind him and gave him a terrific burst of fire at very close range." Crook's victim "rocked violently, then turned over on his back, burst into flames and dived straight down into the sea . . . the pilot made no attempt to get out and was obviously dead". Crook returned to the *mêlée* to find "a nice little massacre" in progress, and soon the surviving Germans broke off and raced for home.[48]

From midday, Kesselring sent about 100 bombers and 200 fighters in another attempt on London. Again, it was driven back and an intense fighter battle developed over Kent. A number of Ju88s reached South London, but the Luftwaffe sustained heavy losses.

The final attack of the day was against the Westland factory at Yeovil. Once again, it was carried out by Heinkels from *Kampfgeschwader 55*, which arrived with a strong escort. Four squadrons attacked them on the way in, and another four on the way out, after the bombers had found their target obscured by clouds and had scattered their bombs ineffectually.

Nearly 50 Luftwaffe aircraft were shot down on 30 September. Fighter Command lost 20, with 8 pilots killed. In the light of the accumulating evidence, Kesselring and Sperrle now decided that all twin-engine bombers should be withdrawn from daylight action unless there was cloud cover to protect them. During October, they would be used almost exclusively on night-time raids.

Instead of mass attacks in daylight, the Luftwaffe now concentrated on infiltrating in small numbers and at great heights, mainly with Me109s and Me110s. Frustrated by Park's targeting of the bombers and avoidance of his fighter-only sweeps, Kesselring converted a third of his Me109 force to carry 250 kg bombs. In theory this would mean that they could not be ignored by the defenders. If they came under attack, the raiders could simply jettison the bomb and revert to pure fighter mode. But the extra load brought significant disadvantages also, as the additional weight further reduced the Messerschmitt's range.

The new tactic caused considerable headaches for Park. A well-placed 250 kg bomb could cause extensive damage. October would become known in Battle of Britain folklore as "Messerschmitt month". Almost all of the southern airfields were hit, as well as Portsmouth, Southampton and London. On 15 October, bomb-carrying Me109s hit London's Waterloo station, closing virtually all its lines out of London.

Me109s crossing the coast at 30,000 feet were beyond the reach of the Hurricane, which made up two-thirds of Fighter Command's strength, and even the Spitfire struggled to get at them. Interception was a patchy business. On one occasion it took only 17 minutes after radar detection for a formation of Me109s to reach Central London. A Mark 1 Spitfire needed 27 minutes to climb to 30,000 feet. Thus, many Spitfires missed the attackers or were caught "on the climb". High-altitude flying in an unpressurized, unheated cockpit was particularly debilitating. Pilots reported stomach pains and sharp aches in the joints from tiny bubbles of oxygen in their blood. The accident rate rose. Park's solution was to detail two "spotting flights" to act as look-outs, flying high, avoiding combat and concentrating on reporting to Uxbridge any approaching aircraft.

But for all the physical wear-and-tear and the losses suffered by Fighter Command pilots during October, the new Luftwaffe tactic was never going to be decisive. There was now no shortage of British pilots or aircraft, and however fast and accurate the German fighter-bombers were, their bombs were too small to affect the course of events that was revealing itself.

On 4 October, Count Galeazzo Ciano, the Italian foreign minister, was present at a meeting between Hitler and Mussolini. Later that day he wrote in his diary that "there is no longer any talk about landing in the British Isles."[49] On 12 October, Generalfeld-marschall Keitel, head of the German armed forces, recorded that "The *Führer* has decided that from now until the spring, preparations for Sea Lion shall be continued solely for the purpose of maintaining political and military pressure on England. Should the Invasion be reconsidered in the spring or early summer of 1941, orders for renewal of operational readiness will be issued later. In the meantime military conditions for a later invasion are to be improved."[50]

The Luftwaffe launched its last substantial daylight effort of the Battle of Britain on 29 October. By now, a small contingent from the Italian air force had joined the campaign on the insistence of Mussolini and, while its outdated bombers attacked Ramsgate, the Luftwaffe raided Portsmouth and London. Most of the enemy aircraft were intercepted and driven back, but a small number got through. The next day there followed a more half-hearted effort, easily repulsed by the ten squadrons Keith Park now had in the air on patrol. On the following day, 31 October, officially deemed the end of the Battle of Britain, for the first time neither side lost an aircraft.

One Me109 pilot, Günther Büsgen of *Lehrgeschwader 2*, had shot down six British fighters and flown nearly eighty sorties during the battle. But he became increasingly disillusioned by the unreality of his orders. On 12 October, over London, he flew his last:

I copped it. On the way home I was attacked by a Hurricane and the hits were unfortunately in the cooling system and when that was hit you had perhaps ten minutes' flying time before you had to bale out.

We were told at that stage that if you were hit over England you had to get back over the Channel. What a nonsense! It was quite impossible. I was shot at 3,000 metres and, not following orders, went into a glide, but noticed that the plane was losing height rapidly. I lifted my cockpit roof and started to get out, but made a mistake and banged my left arm, cutting it. After a few more flying minutes I landed the plane at an aerodrome at Chatham. There were two Home Guards there immediately with weapons, it seemed, out of the Tower of London. "Hands up!" they said. I was quite good at English during my school days and explained, "I can't take my hands up because one is broken."

He ruefully reflected later that, "The flights to London we regarded as completely unnecessary ... They brought no results for us. In October the Battle of Britain was all over — the first part of a lost war."

The Luftwaffe turned its depleted strength to the night-time bombing campaign. The Blitz would continue, with hardly a night's respite, until May 1941, when the German bomber fleets were sent east to prepare for Hitler's invasion of the Soviet Union. By then, some 43,000 British civilians had been killed, about half of them in London, and more than a million homes destroyed or damaged.

But the Battle of Britain — the battle to avert invasion and defeat of the British homeland — had been won.

CHAPTER
NINE

Aftermath

By November 1940, as Fighter Command's ordeal by fire eased, Britain's civilian population took its place in the frontline. In the autumn of 1940, daylight attacks by the Luftwaffe faded out to be replaced by relentless night-time raids, which the RAF could do little to deter. The Blitz, which was to last from 7 September 1940 until 10 May 1941, was Germany's last attempt to try to end the war in the west before beginning her campaign against the Soviet Union. It was a strategy that depended on terrorizing the British people into rising up against their leaders and demanding peace. In Southeast England and in cities across the country, ordinary people had to get used to a life of constant danger and fear.

Gwen Arnold, a young woman living near Bournemouth, remembered the experience vividly:

Throughout that long winter the dreaded siren sounded at dusk every night, and the all clear was not heard until three, four, five or even six o'clock the next morning. Mother, Peggy and I crouched in the tiny cupboard under the stairs all those hours. We sat on boxes with only a candle to lighten the gloom. It was the worst period of the war for me. For hour after hour we listened to the distinctive throb of the German bombers (we could always tell if it was "one of ours" or "one of theirs"), the gunfire and an occasional earth-shattering explosion. At times I physically shook with fear. It was not so much fear of harm to our persons, but fear of losing our home. Home meant everything to us and I could not imagine how we would ever make another home, if we lost the house and our possessions.[1]

Gioya Steinke, a welfare adviser with London County Council Rest Centre Service, remembered that the bombs levelled not only houses but also class distinctions:

As soon as the "all clear" went you had the wardens and the firemen bringing all these people into the rest centres and they were in a pretty terrible state, covered in bomb dust. Everyone was reduced to the same level. You didn't know who was a street market person and who was from the posh flats. They were all reduced down and this I think was the reason for the wonderful camaraderie of the Blitz.[2]

As Steinke suggests, civilian morale stayed firm — and the German strategy failed. Thus, Britain was saved in 1940–I not only by the "fighter boys" and the skill, equipment, organization and leadership of Fighter Command, but also by the refusal of ordinary people, many of them poor, to succumb to either hysteria or recriminations against their political leaders under the weight of the Luftwaffe's bombing.

Churchill's liaison officer, General Hastings Ismay, was clear, though, about the importance of the air battle in averting a British disaster:

> Personally I always felt that if we won the Battle of Britain the Germans would not invade, and that if we lost it they would have no need to invade . . . the Luftwaffe could have proceeded to wipe out, in their own time and without any significant hindrance, first our air stations, then our aircraft factories, then perhaps our other munitions factories, then our ports and so on. The point would have been reached, perhaps quite soon, when we would have been bereft of all means of serious opposition. We could have continued the war from Canada — I hope that we would have done so. But the physical occupation of Britain would have presented [to the Germans] no serious difficulties.[3]

Instead, the Battle of Britain saw the destruction of 1,733 of the Luftwaffe's aircraft as against Fighter Command losses of 915 planes.[4] It was a tally that made the battle, in the view of Luftwaffe General Werner Kreipe, "a turning-point in the history of the Second World War. The German Air Force . . . was bled almost to death and suffered losses which could never

472

again be made good throughout the course of the war."[5]

As for the men of Fighter Command, the Battle of Britain made some of them into celebrities. As the year 1940 wore on, the BBC leaned heavily on pilots to make broadcasts harking back to the great events of the summer. The old reluctance to promote fighter aces, which had been thought bad for group morale, was gone. Certain pilots were pushed towards the newspapers. "Paddy" Finucane, a good-looking flying officer with No. 65 Squadron, became a notable favourite with women readers.

Paddy Finucane

Brendan Finucane, known as "Paddy" to his comrades and admirers, was born in Dublin on 16 October 1920. After his family moved to Richmond in Surrey, he joined the RAF on a short service commission aged eighteen. Finucane was posted to No. 65 Squadron at Hornchurch on 13 July 1940, and the following month shot down two Me109s in two days. With his crinkly hair, square jaw and faraway look he seemed to exemplify the youth and low-key idealism of the pilots, and he was extensively promoted by official propaganda. After he broke his ankle in a non-military accident, Finucane was inundated with get-well letters. "I guess you've received tons of fan mail from hero-worshipping dames all over the country," wrote a Land Girl who gave her address as "Amongst the turnips, Wiltshire". She signed off: "Boy, don't I wish I'd been a nurse."[6]

During 1941, Finucane was a prolific destroyer of German aircraft, shooting down 18 Me109s between August and the end of October. In June 1942, he took over the Hornchurch wing, becoming the youngest wing commander in the RAF. On 15 July 1942, after leading a raid against shipping at Ostend and on German airfields, his Spitfire was hit by fire from a machine-gun post near Le Touquet. He was too low to bale out and the aircraft crashed into the sea. His last words over the radio were, "This is it, chaps." He was not yet 22.

Many of the cast of heroes would not survive the war. Of the 2,917 pilots who took part in the air battles of the summer of 1940, 544 had died. Another 795 would be killed in the remaining years of the conflict.

On 25 November 1940, Hugh Dowding, originally due to retire in June 1939, was replaced as head of Fighter Command by Air Vice-Marshal Sholto Douglas. Park was also moved on, to a training command, and his old adversary Leigh-Mallory took over command of 11 Group. It was a victory for the proponents of the "Big Wing" and of taking the fight to the enemy. Many of the fighter pilots in 11 Group felt that Park and Dowding were the victims of jealousy and intrigue. It seemed to one of them, Al Deere, that they had "won the Battle of Britain but lost the battle of words that followed, with the result that they . . . were cast aside in their finest hour".[7]

Douglas ordered Fighter Command into the offensive. Now, Spitfires and Hurricanes roared over the Channel, hitting targets of opportunity such as bridges and railways, and trying to lure the enemy's fighters into the air in operations known as "Rhubarbs" and "Circuses". They were expensive and wasteful. The pilots had lost the home advantage they had enjoyed during the Battle of Britain, and more pilots were killed during these continental missions than during the summer of 1940. Fighter Command and the Luftwaffe had changed places. Fighters were now called on to escort British bombers on their raids on targets abroad, and British pilots experienced all the difficulties their Me109 adversaries had faced. Pilots disliked, even hated, their new duties.

Fighter Command's military significance began to decline immediately after the Battle of Britain. It was the contest it had been designed for. It went into the fray supported by a superb system of detection and interception, using aircraft that had been bred to excel at their task, which were flown by a body of men fighting for their families, their country and their ideals with skill and courage. These men were led by commanders who, while outwardly apparently unexceptional, had huge inner reserves of resolve, fortitude and intelligence.

The "fighter boys" would never be at centre stage again. But they had given a performance that was unrepeatable. Its brilliance was matched by its significance. The Battle of Britain had immense strategic and symbolic importance. In victory, Britain lived on in freedom to provide a base for the heavy-bomber offensive against Germany and, eventually, a launch pad for the Allied invasion of Europe. The Luftwaffe, which had terrorized Europe, had been humbled. Hitler had suffered his first defeat.

APPENDIX A

Principal Aircraft of the Battle of Britain

RAF
Hawker Hurricane
Supermarine Spitfire

LUFTWAFFE
Messerschmitt Me109
Messerschmitt Me110
Junkers Ju87 "Stuka"
Dornier Do17
Heinkel He111
Junkers Ju88

Hawker Hurricane

HURRICANE MK 1

Wing span	40ft
Length	31ft 4in.
Height	13ft 1in.
Power plant	One Rolls-Royce Merlin III 12-cylinder liquid-cooled engine
Horsepower	1,130hp
Max. speed	328mph at 20,000ft
Climbing rate	2750 ft/min.
Range	505 miles
Service ceiling	34,200ft
Armament	Eight 0.303in. Browning machine-guns mounted in the wings

Below: Hawker Hurricane Mk.1, P3395/JX-B, flown by Flg Off A.V. Clowes, DFM, No. 1 Squadron, Wittering, October 1940

Hurricanes were the most numerous British fighters of the Battle of Britain, comprising 30 squadrons as against 19 Spitfire squadrons. They also shot down more enemy aircraft — 656 as against 529 according to one estimate. Hurricanes were especially successful against bombers, where their deficiencies in speed did not matter so much, and against which they sometimes had free rein while Spitfires occupied the German fighter escorts.

By the end of the 1920s, advances in aircraft and engine design signalled the end of the age of the biplane. In

1930 the Air Ministry issued specification F.7/30, inviting bids from private companies to build a new generation of fast fighters. By 1933 Sydney Camm (1893–1966), chief designer for Hawker Aircraft Ltd at Kingston-upon-Thames, Surrey, had started work on a prototype. It would eventually become the Hurricane.

The new aircraft benefited from the advances made in the early 1930s in aero engineering and aerodynamics. It was to be a monoplane, powered with the proposed new Rolls-Royce 12-cylinder aero engine, and incorporating a sealed cockpit and retractable under-carriage. In other ways it was more traditional — the frame was of metal tubes and wooden "formers" and

"stringers" (vertical frame struts and horizontal strips), covered by a fabric skin, painted with "dope", a lacquer or varnish to reduce drag. This would make the new plane cheaper and easier to make than the metal-skinned Spitfire.

The first flight of the as yet unnamed Hurricane was on 6 November 1935 at Brooklands aerodrome in Surrey. The RAF tested the plane the following February and was impressed. Hawker pressed on with improvements and was rewarded with an order for 600 Hurricanes from the Air Ministry in the summer of 1936.

By October 1937, the first production-Hurricane was ready for testing, fitted with an early example of the Rolls Royce Merlin II engine, which could produce

1,030 horsepower at 16,000ft. The following January, the first Hurricanes were delivered to 111 Squadron Fighter Command. For pilots used to biplanes, the Hurricane looked extremely heavy and it seemed to take an age to get airborne. But the power was hugely exhilarating — it was like nothing they had ever flown, and they found it a surprisingly easy plane to control.

At the beginning of 1939, production switched to a new version with a Merlin III engine and pressed metal, rather than fabric, covering the wings. These now held eight Browning machine-guns, positioned far enough away from the propeller disc to make complicated synchronization gear unnecessary. By the beginning of the war, a little under 500 Hurricanes had been delivered to the RAF.

Further improvements were made, including self-sealing fuel tanks, as well as modifications to the canopy, which was often difficult to open when baling out. The "fixed pitch" propellers were replaced with constant-speed propellers, improving the handling qualities and increasing the ceiling at which the aircraft could operate. A Hurricane Mark 2, delivered in small quantities from August 1940, featured a 1,300hp engine, the Merlin XX, and could reach 342mph.

The Hurricane has entered popular myth as the plain older sister to the glamorous Spitfire. Certainly, it was 1,000 pounds heavier, and so it was not as fast, particularly in the climb and at higher altitudes.

But it could turn more tightly, and its weight and sturdy construction meant that it was a better gun platform and harder to shoot down. "The Hurricane was absolutely viceless provided you treated it right," said 151 Squadron's F/Lt Hugh Ironside. "I think from the point of view of fighting, I would have preferred it to a Spitfire, because it was so much stronger . . . you just couldn't fuss the Hurricane." Many pilots would be grateful for the Hurricane's rugged construction as they successfully landed their badly damaged aircraft.

Supermarine Spitfire

SUPERMARINE SPITFIRE MK I A

Wing span	*36ft 10in.*
Length	*29ft 11in.*
Height	*12ft 8in. (to tip of propeller)*
Power plant	*One Rolls-Royce Merlin 12- cylinder liquid-cooled engine*
Horsepower	*1,175hp*
Max. speed	*362mph at 18,500ft*
Climbing rate	*9.04 min. to 20,000ft*
Normal range	*395 miles*
Service ceiling	*31,900ft*
Armament	*Eight 0.303in. Browning machine-guns mounted in the wings*

Below: Spitfire Mk.1a, X4590/ PR-F, No. 609 "West Riding" Squadron, Middle Wallop, late September 1940

In successive versions, the Spitfire was the only Allied fighter aircraft to be produced from the beginning of the Second World War until the very end — and beyond. Extraordinarily photogenic and a supreme achievement in aeronautical engineering, the Spitfire has earned its place as one of history's most famous and beautiful fighter aircraft.

No combat aircraft can have inspired such depth of feeling among those who fought in it as did the Spitfire. The Hurricane was trusted for its solidity, strength and manoeuvrability; but the Spitfire was, in the words of pilot George Unwin, "the perfect flying machine . . . it was so sensitive on the controls. There was no heaving or pulling and pushing and kicking. You just breathed on it."[1] Although many more Hurricanes than Spitfires were flown during the Battle of Britain, it was the faster, more beautiful and altogether more glamorous Spitfire that seized the public's imagination, becoming, in the words of one of its test pilots, Jeffrey Quill, "a symbol of defiance and of victory in what seemed a desperate and hopeless situation."[2]

The Spitfire evolved from the Supermarine Company's efforts to win the Schneider Trophy. This prestigious competition, held 11 times between 1913 and 1931, tested the speed and endurance of seaplanes (once thought to be the future of long-distance travel) and offered an excellent shop window for aircraft manufacturers. Supermarine had won in 1922, with an aircraft achieving 145mph. Then, the prize went for two successive competitions to the United States with a sleek, streamlined aircraft powered by a Curtiss liquid-cooled D-12 engine. This had already been used in an RAF light bomber and may have inspired Rolls Royce's milestone F.XI engine, the precursor to the Merlin.

The final three competitions, however, all went to the Supermarine Aviation Works Ltd of Southampton, with a succession of monoplane designs by Reginald J. Mitchell (1895–1937), each of which, if the large floats are blanked out, looks more and more like the familiar, lithe shape of the Spitfire.

Supermarine's second victory was in 1929, when the S6, powered by a Rolls-Royce engine, was measured over the course flying at an average speed of 328.63mph. This led directly to the Air Ministry's 1930 specification F.7/30, for a new generation of fast fighters.

Although Mitchell and Supermarine — the company was now taken over by Vickers — won the Schneider Trophy again in 1931 in spectacular style, they struggled for a long time with the different requirements of a fighter aircraft. Mitchell's first effort was a severe disappointment, only reaching some 230mph. In 1934 both Mitchell and Sydney Camm at Hawker (working on the Hurricane prototype) were asked to incorporate into their designs the proposed new Rolls-Royce 12-cylinder Merlin engine as well as the facility for eight machine-guns. Mitchell's team continued to struggle with problems with the propeller and the aerodynamics of their new plane, but on 5 March 1936, two days before Hitler marched into the demilitarized Rhineland in defiance of the terms of Treaty of Versailles, the as yet unnamed Spitfire prototype took its first flight from Eastleigh airport near Southampton.

Three months later, 310 Spitfires were ordered at the same time as 600 Hurricanes. The disparity in numbers was due to concerns that the technologically well-advanced Spitfires would be more difficult to manufacture. This, indeed, turned out to be the case. It was only in August 1938 that the first Spitfires were delivered to No. 19 Squadron at Duxford, and production rates remained low compared to the Hurricane.

As with the Hurricane, further improvements were made to the propeller, to the cramped cockpit — giving the Spitfire its distinctive bubble — and by the addition of armour around the pilot's seat and the insertion of supposedly bullet-proof glass.

The Spitfire had the same engine as the Hurricane, but it was lighter and therefore faster. What had emerged was a more modern and sophisticated aircraft than its Hawker sister. With thin, elliptical wings, and an all-metal fuselage, it was, in effect, half a generation more advanced, as its longer service life would later demonstrate.

The Spitfire's sophistication made it a more difficult and expensive fighter to build than the Hurricane. It was also more complicated to maintain and rearm. Its high nose gave the pilot poor visibility while taxiing, and its forward centre of gravity meant that it was easy to tip it onto its propeller; its narrower wheel base made it harder to land than the Hurricane. But the Spitfire was deemed worth it for its superior performance.

Up against the Messerschmitt Me109 — its great rival — it more than held its own. The German fighter was, with its fuel-injected engine, better in the dive and at very high altitudes. But the Spitfire was sharper in the turn, though not as sharp as the Hurricane, and much more agile at all altitudes. Luftwaffe fighter pilots were said to admire the Spitfire's qualities — and to be shot down by one was no dishonour. In the end, the different strengths and weaknesses of the Me109 and the Spitfire probably cancelled each other out. The contest would be decided by the tactical positioning of the aircraft and by the skill and endurance of the opposing pilots.

Most of the Spitfires deployed during the Battle of Britain carried the same eight-machine-gun armament as the Hurricane, although experiments were made with cannon-firing Spitfires. A Mark 2 model, with a slightly more powerful engine, was introduced in June 1940, though most Spitfires that fought in the summer of 1940 were Mark 1A.

Airmen talked about the aircraft in the language of love. The American pilot James Goodson, who flew with No. 43 Squadron, said: "Once you got used to the Spitfire, of course you loved it. It became part of you. It was like pulling on a tight pair of jeans. It was a delight to fly. I used to smoke a cigar sometimes — against all rules and regulations — but if I dropped my cigar lighter, instead of groping around on the floor, I'd move the stick a fraction of an inch, the Spit would roll over and I'd catch the cigar lighter as it came down from the floor. That was the kind of plane it was. Everybody had a love affair with it."[3]

Messerschmitt Me109

MESSERSCHMITT ME109E

Wing span	32ft 4in.
Length	28ft 8in.
Height	11ft 2in.
Power plant	One Daimler-Benz DB60 1A 12-cylinder, direct-fuel injection, liquid-cooled engine
Horsepower	1,150hp
Max. speed	357mph at 12,300ft
Climbing rate	3,510ft/min.
Range	412 miles
Service ceiling	36,000ft
Armament	Two 7.9mm machine-guns in upper nose (E-3 and E-4) decking with 1,000 rounds per gun; two 20mm MG FF cannon in wings with 60 rounds per gun

Below: Messerschmitt Me109E-3, of 6./JG51, flown by Staffelkapitän Josef "Pips" Priller, Autumn 1940

The Messerschmitt Me109 was, in various succeeding versions, produced in larger numbers than any other fighter of the Second World War. It was, according to fighter pilot Hans-Ekkehard Bob, "an extremely beautiful aircraft. A handsome, racy machine. It handled impressively in the air." It was the Me109 that shot down most of the 1,172 British aircraft lost between July 1940 and October 1940, and which posed the most serious threat to the survival of Fighter Command.

The Me109, like its British rivals the Hurricane and Spitfire, was the brainchild of one man. Willy Messerschmitt (1898–1978) was a designer of extraordinary versatility, whose creativity ranged across gliders, fighters and, later, jets. His aim was simple: to marry the largest engine with the smallest airframe possible. His first 109 was one of four designs submitted in response to a request from the Luftwaffe for a new fighter aircraft to replace its outmoded biplanes. As with two of the other competing designs, the initial Me109, first flown in May 1935, was powered by a Rolls-Royce Kestrel V engine imported from Derby. But in other ways it was radically different, with its enclosed cockpit, all-metal stressed skin, wing-leading edge slats and narrow-track retractable undercarriage. There were faults with the design, some of which were never removed — such as its steep upwards angle when on the ground, which made for poor pilot visibility while taxiing — but the Me109 won the competition and went into further development and production.

The first production-model left the assembly line in February 1937, equipped with a Junkers Jumo 210A inverted-vee 680hp engine, and the following month 16 were flown direct from the factory to Seville during Spain's Civil War, where they were issued to Wolfram von Richthofen's *Jagdgeschwader* of the German Condor Legion to replace their Heinkel 51 biplanes.

The fighting in Spain proved a useful testing

ground for the Me109 in combat. Its three light machine-guns were found to be inadequate, leading to the development of the 20mm Oerlikon cannon. Successive improved versions were produced, with the four-gunned Me109E-1 the first to be fitted with the all new Daimler-Benz DB601A engine with direct fuel injection. This was closely followed by the E-3, equipped with cannon at the expense of two of the machine-guns. By the end of 1939, some 1,500 Me109Es had been built.

The new engine, with a maximum of 1,150 horsepower, was more powerful than the Rolls-Royce Merlin, then being fitted into Hurricanes and Spitfires. The Me109 was also smaller and lighter than its rivals. This would give the Me109 awesome performance but create difficulties as well. There was little space for fuel or ammunition. Its thin, narrow wings, which delivered superb performance in the air, were not so effective as a gun platform and meant that the undercarriage had to be supported by the fuselage; this created a narrow and unstable wheel base and led to numerous crashes on landing.

Unlike the British fighters, the Me109 had an excellent view to the rear; it could out-climb the Spitfire to 20,000 feet and always out-dive it, thanks to its fuel injection. It was less agile than its rivals, but at over 20,000 feet it was undoubtedly the superior aircraft.

Messerschmitt Me110

MESSERSCHMITT
ME110C-4

Wing span	53ft 5in.
Length	39ft 8in.
Height	11ft 6in.
Power plant	Two Daimler-Benz DB601A 12-cylinder liquid-cooled engines
Horsepower	1,150hp
Max. speed	349mph at 22,960ft
Range	530 miles
Service ceiling	32,000ft
Armament	Four 7.9mm MG17 machine-guns and two 20mm MG FF cannon in the nose; one rear-firing 7.9mm MG15 machine gun in the rear cockpit
Bombload	1,100lbs

Below: Messerschmitt Me110D-1 (W.Nr. 3378), S9+DH flown by Hauptmann Martin Lutz, during the Battle of Britain

Known in the Luftwaffe as the *Zerstörer* (Destroyer), the Messerschmitt Me110 was the best twin-engine fighter in the world and markedly superior to the British equivalent, the Bristol Blenheim. It was portrayed in propaganda, and regarded by Hermann Goering, as the Luftwaffe's most devastating modern weapon, manned by the force's best crews. However, as with the Stuka, the Battle of Britain would see the Me110's fortunes and reputation wrecked.

The first Me110 prototype was flown in May 1936. Further tests showed it to be fast and comparatively manoeuvrable for a heavy twin-engine aircraft. The plane went through successive test versions with more powerful engines and did not go into large-scale production until 1939. By the beginning of the war, only some 159 Me110s had been delivered to the Luftwaffe. But the aircraft was given production priority, and by the time of the Battle of Britain there were some 300 of the type lined up against RAF Fighter Command.

Designed for the dual roles of long-distance escort and ground-attack, the Me110 had a top speed only marginally slower than a Spitfire and faster than a Hurricane. Its basic design was highly versatile — amenable to changes in power plant and armament — and it carried three times the fuel of an Me109. Its front-firing weapons — cannon and machine-gun — produced the most devastating effect of any Battle of Britain fighter, as Flying Officer Harold Bird-Wilson testified: "We had a squadron commander who believed in the head-on attack. So he attacked an Me110 head-on and I'm afraid Jerry got the better of him — all we found of him was his shirt."[4]

At the beginning of the war, the Me110 was producing as much fearful speculation as the Me109, and one British air marshal offered a smart dinner in Paris to the first fighter pilot to shoot one down. On 29 March 1940, Hurricanes from

No. 1 Squadron took the prize, reporting in the squadron's diary that the much-feared German aircraft was "very fast and manoeuvrable for a twin-engine aircraft, [but] can be easily outmanoeuvred by a Hurricane". The rear gunner of an Me110, it was discovered, became ineffective during a dogfight because steep turns either caused him to black out or made it impossible for him to aim his armament effectively.

Fighting during the early weeks of the Battle of Britain showed that up against Hurricanes and Spitfires the Me110 had insufficient manoeuvrability and inadequate defensive armament. In spite of its high top speed, its poor acceleration counted against it in a dogfight or when taken by surprise. In a short time, the "Destroyer" had become a liability. In August alone, 120 were lost on operations. The elite Me110 pilots took to forming a defensive circle when confronted with interceptors. This raised their chances of survival, but it was a sterile manoeuvre as they could play no further part in the battle.

Goering was forced to order that his favourite aircraft, designed in part as an escort fighter, should itself have an escort of Me109s. In spite of this, and despite its much-reduced operational use, a further 83 Me110s were downed before the end of September 1940.

Nevertheless, in the hands of the very best pilots, the Messerschmitt Me110 could still be effective. *Erprobungs-gruppe* (Experimental Group) 210, a combination of Me109s and bomb-carrying Me110s, carried out a number of spectacular set-piece raids, achieving surprise by flying at high speed not much off ground level and thereby avoiding radar detection.

Junkers Ju87 "Stuka"

JUNKERS JU87B-2

Wing span	45ft 3in.
Length	36ft 1in.
Height	13ft 10in.
Power plant	One Junkers Jumo 211A-1 12-cylinder liquid-cooled engine
Horsepower	1,100hp
Max. speed	223mph at 13,500ft
Range	370 miles
Service ceiling	26,500ft
Armament	Two 7.9mm MG17 machine-guns in the wings, one 7.9 MG15 machine-gun on a rear cockpit mounting
Bombload	One 1,100 lb bomb carried under the fuselage; four 110 lb bombs under the wings

Below: Junkers Ju887B (W.Nr.3360), T6+HL, of 3./StG 2. shot down over Sussex on 10 August 1940

The *Sturzkampfflugzeug* — better known as the "Stuka" — quickly gained a fearsome reputation. Roaming ahead of the Panzer tank columns, acting as long-range artillery, the dive-bomber hit bridges, communication centres and troop concentrations with impressive accuracy. It was a key component of *Blitzkrieg*. In Poland, and then in the Low Countries and France, the aircraft's steep, almost vertical dive and screaming whistles had a shattering psychological effect on those it attacked.

With its distinctive shape — pointed nose, cranked wings and prominent fixed undercarriage — it was soon the element of the German armed forces most hated and feared by its enemies and most admired by its friends.

The *Sturzkampfflugzeug* was the Luftwaffe's prime weapon until the summer of 1940. The tactic of dive-bombing had been widespread during the First World War, but the first aircraft specifically designed as a dive-bomber was not developed until the 1920s. To avoid postwar restrictions on German aircraft development, Hugo Junkers had established facilities in Sweden, and from here in 1928 emerged the Junkers K47. The aircraft was tested in secret in Berlin, and soon after the Nazis came to power in 1933 a requirement was issued for a new generation single-engine dive-bomber.

Junkers continued developing his aircraft, and in 1935 the first Ju87 was tested, powered with a Derby-built Rolls-Royce Kestrel engine. At trials held the next year, the Ju87 held off competition from three other dive-bomber prototypes to win the contest, and by spring 1937 the Ju87A, now powered by a 635hp Jumo 210 engine, was in service with the Luftwaffe.

Tested in Spain, the aircraft was improved by the addition of diving brakes and a more powerful engine. The Ju87B series was powered by the Jumo 211A direct-injection engine that produced 1,200 horsepower, had more streamlined spats over the landing gear, and was now equipped with an automatic dive control. At the beginning of 1939, the Ju87As were sent to training units and all the *Stukageschwader* (Stuka wings) were equipped with the more powerful Ju87B series. At the beginning of the war, there were 360 available to the Luftwaffe.

In operation, the Ju87 was something of an endurance test. In the dive, the Stuka crew of two could feel the blood draining from their heads. At a height of 1,000 metres an alarm rang in their headphones to alert them in case they had blacked out. At 700 metres (765 yards) above the ground they released their bombs and levelled off. Their undercarriage was fitted with a whistle that shrieked as the planes dived, and the bombs themselves had

cardboard whistles on their tail fins. "That gave quite a psychological effect," said Stuka pilot Werner Roell, "but all these things worked only at the beginning of the war."

The Ju87 had considerable success during the early stages of the Battle of Britain, particularly against shipping and naval targets. But its slow top speed and poor manoeuvrability and rate of climb were its downfall. Whole *Staffeln* (squadrons) were wiped out by the faster and more nimble Hurricanes and Spitfires, and by mid-August 1940 the Ju87 was deployed only rarely. By the end of the month the main units had been withdrawn from combat.

Werner Roell called Stukas "the sharpshooter amongst the bombers. Whereas the horizontal bombers dropped an enormous amount of bombs on an area, the Stuka had a small target and with a small number of bombs, it could erase a target of importance . . . Of course Stukas were slow. They had to be sturdy because they came out of the dive sharply."[5]

For Fighter Command's pilots, Stukas were a welcome sight and "very easy to get out of the sky," according to Teddy Donaldson of 151 Squadron. "We tackled them from the back end and the poor bastards just fell out of the sky."

Dornier Do17

DORNIER Do17Z

Wing span	59ft 1in.
Length	52ft
Height	14ft 11in.
Power plant	Two Bramo 323P 9-cylinder air-cooled engines
Horsepower	1,000hp
Max. speed	265mph at 16,400ft
Range	745 miles
Service ceiling	26,400ft
Armament	Four to eight 7.9mm MG15 machine-guns in front, rear and beam cockpit mountings and ventral (underside) position
Bombload	2,200lbs

Below: Dornier Do17Z, Fl+ET of 9./KG 76, Cormeilles-en-Vexin, France, July 1940

The Dornier Do17 was designed originally, ostensibly, as a fast passenger and mail transport for the German carrier Lufthansa; but it was easily adapted to become a Luftwaffe medium bomber and reconnaissance aircraft. Its slim fuselage, which suggested its "Flying Pencil" nickname (*Fliegender Bleistift*), in fact made it totally unsuitable for carrying passengers.

Benefiting from the latest improvements in aeronautics and aerodynamics, the Dornier Do17 was a highly advanced design for its time. A prototype made its maiden test flight in 1934, and the following year a new version, with two 750hp BMW engines, was tested and recorded a top speed of 230mph. This qualified it as a "fast bomber" and plans for large-scale production were completed by 1936. The following year, the aircraft caught the eyes of the world when, at a military aircraft competition in Zurich, a specially adapted Dornier displayed a speed of 248mph, almost as fast as any of the fighters competing. The same year Do17-E and -F series aircraft entered service with the Luftwaffe. Both were close in design to the 1935 prototype, with the F Series adapted for reconnaissance purposes.

Dorniers fought in the Spanish Civil War, where they proved to be faster than any of the fighters put up against them.

Weaknesses were discovered, however. The cockpit, where all the four-man crew was stationed, was cramped. More seriously, the bomber, which at this time carried a defensive armament of only two machine-guns, was shown to be dangerously vulnerable to attack from behind and below. To remedy this, new versions were developed with a more bulbous cockpit. This sacrificed some of the plane's aerodynamic qualities, but allowed room for a rear-facing gunner, lying down in the "ventral position" (on the underside of the fuselage). By the time of the start of the Battle of Britain, most of the Luftwaffe's Dornier fleet were Do17Zs, each with two 1,000hp engines and six machine-guns.

The Do17 was the most reliable of the German bombers, popular with air and ground crews, but it lacked the load-carrying capabilities of the Heinkel He111 and the speed of the Junkers Ju88. During the Battle of Britain it was probably most effective coming in low over a target and bombing with accuracy.

Experience of fighting in the early weeks of the battle led the Dorniers to increase their defensive armament to eight guns, and, when the bombers were flying in tight formation, the crossfire from all their guns made them a dangerous target. George Unwin of No. 19 Squadron recalled seeing a "lone Dornier going home . . . so I went after him. He had a rear gunner in a dustbin hanging below the fuselage and you had to fix him first and then close in on the aircraft. I could see him shooting at me and I gave him a burst and shut him up. At least I thought I had. As I closed right in again, I suddenly saw the rear gunner shooting back at me with little red sparks . . . suddenly a hole appeared in this glass directly in front of my face. I thought, 'Good God. I must be dead!' "[6]

But the Dorniers suffered too, and a lack of armour around the crew led to a high casualty rate during the Battle of Britain. The oldest of the three main bombers, unlike the He111 and the Ju88 it largely disappeared from frontline units by 1942.

Heinkel He111

HEINKEL HE111

Wing span	74ft 1¾in.
Length	53ft 9½in.
Height	13ft 1½in.
Power plant	Two Junkers Jumo 211-F engines
Horsepower	1,350hp per engine
Max. speed	270mph at 16,400ft
Range	1,212 miles
Service ceiling	27,890ft
Armament	Four to eight 7.9mm MG15 machine-guns in nose, dorsal and ventral (underside) positions
Bombload	4,410lbs

Below: Heinkel He111 H-3, AI+DA, of KG53, based at Lille, France, September 1940

The Heinkel He111 bomber was from the same generation as the Dornier Do17, and it too was facing obsolescence in 1940. Another of the Luftwaffe's "fast bombers", the He111 had a top speed of 270mph — faster than anything it had faced while operating in Spain, but too slow against modern fighters. In fact, it was marginally slower than the Dornier and less manoeuvrable. Against that disadvantage, the He111 could carry as much as twice the bombload. Nevertheless, as with the other bombers in the Luftwaffe, it was in essence a tactical weapon rather than a strategic bomber, designed for speed and flexibility rather than weight of armament.

Designed by twin brothers Siegfried (1899–1969) and Walter Günter (1899–1937), who joined Ernst Heinkel's company in 1931, the Heinkel He111 started life as a hybrid civil-military aircraft, as did the Dornier. Ostensibly a fast mail and passenger aircraft, the He111 was designed from the outset to be able to carry armament and a bombload. It was an elegant and efficient design, and in the mid-1930s it was pretty much the best of its kind in the world.

The first He111 bomber prototype flew in February 1935, and the aircraft went through many different versions, usually involving changes to the power plant, which became progressively more powerful. The greatest design change came with the "P" variant, the first with the trademark streamlined fuselage and streamlined "ventral" gondola (i.e. on the underside of the fuselage). This model started leaving the factories in 1938 and saw service in Poland. By the beginning of the Battle of Britain, many of the "P" series Heinkels had been replaced by the improved "H" series.

Early experience of coming under attack from Fighter Command led to more and more defensive armament, as with the Dorniers. In common with other Luftwaffe bombers, the Heinkels would attempt to stay in rigid formation, the better to deploy crossfire from their guns, which could number as many as eight.

Flying a Heinkel He111 required a completely different approach to that required of a fighter pilot, said Ernest Wedding. "I flew my Heinkel 111 bomber in formation and I had to keep to my station. Even when the British fighters started attacking me, I couldn't do any intricate manoeuvres within the formation or else I would crash into the other bombers. It was a tedious job. All I was doing was watching the aircraft in front and on the left and right and hoping the chap behind was doing the same so that he wouldn't take my tail off. A bomber pilot had to be as steady as a bus driver."[7]

It was Heinkels that bombed Rotterdam on 14 May 1940, and later in the war the aircraft would carry V-1 flying bombs to the English coast. By then, though, He111s had largely reverted to their role as transport aircraft, and nearly 200 were to be lost trying to carry supplies and ammunition to the German pocket at Stalingrad.

Junkers Ju88

JUNKERS JU88A-1

Wing span	59ft 10¾in.
Length	47ft 1in.
Height	15ft 5in.
Power plant	Two Junkers Jumo 211B-1 12-cylinder liquid-cooled engines
Horsepower	1,200hp per engine
Max. speed	286mph at 16,000ft
Range	1,553 miles
Service ceiling	26,500ft
Armament	Six to eight 7.9mm MG15 machine-guns in nose, rear cockpit and ventral (underside) gondola
Bombload	5,510lbs

Below: Junkers Ju88A-1, 9K+AL of 3/KG51, based at Paris-Orly during the battle of Britain

The Junkers Ju88 was the newest aircraft in the Luftwaffe's armoury in 1940 and its outstanding bomber, able to carry a greater load but still outpace and out-range the Dorniers and Heinkels. It was also capable of dive-bombing with great accuracy. It is likely that had the Luftwaffe pos-sessed more of these machines, its assault on Britain might have been more effective.

The Ju88 was conceived by W(ilhelm) H(einrich) Evers and the American designer Alfred A. Gassner — the latter a consultant from the Fairchild Company work-ing in Europe at the time — in response to the Luftwaffe's call in 1935 for a new fast bomber. The first prototype flew in December the following year, but it took a comparatively long time to go into production, with the first test models delivered in spring 1939. By August, the Luftwaffe was taking delivery of the bomber, but only 12 saw action in Poland; the first models were beset with difficulties in the air brakes and undercarriage, problems largely ironed out by the summer of 1940.

The Ju88 was sturdily built and, like the Heinkel, could withstand a lot of combat damage but still make it back to base. Experience against Fighter Command led to an expansion of its defensive armament to as many as six machine-guns — two in the rear fuselage, one underneath, and the rest in the cockpit, where there was even one that could be operated by the pilot. The other forward-firing guns had to be operated by the flight engineer, a weakness of the aircraft.

Flight Lieutenant Charles MacLean had firsthand experience of the Ju88's capacity to soak up punishment. "I caught up with a Junkers 88 and fired every round I could into it and it kept on flying. I flew alongside it and I could see that everyone was killed in it except for the pilot and he was obviously wounded. There were bullet holes everywhere but somehow this old thing plodded on."[8]

The Ju88 achieved several notable successes during the Battle of Britain, particularly in its guise as a dive-bomber. It was also shot down at a lower rate than the other

German bombers, partly because it could dive out of trouble, and not even the Spitfire could keep up with it.

Highly versatile, the Ju88 would serve with distinction throughout the war as dive-bomber, level bomber, torpedo bomber, night-fighter, reconnaissance aircraft and mine layer. Some 15,000 of them were built before 1945, a greater quantity than for any other Luftwaffe twin-engine bomber.

APPENDIX B

Battle of Britain Tables

Equivalent Ranks of the RAF and Luftwaffe

The Nationalities of Fighter Command

Fighter Command Order of Battle, 10 July 1940

RAF and Luftwaffe Losses, July 1940

Fighter Command Order of Battle, 1 August 1940

RAF and Luftwaffe Losses, August 1940

Fighter Command Order of Battle, 1 September 1940

Aircraft Wastage (Hurricanes and Spitfires)

Air Raids on Great Britain, July–December 1940

Civilian Air Raid Casualties, 1940

Equivalent Ranks of the RAF and Luftwaffe

ROYAL AIR FORCE	LUFTWAFFE
Marshal of the Royal Air Force	Generalfeldmarschall
Air Chief Marshal	Generaloberst
Air Marshal	General
Air Vice-Marshal	Generalleutnant
Air Commodore	Generalmajor
Group Captain	Oberst
Wing Commander	Oberstleutnant
Squadron Leader	Major
Flight Lieutenant	Hauptmann
Flying Officer	Oberleutnant
Pilot Officer	Leutnant
Warrant Officer	Stabsfeldwebel
Flight Sergeant	Oberfeldwebel
Sergeant	Feldwebel
Corporal	Unteroffizier
Leading Aircraftman	Obergefreiter
Aircraftman First Class	Gefreiter
Aircraftman Second Class	Flieger

The Nationalities of Fighter Command

A substantial contingent of 574 pilots from countries other than the United Kingdom flew with their British counterparts in the Battle of Britain. The international mix of participants — defined by their flying at least one authorized operational sortie with an eligible unit between 10 July and 31 October 1940 — is as follows.

Nation	No. of pilots	Nation	No. of pilots
Great Britain	2,353	Ireland	10
Poland	139	United States	7
New Zealand	98	Jamaica	2
Canada	86	Egypt	1
Czechoslovakia	84	Austria	1
Belgium	29	Iceland	1
Australia	21	Palestine Mandate	1
South Africa	20	Southern Rhodesia	1
France	13	Unknown	4

Fighter Command Order of Battle, 10 July 1940

Sector	Sqn	Aircraft	Based at	Commander
11 GROUP				
Biggin Hill	32	Hurricane	Biggin Hill	s/L John Worrall
	141	Defiant	Biggin Hill	s/L William Richardson
	610	Spitfire	Gravesend	s/L A.T. Smith
	600	Blenheim	Manston	s/L David Clark
North Weald	56	Hurricane	North Weald	s/L Minnie Manton
	151	Hurricane	North Weald	s/L Teddy Donaldson
	85	Hurricane	Martlesham	s/L Peter Townsend
	25	Blenheim	Martlesham	s/L K.A. McEwan
Kenley	64	Spitfire	Kenley	s/L N.C. Odbert
	615	Hurricane	Kenley	s/L Joseph Kayll
	111	Hurricane	Croydon	s/L John Thompson
	501	Hurricane	Croydon	s/L Harry Hogan
Hornchurch	65	Spitfire	Hornchurch	s/L Henry Sawyer
	74	Spitfire	Hornchurch	s/L Francis White
	54	Spitfire	Rochford	s/L James Leathart
Tangmere	43	Hurricane	Tangmere	s/L John Badger
	145	Hurricane	Tangmere	s/L John Peel
	601	Hurricane	Tangmere	s/L Max Aitken
Debden	17	Hurricane	Debden	s/L R.I.G. McDougal
Northolt	1	Hurricane	Northolt	s/L David Pemberton
	604	Blenheim	Northolt	s/L Michael Anderson
	257	Hurricane	Hendon	s/L H. Harkness
10 GROUP (*Part of 11 Group until 21 July*)				
Filton	92	Spitfire	Pembrey	s/L F.J. Saunders
	87	Hurricane	Exeter	s/L John Dewar
	213	Hurricane	Exeter	s/L H.D. McGregor
	234	Spitfire	St Eval	s/L R.E. Barnett
Middle Wallop	609	Spitfire	Middle Wallop	s/L Horace Darley
	238	Hurricane	Middle Wallop	s/L Harold Fenton

Sector	Sqn	Aircraft	Based at	Commander

12 GROUP

Sector	Sqn	Aircraft	Based at	Commander
Duxford	264	Defiant	Duxford	s/l Philip Hunter
	19	Spitfire	Fowlmere	s/l Philip Pinkham
Coltishall	66	Spitfire	Coltishall	s/l Rupert Leigh
	242	Hurricane	Coltishall	s/l Douglas Bader
Kirton-in-Lindsey	222	Spitfire	Kirton	s/l H.W. Mermagen
Digby	46	Hurricane	Digby	f/l A.D. Murray
	611	Spitfire	Digby	s/l J. McComb
	29	Blenheim	Digby	f/l J.S. Adams
Wittering	229	Hurricane	Wittering	s/l H.J. McQuire
	266	Spitfire	Wittering	s/l R.L. Wilkinson
	23	Blenheim	Collyweston	s/l L.C. Bicknell

13 GROUP

Sector	Sqn	Aircraft	Based at	Commander
Church Fenton	73	Hurricane	Church Fenton	s/l J.W.C. More
	616	Spitfire	Church Fenton	s/l M. Robinson
	249	Hurricane	Leconfield	s/l John Grandy
Catterick	41	Spitfire	Catterick	s/l H. West
	219	Blenheim	Catterick	s/l J.H. Little
Usworth	607	Hurricane	Usworth	s/l J. Vick
	72	Spitfire	Acklington	s/l Ronald Lees
	152	Spitfire	Acklington	s/l Peter Devitt
Turnhouse	79	Hurricane	Turnhouse	s/l Hervey Heyworth
	253	Hurricane	Turnhouse	s/l Tom Gleave
	245	Hurricane	Turnhouse	s/l F.W. Whitley
	603	Spitfire	Turnhouse	s/l G. Denholm
	602	Spitfire	Drem	s/l Sandy Johnstone
	605	Hurricane	Drem	s/l W. Churchill
Dyce	263	Hurricane	Grangemouth	s/l H. Eeles
Wick	3	Hurricane	Wick	s/l S.F. Godden
	504	Hurricane	Castletown	s/l John Sample

Key s/l = Squadron Leader; f/l = Flight Lieutenant; w/c = Wing Commander

RAF and Luftwaffe Losses, July 1940

Aircraft type	Destroyed	Damaged	Pilots killed	Pilots missing	Pilots wounded
RAF					
Hurricane	33	17	23	0	11
Spitfire	34	24	25	0	9
Blenheim	4	1	9	0	1
Defiant	6	1	10	0	2
LUFTWAFFE					
Do17	39	13	30	74	19
He111	32	3	52	85	6
Ju88	39	11	52	67	11
Ju87	13	11	10	12	3
Me109	48	14	17	14	13
Me110	18	4	13	17	2
Other	27	1	19	33	15
RAF total	77	43	67	0	23
Luftwaffe total	216	57	193	302	69

Key Do = Dornier; He = Heinkel; Ju = Junkers; Me = Messerschmitt

511

Fighter Command Order of Battle, 1 August 1940

Sector	Sqn	Aircraft	Based at	Commander
11 GROUP				
Biggin Hill	32	Hurricane	Biggin Hill	s/L John Worrall
	501	Hurricane	Gravesend	s/L Harry Hogan
	600	Blenheim	Manston	s/L David Clark
	610	Spitfire	Biggin Hill	s/L J. Ellis
North Weald	56	Hurricane	North Weald	s/L Minnie Manton
	151	Hurricane	North Weald	s/L Teddy Donaldson
	85	Hurricane	Martlesham	s/L Peter Townsend
	25	Blenheim	Martlesham	s/L K.A. McEwan
Kenley	64	Spitfire	Kenley	s/L A.R.D. MacDonald
	615	Hurricane	Kenley	s/L Joseph Kayll
	111	Hurricane	Croydon	s/L John Thompson
Hornchurch	41	Spitfire	Hornchurch	s/L H. West
	65	Spitfire	Hornchurch	s/L Henry Sawyer
	74	Spitfire	Hornchurch	s/L Francis White
Tangmere	1	Hurricane	Tangmere	s/L David Pemberton
	145	Hurricane	Westhampnett	s/L John Peel
	266	Spitfire	Tangmere	s/L R.L. Wilkinson
	601	Hurricane	Tangmere	s/L W.F.C. Hobson
	FIU	Blenheim	Tangmere	w/c G.P. Chamberlain
Debden	17	Hurricane	Debden	s/L C.W. Williams
Northolt	43	Hurricane	Northolt	s/L John Badger
	257	Hurricane	Hendon	s/L H. Harkness
10 GROUP				
Filton	87	Hurricane	Exeter	s/L T.G. Lovell-Gregg
	93	Spitfire	Pembrey	s/L P.J. Sanders
		Hurricane	Exeter	s/L H.D. McGregor
	234	Spitfire	St Eval	s/L R.E. Barnett
Middle Wallop	152	Spitfire	Warmwell	s/L Peter Devitt
	238	Hurricane	Middle Wallop	s/L Harold Fenton
	604	Blenheim	Middle Wallop	s/L Michael Anderson
	609	Spitfire	Middle Wallop	s/L Horace Darley

Sector	Sqn	Aircraft	Based at	Commander
12 GROUP				
Duxford	19	Spitfire	Fowlmere	s/L Philip Pinkham
	310	Hurricane	Duxford	s/L G.D.M. Blackwood
Coltishall	66	Spitfire	Coltishall	s/L Rupert Leigh
	242	Hurricane	Coltishall	s/L Douglas Bader
Kirton-in-Lindsey	264	Defiant	Kirton	s/L G.D. Garvin
Digby	29	Blenheim	Wellingore	s/L S.C. Widdows
	46	Hurricane	Digby	F/L A.D. Murray
	611	Spitfire	Digby	s/L J. McComb
Wittering	74	Spitfire	Wittering	s/L A.G. Malan
	229	Hurricane	Bircham N'ton	s/L H.J. McQuire
	23	Blenheim	Wittering	s/L G.F.W. Heycock
	266	Spitfire	Wittering	Temporarily unfilled
13 GROUP				
Church Fenton	73	Hurricane	Church Fenton	s/L M.W.S. Robinson
	64	Spitfire	Leconfield	s/L A.R.D. MacDonald
	302	Hurricane	Leconfield	S/L W.A.J. Satchell / s/L M. Mumler
Catterick	32	Hurricane	Acklington	s/L N.M. Crossley
	41	Spitfire	Catterick	s/L H. West
	219	Blenheim	Leeming	s/L J.H. Little
	610	Spitfire	Acklington	s/L J. Ellis
	607	Hurricane	Usworth	s/L J. Vick
Turnhouse	141	Defiant	Turnhouse	s/L Wm. Richardson
	605	Hurricane	Drem	s/L W. Churchill
Dyce	263	Hurricane	Grangemouth	s/L H. Eeles
	145	Hurricane	Dyce	s/L T.P. Pugh
Wick	3	Hurricane	Wick	s/L S.F. Godden
	504	Hurricane	Castletown	s/L John Sample

Key s/L = Squadron Leader; F/L = Flight Lieutenant; w/c = Wing Commander; B'combe = Boscombe; N'ton = Newton

RAF and Luftwaffe Losses, August 1940

Aircraft type	Destroyed	Damaged	Pilots killed	Pilots missing	Pilots wounded
RAF					
Hurricane	211	44	85	1	68
Spitfire	113	40	41	3	38
Blenheim	13	10	6	3	0
Defiant	7	3	7	0	4
LUFTWAFFE					
Do17	71	31	70	129	57
He111	89	15	113	204	35
Ju88	89	32	94	182	19
Ju87	57	16	35	58	19
Me109	217	45	54	91	39
Me110	119	40	80	113	22
Other types	27	4	17	27	10
RAF total	344	97	139	7	110
Luftwaffe total	669	183	463	804	201

Key Do = Dornier; He = Heinkel; Ju = Junkers; Me = Messerschmitt

Fighter Command Order of Battle, I September 1940

Sector	Sqn	Aircraft	Based at	Commander
11 GROUP				
Biggin Hill	79	Hurricane	Biggin Hill	s/L Hervey Heyworth
	501	Hurricane	Gravesend	s/L Harry Hogan
North Weald	56	Hurricane	North Weald	Temporarily unfilled
	151	Hurricane	Stapleford	Temporarily unfilled
	25	Blenheim	Martlesham	s/L W.W. Loxton
				(acting)
Kenley	72	Spitfire	Croydon	s/L A.R. Collins
	85	Hurricane	Croydon	s/L Peter Townsend
	253	Hurricane	Kenley	Temporarily unfilled
	616	Spitfire	Kenley	s/L M. Robinson
Hornchurch	54	Spitfire	Hornchurch	Temporarily unfilled
	222	Spitfire	Hornchurch	s/L J.H. Hill
	600	Blenheim	Hornchurch	s/L David Clark
	603	Spitfire	Hornchurch	Temporarily unfilled
Tangmere	17	Hurricane	Tangmere	s/L A.G. Miller
	43	Hurricane	Tangmere	s/L C.B. Hull
	602	Spitfire	Westhampnett	s/L Sandy Johnstone
Debden	111	Hurricane	Debden	s/L John Thompson
	257	Hurricane	Debden	s/L H. Harkness
	601	Hurricane	Debden	s/L Sir Archibald Hope
Northolt	1	Hurricane	Northolt	s/L David Pemberton
	1 (Can.)	Hurricane	Northolt	s/L E.A. McNab
	303	Hurricane	Northolt	s/L R.G. Kellett /
				s/L Z. Krasnodesbski
10 GROUP				
Pembrey	93	Spitfire	Pembrey	s/L F.J. Sanders
Filton	87	Hurricane	Exeter	s/L R.S. Mills
	213	Hurricane	Exeter	s/L H.D. McGregor
St Eval	236	Blenheim	St Eval	s/L G.W. Montagu
	238	Hurricane	St Eval	s/L Harold Fenton
Middle Wallop	152	Spitfire	Warmwell	s/L Peter Devitt
	234	Spitfire	Middle Wallop	s/L J.S. O'Brian
	249	Hurricane	B'combe Down	s/L J. Grandy
	604	Blenheim	Middle Wallop	s/L Michael Anderson
	609	Spitfire	Middle Wallop	s/L Horace Darley

Sector	Sqn	Aircraft	Based at	Commander
12 GROUP				
Duxford	19	Spitfire	Fowlmere	s/l Philip Pinkham
	310	Hurricane	Duxford	s/l G.D.M. Blackwood
Coltishall	66	Spitfire	Coltishall	s/l Rupert Leigh
	242	Hurricane	Coltishall	s/l Douglas Bader
Kirton-in-Lindsey	264	Defiant	Kirton	s/l G.D. Garvin
Digby	29	Blenheim	Wellingore	s/l S.C. Widdows
	46	Hurricane	Digby	f/l A.D. Murray
	611	Spitfire	Digby	s/l J. McComb
Wittering	74	Spitfire	Wittering	s/l A.G. Malan
	229	Hurricane	Bircham N'ton	s/l H.J. McQuire
	23	Blenheim	Wittering	s/l G.F.W. Heycock
	266	Spitfire	Wittering	Temporarily unfilled
13 GROUP				
Church Fenton	73	Hurricane	Church Fenton	s/l M.W.S. Robinson
	64	Spitfire	Leconfield	s/l A.R.D. MacDonald
	302	Hurricane	Leconfield	S/L W.A.J. Satchell / s/l M. Mumler
Catterick	32	Hurricane	Acklington	s/l N.M. Crossley
	41	Spitfire	Catterick	s/l H. West
	219	Blenheim	Leeming	s/l J.H. Little
	610	Spitfire	Acklington	s/l J. Ellis
	607	Hurricane	Usworth	s/l J. Vick
Turnhouse	141	Defiant	Turnhouse	s/l Wm. Richardson
	605	Hurricane	Drem	s/l W. Churchill
Dyce	263	Hurricane	Grangemouth	s/l H. Eeles
	145	Hurricane	Dyce	s/l T.P. Pugh
Wick	3	Hurricane	Wick	s/l S.F. Godden
	504	Hurricane	Castletown	s/l John Sample

Key s/l = Squadron Leader; f/l = Flight Lieutenant; w/c = Wing Commander;
B'combe = Boscombe; N'ton = Newton

Aircraft Wastage

In the war of attrition that was the Battle of Britain, it was vital that aircraft supply kept up with losses. The damage to RAF fighters was graded according to severity. 'Category 3' meant the aircraft was destroyed or missing. 'Category 2' losses were severely damaged aircraft that, nonetheless, might be repaired or used for parts. 'Category 1' aircraft (not included below) were usually quickly reparable, or even capable of being patched up by the maintenance facilities at the aerodromes themselves.

| | HURRICANE | | | | SPITFIRE | | | | |
Week ending	Production	Cat 2. losses	Cat. 3 losses	Net gain/loss	Production	Cat 2 losses	Cat. 3 losses	Net gain/loss	Total net gain/loss for both types
6 Jul	65	3	4	+58	32	1	5	+26	+84
13 Jul	57	6	22	+29	30	6	15	+9	+38
20 Jul	67	5	13	+39	41	5	6	+30	+69
27 Jul	65	3	12	+50	37	8	14	+15	+65
3 Aug	58	4	7	+47	41	7	11	+23	+69
10 Aug	54	4	16	+34	37	4	12	+21	+55
17 Aug	43	21	82	−58	31	11	40	−20	−78
24 Aug	64	9	53	+2	44	3	21	+20	+22
31 Aug	54	4	70	−20	37	7	50	−20	−40
7 Sept	54	8	84	−38	36	8	53	−25	−63
14 Sept	56	6	47	+3	38	10	26	+2	+5
21 Sept	57	8	34	+15	40	11	21	+8	+23
28 Sept	58	11	40	+7	34	5	35	−6	+1
5 Oct	60	16	29	+15	32	5	10	+17	+32
12 Oct	55	3	28	+24	31	4	22	+5	+29
19 Oct	55	10	28	+17	25	2	9	+14	+31
26 Oct	69	7	34	+28	42	2	9	+31	+59
2 Nov	56	9	16	+31	41	2	14	+25	+56

517

Air Raids on Great Britain, July–December 1940

Target	High explosive (including land mines) Tons	Incendiaries Tons	Number of bombs
London	23,716	2,918	2,951,000
Liverpool and Merseyside	2,114	274	278,300
Birmingham	1,780	141	143,000
Coventry	965	231	234,700
Manchester	933	105	107,000
Bristol	360	112	113,500
Southampton	421	106	108,000
Plymouth	362	95	96,000
Airfields	1,710	28	28,100
Other raids	4,303	211	205,000
Total	36,664	4,221	4,264,600

Civilian Air Raid Casualties, 1940

*under age 16

Month	Men killed (injured)	Women killed (injured)	Children* killed (injured)	Total killed (injured)
July	178 (227)	57 (77)	23 (17)	258 (321)
August	627 (711)	335 (448)	113 (102)	1,075 (1,261)
September	2,844 (4,405)	2,943 (3,807)	1,167 (2,403)	6,954 (10,615)
October	2,791 (4,228)	2,900 (3,750)	643 (717)	6,334 (8,695)
November	2,289 (3,493)	1,806 (2,251)	493 (458)	4,588 (6,202)
December	1,838 (2,962)	1,434 (1,775)	521 (307)	3,793 (5,044)
Total	10,567 (16,026)	9,475 (12,108)	2,960 (4,004)	23,002 (32,138)

Notes

IWM = Imperial War
Museum, London

INTRODUCTION
1. Bungay, Stephen,
   *The Most Dangerous
   Enemy*, 2001.

CHAPTER ONE
ORIGINS
1. Quoted in Bowyer,
   Chaz, *Albert Ball* VC,
   1994, pp. 32ff.
2. Baldwin quotations in
   Hansard (online
   edition).

CHAPTER TWO
**WATCHING, WAITING
. . . AND WITHDRAWING**
1. Quoted in Calder,
   Angus, *The People's
   War*, 1969, p. 42.
2. Freeborn, John,
   interview with author.
3. Richey, Paul, *Fighter*

*Pilot: A Personal
Record of the
Campaign in France*,
1990 (first published,
1941), p. 24.
4. Earp, Richard, IWM
   Sound Archive
   Recording 11772.
5. Churchill, Winston,
   *The Second World
   War*, Vol. 1, *The
   Gathering Storm*,
   1948, p. 257.
6. Richey, op. cit., p. 80.
7. Churchill, op. cit.,
   Vol. 2, *Their Finest
   Hour*, 1949, p. 42.
8. Brothers, Peter, IWM
   Sound Archive
   Recording 10218.
9. Bob, Hans-Ekkehard,
   IWM Sound Archive
   Recording 26965.
10. Schöpfel, Gerhard,

IWM Sound Archive Recording 14770.

11. Kingcome, Brian, *A Willingness to Die*, 1999, p. 137.

12. Vigors, Tim, pre-publication manuscript for *Life's Too Short to Cry*, 2006.

CHAPTER THREE
SQUARING UP

1. Bob, op. cit.

2. Lee, (General) Raymond E., *The London Observer*, 1972, p. 30.

3. Devitt, George, IWM Sound Archive Recording 10667.

4. Young, John, IWM Sound Archive Recording 20468.

5. Bamberger, Cyril, IWM Sound Archive 27074.

6. Roberts, Fred, IWM Sound Archive Recording 26973.

7. Roddis, Joe, IWM Sound Archive Recording 26966.

8. Roberts, op. cit.

9. Brothers, op. cit.

10. Quoted in Escott, Beryl E., *The WAAF: A History of the Women's Auxiliary Air Force in the Second World War*, 2003, p. 5.

11. King, Vera, IWM Sound Archive Recording 10221.

12. Quoted in Crang, Jeremy A. "Come into the Army, Maud": Women, Military Conscription, and the Markham Inquiry', *Defence Studies*, Vol. 8, Issue 3, 2008, p. 383.

13. Orley, Marian, IWM Sound Archive Recording 14764.

14. Quoted in Parker, Matthew, *The Battle of Britain, July–October 1940*, 2000, p. 122.

15. Orley, op. cit.
16. Interview with author.
17. Brand, Stanley, IWM Sound Archive Recording 27347.
18. Clark, Percy, IWM Sound Archive Recording 20982.
19. Pellet, George, IWM Sound Archive Recording 9185.
20. Goddard, Douglas, IWM Sound Archive Recording 20982.
21. Johnstone, Kenneth, IWM Sound Archive Recording 9185.
22. Quoted in Longmate, Norman, *Island Fortress*, 1991, p. 476.
23. Colville, John, *The Fringes of Power: Downing Street Diaries 1939–1955*, 1985, p. 197.

CHAPTER FOUR
BEGINNING THE DUEL
 1. Kingcome, Brian, IWM Sound Archive Recording 10152.
 2. Quoted in *Winged Words: Our Airmen Speak For Themselves*, 1941, pp. 50–2.
 3. Foxley-Norris, Christopher, IWM Sound Archive Recording 10136.
 4. Quayle, Elizabeth, IWM Sound Archive Recording 10609.
 5. Deere, Alan C., *Nine Lives*, 1959, p. 86.
 6. Quoted in Bickers, Richard Townsend, *Battle of Britain*, 1990, p. 111.
 7. Quoted in Ziegler, Frank H., *The Story of 609 Squadron*, 1971, p. 116.
 8. Quoted in Parker, op. cit., p. 140.
 9. Crook, D.M., *Spitfire Pilot*, 1942, p. 32.
10. Deere, op. cit., p. 90.
11. Ibid.

12. Quoted in Parker, op. cit., p. 154.
13. Quoted in Parker, op. cit., p. 155.
14. Page, Geoffrey, *Shot Down in Flames*, 1999, pp. 48ff.
15. Transcript adapted from *www.bbc.co.uk*.
16. Quoted in Kennedy, Irving, *Black Crosses Off My Wingtip*, 1994, p. 4.
17. Quoted by Kieser, Egbert, *Hitler On The Doorstep — Operation "Sea Lion": The German Plan to Invade Britain 1940*, translated by Helmut Bögler, 1997, pp. 274–7.

CHAPTER FIVE
PRODDING AND PROBING

1. Gilbert, Martin, *Finest Hour*, 1983, p. 428.
2. Lee, op. cit., p. 12.
3. Quoted in Overy, Richard, "The Few versus the Very Few", *BBC History Magazine*, June 2000.
4. Quoted in Waite, Robert G. L., *The Pyschopathic God: Adolf Hitler*, 1977, p. 463.
5. Quoted in Townsend, Peter, *Duel of Eagles*, 1970, p. 276.
6. Quoted in Parker, op. cit., p. 159.
7. Quoted in Bickers, op. cit., p. 212.
8. Shirer, William, *Berlin Diary*, 1941, pp. 356–7.
9. Quoted in Bickers, op. cit., p. 213.
10. Quoted in Parker, op. cit., p. 419.
11. Townsend, Peter, *Time and Chance*, 1978, pp. 105–6.
12. Quoted in Parker, op. cit., p. 155.
13. Ibid., p. 142.

14. Quoted in Longmate, op. cit., p. 491.
15. Quoted in Bickers, op. cit., p. 214.
16. Quoted in Mason, Francis K., *Battle Over Britain*, 1990, p. 146.
17. Foxley-Norris, Christopher, interview with author.
18. Deere, op. cit., p. 99.
19. Dundas, Hugh *Flying Start*, 1988, pp. 2–3.
20. Deere, op. cit., p. 103.
21. Goodson, James, IWM Sound Archive Recording 11623.
22. Quoted in Parker, op. cit., p. 262.
23. Wright, Stanley, IWM Sound Recording 11744.
24. Leng, Maurice, IWM Sound Recording 12217.
25. Kup, Edith, IWM Sound Archive Recording 13967.
26. Deere, op. cit., pp. 102–3.
27. Quoted in Hough, Richard Alexander and Denis Richards, *The Battle of Britain*, 1989, p. 202.
28. Haw, Charlton, IWM Sound Archive Recording 12028.
29. Quoted in Parker, op. cit., p. 147.
30. Ibid., p. 166.
31. Steinhilper, Ulrich, IWM Sound Archive Recording 16049.
32. Quoted in Walker, Oliver, *Sailor Malan*, 1953, p. 99.
33. Lee, op. cit., p. 25.

CHAPTER SIX
INTENSIFICATION

1. Colville, op. cit., p. 205.
2. Gillies, Midge *Waiting For Hitler: Voices From Britain on the Brink of Invasion*, 2006, p. xx.
3. Quoted in Parker, op. cit., pp. 189–92.
4. Quoted in 145

Squadron Newsletter, Autumn/Winter 1995.

5. Quoted in Turner, John Frayn, *The Battle of Britain*, 1998.
6. Quoted in Parker, op. cit., p. 152.
7. Quoted in Ziegler, Frank, op. cit., p. 114.
8. Quill, Jeffrey, IWM Sound Archive Recording 10687.
9. Quoted in Allen, H. R., *Battle For Britain*, 1973.
10. Quoted in Mason, op. cit., p. 189 footnote.
11. Batt, L. G., *Sgt Pilot 741474 RAFVR: A Flying Memoir 1938–1959* (privately published) 1990, pp. 39–40.
12. Quotations in Parker, pp. 205–6.
13. Quoted on *www.battleofbritain1940.net*
14. Quoted in Ziegler, Frank, op. cit., pp. 120–1.
15. Quoted in Collier, Richard, *Eagle Day*, 1966, p. 72.
16. Channon, Sir Henry, *"Chips": The Diaries of Sir Henry Channon*, 1996, p. 263.
17. Batt, op. cit., p. 45.
18. Private letter, 15 August 1940.
19. Quoted in Kershaw, Alex, *The Few: The American "Knights of the Air" Who Risked Everything to Save Britain in the Summer of 1940*, 2007, p. 117.
20. Crook, op. cit., p. 50.
21. Ibid., p. 51.
22. Quoted in Parker, op. cit., p. 215.
23. Quoted in Jullian, Marcell, *The Battle of Britain, July–September 1940*, 1967, p. 86.

24. Quoted in Bickers, op. cit., p. 172.
25. Quoted in Ishoven, Armand van, *The Luftwaffe in the Battle of Britain*, 1980, pp. 53–4.
26. Crook, op. cit., pp. 51–2.
27. Brown, Ronald, IWM Sound Archive Recording 12404.
28. Möllenbrook quotations in Parker, op. cit., pp. 217–18.
29. Channon, op. cit., p. 263.
30. From a BBC broadcast.
31. Ismay, James, *The Memoirs of General the Lord Ismay*, 1960, p. 182.

CHAPTER SEVEN
HARDEST DAYS

1. Quoted in Bickers, op. cit., p. 189.
2. *www.battleofbritain 1940.net*
3. Leighton-Porter, Christabel, IWM Sound Archive Recording 11246.
4. Calder, Angus, *The People's War*, 1992 edition, p. 152.
5. *www.battleofbritain 1940.net*
6. Quoted in Price, Alfred *The Hardest Day*, 1979 (paperback edition), p. 114.
7. Colville, op. cit., p. 225.
8. Quoted in Price, op. cit., p. 141.
9. Townsend, *Duel of Eagles* op. cit., pp. 376–7.
10. Quoted in Bickers, op. cit., p. 184.
11. Ibid., p. 228.
12. Quoted in Wheatley, Ronald, *Operation Sea Lion*, 1958, p. 73.
13. Crook, op. cit., p. 65.
14. Ibid., pp. 56–7.
15. Quoted in Parker, op. cit., p. 241.
16. Ibid., p. 245.
17. Quoted in Franks,

Norman, *Battle of Britain*, 1981, pp. 32–3.

18. Quoted in Adams, Perry, *Hurricane Squadron: No. 87 Squadron at War 1939–1941*, 1988, p. 33.

19. Crook, op. cit., pp. 59–60.

20. Quoted in Bickers, op. cit., p. 245.

21. Brothers, op. cit.

22. Townsend, *Duel of Eagles* op. cit., p. 392.23.

23. *www.battleofbritain 1940.net*

24. MacLean, Charles, IWM Sound Archive Recording 10788.

25. Quoted in James, T. C. G., *The Battle of Britain: Air Defence of Great Britain*, 2000, p. 356.

26. Bailey, Jim, "Defiant Survivor", in *Battle of Britain Remembered*, Vol. 1, No. 1, 1999.

27. Deere, op. cit., p. 133.

28. Ibid., p. 147.

29. Townsend, *Duel of Eagles* op. cit. p. 400.

30. Ibid., pp. 404–5.

31. Quoted in Parker, op. cit., pp. 255–6.

32. Townsend, *Duel of Eagles* op. cit., p. 407.

33. Quoted in Parker, op. cit., p. 40.

34. Quoted in Mason, op. cit., p. 256.

35. Townsend, *Duel of Eagles* op. cit., p. 376.

36. Quoted in Parker, op. cit., pp. 249–50.

37. Quoted in Hough & Richards, op. cit., pp. 237–8.

38. Bob, op. cit.

39. Quotations in Parker, op. cit., pp. 259–60.

40. Roberts, op. cit.

41. Townsend, *Duel of Eagles* op. cit., p. 148.

42. *www.battleofbritain 1940.net*

43. Hamilton, Igraine,

IWM Sound Archive 10084.

44. Deere, op. cit., pp. 142–3.

45. Hillary, Richard, *The Last Enemy*, 1942, pp 100–1.

46. Ibid.

47. Brothers, op. cit.

48. Unwin, George, IWM Sound Archive Recording 11544.

49. Bamberger, op. cit.

50. Colville, op cit, p. 235.

51. Quoted in Parker, op. cit., pp. 262–3.

52. Quoted in Franks, op. cit., p. 38.

53. Shirer, op. cit., p. 389.

54. Quoted in Parker, op. cit., p. 262.

55. Quoted in Gelb, Norman, *Scramble: A Narrative History of the Battle of Britain*, 1986, p. 114.

56. Brothers, op. cit.

57. Lewis, Cecil, *Sagittarius Rising*, 1988, p. 60.

58. Unwin, op. cit.

59. Bann, Eric, private letter.

CHAPTER EIGHT
CULMINATION

1. Quoted in Moss, Norman, *Nineteen Weeks: America, Britain, and the Fateful Summer of 1940*, 2003, p. 294.

2. Mason, op. cit., pp. 359–60.

3. Quoted in Wood, Derek and Derek Dempster, *The Narrow Margin*, 1961, p. 346.

4. Quoted in Parker, op. cit., p. 269.

5. Ibid., p. 270.

6. Davy, Horace, IWM Sound Archive Recording 20324.

7. Letter held at the RAF Museum.

8. *www.battleofbritain 1940.net*

9. Johnstone, Sandy, *Enemy in the Sky:*

My 1940 Diary, 1976, p. 118.

10. Quoted in Franks, op. cit., pp. 42–3.

11. Quoted in Parker, op. cit., p. 272.

12. *www.battleofbritain 1940.net*

13. Quoted in Parker, op. cit., p. 272.

14. Robertson, Ben, *I Saw England*, 1941, p. 106.

15. Quoted in Ziegler, Philip, *London at War*, 1995, p. 114.

16. Quoted in *www.battleofbritain 1940.net*

17. Marshall, Walter, IWM Sound Archive Recording 23849.

18. Quoted in Ziegler, Philip, op. cit., pp. 114–15.

19. Quoted in Calder, op. cit., p. 155.

20. Lucas, Laddie, *Flying Colours: The Epic Story of Douglas Bader*, 1981, p. 60.

21. Brickhill, Paul, *Reach for the Sky: The Story of Douglas Bader* DSO, DFC, 1954, p. 44.

22. Quotations from *www.channel4.com*.

23. Quotations in Stahl, Peter, *Diving Eagle: A Ju88 Pilot's Diary*, translated by Alex Vanags-Baginskis, 1984, pp. 60–2.

24. Quoted in Parker, op. cit., p. 281.

25. All quotations in Pile, (General) Sir Frederick, *Ack-Ack*, 1949.

26. Quoted in Lee, op. cit., p. 54.

27. Quoted in Ziegler, Philip, op. cit., p. 115.

28. Crook, op. cit., pp. 61–2.

29. Quoted in Hough and Richards, op. cit., p. 275.

30. Churchill, Vol. 2 op. cit., pp. 295–6.

31. Holmes, Ray, IWM

Sound Archive Recording 2807.

32. Quoted in Parker, op. cit., p. 292.

33. *www.battleofbritain 1940.net*

34. Quoted in Bickers, op. cit., p. 183.

35. Quoted in Turner, John Frayn, *The Bader Tapes*, 1986, p. 87.

36. Unwin, op. cit.

37. Neil, Thomas, IWM Sound Archive Recording 26977.

38. Channon, op. cit., p. 266.

39. Churchill, Vol. 2 op. cit., p. 297.

40. Neil, op. cit.

41. Bennions, George, IWM Sound Archive Recording 10296.

42. Quoted in Ray, John, *The Battle of Britain: New Perspectives*, 1994, pp. 104–5.

43. Nicolson, Harold, *Diaries and Letters*, Vol. 2, *1939–45*, 1967, p. 116.

44. Stahl, op. cit., p. 65.

45. Crook, op. cit., pp. 74–5.

46. Quoted in Hough and Richards, op. cit., p. 233.

47. Quoted in Wood and Dempster, op. cit., p. 366.

48. Crook, op. cit., pp. 80–1.

49. Ciano, Galleazzo, *The Ciano Diaries*, edited by Hugh Gibson, 1946, p. 298.

50. Quoted in Bickers, op. cit., p. 242.

CHAPTER NINE
AFTERMATH

1. Arnold, Gwen, *Radar Days*, 2000, p. 77.

2. Steinke, Gioya, IWM Sound Archive Recording 18724.

3. Ismay, op. cit., pp. 81–2.

4. Figures from Bickers, op. cit., p. 246.

5. Quoted in Terraine, John, *The Right of the Line*, 1985, p. 219.
6. Imperial War Museum Archive Dept, No. 97/43/1.
7. Deere, op. cit., p. 172.

APPENDIX 1
AIRCRAFT OF THE BATTLE OF BRITAIN

1. Unwin, op. cit.
2. Quill, op. cit.
3. Goodson, op. cit.
4. Bird-Wilson, Harold, IWM Sound Archive 10093.
5. Roell, Werner, IWM Sound Archive Recording 12563.
6. Unwin, op. cit.
7. Wedding, Ernest, IWM Sound Archive Recording 26960.
8. MacLean, op. cit.

The website quoted throughout the notes should be: *www.battleofbritain1940.net* and is all one word.

Acknowledgements

Compiling this book has been made easier by the wealth of material amassed over the years by historians of, and participants in, the Battle of Britain. I am particularly grateful to two of the leading historians in the field: FRANCIS K. MASON, author of *Battle over Britain*, which provided the first comprehensive chronology of the summer of 1940, and KENNETH H. WYNN, whose *Men of the Battle of Britain* is the prime reference work on the airmen of Fighter Command. I would also like to record my deep thanks to MATTHEW PARKER, himself a distinguished Battle of Britain historian, for his invaluable help with the research and writing, and I am grateful to VICTORIA KINGSTON, who researched images for the book.

PATRICK BISHOP

Also available in ISIS Large Print:

Hero of the Fleet

William Stone

William Stone died on Saturday 10th January 2009 aged 108. He received a hero's funeral. Born in rural Devon, he joined the navy during the First World War, travelled the globe just before the British Empire's light began to fade and saw action in some of the most significant sea battles of the Second World War. Afterwards, he returned to Devon to run a barber's shop, an altogether more peaceable existence.

Through his years of retirement, he tended his garden, unaware that celebrity was stalking him. As time passed, he became one of a dwindling number of men who served in the Great War. This meant that for some of the most momentous anniversaries clocked up recently — including the 90th anniversary of the end of the First World War — William was a guest of honour. This is his astonishing story.

ISBN 978-0-7531-5247-8 (hb)
ISBN 978-0-7531-5248-5 (pb)

Voices Against War

Lyn Smith

On 15 February 2003, an estimated two million Britons took to the streets of London to protest against war in Iraq. Since the outbreak of that conflict, the anti-war movement has broadened and now has a global reach. Not all protesters would consider themselves pacifists — against all wars and violence — but whatever the basis of objection, their protest is part of one of the most enduring movements in history.

Based on nearly 200 personal testimonies from the Imperial War Museum Collections, this landmark book tells the stories of those who participated in anti-war protest — from the Great War through to the Second World War, the Cold War and up to the present day. This includes the Falkland Islands invasion in the early 1980s, the first Gulf War and the ongoing conflicts in Iraq and Afghanistan.

ISBN 978-0-7531-5243-0 (hb)
ISBN 978-0-7531-5244-7 (pb)

Ground Truth

Patrick Bishop

In April 2006 the elite 3 Para Battle Group was despatched to Helmand Province, Afghanistan, on a tour that has become a legend. All that summer the Paras were subjected to relentless attacks in a gruelling campaign. Two years later the Paras are back. The enemy has been forced to adopt new weaponry and tactics. But how much progress are we really making in the war against the insurgents? And is there an end in sight?

In this searing account of 3 Para's return, Patrick Bishop combines first-person accounts of front-line action with an unflinching look at the realities of our involvement in Afghanistan. Writing from a position of exclusive access alongside the Paras, he reveals the "ground truth" of the mission our soldiers have been given. It's a sombre picture. But shining out from it are stories of courage, comradeship and humour.

ISBN 978-0-7531-5237-9 (hb)
ISBN 978-0-7531-5238-6 (pb)

Bomber Boys

Patrick Bishop

The 125,000 men from all over the world who passed through Bomber Command were engaged in a form of warfare that had never been implemented before. Between 1940 and 1945 they flew continuously, stopping only when weather made operations impossible. There was nothing romantic about their struggle. Often barely out of boyhood, they lived on bleak bases, flying at night on long, nerve-wracking missions that often ended in death. In all, 55,000 were killed, counting for nearly one in ten of all the British and Commonwealth war dead.

In this powerful and moving work of history, Patrick Bishop brilliantly captures the character, feelings and motivations of the bomber crews and pays tribute to their heroism and determination. They were among the best of their generation, who were called on to carry out one of the grimmest duties of the Second World War. *Bomber Boys* brilliantly restores these men to their rightful place in our consciousness.

ISBN 978-0-7531-5675-9 (hb)
ISBN 978-0-7531-5676-6 (pb)

Fighter Boys

Patrick Bishop

Humane and moving, as well as thrilling, Fighter Boys *is a unique chronicle of the decisive conflict of the twentieth century.*

In the summer of 1940, the future of Britain and the free world rested in the hands of the young men of Fighter Command. For most of the 3,000 young British airmen involved, the Battle of Britain, fought in the skies, was their first real experience of combat — and for many, the last. Drawing on extensive new research — including diaries, letters, memoirs and interviews with many of the survivors — Patrick Bishop vividly evokes both the courage and coolness under fire that forged the legend of gentlemanly heroism of the Fighter Boys. This book also explores the darker side of life as a Fighter Boy: the risks, the killing and the fear, the loss of beloved friends. This is a unique study of their indomitable spirit, conveying with unprecedented force what it felt like to be a fighter pilot, in peace and in war.

ISBN 978-0-7531-9914-5 (hb)
ISBN 978-0-7531-9915-2 (pb)

ISIS publish a wide range of books in large print, from fiction to biography. Any suggestions for books you would like to see in large print or audio are always welcome. Please send to the Editorial Department at:

ISIS Publishing Limited
7 Centremead
Osney Mead
Oxford OX2 0ES

A full list of titles is available free of charge from:

Ulverscroft Large Print Books Limited

(UK)
The Green
Bradgate Road, Anstey
Leicester LE7 7FU
Tel: (0116) 236 4325

(Australia)
P.O. Box 314
St Leonards
NSW 1590
Tel: (02) 9436 2622

(USA)
P.O. Box 1230
West Seneca
N.Y. 14224-1230
Tel: (716) 674 4270

(Canada)
P.O. Box 80038
Burlington
Ontario L7L 6B1
Tel: (905) 637 8734

(New Zealand)
P.O. Box 456
Feilding
Tel: (06) 323 6828

Details of **ISIS** complete and unabridged audio books are also available from these offices. Alternatively, contact your local library for details of their collection of **ISIS** large print and unabridged audio books.